The Yanoama Indians
A Cultural Geography

The Texas Pan American Series

The Yanoama
Indians
A Cultural Geography
by William J. Smole

University of Texas Press   Austin and London

The Texas Pan American Series is published with
the assistance of a revolving publication fund
established by the Pan American Sulphur Company.

The publication of this book was assisted by
a grant from the Andrew W. Mellon Foundation.

Library of Congress Cataloging in Publication Data

Smole, William J
  The Yanoama Indians.

  (The Texas Pan American series)
  Bibliography: p.
  Includes index
  1. Yanoama Indians. 2. Human ecology—Parima
Mountains, Brazil and Venezuela. I. Title.
F2520.1.Y3S56 981'.1'00498 75–16167

ISBN 0–292–71019–4

This book is dedicated to the

Yanoama of the Parima highlands,

with the fervent hope that it will never

be used to disrupt their lives.

Contents

Illustrations

Tables

Preface

In fewer than twenty years the world will celebrate the five hundredth anniversary of Columbus's first voyage. During the intervening centuries the Europeanization of the Americas has gone forward inexorably. Yet, a few isolated pockets of the New World have been left virtually untouched. This book deals with one such place, a sparsely populated forest in the headwaters of the Río Orinoco. The people living there call themselves Yanoama.

Notions of geomorphology, kinship, social structure, linguistics, religion, and art forms are not analyzed here per se, since they are amply treated in the existing literature. However, such concepts are incorporated as they are directly pertinent geographically and, particularly, as they apply to Yanoama livelihood activities. A detailed cultural classification is provided as a means of categorizing the Yanoama among tropical American forest cultures, although other classifications could have been used for this purpose.

Terminology is a problem because at least four languages—Yanoama, English, Spanish, and Portuguese—are involved directly, as well as Venezuelan and Brazilian vernacular, and because Yanoama transliteration and orthography are not standardized. The Yanoama used is the Barafiri dialect unless otherwise noted. Barafiri words have been transliterated according to the Spanish alphabet where this is feasible (without diacritical marks), and, except for those used as proper nouns, they are italicized when they appear in the text. Plural forms of Yanoama words are avoided because pluralizing does not follow rules resembling ours. For the sake of clarity, such terms as *teri*, *u*, and *taca* are preceded by hyphens when employed as suffixes.

Yanoama distribution patterns are dynamic. For this reason, and because the great bulk of field data are for the year 1970, conditions and distributions are those of 1970 unless otherwise specified.

Grateful thanks are due people and institutions too numerous for all to be identified specifically. At the University of Pittsburgh, the Faculty Allocations Committee (Faculty of Arts and Sciences) and the Center for Latin American Studies (University Center for International Studies) provided much of the financial support for field work. A grant from the Wenner-Gren Foundation for Anthropological Research for further field study is also gratefully acknowledged. The text could not have been completed without the patience and diligence of the very able Roslyn Lipsky, and preparation of graphic materials was greatly aided by Howard Ziegler. Philip L. Wagner of Simon Fraser University provided valuable insights after reading the manuscript.

Various agencies of the Venezuelan government were very helpful. Among them, special reference must be made to the Servicio Malariológico, Ministerio de Sanidad y Asistencia Social; the Comisión para el Desarrollo del Sur (CODESUR), Ministerio de Obras Públicas; and the Instituto Venezolano de Investigaciones Científicas (IVIC).

Personnel of the New Tribes Mission made the field research possible. Their help as translators, their critical judgments on Yanoama culture, and their generous provisions of food and lodging cannot be adequately acknowledged. Among the many to whom a great debt is owed, two people stand out in particular: Margaret and Wallace Jank. Alas de Socorro and pilot James Hurd kindly made the necessary arrangements for me to fly into the highland Parima study area.

Numerous Yanoama, particularly Buuqui Foo, provided invaluable information and assistance, freely giving encouragement and supplying enthusiasm for the project. For all this, I owe them much.

The Yanoama Indians

A Cultural Geography

Chapter 1

Introduction

T H E Yanoama[1] are an enigmatic people. They, their culture, and their habitat provide special questions for geographic study. In their gardens plantains are of most consequence, although the Yanoama are virtually surrounded by native Indian peoples who cultivate bitter manioc as the staple food crop. The Yanoama are evidently ancient as a culture and as an aboriginal population, with a language classified as independent of the major contemporary linguistic families of South America. They preserve a remarkable degree of cultural homogeneity throughout the territory they have traditionally inhabited. Furthermore, the number of Yanoama (possibly 15,000)[2] and the areal extent of their large culture region (perhaps 30,000 square miles) make findings of more than merely local significance.[3]

The Yanoama of the Parima highlands are still largely unacculturated. The isolation of these highlanders—particularly from Europeans, but also from other Indians—has been almost hermetic for untold centuries. Outside influences are so slight that the study of the Yanoama in this highland core of their territory is virtually a study of the living past.[4] Valuable insights into prehistoric times and the essentials of human ecology in the tropics can be gained from studying them. As a contemporary neolithic people, the Yanoama represent a phenomenon that has become extremely rare in modern times. The few remaining populations are fast disappearing, since they are caught up in the process of acculturation and are even being killed off.[5]

This book deals principally with the Barafiri of the Parima highlands because they are more representative of the aboriginal Yanoama than are other, more accessible groups. The focus is on their livelihood activities, particularly horticulture. Many relevant culture traits are of interest as they mesh with horticulture, and so is the natural habitat itself. All are considered as parts of an ecosystem—the mutual interaction between the Yanoama and their environment viewed in terms of functional areal organization. The general approach is an inductive one: reasoning is from observable or evident particulars to the more general.

Several major themes are embraced here. One is that of Yanoama exploitation of their variegated habitat, including the conceptualization of resources, area, distance, direction, distributions, and location. Another theme involves the spatial dimensions of their culture region and the morphology of Yanoama settlement units. Also important are man-land relationships, particularly as they bear on livelihood. (The simplistic "adaptation" embodied in environmental determinism is not used.)[6] Yanoama horticulture is approached as a functional system in the cultural heartland.

The changes effected by the Yanoama on their habitat and an assessment of the significance of this impact are very important. Implicit in the use of terms like *primitive*, *rude*, or *marginal*, when referring to such populations or cultures as the Yanoama, are a presumed ineffectiveness in their occupation and use of the land and a minimal impact upon the natural environment. Yet the Yanoama, who have been horticulturalists for generations, have made great environmental modifications. The importance of musaceous crop plants to the Yanoama is another theme that threads through these pages, sometimes very subtly.[7]

In seeking a cultural perspective for study of the Yanoama, two different kinds of classifications of aboriginal South Americans are particularly useful. One kind is the comprehensive ethnographic classification, represented by the monumental six-volume *Handbook of South American Indians*[8] and by George Peter Murdock's *Ethnographic Atlas*, which is of worldwide scope.[9] A much narrower kind of classification, the language map as a cartographic portrayal of culture, is well represented by Cestmir Loukotka's "Ethno-linguistic Distribution of South American Indians."[10]

True, in each of these classifications there is a lack of information on the Yanoama. Yet they are specific on one point: the Yanoama habitat is the tropical forest, and they are, therefore, part and parcel of "Tropical Forest Culture."[11] However, the Yanoama constitute only a tiny segment of the aboriginal population inhabiting an enormous and diversified culture region that once extended over most of the Amazon Basin, the Guianas, and the southern half of the area drained by the Orinoco River.

A plausible, if simple, set of four distinguishing culture traits was

established for this entire region in the *Handbook of South American*
Indians.[12] Succinctly, the basic criteria for the Forest Tribes culture
complex are these: (*a*) the cultivation of [bitter] manioc (*Manihot esculenta*
Crantz) as a basic staple food, (*b*) the construction of effective river craft,
(*c*) the use of hammocks instead of beds, and (*d*) the manufacture of
pottery.

Two considered modifications of this set of criteria are also of particular
utility. One of these provides a distinctive and fascinating set of general
features of tropical forest communities: (*a*) multifamily residences (with
the suggestion that such communal architecture might have given rise to
the ceremonial-center concept in certain "high" cultures); (*b*) crop plants
important, but horticultural ritual undeveloped; (*c*) root horticulture,
based on bitter manioc; (*d*) an exaltation of intoxication; (*e*) life generally
riverine rather than sylvan; (*f*) the couvade; and (*g*) women as
horticulturalists, with horticulture strongly secular.[13]

The second takes the position that the most consistently shared cultural
elements are economic, and that "Tropical Forest Culture is a way of life
supported by intensive root-crop agriculture."[14]

However, parts of the tropical forest are—or were—inhabited by
peoples who did not possess all four culture traits established in the
Handbook and certainly not all those of the modified sets cited.[15] Among
these groups are the Yanoama, and some provision must be made for
them. There is wide agreement that a sort of "cultural continental
divide"[16] exists between the bulk of the tropical forest peoples and these
groups that are so different culturally.[17] The latter are often classified as
"marginals,"[18] or "semi-marginals,"[19] and together they are thought to
form "an enormous U-shaped belt of particularly primitive folk on the
periphery of the Amazon basin."[20]

The belt is discontinuous at present, presumably because some of the
different peoples that once might have constituted parts of it have been
culturally overwhelmed by invaders or have utterly disappeared. Among
the fragmented remnants of the ancient distribution pattern are the
Yanoama, evidently representative of a population that was neither
destroyed nor displaced.

Two explanations of these "marginals" and their distribution have been
suggested. One is that they are descendants of early migrants to the
continent who were for some reason isolated over the centuries from
successive immigrant groups and thereby cut off from the diffusion of
new, advanced culture traits that contact might have provided.[21] Another
explanation is that "marginals" like the Yanoama are the culturally
degraded, or involuted, descendants of people who belonged to once-
sophisticated tropical forest agricultural societies.[22]

Chapter 2
The Yanoama and Their Milieu

THE Yanoama are distinguishable among the many "tribes"[1] of the tropical forest in two specific ways: they occupy a site that is particular to them, most of which is used by them exclusively, and they have a unique culture complex—a particular set of cultural features, which together are distinctive.

The Site

Yanoama territory has as its center the Sierra Parima (see map 1) on whose western flanks rise the headwaters of the Río Orinoco and some of its tributaries (Majecodo, Ocamo, Padamo, Ventuari), and on whose east rise the headwaters of some of the Uraricoera-Branco tributaries (most notably the Rio Parima). From the Parima massif, Yanoama are found east along the axis of the Serra Pacaraima, to include on the north the headwaters of important tributaries of the lower Orinoco (Erebato-Caura, Paragua-Caroni), and on the south small headwater streams that enter the Uraricoera-Branco system. In a southwestern extension of the Parima highlands, which is sometimes called the Tapirapeco massif, Yanoama occupy the headwaters of several Rio Negro tributaries (most notably the Demini and the Padauiri), the headwaters of the Río Mavaca (an Orinoco tributary), and the headwaters of the Yatua and Siapa (both tributaries of the Casiquiare-Negro system). The total area effectively

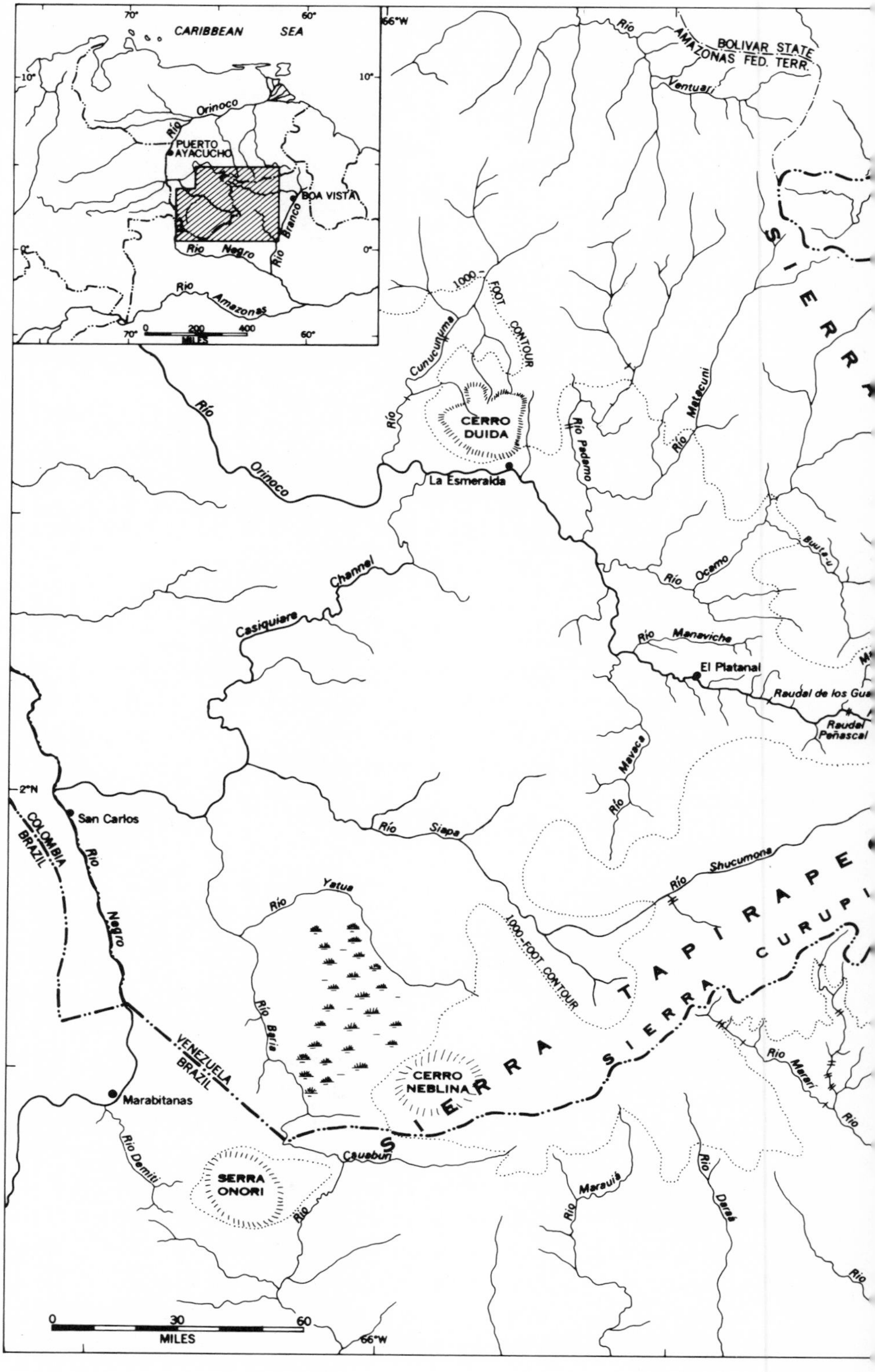
CARIBBEAN SEA
Río Orinoco
PUERTO AYACUCHO
BOA VISTA
Río Branco
Río Negro
Río Amazonas
MILES
BOLIVAR STATE
AMAZONAS FED. TERR.
Río Ventuari
1000-FOOT CONTOUR
Río Cunucunuma
CERRO DUIDA
Río Orinoco
La Esmeralda
Río Padamo
Río Matacuni
Río Ocamo
Casiquiare Channel
Río Manaviche
El Platanal
Raudal Peñascal
Río Mavaca
San Carlos
COLOMBIA BRAZIL
Río Negro
Río Siapa
Río Shucumona
Río Yatua
1,000-FOOT CONTOUR
Río Baria
VENEZUELA BRAZIL
CERRO NEBLINA
SIERRA TAPIRAPECÓ
SIERRA CURUPIRA
Marabitanas
Río Demiti
SERRA ONORI
Río Cauaburi
Río Marauiá
Río Darã
Río Marari
MILES
66°W
2°N

Map 1. Land of
the Yanoama

9
*The
Yanoama and
Their Milieu*

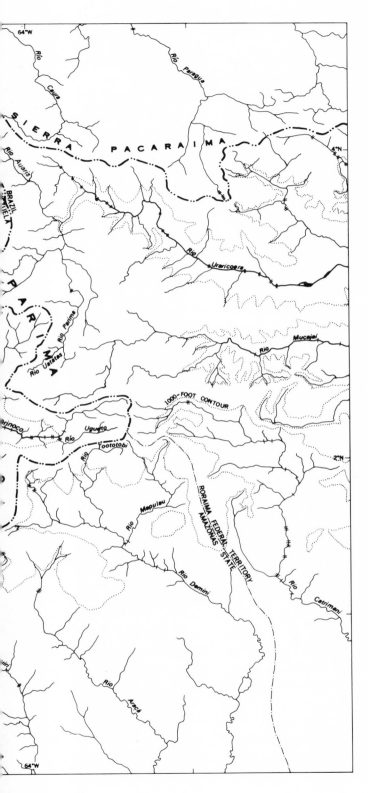

occupied by the Yanoama can be estimated conservatively at about thirty thousand square miles.[2]

This territorial extent is defined in terms of stream names because these are most widely used and most consistent. Prominent elevations, even entire mesas or mountain massifs, are sometimes unnamed on maps and in accounts, or their nomenclature is conflicting. These facts reflect our general lack of information on the Yanoama habitat and the importance to foreigners of stream navigation.

Certain features of Yanoama territory are evident from even this cursory delimitation. The area involved is a large one; it is essentially uninterrupted by alien cultures;[3] and its center is an equatorial highland where several major stream systems rise.[4]

Distinctiveness of the Culture

Students of the Yanoama are not in agreement with respect to their most distinguishing characteristics, and different writers have stressed very different traits. For some students, these people are remarkably "backward."[5] One writer consistently refers to the Yanoama as the fierce people, "because that is the most accurate single phrase that describes them."[6] Another person who spent considerable time among different Yanoama groups describes them as "Gentle. Fierce. Tender. Proud."[7] Still another proposes the designation "men or people of the peach palm."[8]

The Yanoama have been identified above as "marginals" with respect to South American tropical forest culture, largely because of their traditional lack of bitter manioc as the major crop plant and because they do not build effective craft for river navigation. With regard to the latter point, there can be no doubt that the Yanoama are land travelers. As such they contrast with the canoe travelers that predominate in the tropical forest culture. However, the agricultural criterion might be so interpreted as to include the Yanoama rather than exclude them. The horticulture that they practice is based on vegetative reproduction and is thereby consistent with the agricultural technology of South American tropical forest cultivators in general. And, although their principal crop (the plantain, *Musa* sp.) is not included in classificatory schemes, their other important garden staples—*ocumo* (*Xanthosoma* sp.),[9] sweet manioc (*Manihot* sp.), and the native American yam (*Dioscorea trifida*)—are all consistent with autochthonous South American root-crop cultivation. The heavy dependence on musaceous plants, particularly the plantain, is distinctive: the Yanoama are unique among American aboriginals in having the plantain as their most important crop plant in terms of acreage, volume, and religious significance.

Plate 1. Mayobo-teri man. Note Franciscan tonsure, traces of body paint, and large wad of tobacco inside lower lip.

In Yanoama culture an enduring stress is placed on post mortem incineration and ritual mortuary endocannibalism, whereas these have virtually disappeared among the other peoples who once practiced them.[10] Also peculiar is their continuing usage of bows and arrows of "exaggerated length."[11]

Certain other traits also represent considerable distinctiveness. Adult males tie the penis foreskin to a waistcord in a manner rarely used in South America at present, although this trait appears in the archaeologic record.[12] The Yanoama are not known to practice any form of bodily depilation. However, the Franciscan tonsure, believed to have once been widely diffused in ancient South America,[13] is common among both males and females. In their use of tobacco, too, the Yanoama are quite distinctive: large wads of the soft leaves are kept between the lower gum and lower lip almost continuously by many adults (see plates 1 and 5). In general, unacculturated Yanoama find salt (NaCl) repugnant and have no use for it. They also have no kind of fermented (alcoholic) drink.[14]

Otto Zerries has classified some of these, as well as certain other Yanoama culture traits, in terms of their supposed locus of origin. Thus, the avoidance of large streams and of navigation, the exaggerated length of bows and arrows, and the haircut style are relics of a "primitive stratum" of Yanoama culture, presumably developed *in situ*.[15] In contrast, their ritual endocannibalism and the use of rolled green tobacco leaves are "western traits," that is, from the Peruvian Montaña and even the sub-Andean area. Although these practices have become decadent in that western area, the Yanoama continue them.[16]

A Yanoama language is coextensive with these various distinguishing culture traits. It predates the formation of (or at least is independent of) the Carib and Arawak language families that comprise most of the native peoples of the tropical forests north of the Amazon. At the present time it is impossible to ascertain the full range and richness of the language.[17] Native Yanoama speakers have neither alphabet nor orthography, and, consequently, their language has been subject to different interpretations. For example, while one student of the Yanoama says that "the daily vocabulary is much larger than our own," another believes that the language is "scanty in words."[18] Evidently Yanoama is rich in terms dealing with the spatial aspects of their world, but it appears to reflect only a rudimentary conceptualization of time and of precise measurement.

Significant regional variation exists in pronunciation, semantics, and vocabulary. At the time of this study seven dialects had been identified in Venezuela alone (see map 5). With a single exception (the Waika), these appear to extend into Brazil, and each dialect region has as its center some part of the Parima massif or the Tapirapeco massif to the southwest.[19] Differences between certain of the dialects are small, while in other cases dialectal differences are very great. Barafiri speakers, for example, easily comprehend and enjoy recordings made along the Orinoco among people of the Waika dialect. However, they understand Sanoma and, particularly, Cobari only after considerable effort and concentration.

It has been postulated that the Yanoama are diglottic—that, in this special form of bilingualism, they speak two varieties of their language. One variety is the everyday Yanoama to which the dialects belong. The other is a formal Yanoama, *wayamo*, reserved for chanting by adult males during certain ritualized social occasions.[20] This formal Yanoama might be an archaic language, serving as a sort of contemporary lingua franca. It is reasonably comprehensible to male speakers of different dialects when they come in contact and is even assumed to have been "at some time in the past a primary language."[21]

Many Yanoama have a tradition that humanity (i.e., the Yanoama ancestors) originated in the Parima highlands.[22] It is conceivable, therefore, that Barafiri might be the contemporary popular dialect closest to formal Yanoama,[23] since this numerically large group occupies much of the central Parima.

In view of the vastness of the area occupied by possibly fifteen thousand

Yanoama and the physical isolation of most communities, one is led to wonder how a cultural homogeneity could be maintained. The explanation seems to lie in the effective web of kinship and social connections that provides for indirect linkages between all Yanoama, even though the specific individual's operational world is very reduced in size. Several of these functional linkages that provide for continuing interpersonal contact can be identified: a marriage tradition of exogamous lineages, which tends to bind each kin-derived residence unit (*teri*) to others; institutionalized group visiting for the purposes of celebrating with the dead and strengthening friendships (during which the formal, chanted variety of the Yanoama language is used by men); the fusioning of *teri* residence units; and the fissioning of *teri*. There is also a striking cultural conservatism in the Yanoama that discourages inventiveness and experimentation and exists in a context of physical isolation from other cultures.

Isolation

Within the South American tropical forests only a few contemporary peoples, such as the Yanoama, are literally aboriginal. They have managed somehow to retain their cultural distinctiveness and their territory despite pressure and competition from Arawaks, Caribs, Europeans, and finally Creoles.[24]

At present the Indians whose lands border those of the Yanoama are either Carib or Arawak (see map 4). To the east and north are a variety of Carib peoples. To the northwest are the Maquiritare (Maiongong), also Carib in origin. To the southwest and south of the Yanoama territory are lands supposedly occupied by the descendants of Arawaks. These Carib and Arawak peoples are generally classified as typical of the tropical forest culture.

Because of the isolation of the Yanoama lands they can be viewed as culturally analogous to the "driftless area" of glaciated Wisconsin: currents of foreign cultures have advanced and receded about them, leaving the Yanoama themselves largely unaffected. The Parima highlands function as one of the last great cultural redoubts of the South American continent. Thus, even today, the Yanoama are described as a "virgin-soil" population;[25] a population remarkably similar to the pre-Columbian Indians.[26]

They occupy an area that contained no concentrations of sedentary Indians or accumulations of wealth to lure foreign adventurers, nor were there colonial *entradas* like those experienced by so many other tribes.[27] Most of the traditional Yanoama territory is inaccessible by water navigation, effectively protecting its occupants from outsiders. What is more, they were spared the devastation inflicted on many lowland tribes by the rubber and chicle commerce of the late nineteenth and early twentieth centuries.

Contemporary international boundaries, even those deep within the Parima massif, are established and legally delimited as coincident with the divide between the Orinoco and Amazon watersheds (although they are not fully demarcated). Various expeditions have explored some head-water streams up to international points, and most of the major fluvial routes are known.[28]

Yanoama territory, in fact most of the Amazonas Federal Territory (Venezuela) and much of the Roraima Federal Territory and Amazonas state (Brazil), lie well beyond the frontiers of contemporary Creole settlement. It has been said, rather romantically, that "of all the regions of the earth still unexplored, that which extends for hundreds of miles between the Rio Negro and the Upper Río Orinoco, just where the Yanoáma live, is perhaps the most vast and the most fascinating. Since the time of the conquest, all efforts to penetrate the interior of this forest have been useless."[29]

For the Venezuelans and Brazilians of today, this is a sort of *terra incognita*, a "zona pouco conhecida."[30] Some Creole Venezuelans think of the southern third of their country as part of a great storehouse filled with rich resources for future development; others are pessimistic about its potentialities. To date there exists neither a comprehensive inventory of resources nor a clear idea of their dimensions.[31]

EXPLORERS AMONG THE YANOAMA

The highland Yanoama, among the most culturally isolated people of the hemisphere, live alone in an immense territory. These proud people are suspicious and even fearful of things foreign to them. And they are sometimes terrified by certain strange, new objects, such as firearms, cameras, and helicopters, as well as the odd-looking creatures who use them.

Outsiders—whether Europeans, Creoles, or other Indians—are considered foreigners (*naba* in the Barafiri dialect) and the Yanoama are cautious in their dealings with them. However, once they are assured that no harm is to be done them, they are quite frank in their curiosity about foreign things and, particularly, foreign people. They are far more interested in the lines on a *naba*'s face and the hair growth on his face, hands, and chest than they are in his machines—which are largely unintelligible to them anyway.

Unfortunately, most explorers have been unable to appreciate the humanness of the Yanoama. Instead, adventurers helped give them a reputation for being more "wild" (*bravo* or *salvaje* in Spanish), violent, and potentially dangerous than most other Indians of South America. Over the years they have become legendary.

The first European encounter with Yanoama reportedly was in 1758. According to one account, the Spanish officer in charge was Francisco Bobadilla, and there occurred a "bloody fight with Guaica Indians" at the Raudal de Guaharivos [*sic*].[32] In 1760, Apolinar Díez de la Fuente, commander of a Spanish expedition (in which Bobadilla was an officer) charged with finding the source of the Orinoco, heard disturbing reports from his Indian guides. These guides, probably Carib-Maquiritare, told him that the "Guariba" people of the Orinoco headwaters area were very quarrelsome (*guapos*) and valiant, and that the expedition should not go there, "because they would kill me and all my people."[33] The Spanish were within clear sight of the Parima highlands when they decided not to continue because of the dangers that lay ahead.

In 1799 Alexander von Humboldt traveled the Orinoco to La Esmeralda where he, too, heard fearful tales of a tribe of "white Indians," the "Guaicas."[34] Robert Schomburgk proceeded along the upper Uraricoera, over into the Río Erebato–Río Caura headwaters, and then back to the upper Ocamo in 1837–1839. There his porters finally became victims of panic for fear of an attack by "Kirishana" Indians, and he was forced to abandon his plan to continue due south to the Orinoco headwaters, backtracking instead to the Río Padamo, which he followed to the Orinoco.[35]

Alexander Hamilton Rice attempted to cross the Parima massif from the west, via the Orinoco in 1920, and from the east, via the Rio Parima in 1925. On January 22, 1920, in the vicinity of the Raudal de los Guaharibos, a group of well over sixty "Guaharibos" came upon his party. Taking no chances, he killed some of them and then abandoned his plans to continue up the Río Orinoco.[36] In his trip up the Rio Parima in 1925, Rice had a Thompson submachine gun among his weapons. His informants, Carib affiliates who had never crossed the divide between the Rio Parima and the Río Orinoco, told him that the Indians up there were "bad Indians (*bravos*) whom all the others kept away from."[37] Because of the threat of trouble from these Yanoama, the rugged terrain that lay ahead, and his dwindling supplies, Rice accepted "defeat and disaster,"[38] giving up for good his dream of crossing over the Parima massif.

However, the legends live on, and guides are still wary about going into the unknown Yanoama world. One of the scientists on the official 1951 Venezuelan-French expedition to demarcate the source of the Río Orinoco identified a pathological fear among members of the expedition, which he called a "Guahariba psychosis."[39] The leader of an official expedition to the headwaters of Venezuela's Río Paragua in 1956 referred frequently in his account to the fear of "wild" Indians ("Guaikas") felt by his Indian porters and guides.[40]

Perhaps as a consequence of so much misinformation, the Yanoama, as much as any American aboriginal group, have been described in the literature with such abusive appellations as "most primitive," "savage," "wild," "fierce," and "paleolithic."[41]

SUSTAINED CONTACT

To my knowledge, sustained, intimate contact with the Yanoama by non-Indians was not achieved until 1947. At that time James Barker of the New Tribes Mission established himself on Venezuela's upper Río Orinoco, attaching himself to the one group of Yanoama then known to be living near the river.[42] That group, called the Majecodo-teri, had chosen to make themselves accessible to outsiders by relocating near navigable water.[43] The first effective sustained contact with the Brazilian Yanoama was accomplished just prior to 1960 by men also of the New Tribes Mission. By 1962 they had established themselves permanently on the upper Rio Toototobi, a tributary of the Demini. These references are to the time of the first contacts other than ones of a transitory nature. Since those base dates, a variety of other missionary and government establishments have been created and maintained.[44] In most instances navigable river routes were used, and, consequently, contact was made on the lowland periphery of Yanoama territory.[45]

·

Yanoama Origins and Antiquity

Yanoama cultural distinctiveness is usually explained as a function of isolation, and the two hypotheses presented in chapter 1 are most common. One of these incorporates a process of cultural retrogression. According to this hypothesis, the ancient ancestors of the Yanoama were farming people of the central Amazon lowlands who moved north, probably via the Rio Negro–Casiquiare Channel route.[46] The process involved centuries, if not millennia. These particular farming people, like numerous other groups, were weaker than their neighbors, who forced them from the fertile flood plains up into the high interfluves that were unattractive to the stronger tribes. Gradual cultural degradation is thought to have come about with their subsequent isolation, which is an explanation for the existence of most—if not all—of the "marginals."[47]

The second hypothesis is that the Yanoama are direct descendants of (and, possibly, the sole remnants of) one of the earliest migratory waves

Map 2. Routes of Early Human Migration into South America. After Carl O. Sauer, "A Geographic Sketch of Early Man in America," *Geographical Review* 34 (1944).

into South America.[48] These ancient immigrants might have hunted now-extinct large animals, such as the giant sloths, mastodons, and even wild horses, pursuing these herds ever deeper into the South American continent,[49] until finally they reached their present location. Once here, through the succeeding millennia, they remained in a kind of backwater, isolated from both cultural and biological miscegenation. Located far to the east of the Andean mainstream of successive waves of Asiatic immigrants (see map 2), they were effectively cut off from contact with other peoples. Much later, they continued in isolation between the routes used by invading peoples, such as the Arawaks and the Caribs who followed the navigable streams.[50]

Two sets of data have been interpreted to support the second hypothesis, that is, that the Yanoama are directly descended from the earliest immigrants to South America. One of these sets is linguistic; the other is hematological. Reports of glotto-chronological studies suggest that the "languages" spoken by the Yanoama constitute a linguistic conglomerate whose internal divergencies have had at least six to thirty-five centuries ("minimal centuries") to develop.[51] Therefore, it is argued, the various Yanoama subtribes separated from a common group with its own single language perhaps three thousand years ago. Since subtribes that are far removed from one another chronologically live relatively close spatially, the Yanoama are thought to have once occupied a much larger territory.[52] Clearly, these conclusions based on very limited evidence do not prove that the Yanoama ancestors came so early, and they certainly do not obviate the possibility that the Yanoama are descendants of people who emigrated from the Amazon lowlands. The hypothesized divergence of peoples forced from the central Amazon lowland is thought to have occurred so long ago (3500 to 3000 B.C.)[53] that linguistic diversity is to be expected among the various offshoots of a progenitor language that existed at that time.

The second set of data interpreted as supporting the idea that the uniqueness of the Yanoama is due to their hypothesized antiquity is based on analyses of certain blood samples. Only Mongoloid peoples (generally taken to include all American aboriginals) are known to have in their blood the Diego factor.[54] According to one writer, among South American Indians this varies from a frequency of 45 percent for the "Chibcha," to 28 percent for the Caribs, to 12 percent for the Arawaks.[55] The Yanoama, according to all tests that have been conducted, are completely Diego negative; this factor does not appear in their blood.[56] There is no universal agreement among geneticists as to what this signifies, but no one has yet disproved the absence of the factor in Yanoama blood.[57] The discovery of their Diego negativity exposes a currently inexplicable distinctiveness of the Yanoama. It is conceivable that they are one of the most ancient populations of the Americas; few, however, would go further than to recognize this as a distinct possibility.[58] The implication is clear, nevertheless: the ancestors of these people may have arrived earlier than the Mongoloid ancestors of other South American Indian peoples and remained quite separate from them for many thousands of years.

Physical Characteristics

The Yanoama are strong. Both men and women carry heavy loads on their backs.[59] They can move rapidly on difficult trails, and in the high Parima they take chill, damp mornings in stride. Most of the men can withstand arduous, prolonged hunting trips and the heavy labor of clearing new garden sites. When a group travels, the women are expected to act as porters. In size the Yanoama vary considerably. Measurements of adult Barafiri males show a mean height of just under five feet (4'8" is small, and 5'1" is tall).[60] Considerably taller men have been reported, some as much as 5'6" in height.[61] Barafiri women of the Parima highlands average slightly over 4'6" (4'3" is very short, while 4'8" is not unusual). Yanoama women measuring up to 5'2" have also been reported.[62] In a sample Parima highland population, adult men ranged in weight from 90 pounds to 110, and women ranged from 75 pounds to 95. No obesity was observed. In the Orinoco lowlands, particularly where they are in contact with outsiders, Yanoama appear to be more robust than in the Parima. This may be due to the acculturative process that both has brought them into contact with scientific medical attention and has made starchy bitter manioc an important part of their diet.

One of the strongest impressions I derived from my first contact with the Yanoama was that of their redness.[63] That color seemed not only to cover them, but also to cover nearly everything associated with them. The redness is due to the generous usage of *bixa* (*Bixa* sp.),[64] which rubs off easily and has a faint fragrance. Once the *bixa*, dust, and other foreign matter have been removed, Yanoama complexions are light, with the tint ranging from an extremely light yellow to a deep tan. The Yanoama, in fact, are lighter in skin tone than the other aboriginal peoples of Venezuela and lighter than most of the Creoles living in the Amazonas Federal Territory.[65]

The Yanoama never use footwear of any kind, and their feet are tough and calloused, with widely spread toes.[66] The print of such a foot is almost triangular in shape, the heel forming one of the angles. When carrying a heavy load, women tend to walk with knees together, feet apart and toes pointed inward. Strong, even teeth have been reported among groups living near the Orinoco.[67] However, in the Parima highlands, toothache is not unusual, and a common remedy in severe cases is to pry loose or knock out the ailing tooth. Most of these people have a head of thick, straight, black hair, which sometimes glints reddish-brown in the sun. It is unusual to see gray hair, even among the elderly (see plate 2). Baldness, observed on occasion among young children, appears to occur only in relation to malnutrition or some bodily disorder. Normally, body hair is sparse. Most adult Barafiri men are largely free of facial hair, although some few have light moustaches.[68] The broad nose with somewhat flaring nostrils seems to predominate, but narrow shapes are also found. The eyes of the Yanoama tend to look Oriental. Some people have very pronounced epicanthic folds (see plate 3), although among others no eye fold is visible. It is reported that newborn infants have the Mongolian spot.[69] In head shape the Yanoama are predominantly dolicocephalic.[70]

Plate 2. Elderly man from the Niyayoba area. His dog is meek with its owner but very ill-tempered with strangers. This man, probably more than sixty-five years old, is noticeably graying at the temples. Since clothing, such as shirts, trousers, and dresses, are totally foreign, these things are worn indiscriminately by men and women.

Plate 3. Barafiri man holding his peach palm bow. Note arm bands of cotton and his very pronounced epicanthic eye fold. Behind him is a house wall made of *Musa* leaves and palm fronds suspended from poles.

This brief description of the Yanoama is intended only to provide a rough sketch of their physical attributes and to call attention to the considerable diversity within the population.

Ecological Aspects of Yanoama Culture

The Yanoama are a sylvan people par excellence and, therefore, distinct from the great bulk of tropical forest cultures, which are essentially riverine in orientation. While these latter peoples navigate, the traditional Yanoama method of viewing a stream or swamp is as an obstacle to be bridged.[71] Although they are frequently described as nomadic or semi-nomadic, one might seriously question whether they are either of these. Both the riverine and the sylvan peoples of the tropical South American forests have material cultures with a high degree of portability (including the transport of cumbersome, fragile clay pots), and if this is the principal criterion, then all of them might be thought of as at least seminomadic. As with the riverine peoples, the Yanoama community settlement, or *shabono*, is the fixed focal point for all activities until it is finally abandoned to the elements when a new one is built. Another aspect of permanency is the important role of horticulture among the Yanoama as well as the navigating peoples. Their gardens are an indispensable element of the Yanoama ecosystem, and they are not abandoned until new ones have been prepared and come into production. Like *shabono*, gardens are established focal points conducive to permanency of settlement.

Social, political, and economic organization is based upon kinship, specifically on blood ties and formal marriages. Thus, literally every aspect of life is submerged in interpersonal relationships. The tangible manifestation of the socioeconomic, political settlement unit is the circular *shabono* community. When the *shabono* is viewed in terms of the specific family shelters that it comprises, the spatial pattern is an intricate reflection of the intangibles of *teri* kinship. Each Yanoama must identify with some such residence group. Egalitarianism seems to dominate the social structure, and it is equally evident in both economic and political realms. The political organization might best be described as acephalous, although in the literature there are frequent references to "chiefs" and "headmen."[72] Each *shabono* community is practically self-sufficient, with a firm base in horticulture. An important supplement is provided by rather specialized collecting of forest products. Hunting is also significant, but traditionally fishing is not.

Like a few other cultures of the tropical forests, the Yanoama wear no clothing, although they do adorn their bodies frequently for mystical and aesthetic reasons, as well as for the practical purpose of protection from insects. Technology is manifested in a small number of modest tools and crafts, most of which will be dealt with in succeeding chapters.[73]

TRADITIONAL WORLD VIEW

Religion impinges on all aspects of life, without the conceptual distinction between *man, nature*, and the *divine* that characterizes Judeo-Christianity.[74] No omnipotent God exists. There is no material world surrounding the Yanoama and existing independently of them, no world that they view as capable of being dominated and turned to satisfy their own needs. And, in an inexplicable manner, "yesterday" and "tomorrow" merge almost imperceptibly into "today." Mysteriously, man can share a common life with an animal, or even with some natural phenomenon, such as the wind or thunder. People not only live now in intimate association with the monkeys, tapirs, deer, and birds of the forest but also have been—or might be—these very creatures.

There is an easy transmutability among the Yanoama between what are commonly defined as different realms: the human, natural, and divine. This kind of change can be accomplished best by sorcerers, although all adults are capable of it.[75] An important corollary to transmutation is a belief in the alter ego. Thus, adult males share spirits, or souls, with other creatures. Among these, the harpy eagle (*Thrasaetus harpyia*) and the jaguar (*Felis onca* or *Panthera onca*) are particularly prevalent. The alter egos of females are associated spiritually with totally different creatures, such as butterflies. In fact, in Yanoama culture an enormous differentiation exists between male and female, on both human and spiritual planes. In the various versions of the creation legends, the origins of male and female Yanoama are distinctive.

These are people of profound and abiding faith. They believe that certain rituals will train a dog to hunt better, that a woman can prevent conception by sprinkling certain magical powders on her head, that body painting will affect the spirit world,[76] and that powerful sorcerers can cause illness and even death to their enemies.

Culture Heroes. Through untold generations, an oral tradition has kept alive the legends and sacred rites that deal with the great mysteries of existence.[77] In the Orinoco lowlands the most respected spirit is reportedly one called Boreawa. He had been one of the earliest men, transformed later into a spirit being who is credited with having taught mankind (i.e., the Yanoama) necessary truths.

Throughout much of the highland Yanoama territory, however, roughly the same accomplishments are attributed to a spirit being called Omawa.[78] In fact, almost everything the Parima Barafiri have or know seems to be ultimately attributable to Omawa. He is their greatest culture hero, a powerful being who, Prometheus-like, concerned himself with the welfare of mankind. When he discovered that the gigantic she-serpent Rajara had a secret garden in which she grew plantains and other crops, he forced her to teach him to garden so that he could pass on to mankind this knowledge.[79] In general terms, Omawa seems to embody "good" in the context of day-to-day human living, quite unlike Judeo-Christian "good" as a force of cosmic import. His brother, Yowawa (Yoawe, Yoawa), is usually said to be living with him in some far-off place. These are among the few spirits that have proper names (most spirits have the names of plants, animals, or other natural phenomena).

Sorcerers. In Yanoama culture there are few real specialists; most people of the same age and sex category have about the same knowledge and skills. However, some sort of mediator is needed to aid people in dealing with the spirit world. Such a sorcerer, if his magic is powerful, is a very important man. His principal role is to cure the ill or injured in cases where the cause of the problem is considered to be a malicious spirit sent by specific human enemies. Many accidents and all diseases are attributed to spirits.[80] There is no such thing as a "natural" death. Other responsibilities of a sorcerer include sending calamities down upon his enemies and protecting himself and his people from the evil witchcraft of other sorcerers. Each *shabono* community needs at least one accomplished sorcerer for the well-being of the group.[81] A sorcerer's successes and failures are manifest, and success, particularly in warding off evil spirits, enhances a man's social and political position and brings him prestige and leadership responsibilities. Communication with the spirits is possible through the medium of strong drugs, taken by sorcerers as well as other men who wish to contact their own personal spirits (*hecura*). In some settlements along the Orinoco drugs are reportedly taken almost every afternoon by many men,[82] while in the Parima highlands individuals seem to use them infrequently and in moderation. These drugs constitute a sacred, masculine element of Yanoama culture. As such, they are distinctive from tobacco, since tobacco smoke is not considered a significant healing force as it is in other tropical forest tribes and since women can use tobacco freely.

The drugs used are principally hallucinogenic snuffs, which are taken by pairs of men; each man blows the snuff through a hollow reed into the other's nostril. The most prevalent snuff is prepared from "reddish bark resin" of several *Virola* trees.[83] Yanoama know this snuff as *ebena*. Sometimes additional ingredients, such as powdered bark ashes or powdered leaves, are included. The effects are initial excitability, numbing of the limbs, twitching of facial muscles, nausea, then hallucinations, and, finally, a deep, disturbed sleep.[84] Another snuff, which is apparently more widespread among other tribes of the Orinoco and Amazon than it is among the Yanoama, is popularly known among Creoles as *yopo*.[85] It is made from the toasted beans of certain *Piptadenia*, such as *Anadenanthera peregrina* (*cojoba* in Venezuelan vernacular). When this powder, often enhanced with admixtures, is taken nasally, the principal effect is an "intoxication marked by a temporary fury and trance accompanied by visual hallucinations and eventual stupor."[86]

Yanoama and Death. Death triggers the most impressive rituals.[87] The inevitability of death is recognized, and the afterlife is extremely important. If the rituals are performed properly, the deceased will enter a world much like this one but far more agreeable.[88] There, men engage in gardening, hunting, and other important male activities of this life, while women and children also live much as they do on earth. A hot, terrible place is reserved for those who were selfish and stingy in this life.[89]

To avoid that counterpart of hell and the loss of the personal spirit after the death of the body, various ceremonies must be performed. From the moment of death, ritual—and sincere—mourning begins. A deceased person is usually related to many people in his own *shabono*, as well as other communities. When one of the old founders or matriarchs of a *shabono* community dies, the loss brings grief to a great many people. Women shriek and wail, and men often weep freely. Depending upon the circumstances, the body is either taken, wrapped in its hammock, into the forest to decompose or it is burned almost immediately in a pyre constructed in the *shabono* clearing.[90] The personal belongings of the deceased are burned,[91] and if he had a garden it is destroyed. Sons or other close kinsmen occasionally preserve certain weapons or tools for later ritual destruction.

Incineration of the human remains is the *sine qua non* for a peaceful afterlife, because the bones contain the indispensable essence of life,[92] which must evidently be liberated for later use. Even after an attack, bitter enemies will allow the removal of the dead, since the worst thing that can befall a Yanoama is to be denied his post-mortem incineration. This is the only way his immortal ego is released to the spirit world.[93] When the fire has cooled after the cremation, all the bone fragments are carefully picked from the ashes and ceremonially pulverized, to the accompaniment of weeping, in a crude sort of wooden mortar made expressly for the occasion. Some of the powdered bone is then poured into small gourds, which are sealed with wax and distributed among close kinsmen of the deceased. These gourds are extremely valuable possessions of the various male relatives who receive them. Later, when the time is appropriate, a liquid is prepared by boiling peeled ripe plantains in water until they become soft and mushy. Then some of the remaining pulverized bone is sprinkled in. The resulting mixture is called *cowata uba* by the Barafiri, and the rite culminating in the drinking of this liquid is a *reajo*.[94] Preparation of the *cowata uba*, like the preparations for the *reajo* in general, is a male responsibility. Timing for the ceremony is determined by the feasibility of bringing together many close relatives from different *shabono*, as well as the availability of ripe plantains and freshly killed game, which are all requisites. Weeping and lamentations accompany the preparation of the sacred liquid, and men drink it with tear-filled eyes as they remember their departed loved one.[95] The use of these powdered bones is carefully rationed, so that *reajos* can sometimes be performed for years after a person's death. It is particularly important to protract this period of their usage in cases where kinsmen of a dead man are seeking revenge for his death and strong motivation is required to keep alive their hatred.

SPATIAL SENSITIVITY

The Yanoama have a highly developed sense of geography; their spatial sensitivity is acute. They have a keen faculty for perceiving the location of game, wild fruits, tapir licks, honey, and insect life, as well as the plants needed for dyes, adhesives, poisons, narcotics, cording, baskets, and the like. Sometimes, lying in their hammocks, Barafiri men will amuse themselves by testing one another's knowledge of such specific information. One man pretends he is moving through an area, identifying things and places he would see as he zigzags about trying to lose those whom he is testing; when a man becomes lost, he admits it.

Young boys, in play packs, know the forest trails, the multitude of wild plants, the animal creatures, and the cultivated plants of the community gardens. During these explorations, their bare bodies brush against thorns, rough leaves, vines, and rasplike grasses, but there are no audible complaints. Women also develop a familiarity with the habitat. Frequently they form small groups to collect an enormous variety of things, such as edible fruits, amphibians, insects, firewood, and palm suitable for roofing. Except when they fear enemy raids, women range freely through the forest near their *shabono* or campsite in these foraging activities. At all times great caution is shown in the selection of water for drinking.[96] On the trail, a large leaf is folded to make a cup of sorts with which to scoop up a drink. Water is used only where the stream is clear and known to be pure.

Yanoama knowledge of drainage patterns and topography is comprehensive, and their names for features and places are precise.[97] The trails follow direct routes with little concern for avoiding steep gradients. Limits of community territories can be well defined, although there is generally little need to do so since neighboring *teri* have no real concern with precisely demarcated territories.

The measurement of distance is geared to travel time. Direction, too, is generalized, with no evidence of a concept of cardinal directions. In their equatorial habitat, the sun rises in the east and sets in the west throughout the year. Positions between (directions) are used as guides in the approximate measurement of time from sunrise to sunset. Names for directions are also those of populations who live in those directions.[98]

Some of the most convincing indicators of Yanoama spatial sensitivity are to be found in their language. For example, there is a wealth of "position markers," referring to such things as distance, slope, and altitude. These words are used individually and several sometimes appear together in a compound word.[99] The language also includes generic terms for significant features of the physical environment. To the Barafiri, the forest is *urifi*, and conceptually very different from the savanna (*borosi*); a mountain is *febaruca*, while *jefu* is a hill, a waterfall is *bora*, and a river is *mau-u*. A specific savanna or waterfall is identified by the appropriate generic noun accompanied by an identifier (e.g., Niyayoba Borosi or Waiteri Bora). The term for water or liquid is *u*, and it appears as a suffix morpheme in the proper name of any specific stream.[100] Stream hierarchy is well defined; the largest stream known to the people of a particular area is designated as *bada-u* (literally, "big stream"), as well as by its proper name.[101]

The Yanoama have a variety of bases for ascribing proper names to places. For example, they use the term for a prominent physical feature of an area (Oquiyamoba, "where the water gets deep") to distinguish it, or the kind of plant (Cuaisiba, the *Mauritia* palm), or animal (Mayobo, "toucan") that is or was found there, or even some important event (Niyayoba, "to shoot at one another") that occurred there. They never use people's names in identifying places.

In contrast with an acute sensitivity to the natural environment, to location, and to spatial dimension in general, the Yanoama temporal sense appears to be relatively weakly developed. The day is divided into periods that are not related to any measurement unit, such as the hour. Approximate equivalents of these periods are morning (dawn to sunrise), midday (while the sun is high in the sky), afternoon (while the sun is rapidly sinking in the sky), and night (after the sun has disappeared).[102] Evidently the sun must be visible for its position to have any significance, because, when it is covered by thick clouds, the Barafiri lose track of time. When specifying how long a journey will take, or how much time is to be expended on a task, a Yanoama points to where the sun will be in the sky when he is finished. There is no other way for him to measure the period. The passage of the days is counted in numbers of "sleeps," which equal the number of nights elapsed.[103] The sun is believed to be "still inside" the earth before it rises each morning. And, in the Orinoco lowlands during the dry season (November–January), the sun is thought to be closer than it is in the wet season (May–July).[104]

Phases of the moon are observed, and the lunar month is recognized.[105] Usually only a single sequence of phases is used (i.e., the moon "gets big," "gets small," and "disappears"). Although it must be extremely difficult for a Yanoama to put together several of these sequences, there are reports that this is done.[106] Seasons of the year are calculated in accord with the cycle of wild and domesticated plants, and the Yanoama are aware that there is a long time period that lapses between similar harvests. There is a past, and there is a future. But beyond that, there seems to be no clear concept of a specific future time when certain flowers will develop or when certain honeys will become available or of a specific past date when a death occurred.

In their language there are words only for the numbers "one" and "two." No other words exist for precise amounts, and people are obliged to use their fingers to indicate quantities above two.[107] Adding is possible if the sum is no larger than ten (the number of fingers), and some people can even subtract in this manner. Multiplication and division are impossible.

ACCULTURATION

The extent to which the foregoing culture traits can be ascribed exclusively to an autochthonous Yanoama culture is not certain. However, there is convincing evidence that few innovations have been available to them, and that almost none has been accepted by these conservative people. The limited acculturation that has taken place consists principally of the acquisition of material objects, which can generally be seen side by side with the old.[108]

Material Culture. Most of the new objects can be classified as trade goods, such as a variety of steel implements (axes, hatchets, machetes, and knives),[109] aluminum kettles, fish hooks, matches, nylon cord, and sheet plastic. Another category of trade goods, such as cotton thread, cloth, tailored clothing, mirrors, combs, flashlights, beads, manioc flour, and candy, are sometimes highly regarded but economically less useful. The accessibility of *teri* groups and their acquisitive power vary, so that there is an uneven distribution of these objects. When acquired, none of them seems significantly to have affected the Yanoama ecosystem.

Personal elegance has been enhanced by glass beads of varying colors.

Plate 4. Girl from the Niyayoba area, perhaps ten years old. Her neatly cut hair, carefully placed mouth and nose ornaments, and large bunches of feathers and fibers in her ear-lobe perforations indicate that she is prepared for a special occasion.

Plate 5. Mayobo-teri woman and infant. Her body paint is enhanced by ear and nose decorations. She has a wad of tobacco leaves inside her lower lip. Note body painting on the infant and ornaments used by the girls on the left. One girl wears an "apron" of cotton fringe.

Apparently these have become widely diffused only within the past two decades (the Parima Barafiri have had them since about 1960), and some adults in remote *shabono* still have no beads of their own. Along with this innovation, the Yanoama continue to decorate themselves in the traditional manner with body paints, ornaments of string and feathers, and ear plugs; women still place sticks in the perforations of their lips and nasal septa (see plates 4 and 5); and fresh bouquets of flowers, leaves, and fibers are daily put into their pierced ear lobes.

The great variety of traditional vegetable fibers has been supplemented with factory-made cotton thread and nylon and other man-made fibers. Yet, most Yanoama still wear no clothing. These new fibers are used as fishing line and in the manufacture of arrows; pieces of plastic are prized as waterproof containers for valuables, such as feathers or matches.

The traditional Yanoama hammock, which still prevails in the highlands, is made from split vine or strips of bast. These materials, particularly the bast, become brittle, and hammocks made of them have to be replaced frequently. It is not surprising that people find cotton hammocks highly desirable.[110] However, they are very expensive as a trade item and difficult to obtain. As late as 1966, the Jasubowa-teri (who then lived "a few days upstream from Peñascal" and only an hour's walk from the Río Orinoco) had no cotton hammocks.[111] Of nearly 250 people living in a *shabono* of the isolated Niyayoba area in 1968, only two men had cotton hammocks. The Yanoama have traditionally grown cotton in small amounts, spinning the fibers into thread, which they used almost exclusively for adornment of the body.[112]

Aluminum cooking kettles are another kind of trade goods much desired by the Yanoama. Some *shabono* still have a few traditional clay pots in use (frequently concealed from prying foreigners), but, because they are so cumbersome and fragile, such pots are less practical than metal ones.[113] Steel tools are the trade items most eagerly sought after and most ubiquitous today. Axes and machetes have become virtually indispensable for important tasks like clearing the forest for gardens, building *shabono* and camp shelters, and obtaining firewood. Knives are desired, but there seem to be few uses for them among the Barafiri.[114] There is no evidence that the introduction of these tools has significantly affected the acreages cleared for horticulture, the morphology or functions of the *shabono*, or even the amount of firewood used. In short, there seems to have been little, if any, direct ecological impact.

It is also noteworthy that these tools only replace some older Yanoama tools; no new functions have been created for them. Arrowheads are still made of palm wood, cane, or bone; metal points are not used. Nor has metal been applied to the tips of the digging sticks used in horticulture. Acquired metal tools are used to remove the forest cover but not to work the earth. Even in fighting, whether formalized dueling or raiding, the palm-wood club (*nabrushi*) and bow and arrow are indispensable. The traditional agouti-tooth gouging tool is still ubiquitous, but stone tools have disappeared. The *jawa* (see fig. 7) represents what might be the last reminder of a stone tool. This is a small tomahawk, or hatchet, in which a piece of machete or knife blade has been hafted to a wooden handle and tied in place with fibers, just as a polished celt might have been so fastened in days past.

Nonmaterial Culture. It has been widely maintained that the Yanoama culture is essentially preagricultural, and, consequently, horticulture must be a recent adoption.[115] Sometimes it is stated that, if the Yanoama are not preagricultural, then surely they are "incipient" cultivators.[116] Both of these positions seem untenable in view of the kinds of circumstantial evidence used to support them; that is, even though the Yanoama have a deep-seated horticultural tradition that is an indispensable and fully articulated element in Yanoama cultural ecology, it does not appear consistent with many of their other cultural patterns and must, therefore, be new. Following this reasoning, most of the literature classifies planned food production as a cultural innovation among the Yanoama.

Some writers believe that the concept of Omawa, a principal Yanoama spirit being and culture hero, is not Yanoama in origin but has been diffused to the Yanoama "from Carib and Arawakan tribes who have creator-culture heroes with linguistically related names and similar supernatural attributes."[117] I have attempted to corroborate the hypothesis, but it cannot be shown convincingly that the Omawa of the Barafiri is a derivative of the Carib concept of Wanaadi.

Much has been written about the violent and fierce nature of the Yanoama. It is implied that this particular culture trait is as universally distributed over Yanoama territory as the language, the *teri* and *shabono* institutions, and the plantain gardens; it is also implied that it characterizes Yanoama men as much as do long bows and arrows, quivers, and tobacco wads. It would appear, however, that, in contrast to these universal traits, the degree of ferocity is spatially variable like trade goods, fishing, and the use of dugout canoes. Perhaps there is even a positive correlation between these particular variables. Conceivably, certain lowland Yanoama (such as the Orinoco Waika), far removed from the security of their own cultural and spatial dominance, constantly menaced by aliens and foreign values, respond violently as an exaggerated defense to compensate for their insecurity.

Certainly the Yanoama who have moved to sites on or near navigable water are not representative. They are outside their niche in the broadest sense, caught in a squeeze between various adverse influences of "civilization." Perhaps frustration and insecurity lead men in such places to take drugs freely and frequently, and also help explain why they would want to be fierce.[118]

Physical Geography of the Habitat

The Yanoama inhabit a territory that extends approximately from 0.5° to 4.5° north latitude, with no part of it closer to the Atlantic than three hundred miles. Since it includes about thirty thousand square miles of varied terrain,[119] some sort of regionalization of the total contemporary habitat is necessary.[120] In such an equatorial area, geomorphology, particularly relief and drainage, provides a key to areal differentiation and consequent ecological implications.

GEOMORPHOLOGY

The traditional Yanoama territory occupies the Guayana Shield, or Guayana Basal Complex of Pre-Cambrian crystalline rock. Here rise the headwaters of the Río Orinoco and some of its major tributaries, as well as major tributaries feeding into the Amazon system via the Rio Branco and the Rio Negro (see map 1). At the heart of this territory is a highland poorly designated as the Serra, or Sierra, Parima. The Parima is not a true sierra, consisting of a chain of mountain peaks, but rather it is an elevated massif upon whose surface an irregular topography has been sculpted from the bedrock. Evidently neither the Sierra Tapirapeco (and the Sierra Curupira) to the southwest nor the Sierra Pacaraima to the northeast are mountain ranges either.[121] Of these, the Tapirapeco appears to be comparable structurally to the Parima, while the Pacaraima is composed of a series of mesas, cuestas, and hills, cut into the southeastern face of an enormous plateau.[122]

In the Parima massif, low mountains characterize the natural landscape, but there are few of the huge, mesalike *tepuy* formations of the Pacaraima.[123] Cliffs and ledges appear locally where there is sandstone control. Crystalline rock outcrops are rare in the Parima, except at the rather abrupt western edge of the massif, where mesa outliers and gigantic sugarloaves rise above the Orinoco plain. In addition to the western outliers, others are found to the east of the Parima. For example, more than one hundred miles east of the Orinoco headwaters, rising above the Rio Branco lowlands, is the Serra Mucajaí, a great block of igneous rock whose eroded surface reaches 1,500 feet above sea level.[124]

The Orinoco and Amazon systems have cut deeply into the resistant rocks of all these massifs. Drainage is quite complete (the few lakes and swamps are generally small) and intricately dendritic. Rapids, chutes, and waterfalls—the *bora* of the Barafiri—are abundant.[125] Relief is only locally pronounced, particularly where the Roraima sandstone has not been removed. Altitudes of 7,700 feet have been reported in the Tapirapeco, while farther north in the Parima and Pacaraima, extreme elevations hardly surpass 6,000 feet. Precise altitudes are, of course, unknown except for a few specific sites. At the bifurcation of the Orinoco-Casiquiare, for example, the mean altitude of the Orinoco is 374 feet above sea level;[126] at the juncture of the Orinoco and the Ugueto it is about 930 feet.[127] None of these figures gives a clear idea of the considerably greater altitudes of the interfluves.[128]

In the vicinity of the Raudal de los Guaharibos (see map 1) the Orinoco leaves the Guayana Shield. Above this, the river has the characteristics of a youthful mountain stream: numerous waterfalls and a well-defined valley.[129] Below, the Orinoco flows west across a narrow plain that gradually merges with the Casiquiare peneplain.[130] Rapids (*raudales*) replace falls, and all can be shot by small craft in high water, except for the Atures-Maipures rapids just upstream from Puerto Ayacucho. The lower portions of such tributaries as the Padamo and the Ocamo move across this plain in broad, sweeping meanders, just as does the Orinoco. All are seasonally clogged with sand bars.

The Río Orinoco above the Mavaca is contained within its banks throughout the year, so there are no extensive areas where the forest floods, as it does farther downstream, annually inundating thousands of square miles of the Casiquiare peneplain. Between the Mavaca and Raudal Peñascal, the banks get progressively higher. They are particularly sheer on the cutting edge of each meander, but, on the inner edges, swampy lowlands merge with the river terraces. Very few tributaries are visible; on either bank there are only green walls of vegetation. A few spectacular peaks rise above the floor of the narrow plain, some majestically clothed in purple tones that contrast with the green of the forests and the brown water of the Orinoco. These uninhabited outcrops support a cover of scrub and brush, rather than the tall trees of the plain, and on them rock stratifications are identifiable.

CLIMATE

Reliable climatic data for the diverse parts of Yanoama territory do not exist. An important development occurred in early 1970, however, when the Venezuelan Ministry of Public Works began installing dozens of pluviographs and evapographs as well as devices to measure stream level fluctuations, in both lowland and highland locations in the southern part of the country. Unfortunately, most of the data from this new equipment are not yet available, although there is adequate information for lowland stations, such as San Carlos, Puerto Ayacucho, and Boa Vista (see map 1), and some for the Niyayoba area (see map 9) of the central Parima highlands. However, both Puerto Ayacucho and Boa Vista are savannalike in climate type, and, therefore, the data are essentially irrelevant to most of the Yanoama territory.

San Carlos, on the Rio Negro, just downstream from the mouth of the Casiquiare, is at an elevation slightly over 200 feet. It is always wet and warm according to data gathered between 1952 and 1954. The mean annual temperature is almost 80° F, with an extreme maximum of about 91° F. The warmest month (March) averages about 84° F, and the coolest (July) averages about 76° F. Mean monthly relative humidity varies from 85 percent (May) to 91 percent (September). Average annual rainfall, well distributed throughout the year, totals about 143 inches.[131] Throughout much of the upper Orinoco the climate is thought to be sufficiently uniform (and similar to San Carlos) so that it is all classified as selva type;[132] Brazilians classify the western third of the Roraima Federal Territory (just about all of it that appears on map 1) as monsoon type.[133] In both cases the massifs of the international border area are included in the classifications. However, altitude is an extremely important climatic factor: on the massifs, elevation greatly tempers the climate, producing a habitat very different from that of San Carlos or Boa Vista in the lowlands.

Except at some extremities of Yanoama territory, an abundant precipitation is distributed throughout the year (see table 1). It has been reported, for example, that during a period of years more than ten days have never passed at El Platanal (on the Orinoco between the Mavaca and the Majecodo) without rain.[134] Explorers of the Orinoco above the confluence with the Ugueto, also make light of the idea of a "dry" season. For example, during fifty days (January–March 1969) of the "so-called 'dry' season," only two were without rain.[135] During a sample period in the middle of the 1970 "dry" season in the Niyayoba area of the central Parima, it rained—excluding days of drizzle—thirteen days out of thirty-one, and during six of these rain fell most of the day. At that time of the year, the rains tend to come from the north, whereas during the "wet" season they frequently move in from the south.

In the highlands, sporadic rain showers can occur at any time during day or night, but the heavy rains tend to come after 3:00 P.M. Sometimes it is a veritable wall of water that approaches; and, while still thousands of yards off in the forests, one can hear clearly the roaring sound of the falling water. After such a rain, thick clouds might hang against the mountains, dissipating only gradually. An extreme variability of the weather is also evident. Clouds can form quickly, a heavy downpour will follow and

TABLE 1

Annual Precipitation in the Niyayoba Area

(1970)

Month	Precipitation (inches)
January	No data
February	3.00[a]
March	7.19
April[b]	2.95
May	7.63
June	5.20
July	8.82
August	8.24
September	3.27
October	2.28
November	9.52
December	0.62
Total for 11 months	58.72
Mean monthly precipitation	5.34

[a]Estimate.
[b]Excluding April 1–5.

then end abruptly, leaving a crystalline atmosphere with a magnificent sunset behind western clouds. A still morning can precede an afternoon of very strong winds, distressing the Yanoama because of the potential damage to thatch roofing and plantain gardens.

The real seasonal variation of the Yanoama habitat is found in the contrast between the day and the night. In the lowlands, days are hot and humid, and even up in the massifs at 3,000 feet, mean daytime temperatures reach into the low 80's. Throughout the year, days are about twelve hours in length, so that by 7:00 P.M. it is dark, and the big Yanoama *shabono* are quiet except for scattered conversations, occasional coughing, and the crying of babies. Smoke from dozens of hearths hangs low in the humid air. With the advance of the night, it becomes progressively more damp and cool. At the mouth of the Mavaca, in a forested area a little more than 400 feet above sea level, nights are often so cool and damp that blankets are a necessity for foreigners; the Yanoama there, as everywhere, sleep with their hammocks hung very close to their hearth fires. In the higher elevations of the massifs (Tapirapeco-Curupira, Parima, Pacaraima) nights are colder still.

Detailed data on temperature and relative humidity are available for the Niyayoba area (at an elevation of nearly 3,000 feet) in the central Parima during the height of the "dry" season (January through March). The mean daytime temperature was in the low 80's, with a range between 74° and 86° F. The mean nighttime low was about 60° F, with a range between 64° and 54° F.[136] Except for open savanna areas, relative humidity soon after sunset had climbed to between 85 and 95 percent. Most mornings at sunrise it was in the 90's, but within an hour or two it dropped noticeably to about 70 percent.[137] Comparable observations have been made along the uppermost course of the Río Orinoco, where, at an elevation of about 3,000 feet, noon temperatures in the thick forests never rose above 70° F. In this same area, the temperature dropped to 61° F at night and during heavy rains.[138]

Even without a wet-dry seasonality in their headwaters, stream levels fluctuate in response to heavy rainfall during certain months and even to cloudbursts. This applies to all the streams rising in the Yanoama highlands, whether large or small.[139] The Mavaca at its mouth, for example, has been observed (August 20–21, 1964) to drop about one foot in 24 hours. In small streams, such as the Niyayoba-u (see map 9), the volume of rainfall is reflected in the regime with amazing rapidity. A rain of about five-eighths of an inch during an afternoon and evening can cause the stream to rise nine inches by early the following morning.[140] On one occasion a total of nearly one and one-half inches of rain fell over a period of less than thirty-six hours. This caused the Niyayoba-u to rise nearly twenty-seven inches (the maximum level was reached less than 24 hours after the rains had stopped), slightly flooding certain small portions of newly planted Yanoama gardens. Water temperature seemed largely unaffected by increased flow, although a slight variation was measured. For the most part, the water in the Niyayoba-u ranged from 66° to 69° F under a great variety of conditions.[141]

SOILS

Of all the soil types found in Yanoama territory, those along navigable water have been described most often in written accounts, since these are the ones accessible along the routes of penetration. Consequently, there is relatively good information on these alluvial soils and a dearth of data on those where most of the Yanoama live, that is, the interfluves high above the major river plains and terraces. On these stream terraces there are

said to be rich alluvial soils—thick, well drained, and fertile.[142] Along the
Orinoco, near the *shabono* of the Dayadi-teri, for example, the dark topsoil is up to one and one-half feet thick. Below this are red latosol clays
to a depth of six feet, and, underlying these, are thick layers of yellow-
white clays. Up in the Parima massif, which is unlike the Pacaraima in
that it generally lacks remnants of the Roraima sandstones, weathered
granites and other igneous rocks constitute the principal parent materials
of soils. These soils tend to be sandy and at least mildly leached. They
form under a forest floor that has been described as a layer of decompos-
ing organic material, which is virtually alive with shallow roots, bacteria,
insects, mosses, fungi, and even reptiles and mammals.[143] Soils that have
developed under this kind of forest cover are dark, friable, well-drained
loams.[144] Bedrock is sufficiently deep so as not to be a common feature
of the landscape.

Highland savanna soils offer a striking contrast to those of the forests.
Open grassland soils are acidic (pH 4.6 at Niyayoba) and clayey, being
compacted almost to the point of imperviousness. This condition has aggravated sheet erosion, and some surfaces are virtually paved with small
loose rocks, nodules, and concretions.

Frequently in this part of South America, streams are used as indicators
of soil qualities. Most of the streams draining the Yanoama territory were
classed as "black water"[145] in the recent past when the distinction was
made only between "black water" and "white water." These terms are
based on the color of the water: white water, carrying abundant silt and
sediments in suspension, was thought to drain fertile lands and to contain abundant aquatic life; black water, dark brown in color and lacking
silt, seemed to drain impoverished lands and lacked aquatic life forms.
Recently a third category has been suggested, which much more accurately fits the streams of the Yanoama habitat. It is that of "clear water."[146]
As the term implies, water in these streams is largely free of silt particles
and is thought to sustain more life and drain more fertile, productive
lands than do the black waters.

NATURAL VEGETATION

The natural vegetative cover of the Yanoama habitat is tropical rain-
forest, or selva—a type of wooded area that is often described by people
from the middle latitudes as mysterious and very exotic,[147] dark and tran-
quil, and exuberant with life. It is open near the ground (in contrast to
a jungle) and has huge, vine-draped trees arching toward the sky; it is a
warm, humid place filled with the pungent smell of decaying organic matter and the hum of countless insects punctuated occasionally by screech-

ing birds or monkeys. Along streams, or wherever the forest canopy has been rent, veritable walls of vegetation are formed by trees, shrubs, and vines, which compete to fill the space between canopy and ground.

The lowest level of the selva is relatively open because so little light reaches the forest floor that few plants can grow there.[148] It is largely a zone of tree trunks and lianas, among which are the fantastically but-tressed trunks and exposed roots of certain bombacaceous species. The ground is spongy with the decaying remains of leaves, and scattered about are the rotting trunks of fallen trees. A second level of the selva is com-posed of young trees struggling to reach the sunlight. These include both broadleaf evergreens and numerous species of palms. In some highland areas the forest is sufficiently low that palms, such as the *seje* (*Jessenia* sp.), form part of the canopy. These can be found in natural stands, with individual trees reaching 60 feet in height. More commonly, however, the canopy—which forms a third level—is higher. The giant trees occa-sionally reach heights of 200 feet on the lowland stream terraces and average about 120 feet in the central Parima highlands. Many trees are burdened with lianas, and on their trunks and branches are attached an abundance of bromeliaceous plants, epiphytes for the most part. When one of these giant trees falls, it pulls with it a great amount of vegetation and smashes still more, leaving a gaping hole in the forest canopy. For the Barafiri this is *urifi jami*, the "forest place."[149] In contrast to their garden clearings (*taca*) and the savannas (*borosi*), it is largely free of serrated grasses and thorny weeds, and they move through it with relative ease—barefoot and naked.

Savannas, commonplace in parts of the Parima highland habitat but rare in the humid lowlands, support a totally different vegetative cover. This ranges from very scanty grass to thick stands of tall ferns, depending largely on local conditions and the frequency of natural or deliberate burnings. In contrast to the exuberance of forest vegetation and the di-versity of species there, the savannas are very poor in species. Highland savannas are found in all sorts of locations, such as valley bottoms, steep slopes, ridges, and summits. In part because of this pattern of distribu-tion, there is reason to doubt that savanna grasslands are natural in this part of South America.[150]

The species of the forests and savannas appear to be native to tropical America, although there are abundant signs that the "natural" vegetative patterns have been greatly affected by the Yanoama. These people are continuously creating niches and modifying others by such activities as removing the forest for their gardens, selective gathering and hunting, the planting of perennials, and the construction of *shabono* and camps. There is no solid evidence, however, of botanical introductions.

Ecological Implications of the Habitat

Within the total Yanoama territory two major habitat subtypes are distinguishable: riverine lowlands and tropical highlands. On a smaller scale, particularly in the case of the highlands, a variety of microenvironments exist—the result of local relief and drainage patterns, microclimatic variation, soil differences, varying biotic communities, and combinations of these factors.

But it is the Yanoama culture that gives the territory its stamp of distinction. All the natural resources are identified and used in terms of traditional Yanoama needs; only archaic, time-sanctified methods are acceptable in the utilization of resources—otherwise the equilibrium between the spirit world and the Yanoama might be destroyed. Any deviation would be an affront to the controlling spirits and, consequently, unthinkable. Their livelihood activities bring the Yanoama into the most intimate contact with the natural world. They are adept at finding the ecological niches that support their economic system and at creating others: those for horticulture are made intentionally, while those frequented for collecting and for certain kinds of hunting are inadvertently created by the abandonment of old gardens.

IMPLICATIONS FOR HORTICULTURE

Throughout Yanoama territory, only forested areas are cleared for gardening. Among the habitat variables, two are particularly significant for horticulture: soil productivity and climatic seasonality.

In some areas soil fertility and drainage conditions are nearly ideal: gently sloping to undulating bottom lands are fertile, humid, and covered with high forest that is relatively easy to clear. Gardening in such areas can be a productive enterprise. At the opposite extreme, horticulture is considered impossible in the stony, highland savannas, where there is virtually no soil in some places and leached, compacted soils in others. There are also poorly drained or swampy areas, which are avoided. In the highlands, gentle mountain slopes are sometimes used, although small, V-shaped valleys are frequently selected for gardening. In the lowlands, well-drained river terraces are preferred.

In very general terms all of Yanoama territory is warm the year around, but in both the eastern and western lowlands there are pronounced, if brief, droughty spells. These do not usually last long enough to allow the soil to desiccate, but they do permit sufficient drying of felled trees to facilitate the burning of new garden sites. In the higher elevations these droughty periods are rare, so there is no clearly defined time of the year when highland Yanoama can most easily clear and burn the forest for new gardens. In the central Parima, for example, out of desperation people sometimes attempt to burn (or reburn) portions of their new clearings after only a day or two of sunny, windy weather.

These altitudinal differences in precipitation, temperature, and humidity seem also to play a part in the selection of garden crop plants. For example, little cotton is planted in the high Parima, while the cane for arrow shafts seems to yield well in moist highland sites. Musaceous plants, which are the most important to Yanoama horticulture, can be seen flourishing in gardens under 400 feet elevation, as well as in those above 3,000 feet.[151]

The ripening times of garden produce vary considerably with altitude and attendant circumstances.[152] Inter-*shabono* social life is strongly correlated with the availability of ripe plantains, and a *teri* group is proud to be able to invite kinsmen to share their good fortune by feasting on an early, abundant plantain crop. With plantains, too, they can honor their dead in *reajo* mortuary feasting. Peach palm fruit (*Guilielma* sp.), which also has great social significance, ripens much earlier and yields far better at lower elevations than in the mountains. In most cases, guest *teri* are expected to reciprocate with feasts later, when their own plantains (or peach-palm fruits) ripen.

IMPLICATIONS FOR COLLECTING

Collecting is done in old, overgrown gardens and in the forest proper. In both kinds of places there is a rich assortment of plant species that provide raw materials, as well as a variety of foods. Altitude and drainage account for considerable variation in collecting just as they do for horticulture. The distribution patterns of the habitats of many species of plants and animals are dependent on altitude, with some having wider ranges than others. Elevation also affects the timing of plant flowering and fruiting. Distinctive microenvironments, then, may be only a short walk from one another.

Although true stands of trees are supposed not to exist in the tropical forest, there are extensive areas where a single species predominates. Groves of cacao trees, for example, can be found up to altitudes of more than 3,500 feet. There are also veritable stands of such useful palms as *seje* (*Jessenia* sp.), *manaca* (*Euterpe* sp.), and *moriche* (*Mauritia* sp.), with trees ranging from thirty to fifty feet in height. Some, such as the *seje*, are found in well-drained areas, while others, like the *moriche*, prefer swampy ground.

Cashew trees (*Anacardium* sp.) and Brazil nut trees (*Bertholletia* sp.), which grow to gigantic size in the Río Orinoco and Rio Branco lowlands,

are virtually nonexistent in the central Parima massif. The lower altitude
habitats (below 2,500 feet) provide the vines and lianas used for the indispensable Yanoama baskets. Of the various bamboolike plants, the largest are said to produce the best cane at elevations of 4,000 feet and above. Innumerable other plants, many of which are not yet identified botanically, are also sources of edible material, fibers, wood, and gums. These become fewer in number and variety as altitude increases above a few thousand feet.[153]

In addition to plants, a variety of other things are gathered. Insects provide an important nutritional component of the Yanoama diet, particularly ants, termites, wasps, moths, and bees. Children and adults alike are alert for insects on the wing, studying their flight patterns and any signs of swarming, honey making, or nest building. Small amphibians, crustaceans, reptiles, and fishes are other food sources that are found in ponds and streams.

Very little use is made of mineral resources. Stone is rare over much of the smooth lowlands, except at outcrops; up on the Parima massif, fine-grained igneous rock, once preferred for the manufacture of stone tools, was obtained from only a few sites.

IMPLICATIONS FOR HUNTING

The hunt takes place in the forest and in abandoned gardens, both of which offer relatively few game animals (particularly mammalian species) in comparison with the variety of plants they contain. The grass and fern savannas are incapable of providing the food and cover required by game; Yanoama territory is largely without the prolonged droughts of savannalike climate regions—the seasonal droughts that force fish and game alike to congregate at pools and water holes and facilitate hunting and fishing. The Yanoama must stalk his quarry over extensive areas, relying upon his personal knowledge of its habits and instincts, with his bow and arrows as his only weapons.

The most prized animals are taken on the forest floor. These include the greatly esteemed tapir (*Tapirus* sp.),[154] the peccary (*Dicotyles* sp.), and the agouti (*Cuniculus paca*), which are often shot at licks, stream banks, or feeding areas. The most available game species, birds and monkeys, are shot in the forest canopy. A few others, such as the rodent capybara (*Hydrochoerus* sp.) and waterfowl, such as cranes, frequent streams and swamps.

The forest habitat provides little grass for grazing; forest ungulates, such as the tapir, the peccaries, and deer, forage on a wide variety of vegetable foods.[155] Like many other animals and birds, these game species are attracted to producing Yanoama gardens as well as to those that have been abandoned. They are also attracted to some of the same kinds of trees the Yanoama frequent, feeding on the ripe fruits that fall to the ground. Many other animals, such as birds and monkeys, are likewise attracted. These, in turn, tempt carnivores like felines and foxes. The forest contains a diverse and abundant insect life, which supports a variety of insectivores. Among these latter are mammals, such as anteaters and various rodents, as well as numerous bird species.[156]

In general, the altitude ranges of these game species are considerably greater than those of plants. The succulent agouti, for example, is widespread over both highlands and lowlands, as are rabbits, squirrels, curassows (*Crax* sp.), and numerous other species.[157] Certain animals, such as the *baba* (*Caiman sclerops*), which prefer large streams, are not found in the highlands. Lizards like the highly prized iguana (*Iguana iguana*) are also very scarce in the highlands, although huge specimens (well over four feet in length) can be found in the lowlands. As a general rule, elevations under 2,000 feet appear to be better supplied with game species than are the highlands.[158]

Traditional Preferred Habitat

The Yanoama *genre de vie* is intimately linked with their tropical forest habitat and is ecologically intricate.[159] Close inspection reveals the Yanoama preference for the highland forest.[160] It is precisely this kind of habitat that constitutes the heartland of the extensive territory they presently occupy. In the highlands one finds the thick concentrations of their *shabono*, gardens, and old gardens.

More specifically, the strongest preference seems to be for a zone somewhere between the middle of the *tierra caliente* (from sea level to 3,000 feet) and the lower *tierra templada* (from 3,000 feet to 6,000 feet). This is a belt that has as its approximate lower limit elevations approaching 1,000 feet and as its approximate upper limit elevations just over 3,500 feet.

Yanoama territory is but a part of the Guayana highland, an area long recognized as a distinctive South American habitat. When portrayed on a relief map, this highland stands out as a veritable island cut off from all other highlands; it is a "humid low highland" totally surrounded by "seasonally rainy lowlands" to the north and "chronically rainy lowlands" to the south (see map 3).[161] Certain advantages of highland locations to preliterate agriculturalists in the low latitudes have been identified. Among these are the absence of malaria and a reduced incidence of other diseases; and, from a horticultural viewpoint, purportedly there is a lower rate of soil leaching and slower invasion of garden plots by weeds.[162] Ap-

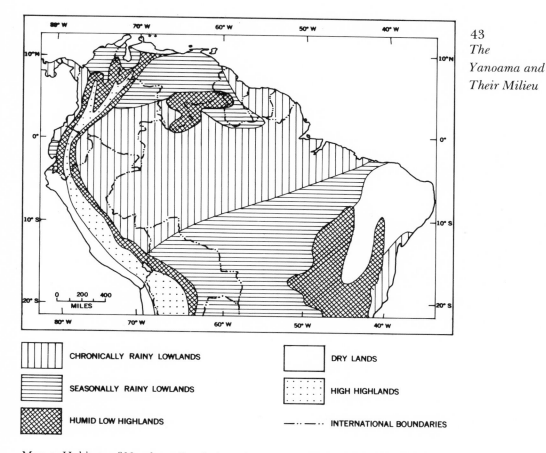

CHRONICALLY RAINY LOWLANDS

SEASONALLY RAINY LOWLANDS

HUMID LOW HIGHLANDS

DRY LANDS

HIGH HIGHLANDS

-- — -- INTERNATIONAL BOUNDARIES

Map 3. Habitats of Northern South America. After Robert S. Platt, *Latin America*.

parently malaria has become a serious problem among certain Yanoama groups only since the 1950's, when they began to move down into the lowlands in significant numbers. Throughout the highlands, noxious insects are not nearly so troublesome as they are in the lowlands, where people sometimes literally run from them. Weather in the highlands is mild, droughts are practically unknown, pure water is abundant, forest soils are productive, and landscapes are majestic.

Helena Valero, a Creole girl kidnapped by the Yanoama and kept among them for twenty years, explains in her narrative how she lived entirely alone for seven months in the southern portion of Yanoama territory. She had no tools whatsoever, and most of the time she was without fire. Nevertheless, she subsisted—living off the forest and the numerous old gardens of the area.[163]

These highlands have been good to the Yanoama. They have contributed to the splendid isolation required to maintain Yanoama cultural integrity. Since 1760, when Díez de la Fuente abandoned hopes for reaching the source of the Orinoco, most other foreigners have reacted similarly in the face of such adversity; they, too, have given up their plans to explore the area, largely because of the difficulties of river navigation. The Yanoama highland core evidently lacks gold and diamonds, as well as the hevea and the chicle that attracted so many ruthless men into the depths of other parts of the American tropical forests.

Certain presumed benefits of contact with Creoles and other foreigners have led some Yanoama groups to abandon the highlands. Among the inducements to do so are safety from attack by Yanoama enemies and access to medical attention and trade goods. Although any adult Yanoama maintains contacts with kinsmen in various *shabono*, there is no person or even a *teri* with factual knowledge about any more than a small part of the total Yanoama population. Between highland and lowland, there is a particularly wide knowledge gap. For the highland Yanoama, lowlanders can be as remote as New Yorkers; for many Yanoama living along the Orinoco, the Parima highlands are some sort of mystical place associated with the ancestors. Little distinction is made between the Yanoama who live there and spirit beings.

An attempt has been made here to set the stage for geographical analysis of the Yanoama as they are found today. Where possible, correlations have been made between culture and habitat. This is, of course, very different from a search for evidence of adaptation to the natural environment. The whole endeavor has been directed toward laying the groundwork for understanding better the intricate complexities of Yanoama cultural geography.

Chapter 3
Distribution Patterns
and Settlement Morphology

T H E Yanoama occupy a territory nearly nine times the size of the island of Puerto Rico. This territory is the most isolated portion of the border area between the modern states of Brazil and Venezuela. However, the Yanoama have no comprehension of either "Brazil" or "Venezuela," so the international boundary holds no significance for them. In fact, the individual Yanoama has no conception of Yanoama territory as a coherent whole. His world and that of his community encompass only a small portion of the Yanoama culture region.

There has been virtually no direct intervention by the Brazilian or Venezuelan states in the functioning of the Yanoama ecosystem. Their rights to occupy and exploit their traditional lands have not been disputed, and no reservation has been created for them.

Areal Extent of the Yanoama Culture Region

Considerable disagreement exists regarding the limits of the Yanoama culture region. *Shabono* communities, the basic settlement units, can be seen and mapped, but campsites cannot be observed from the air, and the boundaries of the territories that pertain to the various *teri* groups living

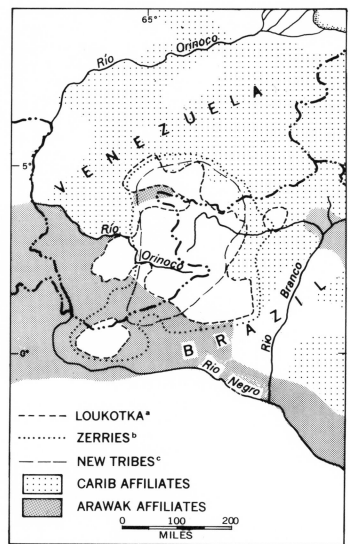

Map 4. Different Interpretations of the Yanoama Culture Area
[a]Cestmir Loukotka, *Classification of South American Indian Languages*.
[b]Otto Zerries, *Waika*.
[c]After maps in *Headwaters* and *Amazon Challenge* (New Tribes Mission).

at the edges of Yanoama lands are quite invisible. On map 4 three different interpretations of the culture region are presented. In spite of the general lack of agreement on what constitutes the limits of Yanoama territory, two observations are beyond dispute: there is no correlation between the Yanoama culture region and any particular stream complex or drainage system, and there is full agreement on the central position of the Parima massif within Yanoama territory.

In contrast to their precise knowledge and terminology for small streams in the highlands, the Yanoama are quite disinterested in such major streams as the lower Ocamo, Padamo, Uraricoera, or even the Orino-co. They have little interest in broad, deep rivers; any large stream that flows beyond their territory is outside their spatial realm of concern. The second, more significant observation suggests that Yanoama territory has a core, or heartland,[1] different from the periphery. If there is a differ-ence, it would appear to be that the Yanoama in the isolated highlands are in their traditional, preferred habitat, at least partially insulated from the culture shock experienced by their fellows who are on the periphery.[2] Territorial limits between the Yanoama and other peoples are said to co-incide with such identifiable natural features as valleys, streams, and ridges.[3] Seemingly there is little need for precise territorial boundaries, since between the Yanoama and most other groups there is an unin-habited belt that functions as a buffer preventing direct contact.[4]

Population Distribution

The Yanoama population is very unevenly distributed, and in their terri-tory extensive areas are virtually empty. These uninhabited (but not necessarily unused) areas frequently fit into one of two categories: the highest elevations of the massifs, and the lowlands.

In the highlands, areas drained by the small headwater streams at 4,500 feet or more are apparently devoid of permanent human residents. One such area lies in the uppermost reaches of the Shabari-u (map 6); it has no producing gardens; it is an inter-*teri* contact zone, where different groups come for collecting and hunting. This phenomenon was reported as early as the 1830's for the "uninhabited upper parts" of the Parima and Uraricapara rivers.[5] The highest reaches of the Río Paragua have been reported as empty,[6] and the Orinoco near its source has been described as an area so free of humans that "nowhere in the vicinity [of the interna-tional boundary] has the virgin forest been cut for banana gardens or set-tlements."[7]

Among the different lowlands, the extensive swamps of the Casiquiare peneplain are judiciously avoided—although this area is sometimes classi-fied as Yanoama territory (cf. maps 4 and 5). Not only is the area hot and subject to widespread flooding through the year, but it is also plagued by an abundant, noxious insect life. As recently as 1950, there was only one Yanoama community, the Majecodo-teri, living along that part of the Orinoco accessible by canoe navigation. In 1960 it was still possible to travel fifty miles up the Río Mavaca (from the Bishaasa-teri settlements adjacent to the missions at the Mavaca mouth) and find no human habita-tion. The lower portions (well under 1,000 feet elevation) of the Ocamo and Padamo were likewise without Yanoama. The same appears to be true of the Rio Negro and lower portions of its tributaries, such as the Demini and the Padauiri, and of the Uraricoera and its tributaries, such as the Parima.[8]

In short, the Yanoama traditionally shunned both broad rivers and hot lowlands. Population concentrations (see map 5) are to be found in intermediate highlands, where the isolated *shabono* is most commonly seen—although groupings of *shabono* communities within a few hundred yards of each other can be found. One of the areas of maximum population density is the central Parima massif and, more specifically, the upper Buuta-u; in a place like this the Yanoama landscape can be seen best.

Precise figures for the total Yanoama population do not exist, nor is it now feasible to obtain them. A sound estimate is that there are at least eight thousand Yanoama speakers in Venezuela and probably a somewhat smaller number in Brazil, yielding a total of about fifteen thousand people.[9] Mean population density over their entire territory is approximately 0.5 person per square mile. Since such a calculation is based upon heavily populated highlands as well as virtually empty lowlands and uninhabited high highlands, the effective density is much higher locally. Observation of the extent to which portions of the high Parima have been transformed into savanna leads to the suspicion that only a few decades ago, if not centuries, population densities there were considerably greater than they are now.[10]

Population Size

Prior to European contact in the fifteenth century, the major epidemic diseases of mankind evidently were absent from the New World,[11] and an isolated population like that of the Yanoama seems to have been safe from these exotic diseases for centuries after some other aboriginal populations were eradicated by them in post-Columbian times. It is probable, too, that in ancient times the Yanoama, like other preliterate populations, were not a "high-fertility, high-mortality" type.[12] They were presumably a healthy people who spaced their children, using techniques like late weaning, abortion, and infanticide, just as they do now.[13] In short, the Yanoama would have been a numerically stable population.

Two contrasting viewpoints exist regarding recent trends toward numerical instability. One view is that the Yanoama are undergoing a demographic explosion that began a century or two ago with their adoption of agriculture, and particularly the cultivation of the musaceous plants.[14] Territorial expansion is thought to have accompanied this rapid population growth.[15] The other view, diametrically opposite, is that epidemics, particularly in the past few decades, have decimated the Yanoama. Documented evidence on the impact of diseases new to the Yanoama shows that these diseases have had disastrous effects on them and that they are probably undergoing a general population decrease. However, this is a demographic process of the present; it does not rule out completely the possibility that more than a century ago the Yanoama underwent a population explosion.

Traditional Ills and New Diseases

Deformed or sickly infants usually are killed at birth. Consequently, the surviving population is a generally healthy one. In childhood, however, nearly every Yanoama becomes host to a wide variety of intestinal parasites,[16] apparently pre-Columbian in origin. But these parasitizations are rarely of more than moderate intensity.[17] During his lifetime any Yanoama is likely also to experience a variety of cuts, burns, bruises, and insect bites.[18] In most cases injuries do not become severely infected.

Mortal wounds can be caused by falls from high places, snake bites, and personal attacks; none of these is peculiar to Yanoama culture. Duels and warfare also contribute to death, although most personal disputes within a *shabono* can be settled without resorting to extreme violence.[19] The Yanoama do not have armies and battle lines; the secret raid is the hallmark of their warfare. If serious hostility develops, only small raiding parties are usually involved. Raids are frequently spaced many weeks, or even months, apart. Consequently, this kind of warfare normally has only a limited impact upon the population size.[20] Nor is hunger a general problem. Locally severe flooding or windstorms might cause damage to the gardens, with resultant hardships because of food shortages. In such cases, the affected population can seek help from friendly kinsmen in other *shabono*.

From the standpoint of a "civilized" person, the Yanoama do not practice basic personal hygiene. For example, they only wash themselves when they are ill, particularly with fever. In the highlands, the Barafiri have a pronounced distaste for getting their bodies wet. On the trail, men will beat wet vegetation with a stick before walking through it, in order to stay as dry as possible. In a heavy rain, outdoor activity stops, as people seek some kind of shelter. They do not brush their teeth, they have no handkerchiefs or even rags, and they have no privies. The Yanoama, however, manage quite well without cleanliness as we know it and without the benefits of scientific medicine.[21] They find a privy repugnant, since filthy excrement is collected there for some purpose incomprehensible to them; handkerchiefs are almost as bad, since mucus is preserved in them.

Beyond the realms of hygiene, medicine, and scientific objectivity lie the most mysterious maladies affecting the Yanoama population—the magical and the psychosomatic. It is probably sorcery—or suspected sorcery, or even the fear of potential sorcery—that is a principal cause of warfare; raiding, as a way of achieving revenge (for an act of sorcery or an overt raid), and the kidnapping of women might be the outgrowths of this basic cause.[22] An otherwise healthy adult might take to his hammock after learning that evil spirits had got control of him and eventually die there, if sorcerers to whom he had access could not help him. Evil spirits sometimes make it impossible for people to walk by getting control of their footprints. If a powerful enemy sorcerer can secretly blow magic powder upon a person's body—or if the victim believes that this has been done—then he might simply surrender to death.[23]

Two Old World diseases are important current causes of morbidity and death among the Yanoama—malaria (particularly *Plasmodium falciparum* and *Pl. vivax*) and yellow fever.[24] In fact, 54 percent of all adult deaths are reportedly due to malaria and other epidemic diseases.[25]

As early as 1935–1940, an epidemic locally called *chavera*, which had fever symptoms closely resembling those of malaria, swept up the Río Padamo. That epidemic is reported to have decimated the Yanoama population of the areas into which it spread.[26] Another particularly destructive epidemic, definitely identified as malaria, raged among the lowland Waika groups between January and August of 1960. It happened to coincide with a time when plantains were in particularly short supply, leaving people undernourished and thereby reducing the effectiveness of the men as hunters. About 10 percent of the Waika population is reported to have died, mostly women and children.[27]

Malaria leaves no immunity and can break out at any time. Infectious diseases, particularly viral diseases, are different. Some people survive an outbreak, and these retain an immunity. The newborn do not have survivor's immunity. Thus, after perhaps fifteen or twenty years, there are other outbreaks among the susceptible, the vectors having been continuously active.[28] Because most Yanoama have had little opportunity to develop immunities or antibodies, bronchitis, influenza, small pox, measles, mumps, whooping cough, and other Old World diseases can be fatal to them.[29] For example, a 1967–1968 epidemic of measles caused numerous deaths: in a sample of seventy-five Yanoama only three were free of measles; of the others, fourteen died, and three experienced miscarriages.[30] The average case fatality rate among all Yanoama from the measles epidemic was calculated at about 8.8 percent.[31] When mumps spread into the Niyayoba area in 1970–1971, even the oldest people caught it.

There is a very pronounced regional variation in the existence and the intensity of these diseases among the Yanoama. For example, malaria is relatively rare in the cooler highlands although it is in the process of moving into progressively higher elevations. Malaria is currently found well above 2,500 feet, which was not true in the 1950's. Infection is particularly frequent in the lowland zones of contact with foreign people who act as carriers. These zones of contact are also the places where Yanoama can obtain medication, if not medical treatment, so that such populations have more benign bouts of disease than do their more isolated kinsfolk. Unfortunately, it is precisely these helpless kinsfolk who are contaminated inadvertently during inter-*teri* social visiting. The sociability of the Yanoama is a major factor in the spread of epidemics among themselves. Even the ill will travel, perhaps hoping to obtain the help of a powerful sorcerer in another *teri*. People also flee *shabono* where disease is rampant, seeking some escape from it. They might move in with friendly kinsfolk or just camp in the forest until they think the danger is past.[32]

Shifting Territorial Limits

Traditionally, the boundaries of Yanoama territory appear to have been quite stable, if not static, although there is no historical record to corroborate this. It would seem that during untold centuries the Yanoama fended off a variety of Carib peoples to their north and simultaneously held at bay an arc of Arawak peoples to their south (see map 4). Thus, neither Arawaks nor Caribs succeeded in destroying Yanoama ancestral culture or pride. A major factor contributing to the preservation of Yanoama territorial and cultural integrity might well have been their lack of river orientation. They did not compete for lowland sites; nor were they even on the access routes preferred by Arawaks and Caribs. Long-term territorial stability could have resulted, because the Yanoama did not threaten the preferred ecological niches of other numerous, more powerful peoples.

Ironically, these peoples pose little threat anymore. They were the first to suffer from exotic diseases and to adopt Creole ways. Along with their decline, there has been developing a political stability of the entire area, due largely to the gradual penetration of Venezuelan and Brazilian authority. It is no surprise, therefore, that the Yanoama are expanding territorially. This expansion has become evident only within the past few decades. It is modest in scale, sporadic, and limited, for the most part, to the relocations of individual *teri* groups. In no way does it resemble planned expansion or military conquest. The Yanoama who move are frequently attracted by contact with outsiders, because they want the trade goods, medicines, and the safety from their Yanoama enemies that such contact can provide. There are also those *teri* who simply move into lands vacated by other Indian cultures. One area of significant expansion can be found in the Sierra Pacaraima. Here, as some Carib tribes abandoned their traditional lands to migrate voluntarily north to the Orinoco lowlands, voids were left locally in the headwaters of the Paragua, Caura, Erebato, and even the Ventuari.[33]

The Yanoama most affected by territorial expansion, at least in Venezuela, appear to be the Sanoma and the Waika dialect groups. The latter, for example, have moved down to occupy numerous sites along the Orinoco. Holes dug where the Bishaasa-teri now live at the juncture of the Mavaca with the Orinoco have yielded potshards and remains of manioc graters typical of Maquiritare culture. Maquiritare oral tradition also suggests that they were occupying this part of the upper Orinoco floodplain as recently as the 1940's.

In parts of the northwest contact zone between Yanoama of the Sanoma dialect and the Maquiritari, the two peoples live together in village communities. This relationship has been described as symbiotic by some, and as virtual enslavement of the Yanoama by others.[34] In such settlements, the Maquiritare are the source of trade goods and of innovation. From them the Yanoama have learned to depend upon bitter manioc, to use loin cloths, to build gable roofs, and to make cotton hammocks.[35] The Maquiritare also provide security for the Yanoama, since the former have firearms for use against enemies and on the hunt.

The Yanoama do menial jobs, such as fetching firewood and water, for the Maquiritare. In fact, they are not needed by the Maquiritare, so essentially no symbiosis exists. The Maquiritare are effective hunters and have their own manioc gardens; they are skilled at making the tools, dugout canoes, baskets, and other things they use. Some Yanoama women are second wives for Maquiritare men, but almost never does a Yanoama man get a Maquiritare wife. There is no slavery, since the Yanoama are free to come and go; and many of them seem to do just that. These settlements are within what might be considered as Yanoama territory, but it is the Carib-Maquiritare who are the dominant population.

Establishing the Distribution Pattern

Years of tedious work were involved in accumulating the data with which to compile even the sketchy details of Yanoama distribution in Venezuela as presented on map 5.[36] In spite of imperfections,[37] the map is the most accurate and comprehensive now feasible.

Each *shabono* shelters at least one extended family, but sometimes more. Virtually no nuclear families or single individuals are to be found who are not part of a *shabono* unit. Even illicit lovers who run from their home com-

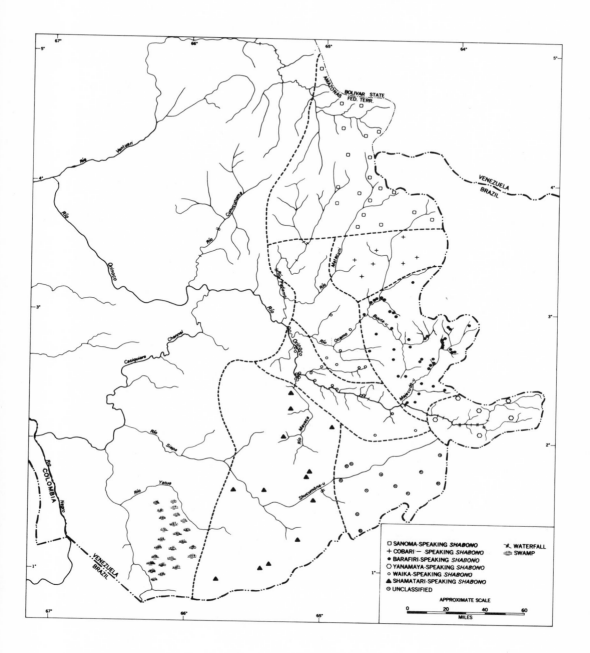

Map 5. Venezuelan Yanoama Dialects

munities soon join some *teri* that will accept them. The name used to identify any specific *shabono* is in fact the name of the group, or *teri*, inhabiting it. In cases where a *shabono* is occupied by more than one *teri*, those names might be retained also.

DIALECT REGIONS

Map 5 includes a comprehensive classification of the Yanoama population into the Venezuelan dialect groupings as we know them at present.[38] The names ascribed to the seven dialects that have been identified in the Amazonas Federal Territory of Venezuela (i.e., Sanoma, Cobari, Barafiri, Waika, Yanamaya, and Shamatari) are arbitrary. Except for the Sanoma, people do not refer to themselves in such terms. The universal self-designation is simply "Yanoama." In fact, words like *Barafiri*, *Waika*, and *Shamatari* appear to signify directions, as well as the peoples to be found in those directions.

For example, the Niyayoba-teri of the central Parima (classified as "Barafiri" dialect) generally refer to the Yanoama living to their west as "Waika," those to their south as "Shamatari," and those to their east as "Barafiri." However, the Mayobo-teri, living about fifteen miles to the east, call people to their east (living in the upper Rio Parima) "Waika." Waika speakers living near the lower Ocamo or the Orinoco refer in turn to the Yanoama to their east (i.e., in the Parima highlands) as "Barajiri,"[39] and those to their south as "Shamatari." Yet, Yanoama living less than forty air miles east of the Parima Barafiri refer to these latter people as "Shamatari." Consequently, these terms are all relative and have meaning only in the context of the speaker's location. "Waika" seems sometimes to refer to populations relatively unknown to the speaker and distant from him, while "Barafiri" does not.

These dialects fall into four major groupings of Venezuelan Yanoama:
1. The northern group, known as the Sanoma, with twenty known *shabono* in the Amazonas Federal Territory.
2. The central lowland group, composed of (*a*) the Orinoco Waika and (*b*) the Ocamo Waika, with a total of twenty-five known *shabono* settlements in Venezuela.
3. The central mountain group, composed of three distinct dialects: (*a*) the Cobari, of the upper Ocamo and Matacuni, with seven known *shabono*; (*b*) the Barafiri, occupying the upper reaches of the Buuta-u and Majecodo rivers, with at least forty-four *shabono*; and (*c*) the Yanamaya of the Orinoco headwaters area, with six known *shabono*.
4. The southern group, which includes (*a*) the Shamatari, with thirteen known *shabono* in Venezuela, and (*b*) an additional thirteen

shabono in extreme southeastern Venezuela, whose linguistic classification is incomplete. Both of these dialects are believed to extend
well into Brazil.

Together, the Yanoama of these specific dialect regions occupy a minimum of 128 *shabono* in the Amazonas Federal Territory of Venezuela.[40]
Conservatively estimating a population of 65 for each *shabono*, the total is
well over 8,000 people.

THE PARIMA BARAFIRI AREA

More than one-third of the *shabono* in Venezuela can be classified as Barafiri speakers. The highlands they occupy constitute an isolated and dense-
ly populated portion of the total Yanoama territory. Unlike so many other
aboriginal peoples of the Americas, however, these have not been forced
into an unfamiliar environment. They occupy the sort of tropical highland habitat that Yanoama seem traditionally to prefer. The Barafiri,
along with the Cobari, have firm tenure of the western portion of the
Yanoama highland core region.

For these reasons the Barafiri can be judged as representative of traditional distribution patterns (see map 6). With minor exceptions, their
settlements are well above the 1,000-foot contour. About half of all *shabono* are paired or clustered, with neighboring *shabono* only a few miles
from each other at most. Certain of the clusters are large; that of the
Comodoroba area, for example, incorporates from four to five hundred
inhabitants. There are other instances, such as that of the Niyayoba area,
where a single large *shabono* temporarily houses the total population of
what until recently had been four separate *shabono*.

The *Shabono* Settlement Unit

Among the Yanoama there are no dispersed single-family houses. The
basic settlement unit is the *shabono*—a large, semipermanent[41] community
residence that is roughly circular in shape, focusing on a central clearing.
The Barafiri term *shabono*, as used here, refers to the entire complex of
individual houses and the cleared space they encircle. Properly, however,
the term applies specifically to the central cleared space. Other writers
have referred to the *shabono* variously as a *village, dorff, ranchería*, or
maloca. The *shabono* houses a community, but it is not really a communal
house. Each adult male builds his own part of the total structure and
maintains that part.

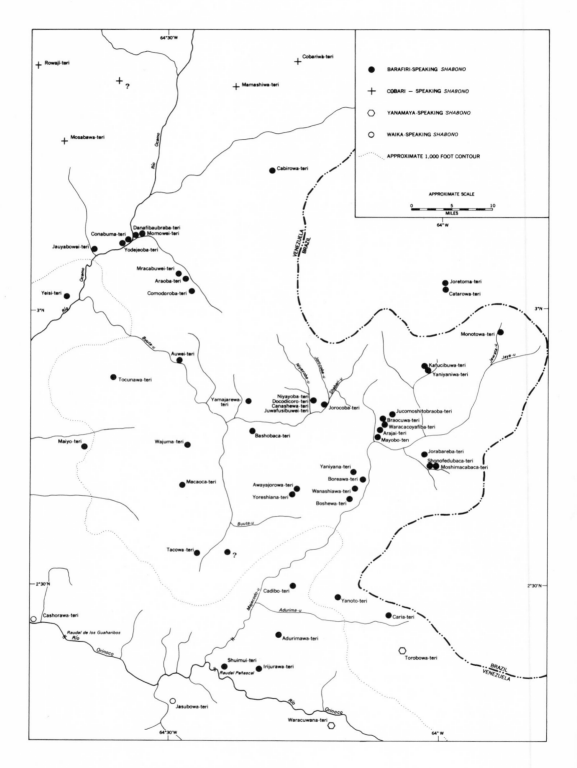

Map 6. The Venezuelan Barafiri

Normally the occupants of a *shabono* are all kinsfolk; in fact, kinship is the raison d'être of the community. It is from this kin group, or *teri*, that both name and identity are derived. Literally, *teri* means "people" or "people of."[42] As a suffix, it forms part of the proper name of a group.[43]

A *teri* might derive its name from a particular plant (Ashitue-teri means "people of the ashi fruit");[44] a bird (Mayobo-teri means "people of the toucan"); an animal (Jaya-teri means "people of the deer"; Jasubue-teri means "people of the jasu toad"); a particular feature, such as a mountain or waterfall, or some other phenomenon (Bashobaca-teri means "people of the spider monkey's home"; Juwafusibuwei-teri means "people of the place where the dead juwa tree is"; Jucomoshitabrauba-teri means "people of the place where the sweet potato vine lies close to the ground").

Frequently the *teri* name is the same as that of one or more natural features of the territory, such as a stream or mountain. The relationship is not clear, but generally the *teri* appear to take their names from places or features, rather than the reverse. Therefore, the *teri* name is geographic.[45] Through time, name changes are as commonplace as changes in the composition of the individual *teri* membership, and multiple names are sometimes the result. Even after fission or fusion or both, old names can be used interchangeably with new ones, although eventually a single new name is agreed upon by a newly constituted *teri*. That name goes with members of the group wherever they might be, whether making new gardens in the forest, collecting, or visiting; and it is ascribed to a place where they are temporarily located.

The linkages between the *teri* members occupying a *shabono* are based upon blood and marriage. Even friendship exists within a kinship context, since only kinsmen (or prospective kinsmen) have any basis for establishing friendships. Consequently, the economic and political functions of a *teri* are accessory to kinship. Each *shabono* constitutes a special microcosm—independent, yet closely bound by kinship ties with numerous other *shabono*. There is no functional hierarchy incorporating the various *shabono* populations, although they vary considerably in size and vigor. In essence, each *shabono* is like all others: simultaneously, it is a tightly knit kin group, a social unit, an economic whole, and a politically sovereign body. The circle of family shelters is symbolic of functional kinship unity. The self-containment of a *shabono* can best be appreciated from the air (see plate 6). Whether isolated or near others, each *shabono* is separate and discrete. The distance between *shabono* is measured in travel time. Where pairs or clusters exist, this may be only a few minutes. However, trips of several days are not unusual for social visits.

Plate 6. Air view of the *shabono* of the Mayobo-teri (cf. fig. 3) on a grassy elevation. The Mayobo area has been occupied by various *teri* simultaneously for uncounted generations. Sometime prior to 1960, there were still at least seven *teri* there. Four of these have since moved away, but another moved in and fission of the Mayobo-teri produced still another, so that there are now five *teri*. In all directions old gardens and small savannas testify to the intensive occupancy of this high, undulating area.

Shabono LOCATION FACTORS

Consistently, certain factors determine the location of Yanoama settlements, the most important of which is security. A new *shabono* ought to be in a place traditionally safe, where it will be secure from any enemies of the builders. Normally a *teri* will build in its own territory, although some might prefer territory belonging to trustworthy kinsmen.

Suitability of an area for horticulture is another critical location factor. Without garden plots the Yanoama could not survive, so it is vital that a settlement be accessible to places deemed good for growing plantains. The best house sites are in clayey areas, since these are unattractive to chigoes (*Tunga penetrans*), a kind of flea.[46]

Under normal conditions a new *shabono* is built in the vicinity of the old one it is to replace, within convenient walking distance of the community's gardens.[47] Since new gardens are cut from the forest in the general vicinity of the *shabono* and existing gardens, people tend not to move very far from an old house when constructing a new one. This proximity also permits a certain degree of leisure during the construction period and simplifies the moving process by allowing each family to move at its convenience. Thus, within a radius of a few miles of a new *shabono* one might find the remains of others in various stages of decay.

A new *shabono* is not usually built until it is needed, such as when the old one has fallen into utter disrepair or has become severely infested with chigoes, cockroaches, and lice. The Yanoama particularly detest fleas; they will even move out of a *shabono* for months on end, hoping that the chigoes will be gone when they return. It is also important that a *shabono* be located near a year-round supply of potable water. Yanoama are careful about what water they drink, obtaining it upstream from toilet areas and trail crossings. The availability of game is another consideration, but not a critical one, since hunters are willing to travel great distances to obtain desirable game animals. Large wild animals tend to shun populated areas, although they are attracted to the isolated sites of abandoned gardens. Like small game animals, they frequent places where there is a good supply of surface water, and they congregate in forest areas where wild fruits are ripening. *Shabono* dwellings are usually constructed in clearings made in the forest, expressly for the purpose. In the Parima highlands, where there are numerous savannas, *shabono* are sometimes built on open grasslands.[48] It is not unusual to find a *shabono* in a clearing at the very edge of the forest, where it borders upon savanna.[49]

THE *Shabono* AS A BASIC UNIT OF OCCUPANCY

The most visible focal point in Yanoama areal organization is the multifamily settlement occupied by a specific *teri*—the *shabono*.[50] Associated with the houses and central clearing, and constituting adjacent parts of a functional whole, are the palisade, trash heaps, and toilet areas. More distant, but as important functionally, are the gardens and the forest that are used by the *teri*. Organizations of this sort incorporate a sort of village-bush dichotomy:[51] here the *shabono* would correspond to the "village," and *urifi* (Barafiri for "forest") would correspond to the "bush."

The Houses. Although not all *shabono* are identical (see fig. 1), one style predominates in Venezuela, and it is to be found with little variation from the Orinoco lowlands up into the highest occupied lands of the Parima massif. This is a roughly circular enclosure of thatch lean-tos, with a central clearing open to the elements. Some of these *shabono* are truly impressive: enormous clearings well over two hundred feet in diameter, circled

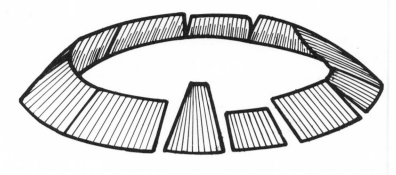

A.   BARAFIRI

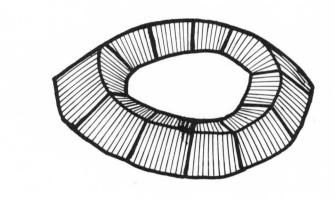

B.   COBARI

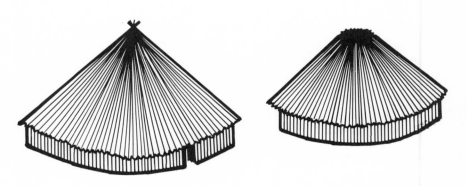

C.   RIO PARIMA   D.   ORINOCO HEADWATERS

Figure 1. *Shabono* Styles. (Not to scale)

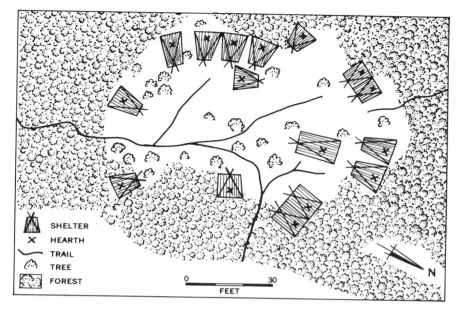

Figure 2. Mayobo-teri Camp

by roofs rising majestically to heights of more than twenty-five feet, with
a general air of neatness and order.

In Yanoama domestic architecture, form follows function. The *shabono* provides for their social organization, demonstrates their technology, and reflects their ecological stability. In the *shabono* live only Yanoama,
a few dogs, and such other pets as birds and monkeys. The mean diameter of *shabono* is perhaps one hundred feet, although variations are considerable.[52] Some of those in the headwaters of the Rio Parima (Brazil)
are largely roofed over, with only a round hole in the center of the roof
to permit the escape of smoke.[53] Such a structure closely resembles certain
of the *malocas* of various South American tropical forest tribes. Some *teri*
of the Cobari dialect group construct *shabono* in which each family is
housed under a ridged roof rather than a lean-to.[54] Like the standard
shabono style, these settlements are also circular, with large open clearings
in the center. Since the shelters coalesce into a ring, with ridge poles
attached to one another, no gables are evident. Other settlement types
have been called *shabono*, although they may represent cultural adapta-
tions from non-Yanoama sources.[55]

For the most part, building techniques and constructional materials
vary even less than *shabono* styles. Framing consists of hardwood poles
lashed together with lianas.[56] Thatching is of palm. The water-loving
Mauritia provides the fronds that are preferred by the Barafiri for thatching, but this species is not easily available to all *teri*. The inferior *bisha*,

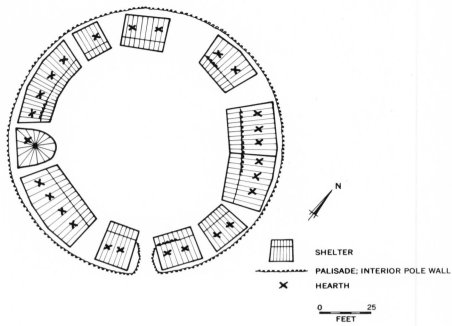

Figure 3. The Mayobo-teri *Shabono*

which is far more widely distributed throughout the forest, is more commonplace as roofing.[57] The roofing technique is quite simple: the lower (basal) part of each frond is hung over small horizontal poles or vines that have been lashed to the roof poles; these latter in turn having been lashed at an oblique angle to vertical supports. On the inside, some of the individual leaflets are tucked under the horizontal supporting pieces; on the outside, they overlap the row of fronds immediately below.[58] If not maintained in good repair, such a roof leaks rainwater like a sieve.

It has been suggested that the *shabono* style developed from a round *maloca* structure with a smoke hole at the top, "by simply pulling the roof away from the center until the smoke hole grew so large that it, in effect, became a center plaza."[59] A more plausible explanation can be found by examining how the Yanoama build their camps. When a group is going to camp for a matter of days or weeks (while collecting, or making new gardens), the men construct a cluster of lean-tos in the forest (see fig. 2). Each of these is very similar to the family lean-to that constitutes part of a *shabono*. The techniques of building, the floor plan, and the use of space are almost identical. A camp shelter, or *bejefa*, is roofed with palm fronds and even *Musa* leaves, which are sometimes only weighted down rather than being attached. The principal difference between campsite shelters and *shabono* shelters is that the latter tend to be somewhat larger, sturdier, and more aesthetic. It would appear feasible that these individual lean-tos

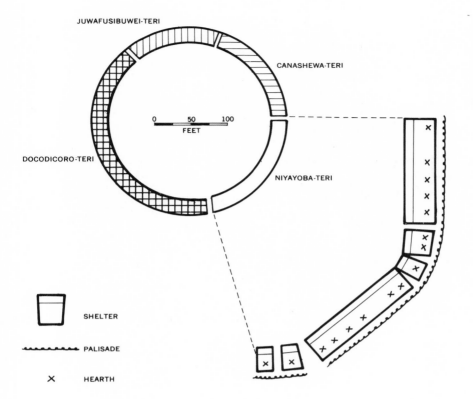

Figure 4. Household Space. Two adjacent examples from the Canashewa-teri.

gradually coalesced at some time into what finally came to resemble a single structure ringing a clearing.

Certain Orinoco lowland *shabono* are almost perfectly circular, with only a break or two in the continuity of the roofs. In other areas, the *shabono* is obviously composed of several discrete shelters, some up to forty-five feet long and containing several hearths (see fig. 3). Even at a campsite several families might build shelters together, while others build at some distance from their neighbors (see fig. 2).

Terminology is quite specific where the *shabono* is concerned. Only an inhabited clearing, a permanent home in Yanoama terms, is a *shabono*. The term does not apply to a campsite, even if the entire *teri* is there. The morphology and the functions distinguish the *shabono*, so that even if it is located on a savanna site, the *shabono* ("clearing") term applies.

In a literal sense each *teri* has its *nano jamo*, or "house place."[60] The individual family shelter is a *nano*, or "house."[61] Each such house has a *jefa* ("front") facing the clearing, and a *shico* ("back part") under the eaves, where firewood is stood vertically to dry. Conceptually, this arrangement of firewood is almost a "wall."

Plate 7. View across the *shabono* of the Jorocoba-teri. Note overhang of the high roof at the front of each house. Walls of palm fronds, *Musa* leaves, and poles (*left to right*) close off the living space. The diameter of this *shabono* is approximately one hundred feet.

Thus, the community occupies a circle of inward-facing individual houses. Each of these, specifically, is a *nano*, and the cleared central space is the *shabono*.[62] The clearing is communal, but each house is private space and is entered only by invitation. The respect for this space is such that if, for example, a young girl is being pursued by another of the community, when she reaches her own house, her safety is assured.

Each household is responsible for constructing its own shelter. Men gather the poles and build the framework; women are charged principally with providing the fronds for roofing and with at least part of the task of thatching.[63] Technically the shelters are the property of male heads of household, while women are reported to own the roofing thatch.[64] Once construction of a *shabono* is finished, the circle of houses is so complete that there is no available space for additional shelters.[65] Use of the *shabono* circumference is so effectively preplanned that any significant change in the composition of the *teri* requires the construction of a new *shabono*. When *teri* fuse, for example, they build anew; the new *shabono* symbolizing their unification. When fission occurs, it is rare for only part of the former *teri* to continue to occupy the old *shabono*.

The ground plan of the roof supports of each lean-to forms a triangle, while the sloping roof is rectangular (see fig. 4). Oftentimes roofs are so

Plate 8. Inside a family living space of the Niyayoba *shabono*. Woman and child sit in her cotton-thread hammock. A hammock of bast strips is visible to the left. Baskets, water gourds, and other possessions hang in profusion from the roof. In the woman's mouth is a wad of tobacco.

fused together that only the smoke stains on them distinguish one household from the next. The high, open front of the shelter faces the clearing, but the focus of each household is its hearth fire. Fires are welcome during the cool nights of the lowlands, and they are a necessity in the highlands. At any time, fires (or at least glowing brands) might be required for cooking. They are also the only source of artificial light, and they lend protection from insects, beasts of prey, and even spirit beings. Hammocks hang very near to the hearth and to one another. In the lowlands there are no dividing walls between households, or walls at the front of each shelter. However, at higher elevations *Musa* leaf dividers, and even walls composed of poles set vertically into the ground, are found (see plate 7 and fig. 3). Thus, a household can have a microclimate that is comfortable during wet, cool weather.[66]

Within the shelter, each family's few personal possessions rest on the floor, hang from the supporting structure, or are stuck into the roofing thatch (see plate 8). The material culture of the Yanoama is limited, and personal possessions are few. Among the most evident are hammocks and stems of ripening plantains. Also visible are some of the possessions of women: large calabashes for water, smaller gourd utensils and containers, various kinds of baskets, cotton-spinning gear, straps for carrying babies

Plate 9. The quarters of a young couple. His hammock is of bast strips, while hers is of cotton thread. A scanty supply of firewood is stacked behind her. His quiver is visible at the top right, and her water gourd hangs at top center. Above the hearth are suspended a few animal bones. A man in the adjacent house can be seen at far left.

and heavy loads, firewood, and personal adornments. Men own hunting equipment (bow, arrows, arrowpoints, quiver), fire-making gear, machetes, axes, *jawas*, personal decorations, and perhaps even clay cooking pots.[67]

If a household has more than three members,[68] then hammocks hang in tiers. The lower ones are only a few inches from the ground and very near to the hearth. Thus, the wife, whose hammock normally hangs in the lower tier, can more easily tend the fire. Hammocks are only inches apart, which means that members of a family can literally reach out and touch one another. Men, women, children, the old, and the very young are all in close proximity (see plate 9). Intimacy is such that one cannot help but observe continuously the lives of others. Emotions can hardly be concealed. Each household merges physically with the adjacent one. Kinsmen are bound tightly together in space as well as by blood.[69]

A simple calculation of the total area of a representative Barafiri *shabono* and its full complement of inhabitants provides a mean of about one hundred square feet of space per person.[70] However, such a figure is unrealistic, since it is in their houses that people spend their time at home, and not in the central clearing. More specifically, it is in the peculiarly small Yanoama hammock that a person spends the night as well as much of the waking day. It is not at all unusual for a family of five to occupy a space of approximately ten by twelve feet, which means that an individual has about twenty-five square feet of living space.[71] Further, there is a tendency within a *shabono*—particularly a large one—for adults not to mingle much with people other than close friends and kinsfolk, although young boys do so freely. Thus, with an enormous territory accessible to them, the people of a *teri* crowd themselves into a very small living space. Egoism is dangerous under such conditions, and the interdependency among inhabitants of a *shabono* mitigates selfishness and conspicuousness.

Only its own *shabono* is home to the *teri*. It is a special place, and only there can important rituals be celebrated.[72] In anticipation of each occasion when they will serve as hosts, the occupants usually refurbish the place, weeding the clearing, repairing rotted roof poles, replacing thatch, and in general making the *shabono* more presentable and comfortable.

The Palisade. Many Yanoama *shabono* are surrounded by log palisades built immediately outside the circumference of the circle of family shelters (see fig. 3).[73] Such a defense is allowed to fall into disrepair when no attack is feared, but during times of conflict these defenses are quickly rebuilt.

A palisade is composed of logs and poles set vertically a few inches into the ground. Logs are placed next to one another in a continuous row and lashed together with lianas and vines. A wall is thus constructed that stands eight to ten feet high. Logs are not uniform in length, and a great variety of woods are used, ranging from dense hardwoods to culmlike *kafu* trunks.[74] These logs are not dressed or pointed.

Rarely do palisades stand plumb. They tend to lean outward, supported by widely spaced logs set diagonally and lashed to the horizontal pole stringers to which the vertical log members are also lashed. Occasionally lashings rot, and the great weight of the palisade brings sections of it crashing to the ground.

A palisade encloses the compound, making it safe at least from arrows fired directly from the outside. It is not unusual to find that certain parts of a palisade are in far better repair than other sections. This would seem to be due to the fact that the real function of the wall is to protect the people living immediately adjacent to it. Thus, it is in the interest of each family to keep its own section of the palisade in good repair. However, not all family heads are equally concerned or equally industrious in this matter.[75]

Logs are generally tied to one another loosely enough that people can escape from the *shabono* if necessary by parting the thatch roof of a shelter, pulling out a log or two from the palisade, and fleeing. Before dark each evening all entries are sealed by putting logs into place.

The Cleared Belt beyond the Palisade. The great majority of *shabono* are located in forested areas, and each has a cleared strip beyond the palisade. This outer circumference of the settlement might be fifty feet in width or more. It soon fills with wild and domestic plant volunteers, although some cultivars might also be planted. Gourds and cotton grow near the palisade or even on waste heaps. Papaya, *bixa*, and medicinal plants can also be observed, but always in small quantities. This belt does not normally function as a garden.[76] One explanation for the cleared strip is that enemies cannot penetrate this kind of vegetation in silence, as they could a forest cover.[77]

Trash Heaps. Refuse generated by the Yanoama is organic, principally vegetable. Accumulated over the years are large amounts of discarded baskets, broken gourds, roofing thatch, cotton and *bixa* pods, and plantain peels, as well as a great variety of other materials. These are usually deposited in a few specific locations immediately outside the palisade. Decomposition occurs rapidly, and trash piles are hardly more offensive than compost heaps. Individual households sometimes allow considerable amounts of trash to accumulate around their own fires and in the adjacent *shabono* clearing before disposing of it. Just as some families are neater than others, so some *shabono* are far more hygienic and neat than others.[78]

Toilet Areas. Certain areas are set aside for human evacuation. The Yanoama are discreet and considerate in meeting these needs, although they exercise little control over infants and dogs. Toilet sites are mutually agreed upon, generally in the forest beyond the outer clearing, but not far from the *shabono*. When the *shabono* is located on an open grassland, specific portions of the savanna are set aside for this purpose, sometimes covering acres.

Water Sources. Well above the toilet areas, and separate from them, are the sources of water for household needs. Each household's water supply is replenished nearly every day, and late in the afternoon women and girls can be seen carrying large calabashes full of fresh water to their own shelters. Normally water is taken from the stream near which the *shabono* was built—usually a distance of several hundred yards.

Gardens. Indispensable to the Yanoama are their garden clearings. These can be classified roughly into three types: the newly made clearings, those in production, and the abandoned gardens. Although gardens yield a variety of products, those of the musaceous plants predominate. Gardens range in size from a fraction of an acre to several acres. And they vary in distance from the *shabono*. Generally, gardens of the three categories are to be found widely scattered throughout the territory that pertains to a *teri*. Travel time from the *shabono* can range from a few minutes to several hours.

The Forest. Each *shabono* is the focus for thousands of acres of forest, which contain the *teri* gardens, prospective garden sites, and collecting and hunting grounds.[79]

Trails. A network of trails radiates out from each *shabono*, although not all trails are equally discernible. The most used and, consequently, the widest of these lead to the producing gardens. Others lead to the places where water is obtained and to friendly *shabono* that are visited regularly. Minor trails, invisible to the untrained eye, lead deep into the forest to hunting grounds and to old gardens.[80]

LEADERSHIP

Each *teri* is autonomous. Political organization is truncated with no hierarchical level of authority superior to the *teri* itself. Nevertheless, any particular *teri* is part of a system of inter-*shabono* linkages. These systems, which greatly overlap each other, are essentially social in nature and rooted in kinship ties.

Overt, explicit manifestations of leadership are not always clearly evident to the foreign observer, and the political organization within the *teri* community has been the subject of varying interpretations. However, there is general agreement that leadership does exist and that it is in the hands of vigorous, mature males.[81] In a *teri* there might be several such men, their personalities varying from offensive extroverts to pensive, tactful men. Similarly, certain *teri* have strong leadership while others do not.

Some writers have called such a leader a headman or chief.[82] Whether or not there is in Yanoama society an institutionalized position of headman, there can be no doubt that a hierarchy of adult males dominates each *teri* and its activities.[83] The authority of an individual leader is circumscribed and temporary. Economically, for example, he is almost powerless in the allocation or distribution of wealth that is not his own. He can enforce his decisions only when he can convince other people that they ought to cooperate.

Nevertheless, there are men who want to be leaders, although those with the necessary qualifications are few. A man who has proven himself to be a powerful sorcerer[84] and who has convinced people that he is clever and fearless (*waiteri*) possesses impressive leadership qualities. Also important is his kinship following. The man with numerous sons and sons-in-law who support him is automatically an influential man. This kind of implicit, informal authority characterizes Yanoama leadership. As long as the decisions of such a man satisfy the people of his *teri*, there is little likelihood of serious competition from other men. A leader wears no special insignia that distinguishes him, except occasionally in his capacity as sorcerer. He is essentially *primus inter pares*. A leader consults with other men, and, as a consequence, all adult males are involved in important decision making.[85] Once a decision is reached, however, each man is still free to do what he pleases.

Certain old people are highly respected and very influential, some of them functioning in a leadership capacity. This is true of a patriarch or matriarch with sufficiently large numbers of offspring and kinsmen to comprise an entire *teri*, or at least a significant portion of one. Certain old men seem to have a tempering influence on some of the high-spirited young males.[86] In fact, young men have relatively little influence. Warfare, a very serious matter, is often decided upon by the mature men.

Apart from matriarchs, younger Yanoama women can also participate in decision making. Some are closely related to and have the ear of influential men. Mature wives and sisters often speak up, loudly, to express their views. From earliest childhood, both males and females have closely observed the life of the *shabono* and have formed opinions on most matters.

All in all this system appears to be quite democratic, but inefficient. There is no effective mechanism for making quick, clear, binding decisions. Men are not obliged to comply with decisions they dislike. Sometimes, too, interpretations of a decision vary greatly. At times of crisis the making of a decision can be delayed much too long. This kind of political organization has been described as follows: "One word from the chief and everyone does as he pleases."[87]

DEMOGRAPHIC FEATURES

Shabono populations vary considerably.[88] The smallest I know is that of the Braocuwa-teri, with only five hearths and a diameter of well under 50 feet. This *shabono* was newly constructed in 1969–1970 within a few hundred yards of friendly *shabono*, all of which are the result of fissioning of the Mayobo-teri. The largest *shabono* I observed is the one in the Niyayoba area built hurriedly to house four different *teri*. This one is more than 250 feet in diameter (see fig. 5). Unlike a true communal house, the *shabono* as an architectural form imposes little constraint on the population size of a community.

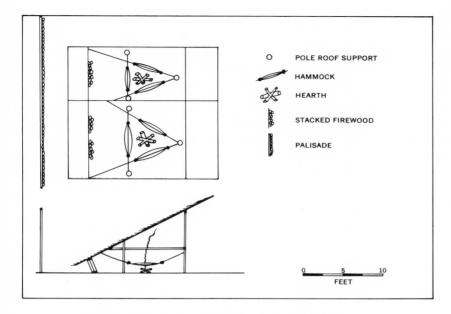

○	POLE ROOF SUPPORT
	HAMMOCK
	HEARTH
	STACKED FIREWOOD
	PALISADE

0 5 10
FEET

Figure 5. The Multiple-*Teri Shabono*. In the Niyayoba area.

A total population of 35 to 40 is unusually small; populations much over 100 are exceptionally large. Most *shabono* house somewhere between 65 and 85 people. A tally of known populations of *shabono* occupied by single *teri* groups in the central Parima highlands yields a statistical mean of 73 persons per *shabono*, with a range from 35 to 180. Approximately the same figures apply to the lowland Yanoama in Venezuela.

Since new *shabono* are built when fissioning or fusion of their populations occurs, *shabono* dimensions coincide roughly with *shabono* populations. In the Parima massif, the Mayobo-teri (about 80 people) occupy a *shabono* 106 feet in diameter with twenty-six hearths; the Waracacoyafiba-teri (about 60 people) *shabono*, with eighteen hearths, is 60 feet in diameter; and the Jorocoba-teri (84 people) *shabono*, with twenty-three hearths, is slightly over 100 feet in diameter.

Shabono with extremely small or very large populations represent temporary, and potentially unstable, conditions. The size at which *teri* communities stabilize seems to be geared to social factors and not conditions of economic power, political prestige, or the natural environment. In most cases, there can be little doubt that the technology and the natural resource base are capable of supporting much larger focal settlements than those built by the Yanoama.

Age and Sex Ratios. Settlements contain youthful populations.[89] For example, of the 210 inhabitants of the Niyayoba *shabono* (see table 2), more than 50 percent can be classified as children. (The term "children" here signifies boys and girls clearly too young to be married.) Among the Niyayoba-teri, 24 (representing nearly 40% of the total population) are children. Another study of an even larger group showed that 32 percent of the population was under fifteen years of age.[90] Yet the Venezuelan and Brazilian Creole populations on the whole are even more youthful, since about 32 percent are under ten years old, and fully 44 percent are under fifteen.[91] Average age is equally difficult to establish, although an attempt has been made. Published conclusions are that the "average estimated age" of males is nearly twenty-one years, and that of females is somewhat over twenty-three years.[92]

There is considerable variation in the data on sex ratios obtained by different students of the Yanoama. So, too, is there variation in the conclusions derived from these data. Some writers have maintained that the Yanoama suffer from a continuing and acute shortage of females in their population[93] and that this shortage is the principal reason for warfare.[94] My data for the Parima highland core of Yanoama territory show a general balance in the sex ratio, with a tendency toward a slight surplus of females (see table 2). This fact is noteworthy, since females are not nearly as visible to the foreign visitor as are males. Females tend to be shy and reticent when strangers arrive, and sometimes men order attractive girls to hide from foreigners.

TABLE 2

Age and Sex Composition of Specific Highland Yanoama Populations

| | Males | | Females | | % | % | % | |
Population	Boys	Adults	Girls	Adults	Male	Female	Children	Total
Niyayoba *shabono*	58	44	54	54	49	51	53	210
Niyayoba-teri	13	15	11	19	48	52	40	58
Jorocoba-teri[a]	17	20	16	20	49	51	52	73

[a]Data on the sex of 11 infants were not available.

A remarkable facet of highland Barafiri culture is the institutionalization of abnormality. Certain adult females, for example, are classified as *wanidi* ("abnormal"),[95] and no man will have such a person as a wife. These women are very few; there were only two in an observed population (Niyayoba area) of well over two hundred. Apparently such abnormals become identifiable well before puberty, and the classification is retained throughout life.[96] It seems to rest upon Yanoama aesthetics rather than any personality trait or physical deformity in a Western sense. The mere existence of such an institution appears to indicate that there is no critical lack of marriageable females, at least in the Parima highlands.

Births. Long-term observations of Yanoama populations are nonexistent. However, there are available comprehensive data for a two-year period (July 1968 through July 1970) on the 210 inhabitants of the Niyayoba area of the Parima highlands.[97] During that period there were 25 live births, with no known stillbirths or abortions of term fetuses. This represents an annual birth rate of approximately 60 per thousand. It would be hazardous to apply this figure to the Yanoama in general, but it can be compared with the 40–44 per thousand for Brazil as a whole, or the 47–51 per thousand for Venezuela as a whole.[98]

During the same two-year period, there was one infanticide, immediately after delivery, but the sex of the baby is not known. An infant boy died about three weeks after birth. The cause of this death was probably pneumonia—aggravated by the rigors of camping in the forest, since the mother went with others to gather wild fruit when the baby was already ill.

None of the twenty-five babies was a twin. In fact, twins are not born to women of the Niyayoba area, or to the other highland *teri* with whom they have direct contact.[99] Of the twenty-three children who survived, eleven were male and twelve were female.[100]

The Yanoama are said to have a "commitment to population control,"[101] which is manifested in various ways. During pregnancy sexual relations are prohibited (at least in theory), and, ideally, continence continues through the entire period of lactation. The total might be as much as five years since full weaning does not occur until a child is able to run about freely. Abortions also limit the birth rate, and possibly so does the use of certain medicinal concoctions to prevent conception.

The number of living children per mother appears to vary considerably. Data obtained from the populations of seven *teri* of the Parima highlands showed that there were 25 women over forty, who had a total of 130 living children. The mean is slightly over 5 living children per woman.[102] However, a mean of only 3.8 live births per Yanoama woman over forty has been reported elsewhere.[103]

Children are inseparable from their mothers for their first few years of life. Boys are sometimes carried, in shoulder slings or tump straps, by their mothers and older sisters until they are several years old. Then, suddenly, the boys become mobile and independent, attaching themselves to play packs. Young girls stay close to their mothers much longer, learning the female role of the Yanoama woman.

Yanoama are indulgent with their children. The youngsters see most of

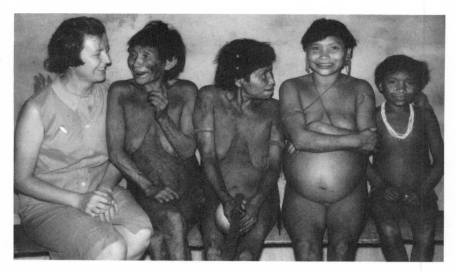

Plate 10. Four generations of a Juwafusibuwei-teri family (with missionary) seated from left to right by age. The matriarch, wife of Ñape Foo, is presumed to be about sixty-five years old, her daughter is perhaps forty-five, her granddaughter is more than twenty-five, and her great-granddaughter is about eight. The old lady's cheeks are smeared black as a sign of mourning. The granddaughter is in advanced pregnancy. Both of the older women are using tobacco.

what occurs in *shabono* or campsite, and they are generally well informed about what they do not see. They, like women, participate at least passively in most events. Children are punished infrequently. However, a severe beating is sometimes given suddenly by an angry parent. Spanking, or other formalized punishments, are not used. The Yanoama are emotional, rather than calculating, in raising their children.[104]

Mortality. Comprehensive data on Yanoama mortality are, like those on births and ages, insufficient to permit any authoritative statement. However, there is reliable information for specific settlements over short periods of time. Probably the most accurate and comprehensive is that gathered during a two-year period (July 1968–July 1970) for the approximately 210 inhabitants of the huge Niyayoba *shabono* cited above. During this period there were seven deaths (yielding for this small sample an annual mortality rate of 17 per thousand).

Three of these deaths were adult males. One man died of what appeared to be a liver ailment; an elderly man died of unknown causes (perhaps pneumonia) while on a visit to the Yoreshiana-teri; and one man in his twenties was killed by enemies during a raid on the Niyayoba area.[105] A boy of about fifteen died of what appeared to be a heart condition, complicated by asthma; and a girl of about fifteen was killed accidentally by her husband while he was punishing her. Two infants died, one by infanticide, as described above.[106] Infant and childhood mortality has been estimated at 18 percent for the Yanoama, described as a low rate by tropical standards.[107]

The Aged. Unsurprisingly, in a preliterate culture such as this, few people reach old age.[108] Those who do are repositories of knowledge and experience, as well as progenitors of much of the population in their own communities. Generally, they are heard when they choose to speak on almost any subject, and they are respected among their kin.

The oldest person among the 210 inhabitants of the Niyayoba *shabono* is a man called Ñape Foo,[109] patriarch of the Juwafusibuwei-teri, who is perhaps seventy years of age. His wife (see plate 10) is probably about sixty-five. The Niyayoba-teri and the Jorocoba-teri have widowed matriarchs,[110] and, in each case, this is an old, highly respected woman whose needs are met fully by her own children, her sons- and daughters-in-law, her grandchildren, and her nieces and nephews. Much concern is shown for such a woman's comfort and well-being.

Marriage. The institution of marriage is an important one, and it is the rare adult who is not or has not been married. Although many men are monogamous, it is not unusual to find men with two wives or more. Sometimes an additional wife is welcomed by an older one; in other cases there is jealousy and even hostility. Frequently, multiple wives are full sisters. Normally, each wife maintains her own household, and the husband lives with his favorite wife of the moment (see fig. 11).

Most females marry soon after puberty, but for men marriage usually occurs later. To qualify for a wife, a young man must have proved himself a capable hunter, and he ought to have had some experience in gardening. It is in this manner that he demonstrates to a girl's family that he can keep a wife and help her parents as well. A marriage agreement generally includes a suitable bride price, a major part of which is the promise on the part of the groom to provide his new wife's parents with meat from the hunt; and not infrequently a groom agrees to do at least some of their gardening for them. Such responsibilities might continue for a matter of years.[111]

These features of marriage make it quite evident why a man finds it attractive to marry sisters and why a girl's family prefers that she marry a mature man. Inexperienced young men are also at a disadvantage in competition with older men for wives, since the older men have had time to make the suitable personal arrangements with a girl's parents long before she reaches marriageable age. Although marriages are sometimes planned for people even before their birth, this is exceptional among the Barafiri. There are known instances of young couples marrying because of sincere affection for one another. In such cases, of course, parental approval is still necessary.

The subject of Yanoama marriage-partner selection is marginal to this research, and considerable detailed information has been published.[112] Generally, cross-cousin marriage is ideal, whereas parallel cousin marriages are forbidden as incestuous.[113] What this signifies is that within a *teri* itself there exist opportunities for satisfactory marriage matches. People, and particularly women, marry outside their home *shabono* only under great pressure. Nor does a *teri* want to lose any part of its population through marriages to outsiders. Compromises are reached in those cases where two or three particularly friendly *teri* groups intermarry, thereby strengthening their bonds.

Yet, marriage is an important mechanism for redistributing people on the land. If a marriage is made between people from different *teri*, the couple decides whether to live with the husband's or wife's kin. A man contemplating the marriage of sisters might well decide to live with their *teri*; however, if a man doesn't feel welcome in a *shabono*, he can take his wife forcibly to live with his own *teri*. If a bride struggles against leaving her parents' hearth, her husband might well grab an arm and pull her away with him. In such cases the female relatives of the bride are likely to hold firmly to her other arm, and a painful tug of war might ensue.

Shabono TERRITORY

Each *teri* has its respective territorial base, or *urifi*.[114] *Shabono*, gardens, old gardens, collecting and hunting grounds are all bound together within this territory by a network of trails into a functional whole. Precisely demarcated territorial limits are unnecessary, since boundaries are not limits of sovereignty. Neighboring *shabono* are intimately linked by kinship, so that the settlement pattern observed at any given time is but a stage in the continuing processes of fission, fusion, and the renaming of *teri* residence groups. Yanoama territoriality reflects this, so an effective means of analyzing this spatial dimension of their culture is to examine the territory of a specific *teri*.

The Jorocoba-teri provide a representative example. This group has not been involved directly in warfare for a generation, its population of eighty-four is close to the estimated mean for all *shabono*, and it has been virtually free from contact with non-Yanoama peoples.

The Jorocoba-teri feel a strong tie with their lands, and they ascribe a permanency to this. They will maintain, for example, that they have "always" lived along the Jorocoba-u. And, from the Yanoama viewpoint, there might be little effective difference between "always" and two or three generations.

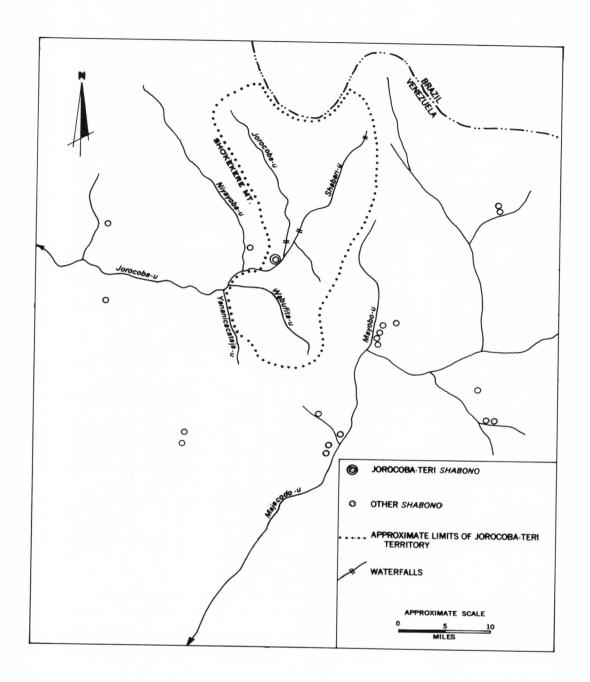

Map 7. Jorocoba-teri Territory (Urifi Jorocoba-teri)

Jorocoba-teri territory, or Urifi Jorocoba-teri (see map 7), is elongated with the present *shabono* in a very eccentric location. The area of this total resource endowment, roughly estimated, is approximately 250 square miles (160,000 acres).[115] Boundaries exist, which distinguish the lands of the Jorocoba-teri from those of their neighbors. These are imaginary lines and therefore not demarcated. Nor are they of particular significance as indicators of territorial exclusiveness.

Territorial limits frequently coincide with drainage divides. Some of these divides, such as Shokekere Mountain, are pronounced ridges more than one thousand feet above the valley floors; others are far less conspicuous. The Jorocoba-teri have all the valley of the Jorocoba-u, which extends north a distance equivalent to at least three days' travel from the *shabono*. Their territory also extends up the Shabari-u to its headwaters, where it abuts upon lands of the Mayobo-teri, and up the Wubufita-u to Boreawa-teri territory.

In some places a stream serves to mark the limits. At the southwestern edge, Jorocoba-teri territory extends to the Jorocoba-u, and then along this stream to the Yananicacataja-u. Yoreshiana-teri territory begins at a huge rock formation, called the "Yananicacataja," located several miles up the river. On the rolling savanna between the *shabono* of the Jorocoba-teri and the Niyayoba area (see map 9), the boundary follows a small creek that rises on Shokekere Mountain.

It must be remembered that these are not boundaries as known elsewhere. The Jorocoba-teri and their land tenure can be understood only in the context of neighboring *teri*, all of which are classified presently as "friends," and with whom they also have kinship bonds. For example, there are numerous marriage ties with the Mayobo-teri.[116] Thus, their Mayobo-teri kinsmen hunt in the upper reaches of the Shabari-u valley. In like manner, Jorocoba-teri hunting parties cross back and forth over the divide when it serves their purposes.

Perhaps because of arrangements made in the 1920's between the Jorocoba-teri and the Docodicoro-teri (see fig. 4) when they lived together in a single *shabono*, these two *teri* still share a certain area southwest of the Jorocoba-teri *shabono*.[117]

Lands northwest of this segment of the Jorocoba-u belong by tradition to the Niyayoba-teri. Nevertheless, far to the south, along an eastern tributary of the Wabufita-u, there are numerous old gardens made by the predecessors of the Niyayoba-teri, where the latter still go to collect. Doubtless, there are more examples of other *teri* sharing portions of the territory of the Jorocoba-teri.

Adult males generally know well this enormous territory, their knowledge derived from intimate use of it. Far up in the headwaters of the Jorocoba-u are the preferred hunting grounds for game, such as the armadillo, sloth, anteater, agouti, spider monkey, and red (howler) monkey. Other specific areas are hunted for big game such as tapir and deer. Scattered widely throughout the territory are innumerable old gardens. The remains of campsites dot the forests, right up to the territorial boundaries—places where, at one time or another, groups camped to collect in the forest, to make gardens, or just to spend the night while on the trail. Several former *shabono* sites can be found also (see map 9). Huge expanses of the total territory are covered with treeless savannas of either grasses or ferns. These open areas, of no real use to the Jorocoba-teri, are burned periodically to help facilitate travel through them.

When a particular area is no longer considered to be suitable for gardening, or for any other purpose, it might be "thrown away." For example, there is a grove of wild cacao trees in the territory of the Jorocoba-teri that has been so classified. Anyone friendly to the Jorocoba-teri is free to collect cacao pods there.

Abundant land resources, particularly forest, are indispensable for Yanoama existence. There is no evidence that any *teri* is without sufficient land. In fact, fission does not occur unless provisions have been made by each group for specific areas in which to garden, collect, and hunt.[118] Wars are not waged for land resources. There is no felt demographic pressure on the land. *Teri* and land are consequently in stable balance.

The Circulatory System

Trails and bridges constitute the indispensable linkages in the Yanoama circulatory system, since people travel only on foot. Many trails are barely visible, and even principal trails are not easy for a non-Indian to follow.[119] Trails tend to follow direct routes between places, rather than to be aligned with relief features or contour lines. Therefore, in the highlands, at least, considerable vertical distance is involved in traveling.

Some trails are used so frequently they can be classified as major routes. In this category are those used regularly for making social visits and those that are used by people carrying heavy loads of firewood or produce from gardens to the *shabono*. Radiating out from the Niyayoba *shabono*, for example, are three important inter-*shabono* routes: the one to the Mayobo area (a five-hour trip for men traveling alone)[120] is used almost weekly by someone or other; the one to the Yoreshiana-teri (a three-day trip for men) is used at least every few weeks, the most regular travelers being an old woman and her *wanidi* daughter; the trail to the Comodoroba-teri area (a four-day trip for men) is used at least once a month. All these trips are made for specific purposes, and, except for the most extenuating circumstances, a person will not travel alone.

Certain improvements are made on these important trails even if the end result is scarcely evident to an outsider. Vines and small trees are cut from the trail, but, if a large tree falls, its trunk is usually incorporated into the trail itself, since the Yanoama much prefer walking on logs to the bare ground. Such logs are sometimes notched, particularly on slopes, to provide toeholds. Steep banks similarly have toeholds cut into them to facilitate the ascent or descent. Along the major trails are resting places. Frequently these are part-way up long ascendants, and, at them, laggards can catch up with the rest of a group of travelers.

The most striking improvements, however, are bridges. These are indispensable, since the Yanoama avoid fording even small streams and have a patent aversion to deep water and fast currents. The most sophisticated type of bridge, both technologically and aesthetically, is the suspension bridge. It consists of poles lashed together to form walkways, which are in turn suspended from lianas attached to trees and poles on each bank. Liana handrails along the walkways are very useful to women crossing with heavy loads. This type of bridge is constructed where water is deep, and, consequently, it is not found in the central Parima highlands, but rather on the fringes of Yanoama territory, crossing the Orinoco and some of the other lowland rivers. A suspension bridge of this type ninety feet long has been reported spanning the upper Orinoco.[121]

In the Parima highlands, two other kinds of bridge prevail. One consists of long poles resting horizontally in the cruxes of pairs of crossed poles that have been pushed into the bed of a shallow stream or a swamp, and then lashed together with vines (see plate 11). In the 1920's the remains of one of these bridges was reported across the Rio Parima at a place where it is 112 feet wide. There were still visible about 75 feet of the bridge, resting on what were described as "piles."[122] Another type of bridge is made by cutting down a tree so that it will fall across a stream at a trail crossing. Widths and lengths vary with the trees growing at the specific sites. Sometimes liana handrails are provided, particularly if women will be using the bridge on a regular basis.

Yanoama Mobility

The Yanoama are a very mobile people. However, this mobility is not to be equated with nomadism. Nomads have no fixed dwelling place, while each Yanoama *teri* has a *shabono* to which it invariably returns. Every group move is to a particular location for a specific purpose, even though to the casual observer it might appear to be an aimless wandering. Group relocations are of two different kinds: the short-term change of residence for the purposes of collecting, gardening, or social visiting, and perma-

Plate 11. Pole bridge across a small creek near the Niyayoba *shabono*, which can be seen in the background. Note the poor condition of the palisade. This group of women, carrying their empty *wuu* baskets, are probably on their way to collect firewood.

nent relocation involving the building of a new *shabono*. The former, or temporary, change of residence, varies in duration from a single night to months.

Occasionally an entire *teri* travels together. If the *teri* is large, it forms a veritable procession on the trail. One such group, the Namoe-teri numbering more than one hundred people, has been described as it traveled to an important *reajo* funerary ceremony.[123] They walked, single file, with women and children in the middle. Each day they began at about 7:00 A.M., continuing at a very slow pace until about 3:00 P.M. For each night's stop, the men would construct shelters in which their families could cook and sleep.

More commonly, the smaller kin groups within a *teri* travel independently of the rest of the community. Among the Barafiri, families tend to schedule their extended absences so that all the *teri* members are away from the *shabono* at the same time. If any people stay behind (i.e., women, small children, old men, and *wanidi*), they move out of the *shabono*, putting up temporary shelters in the forest nearby. This relocation is preferred to remaining alone in the *shabono*.

In the Parima highlands mobility is not geared to seasonality, although January and February are months of considerable inter-*teri* social visiting. The calendar of social events seems to be tied to the availability of plantains (and, to a far lesser degree, peach-palm fruits), rather than annual seasons per se. In the Orinoco lowlands, where seasonality of precipitation is more pronounced and there is far less topographic variation, it has been reported that "most of the intervillage traveling is done from September through April, the dry season."[124]

Certain individuals, particularly aged widows and *wanidi* women, are quite free to move about between settlements. Many *teri* have a person, or persons, of this category who live away from home with relatives for extended periods. In times of warfare, old women can serve as neutrals, providing a communication link between hostile settlements.[125] Those elements of the population least able to move about are, understandably, the crippled, the very ill, and the aged. If it is particularly important that they travel—to a mortuary feast for example—they are carried.

The world of a Yanoama is circumscribed and small, but not all people are equally mobile. On the whole, females stay close to home except for the normal group travels. Men and older boys travel extensively when hunting. If luck on the hunt is poor, they range more widely throughout the forest than if they have early success. Adult males also move about visiting kinsmen for such purposes as acquiring trade items (an ax, a machete, a dog), finding a wife and working out the arrangements for acquiring her, seeking support in the formation of a raiding party, or even raiding another *teri*.

A few case studies can provide the spatial dimensions of the world of a mature, sophisticated male Yanoama. One good example is that of Ñape Foo, a respected Juwafusibuwei-teri man nearly seventy years old. To put his experiences into perspective, they can be compared with those of his son, Rojama Foo, who is about forty years old. Between them, father and son have been to the *shabono* of twenty-five different *teri* at least once. In table 3 these *teri* are listed according to the principal purpose for which they were visited. There are but three areas—at the outer edges of their "known world"—that have been visited by only one of the two men. Only the father has been to the *shabono* of the Cabirowa-teri (northernmost of the Barafiri dialect groups), and only the son has been across the Parima divide into Brazil to visit the Catarowa-teri.[126] The son has also been up the Río Ocamo as far as the Irocoroba-teri,[127] and he has seen the Buuta-u.

Yanoama do not visit *shabono* unless there are people there to welcome them and provide them with food. It is likely, therefore, that in all the *teri* listed in table 3 (except the Bashobaca-teri) there were kinsmen of Ñape Foo and his son. The few *teri* that have been visited with great frequency and for prolonged periods are the ones with which the father and son have the closest bonds of kinship. Currently the Jawafusibuwei-teri

TABLE 3

83
Distribution
Patterns and
Settlement
Morphology

Shabono *Known to Ñape Foo and His Son, Rojama Foo*
(Classified According to Stated Principal Purpose of Visit or Visits)

To Visit with Close Kin	Visits to Trade
Mayobo-teri	Boshewa-teri
Kafucibuwa-teri[a]	Momowei-teri[f]
Niyayoba-teri[b]	Danafibaubraba-teri[f]
Docodicoro-teri[c]	
Waracacoyafiba-teri[d]	Raiding
Arajai-teri[d]	Bashobaca-teri
Jorabareba-teri	
Shonofedubaca[e]	
Moshimacabaca-teri[e]	No Motive Given
	Jucomoshitobraoba-teri
	Cabirowa-teri
To Visit with "Friends"	Yoreshiana-teri
Catarowa-teri	Comodoroba-teri
Yaniyaniwa-teri[a]	Mracabuwe-teri
Wanashiawa-teri	Jorocoba-teri
Monotowa-teri	Canashewa-teri[b]
Irocoroba-teri	

[a]No longer "friends," hence, no visiting at present.
[b]Before Niyayoba-teri, Juwafusibuwei-teri, Canashewa-teri, and Docodicoro-teri joined in a single *shabono* (1966).
[c]Before the Juwafusibuwei-teri and the Docodicoro-teri joined in a single *shabono*.
[d]Fissioned amicably from the Mayobo-teri.
[e]Bitter enemies now; recently moved to present location.
[f]For clay pots.

live in a single *shabono* with two of the *teri* that they used to visit most, the Docodicoro-teri and the Niyayoba-teri. They now most frequently travel to visit the Mayobo-teri.

A third example of traveling experience is that of Buuqui Foo, a mature, experienced Jorocoba-teri man. In his forty-five years of life he has been to the *shabono* of fifteen different *teri* for social visiting and some attendant exchange of goods (see map 8).[128] Spatially, the orientation of his bonds with other *teri* is toward the east (Barafiri), and he has visited just about all the *shabono* in that direction that are specifically known to him. He has also been northwest as far as the Río Ocamo.[129]

A fourth man, Jiiquini Foo, is an effective sorcerer and one of the leaders of the Mayobo-teri. His age is perhaps forty, and his "known world" corresponds roughly to that of the other three individuals. Although he has not been to visit the Catarowa-teri (in Brazil), some of them have come to visit the *shabono* of the Arajai-teri and the Waracacoyafiba-teri in his area (both of these fissioned from the Mayobo-teri).[130]

Map 8 shows that personal travel is not a result of proximity, but of amicable kinship bonds. Travel and visiting are reciprocal acts, and implicit in the map is the inter-*shabono* linkage pattern.[131] The three *teri* (Juwafusibuwei-teri, Jorocoba-teri, and Mayobo-teri) demonstrate personal, specific sets of links; they are friendly to one another and to a similar array of other *teri*, such as the Yoreshiana-teri to the south, the Kafucibuwa-teri to the north, and the Comodoroba-teri to the northwest. People in all the *shabono* known personally to the four men speak Barafiri and, with few exceptions, they occupy highland habitats 2,000 feet or more in elevation.

Distances traveled for social visits vary considerably. It is more than thirty miles in a direct line between the Juwafusibuwei-teri and groups living on the Río Ocamo, although *teri* that share frequent visits are usually located much closer to one another. Men traveling alone can cover fifteen miles or more in a day, but with women and children they move at only a fraction of that speed.

Not all kinsmen are on friendly terms, and personal animosities account in large measure for the bounds of a man's "known world" and for the discordant limits of the four men considered here. As a consequence, an experienced man has intimate knowledge of fewer than ten *shabono* and has visited only about 25 out of a total of more than 128 in Venezuela alone. He knows very little or nothing of the existence of the remaining 100 or so. Areally, he might in a lifetime cover 500 square miles. The men whose experiences are described here have at least passing contact with well over 50 percent of the 44 known Barafiri-speaking *shabono*.[132] A woman's world is far more circumscribed.

The principal reasons to travel to other *teri* appear in table 3. By far the most important of these is social. Travel time, as we have seen, varies from a few hours to a week or more. In any event, people take with them little more than their hammocks, food for the trip, and personal adornments; men also take their weapons. The visit itself is rarely shorter than two days and might continue for a week or more.

A second principal set of reasons to travel is economic: group relocations in order to collect, to hunt, and to garden. Campsites are constructed for this purpose in the area where the specific activity is to take place. Plans are made in advance; before leaving the *shabono*, people know where they are going and why. The heavy work of preparing a new garden induces people to relocate for lengthy periods of time (unless the garden is to be made near the *shabono*). In this way, work on the garden can be combined with scouring the same general area for food, hunting

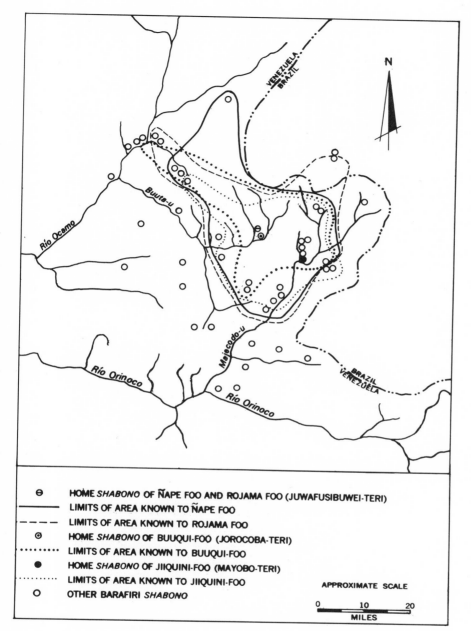

N

VENEZUELA.
BRAZIL

Río Ocamo

Buuta-u

Río Orinoco

Matacodo-u

Río Orinoco

BRAZIL
VENEZUELA

⊖   HOME *SHABONO* OF ÑAPE FOO AND ROJAMA FOO (JUWAFUSIBUWEI-TERI)

⎯⎯   LIMITS OF AREA KNOWN TO ÑAPE FOO

⎯ ⎯   LIMITS OF AREA KNOWN TO ROJAMA FOO

⊙   HOME *SHABONO* OF BUUQUI-FOO (JOROCOBA-TERI)

······   LIMITS OF AREA KNOWN TO BUUQUI-FOO

●   HOME *SHABONO* OF JIIQUINI-FOO (MAYOBO-TERI)

··········   LIMITS OF AREA KNOWN TO JIIQUINI-FOO

○   OTHER BARAFIRI *SHABONO*

APPROXIMATE SCALE

0   10   20
MILES

Map 8. Approximate Limits of Areas Known Personally to Four Barafiri Men.
Shabono locations in 1970.

game, and collecting useful raw materials. In contrast, once a garden begins producing, it is harvested gradually, and plantains and other produce are carried to the *shabono* as needed. No camps are constructed for
this purpose.

When vermin become a serious problem in a *shabono*, the inhabitants
sometimes move out en masse. However, there is more to the move than
simply escaping pests: the Indians will build a camp in collecting grounds
or near a new garden, or they make a social visit with kinsmen.

Hunting and raiding parties have a short duration, and only mature
males participate in these. As a precaution, raiding parties generally do
not build a camp or even light a fire where they might be spotted by the
enemy. As soon as the raid is made, or if it is frustrated, the party immediately returns home. Hunters, like others who must spend a night on the
trail, put up only flimsy shelters, probably spending each night of the
hunt in a different location.

Shabono POPULATION VARIABILITY

One of the frustrating experiences in field study of the Yanoama is traveling to a distant *shabono* only to find it utterly vacant. Yanoama themselves
do not make this mistake (except when raiding), since visiting is done by
invitation. A useful set of specific data on this aspect of Yanoama mobility
exists in the files of the Venezuelan Malariology Service. In the Amazonas Federal Territory, for example, accessible aboriginal settlements
are sprayed periodically with DDT, and malaria medications are also
dispensed at these times. The Parima highlands are not yet effectively
covered by the Malariology Service,[133] but there are accumulated data
for selected Yanoama settlements in the Orinoco lowlands, especially
those of the Orinoco-Waika dialect. These are, in effect, census data collected by spraying teams,[134] and they establish why so many students of
the Yanoama have called them "nomadic," or "seminomadic."

Table 4 synthesizes maximum and minimum populations for six lowland *teri* over a period of nearly five years. The more isolated groups,
such as the Cashorawa-teri and the Jasubowa-teri, which did not live on
the Río Orinoco, were visited far fewer times than the others. The table is
compiled from eighty visits, among which only fifty involved finding any
resident population. Normally, if the people were camped nearby (in
ranchos provisionales), they were tallied there. If no one could be found, the
shabono or other buildings were sprayed and listed as empty.

Fortunately, there is not one of the twelve months for which there are
not a few data, so that both the wet and the dry seasons of this lowland
habitat are represented. Those population figures, which are well above

the norm for a *teri*, probably include visiting kinsmen. Very small popula- tions, such as five or seven for the Shashaiva-teri, are also exceptional. These are probably the people who stayed behind in shelters near a *shabono* vacated when most of its population left temporarily.

Extreme mobility is evident, without a clear-cut seasonal correlation. This is noteworthy, since there are reports that during the particularly rainy months of May through August the Yanoama of the Orinoco lowlands do not travel.[135]

It is to be remembered that these *teri*, unlike their highland counterparts, live on or near navigable water. This might be a factor in their mobility during the rainy months. However, even among the most acculturated groups, there are only two or three dugout canoes for the whole community, making it unlikely that an entire *teri* travels by water.

FISSION AND FUSION OF THE *Teri*

The *teri* has already been described as transitory, since names, locations, population composition, and relations with other *teri* are dynamic. Cleavage (fission) and amalgamation (fusion) of *teri* are continuing processes affecting the *shabono* distribution pattern. In fission, a *teri* splits or cleaves, along kinship lines, into more than one group. One or more of these newly formed groups might remain as discrete *teri* or join with other groups to form *teri*. True amalgamation, or fusion, occurs only at the *teri* level; an entire population accepts a single *teri* name and agrees to occupy a single *shabono*.

Fission has been more regularly observed, and certain causes have been ascribed to the process. Most often it is due to accumulated tensions and factional disputes arising when internal strife and bickering reach critical proportions—a condition increasingly likely as a *teri* grows in numbers.[136] A particularly important cause for disputes within a *teri* involves warfare or the possibility of warfare. A sizeable faction not in agreement with certain warlike actions of the *teri* (or dissatisfied with pacifist actions they interpret as cowardly) might decide to break away. Fission, then, is essentially an outgrowth of a crisis of confidence in leadership. There is no institutionalized chieftainship in Yanoama society strong enough to counteract this tendency toward fission in large *teri* populations. The bitterness between factions is not usually so great that the two or more groups formed by fissioning do not stay in the same general area as amicable neighbors. However, as the years pass and each new *teri* develops its own marriage bonds, physical proximity of the groups might gradually diminish as they pass through phases of separation.

Amalgamation, or fusion, of groups is also a continuing process, involv-

TABLE 4

*Random Monthly Sample of Maximum and Minimum Populations of Selected
Yanoama* Teri *of the Orinoco Lowlands for the Period December 1959 through
August 1964*[a]

Teri	January	February	March	April	May	Ju
Dayadi-teri						
Maximum	51	—[b]	45	—	—	—
Minimum	31	0	0	—	0	
Shashaiva-teri						
Maximum	41	0	30	39	32	
Minimum	21	0	5	—	24	
Yabitao-teri						
Maximum	31	0	0	57	30	—
Minimum	—	0	0	—	—	—
Cashorawa-teri						
Maximum	38	—	—	—	30	—
Minimum	—	0	—	—	0	
Irijimawa-teri						
Maximum	53	33	41	—	33	6
Minimum	0	0	36	—	0	3
Jasubowa-teri						
Maximum	—	92	—	—	—	8
Minimum	—	—	0	—	0	—

[a]Data for August 1964 were obtained by me during visits to all but the Jasubowa-teri
shabono.

[b]No information.

July	August	September	October	November	December	Total No. of Visits
46	53	—	60	66	—	18
—	—	0	—	—	—	
35	32	40	—	20	41	18
14	—	—	0	—	—	
—	34	—	—	65	70	14
0	—	0	—	24	0	
—	—	—	57	38	—	8
0	—	—	—	—	—	
46	—	52	55	—	40	16
—	—	0	—	—	—	
—	—	—	—	—	—	6
—	0	—	—	—	—	

ing relatively small *teri* populations. These might themselves be the result of fission. Or persistent raiding by enemies can reduce a *teri* to a small, terrified group desperately in need of joining with some friendly kinsmen. Epidemics, particularly severe ones, have been known to reduce local Yanoama populations to such an extent that the few survivors in different *teri* find it attractive to unify. However, this is accomplished only after the survivors have conquered their fears and stopped their seemingly irrational flight from spirit beings.

The fluidity of such a mobile people as the Yanoama can best be understood in terms of particular *teri*. The Mayobo-teri presently occupy a *shabono* containing twenty-six hearths (fig. 3), located near the Mayobo-u of the upper Río Majecodo. Some of these people are said to have come from the Canashewa-teri.[137] Another important segment of the population originated from among the Shokekere-teri, now called the Niyayoba-teri.

In about 1957,[138] Jiiquini Foo (referred to above) married a Mayobo-teri woman, leaving his home among the Shokekere-teri to live with her people. He is well versed in magic and cures and has become the most influential individual among the Mayobo-teri. When he made this move, he already had an "older brother," who was a Mayobo-teri. With Jiiquini Foo came his five younger brothers and a younger sister. At some later date his mother, too, joined the Mayobo-teri. All these people, whether originally Mayobo-teri, or formerly Canashewa-teri, Shokekere-teri (Niyayoba-teri), or even Moshimacabaca-teri, are fused together now as the "Mayobo-teri."[139]

For at least the last two decades the Mayobo-teri have flourished demographically. This might be explained by several factors: they have attracted new people from other *teri*, their high elevation and their isolation from Creoles make them relatively free from malaria and other exotic diseases, and since about 1955 they have not been involved directly in warfare.

In conjunction with their demographic growth, the Mayobo-teri have also experienced pronounced fissioning. Three new *teri* (the Waracacoyafiba-teri, the Arajai-teri, and most recently the Braocuwa-teri) have been formed in large part from the Mayobo-teri, building their own *shabono* nearby. Another group, the Jucomoshitobraoba-teri, moved into the Mayobo area about 1968 from a valley approximately ten miles due north. These five *teri* all live close to one another (see map 6) as friends, having amicably allocated their territorial resources among themselves.

Although they have since moved away, several other *teri* were neighbors of the Mayobo-teri as late as the 1950's. This was probably before the formation of the Arajai-teri and possibly even the Waracacoyafiba-teri. The lower Mayobo-u area appears to have had a relatively dense Yanoama population over a prolonged time period.[140]

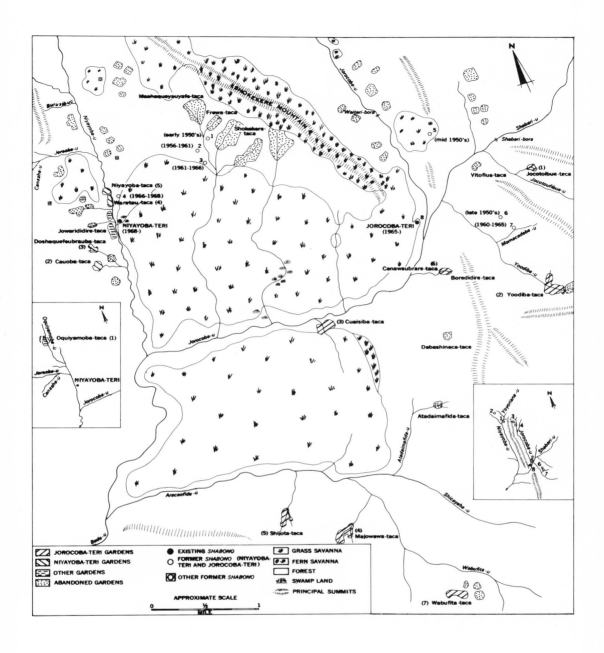

Map 9. The Niyayoba-teri and the Jorocoba-teri. (Garden clearing sequence indicated by numbers in parentheses)

At any particular moment, the site occupied by a *shabono* represents only one phase in the continuous relocation of the *teri* that occupies it. However, tracing these moves through time and space is very difficult for some of the reasons specified. Of particular importance among these are the perishability of Yanoama material culture, the lack of Yanoama concern with the time dimension, the taboo on references to the dead, and the dynamic nature of the *teri*, which is at once evanescent and originative. Nonetheless, an attempt will be made to trace relocations of two sample groups.

The Niyayoba-teri. For many decades this *teri* has existed as a viable community which built *shabono* of its own. Throughout the period these people occupied territory along the Niyayoba-u. Yet, during this time, the name of the *teri* and the specifics of its population composition changed, as did the *shabono* sites; each new *shabono* was built in conformity with the kinship composition of the *teri* at the time.

The oldest name obtainable for the predecessors of the contemporary Niyayoba-teri is Cayuca-teri. This *teri* also lived near the Niyayoba-u, although at that time the stream was known as the Cayuca-u.[141] The time can be very roughly estimated as early in this century. Later, this group became known as the Warata-teri, and the Niyayoba-u was the Warata-u. Still later they called themselves the Shokekere-teri. While they bore this name, at least during the 1920's and 1930's, their principal gardens were on the southwest slopes of Shokekere Mountain. The name Niyayoba-teri was adopted in 1966, when the group moved out onto the savanna that by then had become known as Niyayoba Borosi.[142]

In a general sense, it appears, these people have through the past decades been moving gradually down the valley of the Niyayoba-u, making gardens and building *shabono* with each new relocation.[143] However, only the last four moves (shown on map 9) can be described and located with precision.

About 1956, while still the Shokekere-teri, they moved southwest, across a small stream from the site of a *shabono* on the lower slopes of Shokekere Mountain. The new *shabono* was a small one, constructed on a low, forested ridge.

Then, about 1961, they moved south along the ridge a few hundred yards, building a *shabono* in a forest clearing almost at the edge of the extensive Niyayoba savanna. In these moves, as well as those of four preceding decades at least, they stayed within a few miles of their old gardens. While living here as the Shokekere-teri, they became deeply involved in a war. They were allied with their close friends and neighbors, the Cana-

shewa-teri, the Juwafusibuwei-teri, and the Docodicoro-teri; their enemies were the Moshimacabaca-teri and the Shonofedubaca-teri.

There was such danger of enemy raids by 1966 that some of the Shokekere-teri and their allies moved together. These Shokekere-teri changed
their name to Niyayoba-teri, while others left to live with kinsmen in
friendly *teri·* to the east. In early 1966 the Niyayoba-teri and the Canashewa-teri joined, building a single *shabono* in a clearing cut in a low, poorly drained site at the northwestern edge of the Niyayoba savanna. Before
the end of the year, the Docodicoro-teri and the Juwafusibuwei-teri
joined them, building a second *shabono* for themselves that was tangent to
the first, with a single, continuous palisade protecting the two *shabono* in
the form of the number 8.

By 1968 the structures had fallen into extreme disrepair, and the site
was recognized as uninhabitable; the four *teri* together built a huge *shabono* out on the Niyayoba savanna a few hundred yards south (see fig. 4).
Like the earlier 8-shaped building, this, too, is of poor workmanship and
indicative of the temporary nature of the unification.

The Jorocoba-teri. Like the Niyayoba-teri, the Jorocoba-teri say that they
have "always" lived near the same river, in this case, the Jorocoba-u. Similarly, too, the Jorocoba-teri appear to have existed as an identifiable *teri*
for a much longer time than they have borne this name.

More than fifty years ago, when they were known as the Yoyoriana-
teri, the predecessors of the contemporary Jorocoba-teri had their *shabono*
and gardens at a place called Boocomani. This was on the Racofiba-u,
a small stream feeding into the Yoyoriana-u (see map 9 inset), itself a tributary of the upper Niyayoba-u. During the 1920's, a bitter war developed
between the Yoyoriana-teri, who were allied with the Docodicoro-teri,
and an alliance of the Yoreshiana-teri and the Boreawa-teri. For increased safety from raids, the Yoyoriana-teri and their ally built a single
shabono on an isolated site far from their enemies. They chose a remote
headwaters tributary of the Niyayoba-u, probably well above Boocomani.[144] The location was near a savanna known as Shaishai Borosi, and,
when the two *teri* moved together, they temporarily coalesced, adopting
the name Shaishaiwa-teri.

During the 1940's, mutual raiding gradually fell off; and when hostilities had totally abated, the Yoyoriana-teri and their ally separated. The
Docodicoro-teri stayed in the valley of the Niyayoba-u, while the Yoyoriana-teri crossed over into the watershed of the Jorocoba-u. For several
years the latter remained isolated in the headwaters area and built at least
two different *shabono*.

By the 1950's, the group was calling itself the Jorocoba-teri. With increasing confidence that the war was, in fact, over, they moved into the lower Jorocoba-u—a move in the direction of the former enemy.[145] Since the mid-1950's, they have occupied several *shabono*, the last four of which are clearly identifiable (see map 9). All are within about a mile of one another.[146] The site used in the mid-1950's is in an extensive area of savanna and scrub forest that cover their old gardens. The next two sites are overgrown with forest that has encroached upon them. The present *shabono* stands in a forest clearing on a terrace seventy-five feet above the Jorocoba-u, at the very edge of the Niyayoba savanna.

The Bonds between the *Teri*

Since each *teri* tends to be an economic and political unit, it is largely self-sufficient and similar to all the others functionally. No *teri* exists in a vacuum or in a totally hostile world. It is an integral part of a complex web of inter-*shabono* social linkages based upon personal kinship bonds. No individual Yanoama is aware that this web is culture wide, since its impact is local. Mobility and marriage requirements both militate against the possibility of there being adults who do not have strong kinship ties with *teri* other than their own, even though they are not always on good terms. These bonds, often based on marriage initially, grow into blood ties as children are born, and they are fortified by frequent social visits. Even exchange patterns are completely submerged in kinship bonding patterns.

THE BONDS OF MARRIAGE

Marriage between friendly kinsmen is standard procedure, and, in theory, one need not leave his own *teri* to marry. Among the Barafiri of the Parima highlands, there is a strong preference to marry at home within one's own *shabono*, and this preference is felt by all concerned: the man, the wife, and their parents.[147] Yet, marriages between *teri* are commonplace. Two *teri* from the highlands—the Niyayoba-teri and the Jorocoba-teri, which have already served as samples—can provide specific information on marriage as an institution that binds together the *teri*.

The Niyayoba-teri. The Niyayoba-teri, numbering fifty-eight, are an extended family based upon three siblings—two brothers and a sister. One of the brothers is deceased, but he is survived by two wives and their descendants. The other brother, a distinguished patriarch, has two wives and several descendants. The third sibling is a younger sister, who is married and has descendants of her own.

Among the surviving old folks, their children, and their grandchildren, numerous marriages have been made with people from other *teri*. In total there are nine females and four males who have married into the Niyayoba-teri, and at least five females and three males known to have married outside and to have moved away.[148] By far the strongest marriage bonds are with the Juwafusibuwei-teri, from whom five females and one male have married into the Niyayoba-teri. An imbalance in the relationship is evident, however, favoring the Niyayoba-teri, since only two females have left them to join the Juwafusibuwei-teri.

Links with other *teri* are much weaker but still important since they involve the marriages of adult males. For example, two men have come from the Yaniyaniwa-teri, although no one from the Niyayoba-teri has gone there. An adult Mayobo-teri male has married into the Niyayoba-teri, and two Niyayoba-teri females have gone to live with Mayobo-teri husbands. Another male has moved to the Jorocoba-teri, and a female has come from there. In view of the fact that the Niyayoba-teri have lived with them since 1966, marriage links with the Docodicoro-teri and the Canashewa-teri seem weak. One male and a female married into the Docodicoro-teri, which are a relatively large and haughty group; another male has gone to the Canashewa-teri, and a female has come from them.

One must be mindful that these are identifiable, contemporary marriage bonds only. Even so, effective ties with six neighboring *teri* exist, and there are numerous other neighbors with whom there are weaker bonds. The current trend among the Niyayoba-teri is for females to be married outside and to move away, a development that is not desirable from the viewpoint of the Niyayoba-teri.

The Jorocoba-teri. This group, too, is an extended family, founded by three brothers. One of the brothers (now deceased) had as wives two sisters who were Wanashiawa-teri; another had as wives three sisters (two of whom are deceased) from the Boreawa-teri; the third has never married. The lineages of the Jorocoba-teri are presented in table 15 and figure 11.

Like the Niyayoba-teri, the Jorocoba-teri include three living generations with strong marriage bonds linking them to other *teri*. However, in this case nearly all the marriages have brought people to the Jorocoba-teri. Only one woman has left on marrying, while sixteen females and five males have joined the Jorocoba-teri as the result of marriages, thus accounting for a significant segment of the total population.[149]

Marriage bonds with the Mayobo-teri are the strongest; all five males have come from that *teri*, and three females as well. Of the remaining thirteen females, four are from the Docodicoro-teri. Two middle-aged women are said to have come from the Shokekere-teri; and a young woman is identified as having been a Niyayoba-teri.[150] Another woman is said to have been of the Joreaba-teri originally.[151]

Again, marriage bonds are between neighboring *teri*. The spatial orientation is shifting, however. The marriages with groups now to the south, such as the Boreawa-teri, were made more than forty years ago, while the more recent marriages are with the Docodicoro-teri and, particularly, the Mayobo-teri.

FORMAL VISITS

Two kinds of inter-*shabono* social visiting are distinguishable, both of which also perform important political and economic functions. The most powerful manifestation of the strength of the kinship bonds between different *teri* is found in the celebration of the *reajo*, or mortuary ritual. Each performance of the ceremony brings even closer together the participants, already tightly bound by kinship and their affection for the deceased kinsman. While gathered for this purpose, people can share news of interest to them all;[152] there is time for protracted social visiting; the afflicted have an opportunity to benefit from sorcerers other than those of the home *shabono*; and it is an occasion for people to acquire new possessions in a setting of trust where kinsmen can exchange gifts.

But, most important of all, the ceremonial itself is the stuff that binds together different *teri*. This is very effectively revealed in the account by Helena Valero of her own dead Yanoama husband's incineration ceremonial.[153] Eleven small gourds were filled with his pulverized bones, and these gourds were then distributed in the following manner: six remained within his own group, the Namoe-teri (two went to his brother, and four were left in the charge of the oldest of his five widows, to be saved for his sons when they grew up); three went to an uncle and a male cousin, who were of the Patanowa-teri; one went to an Ashitue-teri kinsman; and one went to a Hasubue-teri kinsman. Thus, nearly half of the gourds were distributed to participants from three groups other than the Namoe-teri themselves.

Valero also describes in detail a *reajo* for a respected woman, held some months after her death but immediately after her bones were incinerated and pulverized. This particular ceremonial served to bring together on a friendly basis, at least momentarily, three *teri* that had fissioned from the Namoe-teri years before and were on bad terms with each other.[154] Of course, it is equally possible for the bereaved kinsmen of a murdered man to rededicate themselves to the goal of avenging him at each *reajo* in his honor. With careful rationing, the dead man's powdered bones can be so used for years.

The second type of inter-*shabono* social gathering is the *showao*, a feast held to celebrate an abundance of food, and, particularly, a good supply of ripening plantains. Such a feast also brings together large numbers of people from different *teri*, although in theory it lacks the religious basis of the *reajo*. Among the Barafiri Yanoama, the *showao* is held very infrequently.[155] It appears that when a *teri* is proud of the ample food supply in its gardens, its preference is to share it with kinsfolk in the celebration of a *reajo*. Since the *reajo* requires enormous amounts of food for days of feasting in conjunction with the religious ceremonies, the *showao* and *reajo* are usually combined.

Whether the celebration be either or both, in no case will a group of people from one *shabono* visit another unless an invitation has been extended to them. Therefore, provision is always made for there to be "hosts" and "guests."

Yanoama Immutability

Throughout the foregoing discussion the Yanoama come through as a population that is stable both culturally and spatially. They have a *genre de vie* that suits them, and they are unwilling to change it; they move about frequently according to certain norms, but they are certainly not nomadic. Although they have been categorized as marginal on the basis of selected specific culture traits, the Yanoama culture is complex and steadfast.

Overall, they are sparsely distributed in an enormous territory. Yet, they are crowded into communities where personal space is at a premium. Sometimes the *shabono* communities are clustered, making local densities remarkably high. The spatial separateness of the *shabono* does not signify functional autonomy, however. Every *teri* has strong bonds of kinship with others—bonds that signify heavy social obligations with deep-seated political and economic overtones. This focus of human organization, the *teri*, is an institution subjected simultaneously to the processes of fission, fusion, relocation, and warfare; and yet it remains remarkably stable.

Each *teri* has its own territorial resources within which the nodal settlement, itself structured spatially along kinship lines, is fundamental to any comprehension of settlement patterns and resource utilization. In addition to the *shabono*, integral parts of this functional whole include collecting and hunting grounds, as well as garden clearings. Without all these, life would be untenable. Gardening, collecting, and hunting are bound up inextricably into a single ecosystem whose stability and probable antiquity are suggested by its uniformity over diverse and extensive habitat zones.

Chapter 4

Yanoama Livelihood

F o r untold generations the Yanoama have been supported by a stable economic system.[1] This system is here viewed as a category of activities fully articulated with many other systems in the culture and not simply as the means whereby the Yanoama earn a living. Fundamental to all these systems is the multifamily *teri* community.

A *teri* embraces several basic economic units—"basic" here implying that they are both economically identifiable and functionally irreducible. Each is headed by an adult male gardener. In many cases the basic economic unit consists of a single household composed of a nuclear family; it may include more than one household, depending on the nature of a man's social responsibilities.[2]

The Yanoama in a *teri* are tightly knit and economically interdependent. What is more, they normally accentuate their individuality by maintaining a spatial separation from the *shabono* and the territories of other *teri*. Consequently, more than the basic economic unit described above, the *teri* itself is the most discrete and thus the most evident economic entity. Not only is the *teri* a sociopolitical unit, but it also functions broadly as a production unit, as a unit of apportionment, and as a consumption unit. The level at which it operates can be described as one of subsistence.[3] Each *teri* is capable of producing the full complement of its survival needs, making it economically self-sufficient. Yet, the individual Yanoama cannot conceive of an existence without other Yanoama.[4] This means that, although the *teri* is capable of economic viability, it is not capable of social self-sufficiency.

The combination of *teri*, *shabono*, and corresponding territory, viewed as a spatial organization, constitutes the effective ecosystem for the individual Yanoama.[5] Natural resources are not available exclusively to any particular person or household per se, but to the *teri* as a whole. Land, for example, does not belong to an individual or even a family.[6] The same can be said of plants growing wild and of game animals. In contrast, any form of vegetation that has been planted, whether recently set out or old and even feral in appearance, is subject to individual ownership. So, too, are the products of such a plant. Among the Yanoama, then, as with many preliterate societies, land is a free good. Crop plants, and even pet animals, that have been removed from the domain of Nature, are not.

There is no domesticated animal but the dog, whose economic utility is open to serious doubt. And, as with others of the most conservative American aboriginals, there is no economic role whatsoever for fowls, pigs, or even cats when these are made available.

Major Economic Activities

Of all the interrelated segments of the Yanoama economic system, horticulture is the keystone.[7] Horticulture is a thoroughly assimilated part of the ecosystem and indispensable to the Yanoama life style. Without this dependable, planned food production, it is doubtful that they could survive. Gardening activities must continue during wartime as well as when there is peace. If a relocation of residence to a distant place is planned by a man or by a *teri*, gardens must be prepared there first. Only after these gardens are in production can people make the move permanent.[8] All members of the society are familiar with gardening; many adolescents and most adults actively participate in this activity. It is a well-established, integral part of Yanoama culture.[9]

Collecting constitutes a continuing and important complement to horticulture. Hunting is an exclusively male activity that is economically subordinate to both gardening and collecting, although all three are functionally meshed.

Surpluses and Storage

Traditionally, the Yanoama produce no effective surpluses beyond their own needs. Of all the varied products of horticulture, collecting, and hunting, foods are the most important goods. In addition to normal dietary requirements, periodic ceremonial feasting demands enormous amounts of foodstuffs. On these occasions, such as the *reajo* and the *showao* described above, it is supposed that guests, like their hosts, will eat in great quantity. An adult male, for example, can eat continuously until he has consumed a few pounds of meat and perhaps ten plantains, or more. After a brief respite, he is expected to begin eating again. On feast occasions, too, hosts make generous gifts of food to their departing guests. From the Yanoama viewpoint, food used in this manner is not a surplus with alternative uses.[10]

There appears to be little concern with the preserving and storing of goods, including food, although the Yanoama are technologically capable of doing so to a modest extent.[11] Generally, food is eaten when available or soon thereafter. Even though periods of hunger are anticipated from time to time, there is always confidence that the gardens can be counted on to supply food in some immediate future. At times a piece of game is hung over the hearth fire to smoke, and, on rare occasions, this might still be edible ten days after the kill. Bunches of plantains and bananas are brought green to the *shabono* or campsite and hung from the roof poles to ripen slowly. But, again, this represents merely a few days' food supply. The firewood stored at the back of each family shelter in the *shabono* is normally only enough for a few days.

Exchange

Kinship provides the vital channels for economic intercourse, since inter-*shabono* social visits afford the setting for most exchanges of goods, including food. Traditionally, exchange among the Yanoama consists of giving and receiving gifts. The ultimate governor in these exchanges is reciprocity—a reciprocity gauged to the Yanoama value system, without fixed equivalents. Response need not be immediate, since the reciprocal act, or acts, can be postponed for lengthy periods of time. Requests for gifts are frequently made with a formal chant in which something specific, such as a machete, is requested by a man of his close kinsman. This gesture has been interpreted by non-Yanoama as begging.[12] When such a formal request is made, it is almost impossible to refuse.

Much gift giving these days involves trade goods—manufactured items, such as steel tools, glass beads, and metal pots—that are exotic to Yanoama material culture. There are also those goods that have been traditionally exchanged in like manner, such as objects made by exceptional people. These include very personal items, like the ubiquitous arrowheads, which men give and receive with animated enthusiasm, and strong, high-quality narcotics. Yet another category of traditional exchange goods includes certain raw materials that are scarce locally within the total Yanoama habitat. For example, some *teri* lack within their territories such things as the vine used to make strong baskets, or high-quality cane for arrow shafts, or the bamboolike *guadua* (*Guadua* sp.) from which quivers are made. Most of these materials hardly qualify as important gifts, however, since friendly *teri* can collect them in one another's territories. When both producer and consumer goods are lacking in a *teri*, the need for the former takes priority. This means that a man desires an ax far more than a shirt, if he has neither.[13]

Linkages in the exchange network are effective if indirect. For example, until a permanent Christian mission was established near them in 1968, the people of the Niyayoba area obtained the bulk of their trade goods from friendly Yoreshiana-teri kinsmen.[14] The Yoreshiana-teri, in turn, got some of these goods from other friendly *teri* living near the lower Majecodo-u, and some came from Bashobaca-teri kinsmen. These latter had acquired them from the Auwei-teri, who themselves obtained these goods directly from priests who periodically travel from their mission base on the lower Río Ocamo as far up the Buuta-u as the Auwei-teri *shabono* (see map 6). Normally, little effort is made to jump any of the connections in such an exchange network. For example, the Niyayoba-teri did not go to the Ocamo mission—or even to the Auwei-teri—for trade goods, knowing all the while the roles of both.

It is possible for goods to pass quickly through an area. If a *teri* is visited frequently by kinsmen who "beg" for their possessions, they are able to keep their trade goods only briefly.[15] Sometimes, in fact, hosts hide their valuables in the forest when they expect visitors, so as to avoid being asked for them.

The distribution of foods between *teri*, principally garden produce, occurs within the context of social feasting, which also conforms to the rules of reciprocity. Redistribution patterns, then, consist essentially of direct gift exchange. There is economic interdependence between *teri* only in a social context. Just as there is no place in Yanoama society for a person rich in material possessions, so there is no place for intermediaries in the exchanging of gifts.[16]

Regional Variation

There is little regional variation in the Yanoama economic system. Hunting and collecting vary principally in terms of elevation and drainage, factors that affect the availability of plant and animal species, the seasonality of insect life, the kinds of honey, and the ripening times of wild fruits.

In the pursuits of hunting, collecting, and gardening there is no significant regional variation in the traditional tools and techniques utilized.

In horticulture, the emphasis on plantains is invariable. Crop associations, however, do vary with the degree of acculturation. Maize is important in some of the gardens along the Río Orinoco, particularly near missions. And one of the clearest indicators of acculturation is a prevalence of bitter manioc in Yanoama gardens. Its production is encouraged by Creoles and it is the staple crop of the aboriginal cultures with which Yanoama might come in contact. In the temperate, isolated Parima highlands, the principal crops continue to be plantain, *ocumo*, and sweet manioc.

Stability of the Economic System

Clearly the entire economic structure rests upon a horticultural foundation, although it is impossible to determine precisely when this form of agriculture—and resultant planned food production—was incorporated into Yanoama culture. Their horticulture is impressively stable, and part of the explanation would seem to be due to isolation from other cultures. The highland habitat, surrounded as it is by a veritable sea of hot lowlands, may also contribute to stability by virtue of its distinctiveness in comparison with adjacent habitat types.

Certain other factors, more widely applicable, merit consideration. For example, the Yanoama economic system requires relatively little technological specialization; essentially the same skills are required of all men and of all women so that each adult needs and acquires about the same knowledge as all others of that sex category. What is more, the spatial distribution of their varied natural resources continually stimulates a dispersal of effort in many directions:[17] the attention of a *teri* is drawn simultaneously toward their numerous gardens, toward all sorts of ecological niches where they collect a variety of commodities, and toward diverse hunting areas. Long-term cooperative economic effort is not mandatory. Consequently, sophisticated organization does not develop, nor does labor specialization. One result is changelessness.

Another factor is numerical stability of the population. The Yanoama, like so many other "primitive" populations, have effective mechanisms (prolonged lactation, infanticide, and abortion) for keeping their numbers small in relation to their total resource base. Diseases also take a high toll of life. Consequently, pressures to subject land to permanent cultivation, or even to intensify cultivation, have not developed.[18]

Yields constitute yet another factor. Shifting cultivation, as practiced by the Yanoama, provides high yields in terms of energy expenditures—certainly much higher than does hunting. The heaviest labor is that of clearing new garden sites, and this is broken into work periods interspersed with leisure and hunting. With the recent acquisition of steel tools, clearing the forest has become far less awesome a task than it used to be. Two or more men, or a man and his family, may work together, thus alleviating the tedium with conversation and humor. Some days a man's work consists of preparing and carrying to his garden a single load of plantain suckers, or of planting such a load. Within an hour or two he is finished. Other days, more than five hours might be spent working—or none at all.[19]

There is no burst of activity at a specific time for planting or harvesting, since neither of these is clearly defined as a piece of work and since they occupy overlapping time periods. Here is an economic system that allows considerable free time. People can spend long hours resting in their hammocks, while preparing food in a leisurely way or snacking. In their hammocks women sometimes spin, seed cotton bolls, or nurse infants; men might work on arrowheads. Conversation is threaded through these periods of relaxation. Even during a food shortage, ample time is spent at ease.[20]

And, finally, there is the factor of habitat preservation, or resource conservation. The horticulture practiced by the Yanoama does not in itself require degradation of the environment.[21] In fact, cultivated plots resemble the pre-existing natural ecosystem. Each garden contains a great number of cultivated species occupying vertically several vegetation levels, and with a closed cover so that soil is not exposed directly to the elements. Neither hoe nor plow ever disturbs the ground.

In spite of a superficial appearance of untidiness and disorder, the uses made of light, moisture, soil fertility and texture, and slope are very practical and effective. The principal cultivated plants are autochthonous, rather than exotic introductions—with the possible exception of the musaceous plants. After a year or two of steady food production, a garden is already well into the recycling process that will return it to the tropical forest. Barring some severe disturbance, like a fire out of control, it will remain as forest until it might again be put to use briefly as a garden.[22]

Obviously, this is a stable population. With abundant reusable land resources, with supplementary sources of wild plant and animal food available through collecting and hunting,[23] and with an agriculture yielding sufficiently for their needs and still allowing ample leisure, these people are not likely to change their economic system. Why should they? The Barafiri are already affluent.[24]

Chapter 5

Horticulture

THE Yanoama practice an ancient kind of tillage, a form of shifting cultivation that is thoroughly characteristic of aboriginal tropical American agriculture; it probably has spontaneous origins completely independent of Old World influences. In Venezuela the Creole term for a plot so cultivated is *conuco*,[1] while in Brazil it is known as *roça*.[2] In the Barafiri dialect *ficari* is the word for garden.[3]

In "shifting," or "migratory," cultivation, it is the land that is consistently rotated, rather than the crops. Yet, enigmatically, as practiced in South America it is also perennial. The Yanoama, for example, plant their gardens principally in stem and root cuttings, using the technique of cloning. Seeds are largely ignored, except as foods of minor importance. Thus, there is an important contrast with the essentially annual character of Mesoamerican milpa shifting cultivation, where the stress is on maize and other seed crops.[4]

Yanoama horticulture, like collecting, appears to be essentially secularized, at least from a Western viewpoint. However, a few rituals do exist,[5] and certain incantations are made to the forces of the winds, the rain, and the spirits of animal predators when any of these threatens harm to garden plants.

Technology is relatively simple; the major tools—even among contemporary Creoles in Venezuela and Brazil—are the ax, machete, digging stick, and fire. Ashes from the burned vegetal cover constitute the only fertilizer—and an effective one. No draft animals are used.

Gardening is a male-dominated, adult occupation; men make the major decisions and provide most of the labor for clearing, planting, and tending the gardens.[6] Each garden plant is the property of the man who put it there, even though functionally it belongs to his household; and a man takes considerable pride in having a good garden, one that is neat and produces well. The Barafiri refer to a good gardener (i.e., one who spends considerable time at work in his gardens) as *coyeriwa*.[7] Men know well the details of the horticultural patterns within their respective *teri*, such as the names and locations of all the gardens, what crops are there, ownership of many of the plants, and their anticipated ripening times. In the Parima highlands even boys do some gardening, in conjunction with their fathers or some older kinsmen.[8] The age at which a male clears and plants the first garden of his own depends on conditions within his family and his personal inclinations. Normally, by the time he is well into his adolescence, a young man has assumed certain responsibility for gardening activities in his family. To qualify for a wife it is generally necessary for a young man to have a garden. Frequently, to compensate for the wife, he is obligated to work also in the garden of his parents-in-law and to provide them with game.

Women do not have garden clearings of their own, and the Barafiri are somewhat surprised that this might be conceivable. Occasionally, an elderly widow, or a *wanidi* woman, will plant a small portion of a garden clearing prepared by her close male kinsmen. The plants she sets out are hers to use as she chooses, thus making her less dependent on her relatives for food. This is unnecessary for wives and daughters who are being provided for entirely by their men. Sometimes women assist in planting, to the extent that they transport to the gardens some of the heavy loads of suckers and cuttings. Rarely, if ever, do they themselves set out plantains, bananas, or other crops.[9] However, while men plant, women might keep their menfolk company, perhaps using the time to cut firewood, or just watching. Women also do some of the harvesting. Their most strenuous job in horticulture is to carry the heavy bunches of ripening plantains, or basketloads of tubers, back to the *shabono* or campsite where they will be used. In spite of this significant role, gardening is not basically women's work, and girls rarely work in the gardens. This is in striking contrast with many other aboriginal South American horticultural peoples, where women are economically indispensable in gardening. Among the bitter manioc cultivators, for example, the garden becomes an exclusively female realm just as soon as the forest has been cut and burned by men.[10]

The Gardening Process

Horticulture is a continuing activity, with all the various stages in the gardening process visible simultaneously. At any given time, the various horticultural segments of the *teri*-based economic unit are in different stages of development. There are the gardens in production—those from which the *teri* is currently "eating." There are the new sites that are being prepared for gardening activities—the *dude taca* in Barafiri, or "young clearings." And there are the numerous old gardens—the *suwabada taca*, or "old woman clearings," which are in varying stages of abandonment. With the exception of those who are making their first gardens, each man is likely to have at least one producing garden and several old ones. The distribution pattern formed by a *shabono* and its gardens reflects Yanoama values. It visibly demonstrates their view of what constitutes a complete community and the spatial dimensions of such a unit (see map 9).

GARDEN-SITE SELECTION

Each man chooses his own garden sites, considering a variety of factors of relative and absolute location. He is, of course, limited to the territory of his own *teri*, normally an area covering hundreds of square miles. Old gardens and unforested areas are scrupulously avoided. He takes into account the locations of his existing gardens and those of his kinsmen, as well as the *shabono* location. Rarely will he make a new garden more than a few miles from any of these. In fact, new clearings are frequently extensions of existing gardens.

Different location factors weigh particularly heavily at different times. If warfare is anticipated or underway, then a man must take into account just how vulnerable a new garden would be to surprise attack by the enemy.[11] In the case of the warring Niyayoba-teri, for example, other factors are subordinated to that of safety. They have made their new gardens on the normally undesirable flood plains of small streams in order to stay as close as possible to their palisaded *shabono*. Even so, they are extremely cautious, entering their gardens in pairs or small groups, sometimes with their bows drawn. Gardens—like forest glades—are places traditionally preferred for surprise attack. Similarly, if a *teri* is in the process of fissioning, new garden sites are selected accordingly. And, when a man contemplates marriage with a woman from a distant *shabono*, he must decide where he will live and, consequently, where he will make his gardens.

In addition to these considerations of relative location, a judgment must be made on the features of a prospective garden site itself. For the Barafiri gardener, the critical factor is whether a site is *ishabena* or not. To

find out, he takes into account relief, altitude, drainage, and soil qualities, principally to the extent that these influence the natural vegetative
cover of the site. Invariably, a place must be forested even to merit consideration for its *ishabena* qualities.[12] The term *ishabena* has slightly varying definitions among men of the Parima highlands. The most consistent
interpretation is that one finds *ishabena* where one or more of certain large
tree species (such as the *abia, quefi, shodocoma*, and *jocotofi*) grow naturally.
Some men say that *ishabena* exists where these large trees grow in association with a *Heliconia* they call *alemasijenaco*.[13] Still others judge *ishabena*
to be present where there are very few small trees growing—that is, where
there is an absence of undergrowth. Essentially, to be *ishabena* is to be
"good for plantains," or to be "good for *cowata*."[14] It is on the basis of
aptness for plantains, then, that the Yanoama choose the sites for their
gardens. So important is *ishabena*, that a group will sometimes risk enemy
raids by making gardens far from the *shabono* if they are convinced they
must go that far to find a place with excellent *ishabena* qualities.[15]

The final decision on where to make a new garden is an important one.
Often it is made months in advance of the actual clearing phase, and only
after the merits of the site have been discussed with experienced kinsmen.
The net impact of the application of these location factors in the Parima
highlands is a pattern of widely distributed gardens on steep slopes and
small, V-shaped valleys.[16] Smooth areas, such as flood plains, ridges, and
knobs, are generally avoided, as are mountain tops. Sometimes, a single
garden clearing stands alone, surrounded by high forest. More often
than not, however, clearings are clustered. Instead of opening up an entirely new part of the forest each time a garden is needed, men seem to
prefer to cut back into the forest adjacent to their existing gardens, con-
veniently adding new crop land. Each of these additions is a new clearing,
comparable in size and shape with those made in isolated places, and one
whose life cycle will be entirely independent of those of adjacent, older
clearings (see plate 12).

The development of a cluster of garden clearings begins with a nucleus,
an isolated clearing cut from the forest where before there was none. Of
course, this original clearing was made on the spot deemed to have the
best possible *ishabena* of the general area. If the place is well situated, and
has around it adequate *ishabena*, new clearings are made next to it. For
year after year, new clearings might be added successively, until a cluster
has grown to include numerous different clearings. New gardens might
be next to the original nucleus, or many hundreds of yards from those old
gardens that are reverting to forest. When cutting a new garden clearing
adjacent to an existing one, particularly if the latter contains plantings
easily subject to damage, a narrow belt of forest is left standing between
the new clearing and the older one (see plate 13). Consequently, individ-

Plate 12. View north across a cluster of gardens belonging to the Arajai-teri and the Waracacoyafiba-teri of the Mayobo area. Here old gardens merge with producing gardens and newly cleared additions. Downslope, and adjacent to a garden area in the process of being abandoned, is a large tract of savanna (*background*). At the right edge of the savanna, on a promontory, is the present *shabono* of the Waracacoyafiba-teri.

Plate 13. Jorocoba-teri man standing among young plants in a new addition to Yoodiba-taca, one of his group's largest garden clearings. In this upslope area the *Musa-ocumo* region and the manioc region merge. Manioc predominates in the distance, while in the foreground *ocumo* and *Musa* plantings are most numerous. Yoodiba-taca has good *ishabena* qualities, with heavy, dark soils.

ual gardens do not always merge together. One such cluster (Yoodiba-taca), belonging to the Jorocoba-teri, covers tens of acres (see map 9). The Juwafusibuwei-teri have what might be an even larger cluster (Oqui-yamoba-taca), straddling the upper Niyayoba-u. In keeping with Barafiri preferences, the nucleus tends to have been either a clearing extending up the sides of a narrow, well-drained valley or one in a small cove far up a mountain side in the headwaters of a local drainage system, where streams are only intermittent. New clearings are added in any direction—up slope, down slope, or into lateral valleys—until all the desirable lands in the vicinity have been occupied. After that, no more clearings are added to the cluster. The Yanoama have a clear grasp of slope and drainage patterns. When a new clearing is made up slope, or upstream, it is identified with the suffix *ora*, which in Barafiri means "the uphill part" (or "the upstream part" of a water course). If the addition is down slope, it is identified as *bosi* ("downhill part"), or *cora* or *coro* (both of which mean "downstream part" as well as "downhill part").[17]

NAMING THE GARDEN CLEARINGS

The Barafiri have a word for their garden clearings: *taca*, a generic term.[18] Every garden clearing has at least one proper name of its own, in-

Plate 14. Mayobo-teri men chopping down a tree with steel axes. This particular tree is being removed in order to make it safer for airplanes to use an adjacent airstrip, although the technology is the same as that used in gardening. In the background are extensive old gardens.

cluding the suffix *taca*. Each name tends to incorporate some feature of the place or some event that occurred there.[19] It is impossible for a clearing to bear the names of the men who made it because of the stringent personal-name taboo. Frequently, men of the *teri* have already ascribed the name to a site before it is cleared. Literal translations of some of the proper names used in the central Parima highlands include:

> Cuaisiba-taca: "Moriche-palm-place clearing"
> Wabufita-taca: "Wabu-tree-place clearing"
> Canawaubrare-taca: "Cedar-tree-standing clearing"
> Dabashinaca-taca: "Anteater-tail clearing"
> Boredidire-taca: "Jaguar-in-it clearing"

From the southern Yanoama the name Wakawe-taca ("Red-earth clearing") has also been reported.[20]

PREPARING THE GARDEN SITE

There is a clear distinction between what the nouns *garden* and *clearing* signify. When a man clears a place in the forest so that he can put in a new garden, he usually does so in conjunction with kinsmen who also want new gardens. What they prepare is a single cleared space, or garden clearing.

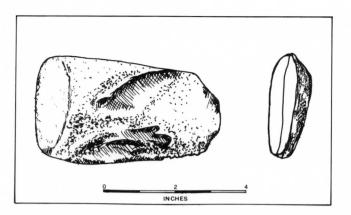

Figure 6. Polished Stone Celt. This celt, or *boo*, represents the type once hafted to handles for use as axes and tomahawks.

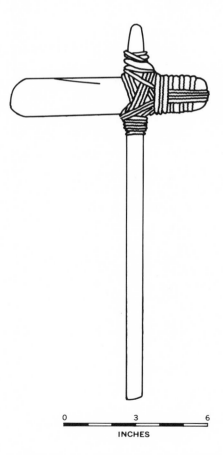

Figure 7. Contemporary *Jawa*, or Tomahawk. A tool manufactured in much the same manner as the stone axes except that it has a piece of machete for a blade.

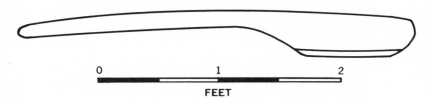

Figure 8. Palmwood Hatchet. Presumed appearance of "hatchets" once used by the Barafiri to clear the forest. About three feet long, this tool had a handle and a sharpened leading edge for chopping.

Within that space, each of the men will plant his own garden in the part he himself cleared at his own pace. It is extremely unusual to find only a single garden in a clearing. Instead, anywhere from two to eight kinsmen, or even more, might share it. Since their parcels are contiguous, sometimes men can be seen working side by side. Frequently, too, they help one another, particularly in the difficult task of felling the largest trees. And, if a man has a son old enough to help, he might work at his father's side. For these reasons, the preparation of individual gardens can give the impression that it is a communal activity. In a strict sense, however, this is not the case. Individual men make and use gardens for themselves and their families; similarly, individuals build shelters to form a *shabono*, but do not construct a communal house.

At almost any time of the year someone or other in a community might be in the process of clearing land for a new garden.[21] This is the most arduous and prolonged job a Yanoama male must face. He is fortunate that today his tools are metal (see plate 14). Steel tools apparently did not begin to reach the central Parima highlands of Venezuela, even sporadically, until the 1920's. Before then, the Barafiri were limited entirely to stone and palmwood equipment, and fire, in clearing the forest for their gardens. The population size and per capita garden space were perhaps much the same as they are now, signifying that men evidently enjoyed somewhat less leisure time.[22] Most trees were felled with *boo* (stone axes), hafted in much the same manner as contemporary *jawa* (tomahawk) blades are bound with fiber cords to wooden handles (see figs. 6 and 7).[23] There are no reports of girdling, but, in the case of very large trees, the branches were lopped off rather than cutting through the trunk. Small trees, and other growth only a few inches in diameter, were chopped down with palmwood "hatchets"—poles with flaring, sharpened edges (see fig. 8). Other small, woody growth was broken and killed with palmwood poles, not unlike the contemporary *nabrushi*. One end of the pole was sharpened, and with this a person would pound against small tree trunks until they were weakened enough to push over.[24] Such a pole could also be used as an effective lever. After the dead vegetation had dried out, fires were started with firedrills identical to those still in use. In fact, little of the gardening process appears to have changed with the introduction of steel tools.

Those men who will garden in the same clearing decide on the boundaries of their respective gardens and the consequent dimensions of the entire clearing, while the forest is still standing. Clearings tend to be roughly oval in shape, although exceptions are numerous. Cutting begins with saplings and other small trees toward the center of the area to be cleared.[25] In this phase, women and children provide considerable help in some families, occasionally using sharpened peach palm poles in the ancient manner of hitting the tree trunks with the pointed end until the trees can be pushed over. Men fell all of the larger trees, which are the last to be cut. In ravines and narrow valleys, trees are felled down slope, often forming a thick jumble of trunks and branches at the bottom. Trees are cut so as to fall away from the forested outer edge of a clearing. Some of the trees of the highlands measure well over 120 feet in height, with enormous, buttressed trunks (see plate 15). Such a giant requires the construction of a pole scaffold perhaps twenty feet from the ground level, above most of the buttresses, so that the bole of the tree can be attacked directly with axes. Girdling is rarely, if ever, used as a technique to defoliate trees, even the largest ones. Occasionally a solitary tree or two might be left standing in a clearing.[26] Men use their steel tools deftly, so that an acre of hardwood forest can be cut in a week or two, if the effort is reasonably continuous.[27]

After cutting, the vegetation is left to dry out in preparation for burning. The fires kill all manner of pests in the surface layers of the soil, as well as spores and seeds that are the germ of potential competition for the crop plants to be set out. What is more, the fires reduce much of the timber to fertile ash. The Barafiri believe that without having been burned first, a place is no good for gardening.[28]

Burning presents certain problems. In some cases, for example, the litter of green wood (trunks and branches) is so dense that it covers perhaps 30 percent of the total surface of the prospective garden (cf. maps 11 and 12). Even though some of the more resinous species might burn completely after only a brief drying period, other species are difficult to burn until they are thoroughly dried out. This exposes an even more severe problem for Yanoama gardeners of the Parima highlands, where relative humidity is high, and heavy showers can come at any time of the year. Even the "dry season" (November through February) brings frequent rains from the north. A few sunny, windy days in succession are about the best that can be hoped for. So, between showers, frequent attempts are made to start fires in different parts of the new garden clearings. Sometimes dry kindling is brought from the *shabono* or camp shelter. Occasion-

Plate 15. Newly planted garden clearing of the Docodicoro-teri. This particular
tree was nearly 150 feet tall. In the distance stands the buttressed stump and the
platform constructed as an aid in chopping down the giant tree. It is probably
some species of *Mora*.

ally, almost out of desperation, a wife, a child, or an elderly female relative of the man who has cut a new garden spends whole days there tending small fires in an attempt to burn at least some of the large branches and trunks scattered about. In the Orinoco lowlands, burning is often timed to precede the heavy rains of April or May. This is the end of the "dry season," when the Yanoama gardener can hope for several rainless days in succession, thus permitting felled trees to dry out sufficiently to burn well. Sometimes, however, dry firewood might also be used to get fires started and even to keep them going.

Because cutting and burning the forest for new gardens is so protracted a job, it is common for the families involved to camp nearby during at least part of the time. Here, they combine collecting activities in the vicinity with work on the garden site, supplementing what they forage with plantains, and perhaps tubers, brought from their producing gardens. This is the only time in the life of a garden that people camp near it, since planting, maintenance, and harvesting do not require prolonged periods of intensive labor.

Occasionally, overgrown portions of producing gardens are cleared for reuse after only a year or two. The weeds and thorns are cut and burned; then the area is almost immediately replanted. The Barafiri are even known to dig up and remove plantain and banana suckers from weedy, overgrown gardens, then cut the scrubby growth, burn the area, and later replant the suckers.

Within a clearing, garden boundaries are invisible. For one thing, the Yanoama build no fences. Far more important, the kinsmen who share a clearing share the different kinds of land contained within it. Three land types are particularly significant: the low-lying, humid areas, which are best for tobacco and plantains; the higher, steeper slopes where manioc does well; and the intermediate slopes. This means that within a clearing a man can have more than one garden or that his garden might be fragmented. Each man who gardens the clearing knows the dividing lines, since he knows where he and the others cleared and where they planted. But the stranger does not. Garden boundaries do not normally coincide with land types, with contour lines, with crop types, or even with such natural features as water courses (see map 10). The entire clearing reflects the unity of the kinsmen who created it. Yet, the functional unit is the garden belonging to a man and his household; it is not the clearing as a whole.

KINDS OF CULTIVATED PLANTS

The Yanoama use their garden space judiciously and with a clear understanding of specific plant requirements. With scant exceptions, they plant

vegetatively (using cuttings) rather than using seeds. This makes for
perennial cloning and, coincidentally, eliminates virtually all possibility of
cross-fertilization and resultant hybridization.

Intercropping is standard procedure, with nearly all the plants in a
garden destined for use as food. However, a great variety of plants grown
for other uses are also included, although there are only a few of each
species. In the Parima highlands the traditional garden plants meet
virtually no competition from new introductions. Through time, however, certain of these traditional crop plants might gain or lose acreage in
relation to one another as emphases and preferences shift. With rare
exceptions, each garden contains the tall *Musa* (plantains and bananas),[29]
their enormous leaves rustling with the breeze; the large, heart-shaped
ocumo (*Xanthosoma* sp.) leaves on thick, sturdy stems; the shrublike sweet
manioc plants; and the climbing yam vines. These provide impressive and
visible signs of the huge store of starchy foodstuffs that is being accumulated in the garden.[30] Once their fruits and tubers begin to ripen, the garden will yield an almost continuous supply of foods for a period of two
years or so. In addition, it provides some seeds, as well as a wide variety
of nonedibles.

Unequivocally, musaceous plants are everywhere the hallmark of traditional Yanoama horticulture. This is such an evident feature of the cultural landscape that outsiders frequently refer to a Yanoama garden as a
"banana plantation" or "plantain plantation" (*platanal* in Spanish).[31]
Consistently, plantains are the principal food source and occupy more
garden space than any other species. Among some Yanoama groups it is
reported that 90 percent of their cultivated land is used for musaceous
plants.[32] It has also been estimated that the "cooking banana" (plantain)
alone "probably contributes at least 70 percent of their total calories."[33]
Of the varieties of food available to them, the Yanoama most highly esteem plantains and meat (from game animals), which they like to eat
together. The plantain is the most prestigious of all plant foods by far,
corresponding to rice among some Oriental peoples. This important position for plantains is not a recent development. More than a century has
passed since foreign travelers made personal contact with the Yanoama in
their own habitat, and those men recorded similar observations. The
earliest was Robert Schomburgk (in 1838), then Theodor Koch-Grünberg (in 1912), and A. Hamilton Rice (in 1920 and again in 1925).[34]
The spatial scope of our record is even more impressive, since we have
recent data from various and diverse parts of the Yanoama territory:
for the southwest, Helena Valero and Gottfried Polykrates; for the southeast, Hans Becher and Otto Zerries, among others; along the Orinoco,
Pablo J. Anduze, Napoleon A. Chagnon, and numerous others; for the
far north, Cándido Montoya Lirola and others; and, for the central high-

lands, James V. Neel and myself.[35] It is no surprise that observers have been quick to characterize the Yanoama by their cultivation of plantains and bananas. In having musaceous plants for their staple, they provide a striking contrast to most, if not all, other aboriginal South American cultivators.

Musaceous Plants. Numerous varieties of plantains (*Musa paradisiaca* L.) and bananas (*Musa sapientum* L.) are cultivated by the Yanoama, their names varying with dialect groups.[36] Certain varieties of these musaceous plants are widely dispersed, ranging at least from the Parima highlands (where gardens are found at elevations over 3,500 feet) to the Orinoco lowlands (only a few hundred feet above sea level).

1. *The Plantains.* Most highly prized of all the *Musa* is a plantain called *cowata* by the Barafiri, and *culata* (*corata, kurata*) by the Orinoco Waika. If there exists in the Yanoama language a generic term for plantains, these are versions of it.[37] Among foreigners, only an expert could distinguish the *cowata* plant from other plantains. Yet, even Yanoama youngsters can unfailingly identify this and other musaceous plants, even before inflorescence. The *cowata* fruits are small for plantains in South America, averaging only about seven inches in length, with a maximum diameter of about one and one-half inches. The skin turns a pale yellow when the fruit is fully ripe, although the Yanoama frequently prefer to eat *cowata* while the skin is still green. Before ripening, the flesh is dry and almost white. When ripe the flesh is yellow, is firm in consistency, and has little flavor.

Various other plantains are also widely grown. After the *cowata*, the most popular among the Barafiri is the *baushimi* (called *baishimi* by the Orinoco Waika). When ripe, this fruit is much like a banana in appearance, with a yellow skin. However, its orange-colored flesh tastes more like a plantain than a banana.[38] Another important plantain is the *bareamo*, a large fruit attaining a length of eight to ten inches.[39] However, each bunch is composed of few fruits. In contrast, the *monarimo* is a plantain whose bunches contain many full hands of fruit. Each fruit is only about six inches in length, but thick. Finally, there is the *irocaco*, a plantain whose fruits have a purplish color.

These five varieties of plantains, in the order discussed, are unquestionably the most important to the Barafiri of the central Parima highlands. However, other varieties were and are grown in their gardens. For example, a Juwafusibuwei-teri man remembers that in the 1930's people planted significant numbers of two other kinds of plantains. These were the *yadadorimi*, which grows on a plant that rarely reaches five feet in height, and the *wakawakarima*, which produces red fruits. A variety called *areshimawa* has also been reported.

2. *The Bananas.* Fewer varieties of bananas than plantains are used by the Barafiri, and the volume of production is very small in comparison. Three varieties predominate: the *rapaima*,[40] with rather large, long fruits; the *faturimo*, which is produced on a very small, low plant; and the *dabada-borima*, a small, thick banana, whose name literally means "fat kind." Middle-aged people remember when the *makamakawa* was also planted with some frequency. Elsewhere, Yanoama widely use the *rocomo* (*rokomã*),[41] and a *rocomo naba* (or *rokomo nabe*) has been reported for the Orinoco lowlands.[42] What is remarkable about this last banana is that the name means "foreign *rocomo*." The *ushiborimo*, a "blue," or "purple," kind of banana, is also reported for the Orinoco lowlands. Two other bananas, the *nakaximi* and the *rokoja*, have been ascribed to Surára and Pakidaí gardens.[43]

Even in this very brief survey of the musaceous garden plants used by the Yanoama, it is rather evident that there are available more varieties than a *teri* normally uses. It is also clear that botanically sound information on Yanoama cultivars is severely limited.

Tuberous Crop Plants. A group of tuberous plants rank second in importance after the plantains, in terms of both acreage and dietary significance (see table 5). Various observers of the Yanoama and their culture have noted the importance of certain starchy tubers, but scant attention has been paid to this particular aspect of their horticulture.

Among these tubers, *ocumo* (*Xanthosoma* sp.)[44] comes closest to ubiquity, often intercropped with musaceous suckers in new plantings. It is the fleshy rhizomes, or subterranean stems, that are eaten. Above ground, the enormous, heart-shaped leaves of the plant grow at a height of well over three feet on the ends of long, fleshy stems. To the Barafiri this plant is *ofina*. New World yams (*Dioscorea trifida* L.) are also widely cultivated.[45] Three varieties are identifiable, one with white tubers, one bearing purple tubers, and another called *shibujurimo*. No other typology is available at present. Creole Venezuelans are also familiar with both purple and white *Dioscorea* in their *conucos*, markets, and kitchens. Sweet potatoes (*Ipomoea batatas* L.) constitute another important garden crop plant, their tuberous roots being "extremely nutritious."[46] However, far less effort is expended on this plant than on either the *Xanthosoma* or the *Dioscorea*. A fourth important tuberous root crop is manioc (*Manihot dulcis* [Gmel.] Pax.). It must be emphasized that this is sweet manioc and not the poisonous, "bitter" manioc (*Manihot esculenta* Crantz, or *M. utilissima* Pohl), which is so widely cultivated as a staple by other aboriginals.[47] Both bitter and sweet maniocs have striking attributes: in terms of the total effort expended, caloric yields from manioc are very high when compared with other autochthonous crop plants (see table 13); what is more, the

Principal Barafiri Crop Plants

English Name	Most Common Barafiri Name	Venezuelan Vernacular	Genus and Species[a]	Orinoco Waika Name
plantain	*cowata*	*plátano*	*Musa paradisiaca* L.	*culata*
banana	*rapaima*	*cambur*	*Musa sapientum* L.	*rabarimo*
"yautía"; "tania"	*ofina*	*ocumo*	*Xanthosoma sagitti-folium* (L.) Schott.	*ojina*
yam (purple)	*waja anaco*[b]	*mapuey* (*morado*)	*Dioscorea trifida* L.	*cabiromo*
yam (white)	*aja aco*	*mapuey* (*blanco*)	*Dioscorea trifida* L.	*aja aco*
sweet potato	*jucomo*	*batata*	*Ipomoea batatas*	no data
sweet manioc	*nashi*	*yuca dulce*	*Manihot dulcis*[c] (Gmel.) Pax.	*nashi*

[a]According to L. Schnee, *Plantas Comunes de Venezuela.*
[b]Sometimes *wajaa naba* with the second word meaning "foreign."
[c]Sometimes *M. utilis.*

tubers can be left in the ground for months after maturing, to be dug up when needed.[48] Of the two, bitter manioc is reputed to yield better than the sweet.

The great bulk of the Barafiri diet is obtained from the combination of only the few cultigens discussed here. They are the fruits of the herbaceous *Musa*, the tuberous rhizomes of the herbaceous *Xanthosoma*, the tuberous roots of the *Dioscorea* and of the creeping *Ipomoea*, and the tuberous roots of the bushy *Manihot*.

Tree Crops. Certain trees are also planted, although the number of genera is small and the garden space allocated to trees is very limited. One species in particular is consistently reported as very important economically and socially. This is *rasha*: a palm called *pijiguao* in Venezuelan Spanish, *pupunha* in Brazilian Portuguese, and pejibaye or peach palm in English. Unfortunately, there is disagreement on the botanical identity of *rasha*. Some writers classify it with the genus *Bactris*, while others identify it as *Guilielma*.[49] Most likely, the Barafiri *rasha* are peach palms, and constitute one or more species of *Guilielma*. The *Bactris setulosa* [Karst.] (*corozo, macanilla,* or *albarico*) and the *Guilielma gasipaes* [(H.B.K.) Bailey] resemble one another morphologically, since both have pinnate leaves and bands of long spines on their trunks. However, there are important differences, such as inflorescence, rachis, and fruit. The *Guilielma* attains heights of

more than sixty feet, while the *Bactris* reaches only about half that size.[50]
Most important, the peach palm is distinguished from the other palms
used by the Yanoama in that it is found only where it has been planted.
This palm is not known to exist in a wild state, nor does it freely volunteer.

There is no uniformity in the distribution pattern of the peach palm in
Yanoama territory. It grows and produces best at elevations well under
3,000 feet. Here, in the hot lowlands, veritable groves can be found in
abandoned gardens—groves that were begun when peach palms were
intercropped with other plants, such as plantains. They thrive in areas
where soil is deep and rich. In the high Parima, peach palms are relatively scarce, and the fruits ripen later than in the lowlands.[51] The drupes
(fruits) are highly regarded as food. Flavor and size vary greatly, and
fruits more than two inches in diameter are rare. The starchy layer enclosing the seed (an ovaloid "nut" about one-half inch in diameter) is
edible and nutritious.[52] Some drupes contain no seed or nut, being
completely edible except for the epicarp, a thin outer skin. All are boiled
whole before being eaten.

Occasionally, *afai*, or avocados (*Persea americana*), are planted in Barafiri gardens. Unlike the peach palms, these are planted only singly, so
they are far fewer and more widely scattered. There is no information
available currently on whether this avocado is a cultigen, although it is
not known to grow wild in the Parima highlands.

The papaya (*Carica papaya*) is a tree whose seeds are planted in gardens
and in the vicinity of *shabono*. Sometimes, too, plants volunteer at *shabono*
trash heaps and bear fruit for years after the place has been abandoned.[53]
The papaya is classified as a tree of the *tierra caliente*, growing at elevations below 3,000 feet.[54] Yet, I have seen in the Parima highlands (at
about 3,000 feet) healthy specimens more than fifteen feet tall and bearing fruit. Unlike all the food plants identified heretofore, the papaya has
little or no starch (and consequently little carbohydrate). It contains from
7 to 9 percent sugars and proteolytic enzymes that greatly aid the diges-
tion of proteins.[55]

At least two other kinds of trees are planted: one, *bixa*, yielding an important vegetable dye,[56] and the other (an acacia) serving as the source of
a narcotic drug. *Bixa*, or arnotto (*Bixa* sp.),[57] is called *nana* by the Barafiri. Botanically, the plant is classified as a tree that can grow to a height
of more than twenty feet, although it much more frequently resembles a
bush. In addition to an abundance of large pink flowers, each plant yields
numerous reddish seed pods covered with soft spines. The crushed seeds
are a necessary element of Yanoama culture, providing the fragrant red
coloring that is freely applied to the body, baskets, arrowheads, and ornaments. By diluting with water or adding other ingredients, such as wood

ash, a variety of colors from light pink to dark purple are obtained. *Bixa* is planted in gardens and near *shabono*, sometimes also volunteering near house sites. Nearly all hallucinogens are prepared from substances obtained from wild species. However, at least one species of *Acacia* is believed to be planted occasionally. The "bark" of this tree, when pulverized and processed, yields one of the various narcotics the Barafiri call *ebena*.

Minor Crop Plants. All remaining crop plants are relatively insignificant in area occupied and in volume of production, although some of them are of great importance to the Yanoama. These plants are so diverse in appearance and in function that the most meaningful way of grouping them is in terms of the method of planting.

1. *Planting of Cuttings.* A group of gramineous plants is represented in Barafiri gardens. Among these are certain grasses—some of them aromatic—cultivated for medicinal purposes and for magic, both of which are intimately interconnected.[58] There are also specimens of certain bromeliaceous plants that are grown for the fine, tough fibers that can be obtained from their fleshy leaves. *Sonamacasi* plants are cultivated for their razorlike leaves, which are used for cutting.[59]

Far more obvious is the cane (*sharaca*) from which arrow shafts are obtained. It is a gigantic grass that grows in large clumps. These plants are believed by some Barafiri to yield the best quality arrow shafts when they grow at elevations well above 2,000 feet. Yet, they are also reported growing in gardens of the Orinoco lowlands.[60] Irrespective of the preferred habitat, no Yanoama group at any altitude can tolerate an absence of cane for their arrow shafts. The stalks, whose feathery tops in flower greatly resemble sugar cane, can grow taller than fifteen feet; they are light, strong, and without any jointing. At the base, once the overlapping outer leaf sheaths are removed, the stalk itself is less than an inch in diameter.

Sugar cane is another giant grass that can be found in many Yanoama gardens, although there is more frequent mention of it as a food plant of the Brazilian Yanoama than of those in Venezuela. This Old World plant is known to the Barafiri as *buu*—a word that also means "honey." It is impossible to ascertain when Barafiri began planting sugar cane and where it was introduced.[61] It appears to grow well, even in the high Parima, but a few clumps are all that are ever found in a garden, and sometimes there is none at all.[62]

2. *Transplanting.* Tobacco (*bee najeco* in the Barafiri dialect) is distinctive in that it is invariably transplanted while still young. The plant is extremely important and practically no adult would be without his or her wad of rolled tobacco leaves.[63] Seeds from mature tobacco plants (*Nico-*

Plate 16. Jorocoba-teri man setting out tobacco seedlings. When he came to his garden to plant them he brought one leaf packet containing the seedlings and another full of dark, damp mud. A ball of mud was squeezed around the roots of each plant before it was set into the ground. His extended right hand is between a white, ash-covered spot where he is planting and the leaf upon which the mud lies.

tiana tabacum L.) are collected and saved, to be sown at an appropriate time in small seed beds. Planting is sometimes done by blowing the tiny seeds onto the prepared soil; later the tender seedlings are often shaded from the sun by *Musa* leaves resting on a framework of sticks.[64] Only men engage in tobacco cultivation, and each keeps watch over his own seed bed. When the sprouts have become a few inches tall, they are carefully transplanted into the garden proper (see plate 16). A tiny patch of tobacco is all that a family requires, so this crop can be easily overlooked in Barafiri gardens.

3. *Planting of Either Seeds or Cuttings.* Cotton (*shinaru* in Barafiri) is planted in two different ways. Sometimes the seeds are put directly into the ground; sometimes six- to eight-inch sections are cut from the stalks of mature plants, and these cuttings set out. The technique used seems to depend, at least in part, on just how soon a harvest is needed. Occasionally cotton plants can be seen growing in the clearings outside the *shabono* palisades, but most of them are found in gardens.

Unfortunately, we do not yet know which species are used by the Barafiri although there can be little doubt that the genus is *Gossypium*.[65] Cotton fibers are important and are universally used for decorative and symbolic purposes. The fibers are spun into the thin cords that are tied around people's waists, arms, and legs, crossed over the breast, and sometimes tied through the perforations in earlobes. From thick cotton thread, women make fringes, which they wear like short aprons, and the beltlike bundles of thread that adorn men's waists on special occasions. It is the exceptional cord that is not colored red from *bixa*.

Cotton bolls do not ripen well in the Parima highlands, perhaps because the climate lacks a lengthy period of dry, sunny weather. To dry out their cotton before removing the seeds, the Barafiri suspend clusters of bolls over their household fires for days on end.

It is frequently reported that cotton is a relatively recent introduction to Yanoama culture,[66] but there is no firm evidence that the growing of small amounts of cotton, to be hand spun into thread for use on the body, is not an ancient Yanoama tradition. However, there can be little doubt that the cotton thread hammock might be an innovation. Even so, after having recently learned to covet cotton hammocks, and knowing how they are made, the highland Barafiri still grow only the very small amounts of cotton that meet their traditional needs. Down in the Orinoco lowlands, however, cotton is grown in such quantities that the Waika have a surplus of thread for barter.

4. *Seed Sowing.* Plants whose seeds are sown constitute a relatively minor group of cultivars. Of these, one species in particular is found in Barafiri gardens with the greatest frequency. This is a creeper, generally

intercropped with plantains, that produces the small, yellowish, gourdlike fruits the Barafiri call *shokadama*.[67] Its botanical classification is elusive at present, although it is probably a cucurbit. The edible seeds are removed from the fruit and toasted in the ashes of a hearth fire. Later, after the ash has been sifted out through a shallow basket, the seeds are split and eaten. In the humid, plantain-shaded portions of producing gardens are to be found the remnants of many of these fruits: the hard, ripe outer shells lie where they were smashed open so that the seeds could be pulled from the fibrous flesh. Only the seeds are carried away from the garden.

The highland Yanoama also have the bottle gourd (*Lagenaria* sp.),[68] or a very similar plant, from whose fruits they fashion water containers and other vessels (see plate 9). Very few of these plants are required to meet their needs. The calabash tree, or *totumo* in Venezuelan vernacular (*Crescentia cujete* L.), appears to have been absent from Barafiri territory.[69]

Pepper (*braqui* in Barafiri) is occasionally reported as a Yanoama garden plant—undoubtedly some species of *Capsicum*. These are "hot" peppers, which seem to have more importance as substances used in magical rites than as items of the diet. There is one report from the high Parima of peppers being smoked over a hearth fire.[70]

Two different kinds of maize, both apparently *Zea mays*, are planted in very small quantities by the Yanoama of the Parima highlands. One kind, seemingly a traditional cultigen, is known as *shidi* to the Barafiri. This is a small plant, no more than five feet tall, producing small ears. The second kind, a type of hybrid, is known to have been introduced to them directly by missionaries since 1960. The Yanoama are impressed with the large size of this new maize plant and by the large ears it produces. In both the Parima highlands and the Orinoco lowlands, where it was also introduced by missionaries since 1950, the new maize is known by a single root word, *yono*.[71] In planting, dried maize kernels are placed directly into small holes, which are poked in the ground with the finger or a stick (see plate 17).[72] The Barafiri explain that they plant very little maize, because they do not particularly like to eat it. They believe maize to be a potentially harmful plant and one that frequently causes diarrhea in children who eat it. On those relatively rare occasions when roasted maize ears are eaten, it is invariably their traditional kind, rather than the larger, new *yono*.

Along with the new maize, there are other seed-sown garden plants known to have been introduced to the highland Barafiri since 1960: these are beans, tomatoes, and squashes. Of the beans, one can be identified precisely. This is the Brazilian black bean (*Phaseolus* sp.), or *feijão* in Brazilian Portuguese. It was introduced by Brazil-based missionaries in 1961,

Plate 17. Young Niyayoba-teri man planting maize in his portion of a new garden clearing. Note the abundance of charred wood and the ash-covered surface of the garden. This man, who is wearing exceptionally large feathered ear ornaments, carries his maize in a small tin can.

and even the Barafiri name *feshao* (or *feshawa*) is of Portuguese origin. The tomato (*Lycopersicum* sp.) was introduced at about the same time and in the same manner. It is called *tomashi* in Barafiri, a word nearly identical in sound to Brazilian pronunciation of the Portuguese word *tomate*. Squash (*Cucurbita* sp.), whose seeds the Barafiri call *suru moba*, was introduced after 1968 by missionaries.

These highland Yanoama do not like maize, and they simply reject beans, tomatoes, and squash as food. It was the possibility of barter that induced them to experiment with new garden plants. Men accepted seeds originally as a novelty, and as long as the produce continues to have value in bartering they continue to replant. The only utility of beans, squash, tomatoes, and "new" maize lies in exchanging them, since they are inherently useless to the Barafiri. Traditional food preferences were established long ago, and the Yanoama are extremely resistant to change. Beans have virtually disappeared from Barafiri horticulture, since Venezuela-based missionaries, who have been in the area since 1968, show no interest in bartering for them.[73] However, because the missionaries do have some interest in obtaining tomatoes and squashes, these can still be found occasionally in a Yanoama garden. In fact, they seem to thrive there. On a single healthy tomato plant, for example, are to be seen an abundance of flowers, green fruits, and ripe fruits.

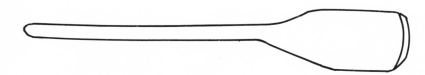

FEET

Figure 9. Palmwood *Fimo*. Presumed appearance of the shovellike tool once used in Barafiri horticulture. About five feet in length, it had a long handle and a broad sharpened blade.

PLANTING THE GARDEN

Planting is done, like so many other tasks, in a seemingly relaxed, casual manner. Men work at this job no more than a few hours a day. If the garden being planted is several miles from the *shabono*, the round trip must be made each work day, since camps are not established for the purpose of planting. The planting of a new garden is done gradually, sometimes covering a span of months. Part of this is due to the fact that in the Parima highlands rains often frustrate planting schedules, just as they hamper the burning of new gardens. In the highlands, therefore, an entire garden is not burned completely at one time, nor can it be completely planted in consecutive days. Before the burning phase is completed, some planting has begun in those parts of the clearing that have burned well. Weeks later men are still planting humid parts of a garden, while in other parts their new plants have rooted and are leafing out.

Traditionally, a special tool was used in planting. Known as a *fimo*, this shovellike device about five feet long was made from a single piece of the heart wood of the peach palm (see fig. 9). The edge of the broad lower part was sharpened. Used exclusively in horticulture, its functions were to loosen suckers from parent musaceous plants and to dig holes in new gardens where these suckers were being planted. The principal planting tool today is the machete, supplemented occasionally by sticks. When a Barafiri needs a stick for making holes in the ground, he merely picks up one that is handy. Sometimes he sharpens one end and sometimes he does not. Normally the soil in new gardens is so loose and friable after burning that the surface is easily worked. However, some tool, such as a machete, is needed to excavate the deeper holes that will receive plantain and banana suckers and the larger cuttings, such as *ocumo*.[74]

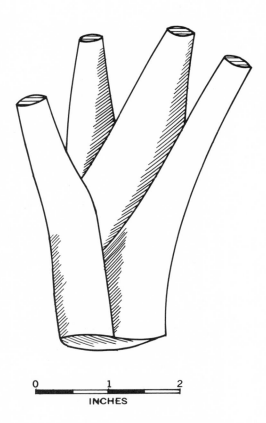

Figure 10. Trimmed *Ocumo (Xanthosoma)* Cutting

Propagation of Staple Crops. Propagation of the principal staples—plantains, *ocumo*, and manioc—is achieved by means of transplanting either suckers, rhizomes, corms, or stem cuttings.

1. *Plantains.* Sometime after a plantain has produced a bunch of fruit, the pseudostem is cut down. By then several suckers have already sprouted from the large basal corm of the plant. Two or three of these are left to develop in order to provide future harvests from the parent, while other suckers might be removed for transplanting in a new garden.[75] The suckers are separated from the corm with a stick or a machete, although formerly the *fimo* was widely used. The leaves are cut from each sucker, and some of the roots are also cut off. Even after trimming, suckers are heavy, weighing between three and one-half and four pounds each. They are also bulky, and only about twenty or so can be fitted into one of the sturdy carrying devices manufactured expressly for their transportation.[76] Each such carrier (*basha afi* in Barafiri), made of lianas and green leaves and fitted with a tumpline, is normally disposed of at the planting site after having been used but once.

In the new garden, the suckers are kept shaded in the carrier or covered

with leaves from *Musa* or *Heliconia* until they are planted. Each is set into
a hole a foot or less in depth, with the trimmed leaf sheaths exposed
above ground. Plantains are spaced from eight to twelve feet apart, a distance that allows full-grown plants to overlap leaves, but not to shade
one another. Neither rows nor other geometric forms are utilized intentionally (the abundance of logs and stumps would make this difficult),
and the distance between individual plants varies considerably.[77] Each
plant is expected to produce a bunch of fruit between nine and
thirteen months after the sucker is set out. Subsequently, by proper
pruning of suckers, a parent stool can be expected to yield three more
bunches of fruit spaced about eight months apart. In contrast, most of
the *ocumo*, yams, sweet potatoes, and gourds planted among the musaceous plants will provide only a single harvest.

2. *Ocumo.* During the same weeks that a man is setting out his plantains, he occasionally brings a load of *ocumo* cuttings to be planted
among them. Each cutting consists of a portion of the subterranean corm
from which the roots have been cut. The leaves are cut off at the base
of the stems (see fig. 10). These trimmed cuttings are smaller than
trimmed plantain suckers and easier to handle. Like plantains, they can
be transplanted at any time of the year in the Parima highlands. They
are transported to new gardens in carrying devices very similar to those
used for plantains, although smaller.

3. *Sweet Manioc.* Manioc is easier to propagate than either *Musa* or
ocumo. The stems of mature plants are cut into lengths of approximately
twelve to sixteen inches. Lightweight and free of any adhering soil, stem
cuttings are hardy and extremely portable. At the planting site, preferably with a sandy soil, the cuttings are shoved a few inches into the
ground by twos or threes. No rows are used, but care is taken to set the
cuttings at a sharp angle. Manioc stem cuttings have no top or bottom;
that portion above ground leafs out, and the part that is buried sets
roots.

Staggered Plantings. There is no evidence of a systematic staggering of
crop planting in the Western sense of producing a sequence of closely
spaced ripening periods in a garden. Yet, an effective approximation of
this is seen in the Parima highlands.[78] The accepted time to plant a garden is immediately after it has been burned. In the Orinoco lowlands
this is a reasonably well defined climatic period, and burning is not a
serious problem. However, in the cooler, humid highlands the weather
is capricious. No time of the year is ideal for burning; consequently,
there is no well-defined planting season. Likewise, in producing gardens
and in many old gardens, some *Musa* suckers are always big enough for
transplanting—as well as *ocumo*, yam, sweet potato, and manioc plants

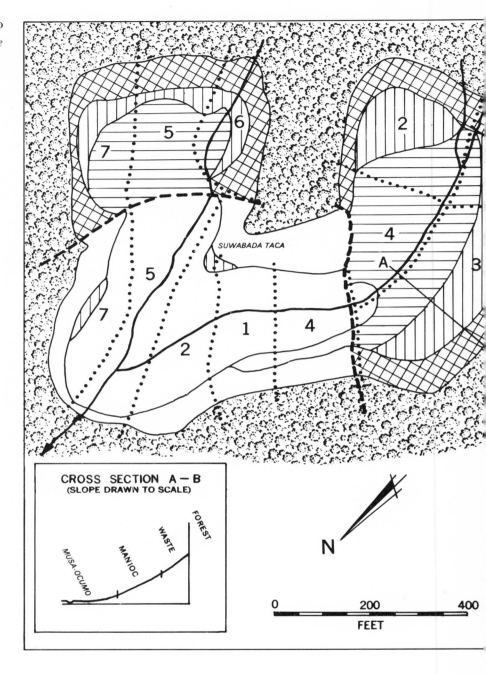

Map 10. Garden Regions. The example of Majowawa-taca.

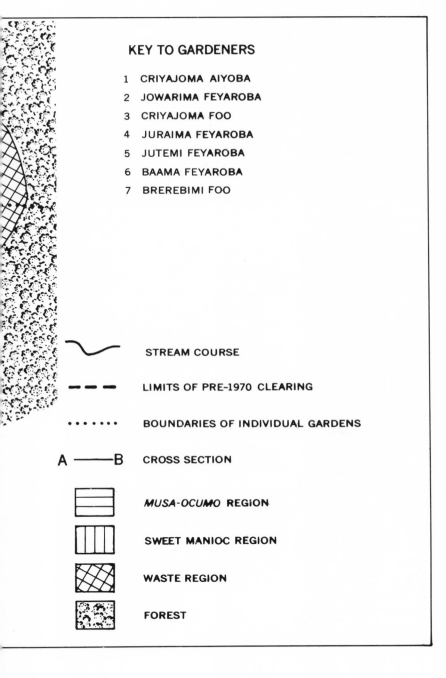

KEY TO GARDENERS

1 CRIYAJOMA AIYOBA
2 JOWARIMA FEYAROBA
3 CRIYAJOMA FOO
4 JURAIMA FEYAROBA
5 JUTEMI FEYAROBA
6 BAAMA FEYAROBA
7 BREREBIMI FOO

STREAM COURSE

LIMITS OF PRE-1970 CLEARING

BOUNDARIES OF INDIVIDUAL GARDENS

A———B CROSS SECTION

MUSA-OCUMO REGION

SWEET MANIOC REGION

WASTE REGION

FOREST

from which cuttings can be obtained. Since it is very rarely too dry or too wet in the highlands for transplanting, propagation is at least theoretically conceivable at any time of the year. And, indeed, men are to be seen preparing and planting new gardens in the height of the "wet" season and clearing, burning, and replanting small sections of their producing gardens in both "wet" and "dry" seasons.

For these reasons one finds crop plants in varying stages of development in a producing garden. Among the plantains, for example, some plants have bunches of ripening fruit, while others are only forming bunches, others are beginning to flower, and still others are just leafing out.

GARDEN REGIONS

A clearing, or *taca*, normally contains the gardens of different men. It also includes various crop regions, the boundaries of which do not correspond to those of the individual gardens, since the regions are in effect shared by the various gardeners. In fact, the clearing of a particular site is designed to provide for a set of distinctive garden regions rather than uniformity throughout the clearing. Specific crop plants are designated for particular areas long before they are actually planted. Slope is a particularly important criterion in establishing garden regions, with flat sites generally avoided.[79] Within a clearing relative relief is frequently great. It is not unusual to find an altitude range of well over two hundred feet and consequent vertical zonation. This provides the variety of different kinds of planting sites, or microniches, which the Barafiri prefer and use in a consistent manner.

In most clearings, each gardener has a parcel (or parcels) that provides for the specific requirements of his different crop plants, in terms of soil porosity, fertility, and humidity.[80] Because the kinsmen who share the clearing use the identical complement of crop plants, their needs are almost identical. Thus, they must share these different regions where optimal conditions exist for specific crop species. Since each of the various cultivars is normally planted in sites corresponding to its needs, and since intercropping is commonplace, in essence specific crop associations constitute uniform regions within garden clearings. The three principal types of garden regions are presented in map 10. A representative Jorocobateri garden clearing, Majowawa-taca, is depicted in plate 18. Majowawa-taca is shared by seven gardeners; it contains an abandoned portion (*suwabada taca*), a producing section, and two new additions.

The low, alluvial portions of a clearing, where soils are deep, dark, heavy, humid and yet well drained, are reserved principally for the musaceous plants.[81] Among the plantains and bananas, *ocumo* is also set out,

Plate 18. View south across part of Majowawa-taca (see map 10). In the foreground, the lowest part of the clearing, mature musaceous plants stand tall and thick. On the slope to the left is a *suwabada taca*. Beyond is seen one of two major additions to the clearing. Planting there has already taken place, following the same pattern of crop regions as those of the producing areas. Some slopes in the new part are 30° or more, and the higher reaches of the clearing are at least 150 feet above the valley floor.

as well as sweet potatoes, yams, and the gourdlike *shokadama*. The *ocumo*, yams, and sweet potatoes develop in a few months, and they are dug up for their tubers before the musaceous plants grow large enough to shade the ground. The gourds are pulled loose for their edible seeds within a few months. Thereafter, this portion of a garden becomes a region occupied almost exclusively by musaceous plants, particularly *cowata* and *baushimi* plantains. Two other kinds of crop plants also are found in this region. One of these is the peach palm, whose root sprouts or nuts, if available, are planted. In the Parima highlands they are relatively few since the peach palm is principally a lowland species. Tiny patches of tobacco can also be found where the seedlings have been transplanted, preferably on or near thoroughly rotted logs or stumps. Essentially, this portion of a garden is an ingenious replica of the forest in miniature. Under the mature *Musa* plants it is cool, dark, and humid, even at mid-day.

Somewhat further up slope is a well-defined second region, the distance depending upon soil qualities, gradient, and the size of a particular garden. This is a zone where sweet manioc predominates. *Ocumo* is often found intercropped in the lower parts of this region, and farther up slope cotton is sometimes intercropped with the manioc. In the highest, best-drained portion of a garden, virtually nothing but manioc is planted. Both these garden regions are distinguishable in terms of principal staples rather than "minor" plants, although there is also a tendency for each of these to be found in one of the regions.

A man plants his new garden in coherent segments, gradually building up the areal differentiation within his particular portion of the entire clearing. In essence, planting by segments is planting by crop types. For example, on a day when he is planting, a man usually brings from an old garden only one load of cuttings to be set out. These cuttings might be either plantains, bananas, *ocumo*, yams, or manioc. Only one kind of crop is planted, and he works in only one segment of one region of his garden. Cuttings are prepared (separated, trimmed, and cleaned) in the old garden from which they were removed or at the *shabono* or campsite where the man is living, so that no extra weight need be carried to the new garden. Immediately on arrival at the planting site, the man starts to work, hardly stopping until the entire load of cuttings has been set into the ground. He is likely to begin the planting of a new garden with musaceous plants, spending more effort on the setting out of plantains than anything else.

By the time a garden clearing begins to produce, there sometimes appears a fragmentary belt with no crops—a zone of scrubby brush and weeds growing among charred logs and stumps. This constitutes a third distinctive garden region.[82] It is "waste" land of sorts, easily observed from a distance and appearing to be a zone of transition between cropland and forest. In some places, this land was cleared but never planted;

in other cases, it was used briefly (for such crops as manioc or *ocumo*) and then abandoned to begin the reversion to forest while the rest of the garden continued to produce. This kind of region varies in width from less than twenty feet to one hundred feet or more. In the Venezuelan Parima its vegetation characteristically includes fast-growing volunteers, such as ferns, *kafu* trees, diverse *Heliconia*, thorn bushes, needle leaf palm, and even *seje* palm (*Jessenia* sp.), as well as a variety of grasses.[83] This third region frequently occupies the up-slope edges of gardens above the rest of the clearing, although this is not always the case. Such areas are sometimes considered too dry for any planting. Similarly, the lower edge of a clearing might be too wet for crops and also part of the waste region.

It is often said that an area becomes waste because "it won't burn well." And, since trees are cut to fall down slope in the clearing process, there is relatively little combustible material at the upper edges of a clearing. Without adequate burning, vegetative cover and faunal pests are not effectively eliminated, and no ash is added to the soil. Consequently, no effort is made to plant such places, unless they are reburned. There are other plausible explanations for such a region. In the humid Parima highlands, cutting extends farther into the forest than the anticipated limits of the garden clearing, so that at least the unshaded center will dry out well enough to burn. What is more, a belt of wasteland can also serve as protection from enemy raiders, since it is almost impossible for a raider to fire point blank at a man in his garden and still have the cover of the forest.

GARDEN SIZE

The *shabono* settlement unit is composed of a number of individual households. As a general rule, each married man is head of at least one household and is responsible for his own wife (or wives) and children. Before making a new garden, a man calculates his household needs for food and other materials as well as his existing garden resources, and then he clears and plants accordingly. There are also rare cases of men who garden for only themselves and perhaps another person such as a nephew, and there are instances where an old woman or a *wanidi* woman might garden a tiny plot prepared for her by some male kinsman. These are, however, striking exceptions to the general composition of household units. Yanoama horticulture cannot be understood without information on just how much land is being actively gardened by a community at any given time. As a means of revealing this facet of their economic system, specific data for two *teri* are analyzed below. The Jorocoba-teri, numbering eighty-four, occupy a *shabono* of their own (see fig. 11) and are engaged in no warfare. In contrast, the Niyayoba-teri, who number

TABLE 6

Principal Garden Clearings of Two Sample Teri[a]

Name of Clearing, or *Taca*	Number of Gardeners	Approximate Acreages				
		New	To Be Reburned[b]	Producing	Waste	Total
The Jorocoba-teri						
Wabufita	6	5.2	0.6	—	0.1[c]	5.9
Boredidire/ Canawaubrare	3	2.1	0.7	—	1.9[d]	4.7
Shijota	7	6.2	—	—	1.5	7.7
Majowawa	5	4.8	—	3.8	2.9	11.5
Cuaisiba	8	0.2	—	6.1	2.1	8.4
Yoodiba	8	1.4	0.6	2.3	4.6	8.9
Jocotoibue	1	—	—	0.5	—	0.5[e]
Total		19.9		12.7		47.6
The Niyayoba-teri						
Waratau	3	3.7	—	—	—	3.7
Niyayoba	5	3.3	0.3	—	—	3.6
Doshaquefe ubrauba	2	1.0	0.1	2.0	1.0[f]	4.1
Cauoba	8[g]	0.4	—	3.1	0.5	4.0
Oquiyamoba	2	0.3[h]	—	1.3	0.2	1.8[i]
Total		8.7		6.4		17.2

[a]Excluding old gardens, or *suwabada taca*. Cf. map 9.
[b]A reflection of optimism, since most will not be recleared and reburned.
[c]A significant proportion of this garden clearing is granite outcrops.
[d]Much of this "waste" area is due to the severe illness of one of the gardeners.
[e]Jocotoibue-taca is an old garden, largely abandoned.
[f]Most of this particular area has already yielded *Musa* and tubers.
[g]In addition, two women have small gardens here.
[h]An area recleared from overgrown portions of the existing clearing.
[i]Oquiyamoba-taca is a large clearing belonging principally to the Juwafusibuwei-teri. Of the five acres or so belonging to the Niyayoba-teri, all but 1.8 acres have been abandoned.

about fifty-eight, are actively involved in a war, and, as a consequence of this condition, they share a *shabono* with three other *teri* (see fig. 4). In each case the average household size is between five and six persons, including nursing infants.

Each *teri* has several garden clearings in varying stages of development, and these clearings and their characteristics are presented in table 6. In certain clearings up to eight different men have garden parcels, while others contain the gardens of only two or three men. Some clearings are almost totally new, not yet having yielded anything; others contain the producing gardens that people currently eat from; and still others, such as Jocotoibue-taca and Oquiyamoba-taca, are nearly phased out. Those areas that have been cleared but require further reburning before being planted are relatively insignificant. However, the "waste" land of the Jorocoba-teri totals more than 13 acres, while that of the Niyayoba-teri is nearly 2 acres. In some cases, especially in new clearings, this is land that has begun to revert to forest without ever having been planted in crops. The bulk of the "waste" land, however, comprises parts of gardens that have already yielded their produce. In essence tracts that are so classified are abandoned lands, scattered among parcels that are still in production.

The fifty-eight Niyayoba-teri have approximately 6.4 acres of garden land in production, and 8.7 acres newly prepared. The eighty-four Jorocoba-teri have well over 12 acres in production, plus nearly 20 acres in new gardens. In all cases, this excludes their numerous abandoned garden clearings (*suwabada taca*) from which food and other useful materials are also obtained regularly. Among the warring Niyayoba-teri, the situation is far from ideal. There is a mean of only 1.7 acres of garden land for each of the ten men who garden, a figure incorporating newly cleared or planted gardens, gardens in production, areas to be reburned, and "waste" regions within new or producing gardens. This means that the per capita garden area is slightly under 0.3 acre. Of this, only a little over 0.1 acre is in production for each person of the *teri* community, and another 0.15 acre of new garden land per person is worked.[84] Conditions among the Jorocoba-teri are better and probably far more representative of Yanoama horticulture in the Parima highlands. For each of the sixteen Jorocoba-teri men who garden, there is an average of nearly three acres of garden land, excluding, of course, the abandoned gardens. Viewed differently, there is a mean of about 0.57 acre of garden land per person. Of this total, 0.15 acre is producing and 0.24 acre is newly cleared or just planted.

These figures are really quite remarkable, comparing favorably with garden acreages among tropical lowland tribes in diverse parts of South America. Among the Cubeo of Colombia's upper Río Vaupés, for example, the mean size of manioc gardens is about 0.2 acre per person.[85] The Kuikuru, located on a headwater tributary of Brazil's Rio Xingú, are reported to have under cultivation at any one time slightly over 0.65 acre per capita.[86] These data from the Parima highlands are also strikingly different from those obtained in a Waika settlement of the Orinoco lowlands studied in 1968. This latter community was reported to have less than 15 acres of newly cleared garden land for a population "probably between 150 and 200,"[87] a mere 0.07 to 0.1 acre per person.

Only very superficial data are currently available on pests and the extent to which they affect Yanoama horticulture. Bacteria, fungi, and other kinds of disease-causing organisms are not overtly recognized by the Barafiri as harmful in gardening. Nor are infestations of epidemic proportions known to exist, although one can observe cases where individual plants (i.e., tobacco, maize, and plantains) are obviously under insect attack. The only pests specifically identified, however, were leaf-cutter ants and caterpillars. A factor of critical importance in shifting cultivation is the protective burning a garden undergoes while it is being prepared. The intense heat quite literally sterilizes the site, destroying insect larvae, eggs, and grubs, as well as other organisms. The destruction of a belt of forest at the edges of the planted area itself, the "waste" region described above, might also serve as a means of purifying the garden proper.

More than insects and microbes, the biotic threat to a garden lies in the larger species of native fauna, particularly birds and mammals. Among the southern Yanoama, such garden pests as hummingbirds and rats are reported to cause damage.[88] Certain monkeys and many birds are attracted to ripe bananas and plantains, but they do little harm because the bunches of fruit are removed green from the gardens. Root crops appear to be the least vulnerable to pests.[89]

Nearly all these pests—insects, birds, and mammals—are themselves food sources for the Barafiri. In the vicinity of *shabono* and producing gardens, they are quite effectively collected or hunted. Only infrequently do the bigger game animals, such as peccary, deer, or tapir, venture near a new or producing garden, but they are strongly attracted to abandoned gardens. A man generally goes to his gardens armed with bow and arrows; and while on the trail or at work in the garden, he is alert to the possible presence of game of any sort.

Among the Parima highlanders, it would appear that the loss of a crop or an entire garden is very rare. When it does occur, it is due to some human agency, usually personal or group hostilities, and not to pests.

MAINTENANCE

In highland Yanoama horticulture there are no fields as such, and there is virtually no tillage, fertilization, irrigation, or systematic removal of weeds. Yet, one cannot dispute that a man does maintain his gardens, even though they are frequently miles from his *shabono* and cannot be attended to daily.[90] It is standard procedure to combine garden maintenance with other activities. For example, a man might go to his garden to finish certain new plantings, or to gather a load of ripe tubers and green plantains, or simply because a hunt or some other activity has brought him nearby. On these occasions a rather effective maintenance is accomplished.

Once in his garden, a man looks over the area in general, checks for pests, and takes note of how his own and his kinsmen's plants are developing and what might be ripe. He also looks to see whether anything has been stolen or gathered without his knowledge. The Yanoama gardener is often obliged to provide supports for his musaceous plants, since strong winds can cause severe damage. As the bunches of fruit begin to form, the plants (some of which attain heights of more than twenty feet) get very top-heavy. When a gardener notices this condition developing, he generally props a long pole tightly against the pseudostem, stabilizing the end of it in the ground. Less frequently, slender lianas are tied high up on the pseudostem, pulled tight, and then fastened to nearby logs or tree stumps (see plate 19). From time to time these supports are checked for their effectiveness.

In a new garden, fire has generally removed all competition for the crop plants, but soon thereafter the weed invasion begins. Thus, even if systematic weeding is not conceptualized by the highland Yanoama, weeds certainly are. Among these noxious plants are a variety of creepers, shrubs, trees, and grasses. One of the most offensive is a certain treelike plant, called *shaa* by the Barafiri, which is almost literally covered with thorns. Sometimes it attains a height of well over ten feet.[91] In contrast, a volunteer tree, the *kafu*, is protected, since it yields edible fruits. A weed called *eroerorimo*, which bears a striking resemblance to middle-latitude pokeweed (*Phytolacca* sp.), serves no useful purpose for the Barafiri. In the plantain-*ocumo* region, more than anywhere else in a garden, weed growth is greatly hindered once the musaceous plants get large enough to shade the ground completely.

Yanoama of the Orinoco lowlands are reported to practice careful weeding of their gardens, particularly when their crop plants are still small,[92] but, after the first two or three years in the life of even a lowland garden, all weeding has stopped. Evidently the highland Barafiri are less fastidious in this particular facet of garden maintenance, although they, too, are careful when they pull or cut weeds, and they are attentive to the weed competition for their young plantings. Unquestionably, much more weedy growth is tolerated by them than by Western gardeners.

GATHERING THE PRODUCE

The gathering of vegetable produce from a garden is a protracted process. It begins only a few months after initial planting, when the first

Plate 19. Deep within the *Musa-ocumo* region of a large garden clearing belonging to the Arajai-teri. This is a producing garden in which some of the *Musa* have already borne fruit and suckers of the parent plants are large. Note particularly the pole props and vines used as guys to keep some of the pseudostems erect. Peach palms several feet tall can be seen among the musaceous plantings and the charred logs and stumps.

gourds and tubers (particularly *ocumo*) have become edible. It continues virtually without interruption, although in gradually diminishing volume, for years after the garden has been abandoned as a planting
ground. Much of what grows in a garden never leaves it; only edible or
otherwise useful parts of plants are normally removed. The remnants of
crop plants make a sort of mulch, and so do the weeds that are cut or
pulled.

In this tropical upland habitat, there is no clearly defined horticultural
seasonality, other than that of the life cycles of the different varieties of
cultivated plants themselves. People harvest those parts of their mature
plants that they want, as they have need for them.[93] A garden is not
emptied of its produce at one time. Some fruits, such as plantains, must
be picked as they ripen, while tubers, like manioc, can be left in the
ground for months. The only period that vaguely approximates a harvest
time in the middle-latitude sense occurs when a new garden clearing begins yielding large quantities of *ocumo* or plantains, especially if the local
teri has been experiencing food shortages. Then, ripening of the plantains is cause for jubilation. The Yanoama are utterly dependent on their
garden produce, and if for some reason this food source is cut off or delayed, they are forced into the forests to gather foods.

The products of a plant are gathered by the specific owner who set
out that plant or by members of his household. Sometimes a man will
gather produce in the adjacent gardens of his kinsmen and bring it home
to them. The interdependence between *teri* households is great, and such
an act is theft only if it is done surreptitiously.[94] Adult males and females, as well as youngsters, may gather garden produce, although much
of the routine work of gathering it and carrying it home is done by
women. Gathering in a garden can consist of no more than a person's
casually breaking off an ear of tender maize; or digging up a few small
manioc tubers and eating these raw as a snack; or pulling loose a few
bixa pods, crushing the seeds between the hands, and smearing the red
coloring on the body. More commonly, however, a variety of produce is
gathered to be carried home: perhaps a few *ocumo* tubers, some gourd
seeds, a few leaves of tobacco, some *bixa* pods, and a bunch of green
plantains. Small or loose items are wrapped in large leaves (*Heliconia* or
Musa), then tied with vines to form a neat package. A man will hang such a
package around his neck or to his waistcord, leaving his hands free. A
woman comes to the garden with her large carrying basket, or *wuu*, and
into this she puts everything, including leaf packages.

Apart from this continuous flow of produce from a garden, there is the
periodic and massive gathering of plantains for ceremonial purposes.
The *reajo* for the dead, in particular, requires large quantities of plantains. Adult males, with some assistance from older boys, gather and pre-

Plate 20. Docodicoro-teri men peeling *cowata* plantains in one of their garden clearings. This is part of the preparation for a *reajo* funerary feast. Some of the boys are helping, although most just watch. No females are present. The man standing to the left, wearing an armband from which is suspended a toucan breast, is one of the leaders of this *teri*.

pare the plantains for a *reajo*. The fruits are peeled in the gardens (see plate 20), then carefully packed into *wuu* baskets and carried to the *shabono*. Even a ceremonial for only a few guests demands several basketsful, since all participants eat heartily. Each ceremonial presents the occasion par excellence in Yanoama culture for conspicuous consumption, particularly of garden produce. The enormous volume of food consumed during the several days' duration of a feast and the frequency with which these ceremonials are held place heavy demands on the gardens. Plantains are roasted, or boiled unpeeled, or peeled and boiled until mushy in a soup or gruel (*cowata uba*). The Yanoama do not ferment plantains, or any other substance, in order to produce alcoholic drinks, such as the manioc "beer" that is consumed by so many of the other tropical forest cultures of South America. Nevertheless, the institutionalized feasting patterns are similar to those of other tropical forest peoples.

Yields of Producing Gardens

Horticulture accounts for the bulk of Yanoama caloric intake, although much of the protein and fat of their diet is obtained from collecting and

hunting. The sizes and quality of their gardens are directly correlated to
the morale of a *teri*, just as is the quality of their *shabono*. To obtain information on the productivity of Yanoama horticulture, intensive field
study of both new and producing gardens is required. The following
discussion is based upon numerous examples from the Parima highlands.

In one new garden, a recently planted sample area of 2,500 square feet
was mapped for analysis (see map 11).[95] This area contains forty-eight
Musa plants (of which 42 are of the *cowata* plantain type), forty-two
Xanthosoma plants (of which 28 are *ocumo*), plus six tobacco plants, and
two yam plants (see table 7). Rendered in acreages, this represents the
equivalent of more than eight hundred *Musa* and well over seven hundred *Xanthosoma* per acre. Another new garden, Canawaubrare-taca,
which belongs to the Jorocoba-teri, provides useful data on the planting densities of sweet manioc (see map 12). A sample area covering 1,200
square feet was selected near the top of a steep slope, at the center of a
garden region planted almost exclusively in manioc. In the sample are
116 plantings, much more closely spaced than are either *Musa* or *ocumo*,
each consisting of two or three stem cuttings set into the ground together.
This represents the equivalent of more than 4,200 plantings per acre. No
data are currently available on how many pounds of edible tubers are
obtained by the highland Yanoama from each planting of sweet manioc. However, annual yields of more than five tons of unpeeled, bitter
manioc per acre have been reported for forested lowlands.[96]

TABLE 7
Planting Densities of Selected Garden Crop Plants

Plant Type	Plants in Sample Area (2,500 sq. ft.)	Equivalent in Plants per Acre
Musa (total)	48	835
cowata	42	731
baushimi	3	52
faturimo	2	35
rapaima	1	17
Xanthosoma (total)	42	731
ocumo	28	487
others[a]	14	244
Dioscorea	2	35
Nicotiana tabacum	6	—[b]

[a]Including varieties the Barafiri call *jayurama*, *guaica*, *shitolao*, and *mayobo*.
[b]Only small patches of tobacco are set out, and, consequently, it is unrealistic to think in
terms of tobacco acreage.

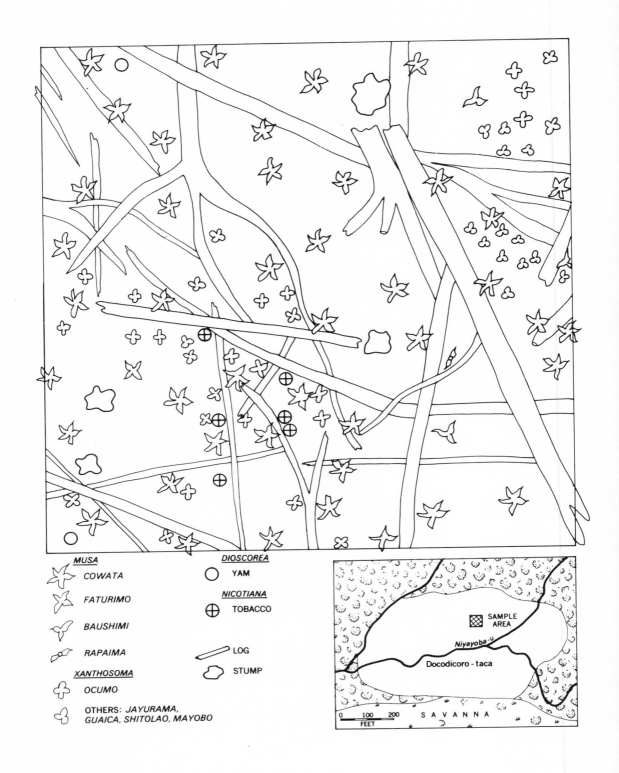

MUSA
✳ COWATA

✴ FATURIMO

🌿 BAUSHIMI

🌱 RAPAIMA

XANTHOSOMA
❀ OCUMO

❀ OTHERS: JAYURAMA,
GUAICA, SHITOLAO, MAYOBO

DIOSCOREA
○ YAM

NICOTIANA
⊕ TOBACCO

▭ LOG

⬭ STUMP

SAMPLE
AREA

Niyayoba-u

Docodicoro - taca

0   100   200
    FEET

S A V A N N A

Map 11. Sample *Musa-Ocumo* Plantings in a New Garden

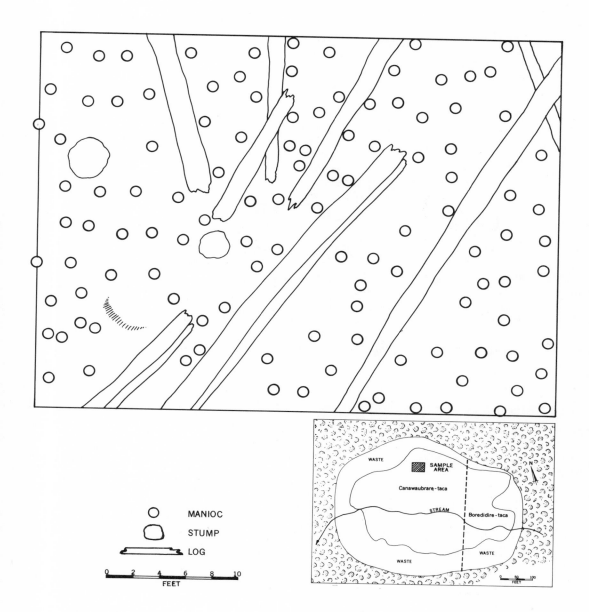

MANIOC

STUMP

LOG

0 2 4 6 8 10
FEET

WASTE

SAMPLE
AREA

N

Canawaubrare-taca

STREAM

Boredidire-taca

WASTE

WASTE

0 50 100
FEET

Map 12. Sample Sweet Manioc Plantings in a New Garden

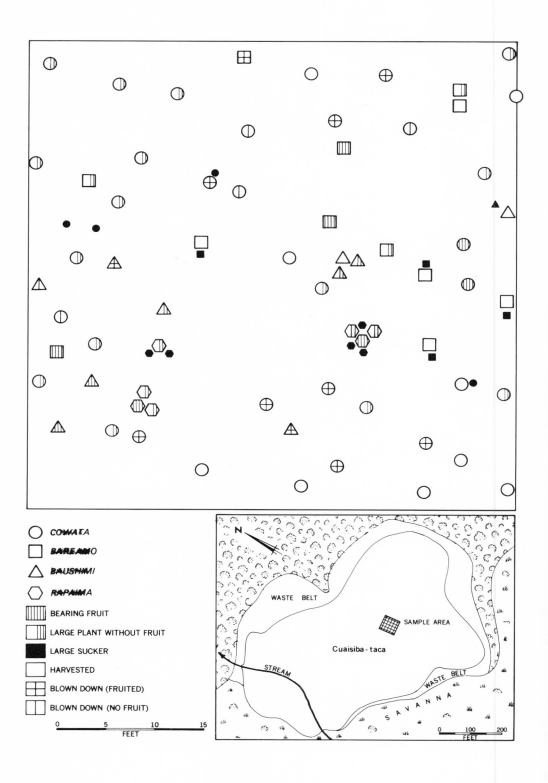

Map 13. Sample of *Musa* in Production

Mere numbers of new plants cannot alone provide a comprehensive picture of yields, nor can new gardens. Consequently, a sample area (2,500 square feet) was selected from the center of the *Musa-ocumo* region of a producing garden. This is Cuaisiba-taca, a Jorocoba-teri garden that is well over a year old (see map 13). As such it provides data on garden yields through time. Within the sample area nearly all the *ocumo*, originally planted with the *Musa*, had been dug up months before. Parts of the garden are virtually overgrown with weeds, although some sweet potatoes and yams survive tenaciously, as well as a small number of *ocumo* plants. However, all these together are insignificant in comparison with the musaceous plants.

Within the sample area there are (excluding young suckers) a total of 81 *Musa* plants in various stages of development (see table 8). When these plants are mapped (map 13), important patterns appear. An original planting of 62 *Musa* in the area is discernible, and so are the distributions of the different varieties of *Musa*. Also, the perennial quality of musaceous plants is evident: several large suckers might be found growing from a single stool—the parent sucker that was set into the ground at planting. To get more than one harvest from a planting, the Yanoama chop down the large pseudostem after cutting or breaking the bunch of fruit from it.[97]

TABLE 8

Stages of Development of Musaceous Plants in a Producing Garden

Variety	Original Planting (estimate)	Plants Visible (map 13)	Bunches Accounted For A	B	C	Bunches Expected D	E
Plantains							
cowata	40	42	9	12	2	15	4
bareamo	11	16	5	1	3	3	4
baushimi	8	11	2	3	2	3	1
Bananas							
rapaima	3	12	0	0	2	5	5
Total	62	81	16	16	9	26	14

A. Bunches gathered.
B. Mature plants blown down.
C. Plants bearing bunches.
D. Plants in flowering stage. These are mature pseudostems in flower, about to flower, or already having flowered.
E. Suckers at least three feet high. Smaller ones are not included in this tabulation, although some of them will eventually bear bunches of fruit.

Of the 81 plants plotted, 69 are plantains (mostly of the *cowata* variety) and 12 are bananas. Out of this total, 16 plantain bunches have already been gathered and their pseudostems cut down. An additional 16 mature plantain pseudostems have been uprooted or broken off by strong winds.[98] This is an impressive loss, in theory representing an equivalent of 278 bunches per acre, although in fact the damage is highly localized within this particular garden clearing. Nine plants are bearing bunches of fruit, while 26 others are large enough to have reached the flowering stage. A conservative estimate of the *Musa* yields from this small sample area during a span of two years or less is approximately 51 bunches of fruit.[99] Only 7 of these are bananas, and they probably are destined for barter with missionaries in the vicinity.

It is the plantains, then, that must be stressed if realistic estimates of yields are to be obtained (see table 9). In the sample area approximately 59 plantains were set out (equivalent to more than 1,000 per acre), although only 44 bunches of fruit (equivalent to about 765 per acre) can be expected within two years of planting.[100] The discrepancy is due in large measure to severe wind damage. Even so, it compares favorably with densities on commercial plantations.[101]

TABLE 9

Estimated Plantain Yields

	Number of Plants Set Out		Potential Number of Bunches[a]	
Variety	Sample	Per Acre Equivalent	Sample	Per Acre Equivalent
cowata	40	696	26	452
bareamo	11	191	11	191
baushimi	8	139	7	122
Total	59	1,026	44	765

[a]The sum of bunches gathered, plants bearing bunches, and plants in flowering stage. See table 8, columns A, C, and D.

Consistently, the highland Yanoama show a preference for the *cowata* type of plantain and, among the few bananas they plant, the *rapaima* is most evident. Certain advantages of the *cowata* and *rapaima* become apparent when bunch size is examined.[102] Among the plantains, the mean weight of bunches of fruit, when they are removed from the gardens to ripen, is about thirty-six pounds (see table 10). However, among bunches of *cowata* alone, the mean weight is forty-nine pounds. Similarly, while the mean bunch weight for all bananas is forty-three pounds, for the *rapaima* it is fifty pounds. Obviously, in this Parima highland sample at least, the *cowata*, among the plantains, and the *rapaima*, among the bananas, yield best. The heaviest bunch observed was a *rapaima* that weighed sixty-five pounds; the heaviest single bunch of plantains was a *cowata* weighing fifty-nine pounds.[103] In order to obtain a realistic measurement of what this means in terms of food production, the waste must be subtracted from the weight of each bunch of fruit. The stem and the inedible skins that are peeled from the fruit account for approximately one-third of the total weight of the entire stalk of fruit.[104] Consequently, a forty-nine pound bunch of plantains yields somewhat less than thirty-three pounds of edible pulp (see table 10).

TABLE 10

Estimated Edible Musa *Yields*

Plant Variety	Mean Bunch Weight (pounds)	Mean Edible Fruit Weight (pounds)	Edible Yield (pound/acre[a])	Annual Edible Yield[b] (ton/acre[c])
All plantains	36	24	18,350	4.6
cowata	49	33	25,250	6.3
others	28	19	14,550	3.6
All bananas	43	29	—[d]	—
rapaima	50	33	—	—
others	36	24	—	—

[a]Based on 765 bunches per acre over a two-year period. See table 9.
[b]Adjusted successively to indicate what yield would be if the 765 bunches were all kinds of plantains, only *cowata*, and all kinds except *cowata*.
[c]U.S. short tons.
[d]Bananas are insignificant on an acreage basis.

In addition to the volume of production, the energy-generating capacity of their staple crops is also of critical importance to a horticultural people. In table 11, a comparison of the caloric yield per acre of Yanoama *cowata* with a staple like manioc reveals that the former is clearly competitive. However, in calculating and comparing nutritional yields per acre, serious problems are encountered; and this tabulation must be seen merely as one of estimates. A major problem lies in the fact that most data are presented in terms of annual yields. Among many tropical forest cultures, this annual basis of calculation is logical because the practice of replanting is commonplace, even though gathering of manioc might not even begin until two years after planting.[105] Where bananas are produced on plantations, there is a pronounced annual rhythm. However, the Barafiri horticultural system is not geared that way. The highland Yanoama seldom replant as they gather their garden produce. Occasionally a man clears and replants a segment of his garden, and sometimes the tuberous roots of cultivars sprout spontaneously, but these instances are very different from the perennial nature of *Musa* (new suckers shoot for years from a single parent stool) or the peach palm.[106] Another problem is establishing how much edible food is left after waste removal. This applies particularly to bitter manioc, which is normally converted (by peeling, grating, squeezing, and toasting) into flour or *cazabe* cake before being eaten, although available published caloric values are for fresh, moist tubers. For example, a pound of freshly dug tubers yields nearly five hundred calories. Yet, fifty to sixty pounds of fresh tubers might convert into only "two large manioc cakes."[107] Thus, even if two cakes weigh several pounds apiece, the edible material is only a small fraction of the gross yield. Finally, there is the problem of establishing the caloric values of tropical staples, since

TABLE 11

Comparative Calorie Yields of Selected Staple Crop Plants

Crop Plant	Annual Yield (pounds/acre)	Gross Yield over 2-Year Period (pounds/acre)	Edible Yield 2-Year Period (pounds/acre)	Calories per Pound[a]	Yield over 2-Year Period (calories/acre in millions)
Cowata plantain	no data	37,500[b]	25,250[c]	500	12.63
Manioc (Cubeo)[d]	12,000	24,000	6,000[e]	495[f]	2.97
Manioc (Kuikuru)[g]	10,000	20,000	5,000[e]	495[f]	2.48
Banana (plantation)[h]	15,500	31,000	20,650	415	8.57

[a]Based on Simmonds (*Bananas*), Miracle (*Maize*), and Ochse (*Tropical Agriculture*).

[b]This calculation is for the intercropped *Musa-ocumo* region. It is based on the assumption that all plantains could be of the *cowata* type (cf. table 9). If the bananas (see table 8) of this region were also *cowata* plantains, the total yield could be nearly 43,500 pounds per acre. This would still exclude the *Xanthosoma* and other minor crops of the region.

[c]See table 10.

[d]Goldman, *Cubeo*, pp. 35, 59, 85. He writes of an annual "acreage yield [of] between five and six tons" (p. 85). In this table the figure used is six short tons.

[e]Manioc flour. Schwerin accepts a yield of one pound of manioc flour for each four pounds of tuberous roots ("Apuntes sobre la Yuca y sus Orígenes," p. 24).

[f]Raw tubers.

[g]Carneiro reports that a garden "produces about 4 or 5 tons of manioc tubers per acre per year." However, perhaps nearly half of the total manioc harvest "is lost to peccaries, and to leaf-cutter ants" ("Cultivation among the Kuikuru," p. 48). The figure used in this table is five short tons, and no deduction is made for losses to pests.

[h]Based on Simmonds (*Bananas*, p. 190) and Ochse et al. (*Tropical Agriculture*, I, 384). In this table a yield of about seven English long tons is used.

published data vary enormously. This is particularly true of the plantains, where the range is at least from 75 calories per 100 grams to 119 calories per 100 grams.[108] An estimate of 110 calories per 100 grams is very conservative, particularly in view of the fact that the Yanoama consume most of their plantains before complete ripening, when starch content is very high. For bananas, a reasonable 91 calories per 100 grams is used in table 11.[109]

Intercropping is an important feature of Yanoama horticulture. Consequently, yields are best appreciated when viewed in the context of garden regions as described above. Table 12 examines the heavily intercropped *Musa-ocumo* region, which occupies roughly two-thirds to three-fourths of the cultivated land in highland gardens. Reliable information is unavailable for acreage yields of Barafiri *Xanthosoma* (see table 7) and minor crops, such as yams, sweet potatoes, gourds, and peach palms, but together these certainly account for significant food production. Of the total caloric yield from just the musaceous plants in this garden region at least half is provided by the *cowata* plantains, while as much as 98 percent may come from all plantains.[110] Over a two-year period, an acre of the *Musa-ocumo* region yields nearly 12 million calories from the *Musa* alone (table 12). If we assume a very generous daily requirement of 2,400 calories per person of any age or body build (equivalent to somewhat over 1.7 million calories in two years), the musaceous plants in a single acre are capable of supplying the annual needs of nearly seven people.[111] If all these musaceous plantings were *cowata* plantains, yields would be even higher (see table 10).

These are broad generalizations, of course, and corroboration de-

TABLE 12

Edible Yields of Musa *When Intercropped*[a]
(Calories per Acre over a Two-Year Period)

Type of Musa	Estimated Yield in Edible Pounds per Acre	Calories per Pound	Calories per Acre (in millions)
Cowata plantain	14,900	500	7.45
Other plantains	5,900[b]	500	2.95
All bananas	3,500[c]	415	1.45
Total			11.85

[a]Excluding *Xanthosoma*, yams, sweet potatoes, gourds, and peach palms, which are intercropped with them.
[b]Based on 19 pounds per bunch.
[c]Based on 29 pounds per bunch.

pends upon detailed research in Yanoama nutrition. Under no circumstances other than feasting, for example, are young people and women ever likely to consume 2,400 calories a day. The great bulk of calories produced by Barafiri horticulture is in the form of carbohydrates, which do not by themselves constitute a balanced diet.[112] However, collecting and hunting relieve the gardens from full responsibility for sustaining these people. Their virtual rejection of available cultivars, such as peppers, tomatoes, beans, squash, and maize, effectively deprives the highland Barafiri of significant potential sources of vitamins and proteins.

Manioc is notoriously rich in carbohydrates, although most research has dealt with the poisonous, "bitter" varieties rather than the "sweet" varieties the highland Barafiri cultivate. The processing of bitter manioc into palatable flour or cakes by tropical forest peoples generally involves an enormous weight loss, whereas the Barafiri method of roasting manioc tubers on embers involves a loss only slightly greater than the skin itself. Among the *Musa*, plantains have considerably more calories than do bananas, or even white potatoes, since they are relatively dry and consequently higher in percentage of carbohydrate content (see table 13). Likewise, unripe plantains and bananas are more starchy than are ripe fruits. Plantains in particular retain this quality "until a very advanced stage of ripeness."[113] It is precisely in this unripe stage that the bulk of their plantains are cooked and consumed by the Yanoama. The cooked, unripe banana is "closely comparable with the potato" nutritionally.[114] What is more, plantains are reported to be good sources of ascorbic acid (vitamin C).[115] Nevertheless, like manioc, plantains are particularly poor in proteins and fats and thus similar to other aboriginal American agricultural staples.

Abandonment of the Garden Clearing

The territory of the highland Yanoama is replete with old garden sites.[116] On the trail far from any *shabono*, for example, specific tracts of the forest are frequently identified by the Barafiri as being *suwabada taca*. This term translates literally as "old woman clearing," and is the generic term for all old gardens, no matter how long it might have been since they were abandoned.[117] Conceptually, such a clearing is distinct from a garden clearing in production and from a *dude taca* ("new clearing" or "young clearing"). Unlike the new or producing garden clearings, however, the "old garden" category spans a time period that can be calculated in decades. This means that some clearings date from past generations, while others might be only a year beyond the phase of full

production. Some *suwabada taca* are isolated in places remote from contemporary gardens and *shabono*, while others are juxtaposed with new and
producing garden clearings so that all coalesce into areas covering tens of
acres. Like the new and the producing clearings, each old garden clearing
has a proper name, which it retains through the years.[118] Each also belongs to the men who made it, in that they (or their kinsmen and descendants, as surrogates) have full rights to the plants there.

The abandonment of a garden is a gradual process that normally
takes many years to accomplish. As such, it is distinctive from the abandonment of fields by cultures that sow them in annuals. We have already
seen the difficulty of ascribing labels—such as "new," "producing," or
"old"—to garden clearings. Even when a new clearing is being made, a
strip of waste or abandoned land is sometimes evident. Or, after an early
harvest of manioc, parts of a producing garden are, in effect, aban-

TABLE 13

Nutritional Values of Selected Crops (Percentage of Content)

Item	Bananas[a]	Bananas[b]	Bananas and Plantains[c]	Manioc[d]	White Potato[e]	Peach Palm[f]
Water	75.3	75.0	70.0	64.1	78.0	48.8
Carbohydrates	22.0	20.0	27.0	32.5	19.0	40.9
Protein	1.3	1.2	1.2	1.2	2.0	2.8
Fats (oils)	0.6	0.2	0.3	0.2	0.1	6.7
Ash	0.8	0.8	0.9	0.8	1.0	0.8

[a] Ochse et al., *Tropical Agriculture*, I, 697 (copied from Popenoe and Jiménez).
[b] Ibid., p. 638 (taken from Chatfield and McLaughlin).
[c] Simmonds, *Bananas*, p. 257 (taken from Chatfield, Watt, and Merrill).
[d] Milton de Albuquerque, *A mandioca na Amazônia*, p. 121.
[e] Simmonds, *Bananas*, p. 257 (taken from Chatfield, Watt, and Merrill).
[f] Ochse et al., *Tropical Agriculture*, I, 697 (copied from Popenoe and Jiménez).

doned. Similarly, crop plants, such as plantains and peach palms, continue to yield years after a garden clearing has been abandoned in the
broad sense. Almost with its creation, the invasion of a garden clearing
by unwanted vegetation begins. Quickly some of the hardy tree stumps
sprout, and grasses (including certain large *Guadua*) move in. More gradually, creepers, epiphytes, bushes, and trees begin their takeover. Within only a few years a thick jungle is formed. After two or three years of
regular gathering of garden produce, maintenance of the clearing has
practically ceased, and visits to the garden become less and less frequent.
The principal reason to abandon a garden clearing seems to be this in-

Plate 21. Gathering plantains in Jocotoibue-taca, one of many old gardens on the southern slopes of Shokekere Mountain. The man (with a large wad of tobacco in his mouth) holds plantains picked from a small bunch ripening on the plant behind him. In the old garden, which was cleared about 1963, more than one hundred musaceous plants (mostly *cowata*) are still producing pseudostems and bunches of fruit from the original stock. The place is a veritable thicket of regrowth; in addition to the plantains, there are some peach palms and even a few gourds and sweet potatoes.

vasion by plants that choke out and shade the crop plants. It is obvious to the Yanoama that more effort is needed to combat these developments than to make a new clearing. Loss of soil fertility is not evident as a motivation for the Parima Barafiri to abandon their gardens.

Nevertheless, the old gardens are of considerable economic importance, even if their contributions cannot be calculated with precision. For example, they supply many of the suckers for the propagation of *Musa* in new gardens. More important, the *suwabada taca* provide significant quantities of vegetable foods. These are obtained directly from survivors among the crop plants that were set out and from their progeny. For example, peach palms flourish for decades, and some of the musaceous plants continue to yield bunches of fruit for years after abandonment (see plate 21). In the old gardens musaceous plants are not normally tied or propped to protect them from wind damage, nor are competing suckers systematically thinned out. Nevertheless, I have seen a sixty-pound bunch of *rapaima* bananas picked from one of the Jorocoba-teri abandoned gardens.[119] Musaceous plants are characterized by a lengthy life span, and, in theory, they are immortal. The life of commercial banana fields is five to twenty years, but in Uganda "many [banana] fields are thirty years old and fifty to sixty years is not an uncommon figure."[120]

These *suwabada taca* of the Parima highlands are the "old *roças*" of the southern Yanoama, the long-abandoned gardens in forests presently uninhabited, where *bixa* (*urucú*), *ocumo* ("potatoes"), peach palm (*pupunha*), cotton, arrow-shaft cane, and "many bananas of different kinds" are to be gathered.[121] The food supply is so abundant in some of the old Yanoama gardens, in both highlands and lowlands, that groups will camp in them during extended periods, gathering ripening fruits as well as various raw materials. Food is also provided by certain plant volunteers in the secondary forest. One of the most important of these, the *kafu*, bears fruit that is greatly prized in season. This highland *Cecropia* grows very rapidly and appears as the dominant tree in the early phase of forest reestablishment.[122] The tender shoots of young needle leaf palms are also eaten, usually raw. The old gardens, with their thick cover of low vegetation and browse, as well as a residue of food plants, are attractive to game animal populations. Thus, they tend to be relatively productive hunting grounds for birds, monkeys, agouti, and even deer, peccary, or tapir.[123]

Until a growth of tall trees has returned, an old garden is not suitable for reuse, since it does not have the *ishabena* qualities that would make it attractive to Barafiri farmers. There are no reliable data on the time interval required for gardens of the Parima highlands, or of the adjacent lowlands for that matter, to be converted back into selva ecologically approximating virgin forest of the area.[124]

Chapter 6
Collecting

A N enormous variety of things is collected by the Yanoama from their large and variegated habitat. It is impossible to enumerate all of these items, but it is possible to provide an idea of their diversity and the scope of collecting as an economic activity.[1] Collecting is an important part of the economy, complementing horticulture and providing many kinds of foods and raw materials. Much of the time, collecting provides tasty additions to garden fare, but when gardens are not yielding sufficiently, it can temporarily become a community's major source of sustenance. No religious rituals are known to accompany this activity, which is highly secularized and open to all members of a community. Women are excellent foragers, but they are not expected to do strenuous tasks, such as climbing or felling trees. All but the very young are constantly alert to the sights, sounds, and smells around them: the whir of insects in the air, the distant croaking of frogs,[2] the swarming of honey bees, or the smell of blossoms. Normally new foods are eaten only when recommended by someone, although mistakes are made occasionally by children who experiment. Adults try foods new to them only upon recommendation or if they have seen monkeys eat them.[3] All in all, the Yanoama are extremely conservative in their eating habits.

In the forests, ecological niches exploited by collectors range from a few hundred feet above sea level to an upper limit whose elevation has not yet been established. In contrast to the utilization of the forests, two sets of niches available to the Yanoama are traditionally ignored: the major rivers and the open savannas.[4] Of the myriad products of their forests, the palms stand out as particularly important plants; and, among the fauna, insects appear to be of special significance. Most of the effort expended in collecting is for food; obtaining materials such as thatching, resins, and fibers is almost incidental. Yields can be very high: the volume of fruit obtained in season from certain trees is great, and the abundant larvae and pupae of some insects are remarkably nutritious.

The Yanoama are constantly collecting in a casual manner. While on the trail, or at any other part of the waking day away from the *shabono*, they are on the lookout for edible items or other useful materials. But this casual form of collecting is quite insignificant economically. The important collecting is done by groups whose purpose and plan are to collect particular things they expect to be available in certain places at specific times. The group might consist of a few households, a lineage, or possibly an entire *teri* population, and they construct a camp in the forest expressly for the purpose.

It is in this manner that collecting contributes significantly to the community food supply, meshing subtly with horticulture and hunting. All three economic activities are engaged in simultaneously in these encampments, which are frequently made in or adjacent to abandoned gardens. Collecting and gardening are so intimately interrelated because much of what is collected has been provided by the Yanoama themselves through their gardening activities. The peach palms, whose fruits they collect, have invariably been planted. Similarly, plantains, bananas, cotton, papaya, and *bixa* (and possibly avocados) are collected in old gardens or abandoned *shabono* sites where they were planted or have sprouted from refuse heaps. The fruits of such volunteer trees as the *kafu* are also highly appreciated. And, a variety of insects and game animals are attracted to these old gardens.[5]

Except during wartime, people return to these old gardens—their *suwabada taca*—year after year,[6] each time building a new camp near the previous ones. They will remain there for many weeks if the supply of food is sufficient to warrant it. Daily, small groups will fan out into the high forest, collecting wild species, or hunting, as they go. It is commonplace for groups to camp near new garden clearings they are preparing in the forest. In this way, men can spend part of their time hunting, they can work in their gardens, and they can do some collecting, while women and children forage and rest. Their diet during these periods is often a mixture of collected foods, game, and garden produce (particularly plantains, but also *ocumo*) carried in from producing gardens or gathered from old gardens. When the general area has been gleaned and the garden tasks completed, the group may move on to make camp elsewhere before returning to their *shabono*.

Except for some fresh fruit, foods are not generally consumed where collected. Instead, quantities of foods, such as honey, tadpoles, and tree fruits, are carried in baskets back to the camp or the *shabono*, even if they are to be eaten raw. Most things, however, are taken back to the hearth fire for cooking. Certain items, such as small birds, frogs, and little fish, are prepared where they are obtained. They are gutted, sometimes the heads are twisted off, the feathers or fins pulled off, and perhaps they are even skinned. Then the remains are wrapped neatly in packages made of green leaves and secured with lianas or fibers. Considerable agility is shown by the men and boys who climb trees to obtain fruits, insects, eggs, and the young of birds, although occasionally someone is seriously injured in a fall. Women, and the children who are their apprentices, have keenly honed senses when it comes to ferreting out all manner of food sources.

Few tools are used in collecting. Except for sharpened digging sticks, about the only special tools are the machete (a relatively recent introduction) and the traditional *jawa*, a kind of tomahawk (see fig. 7). Formerly the *jawa* blade might have been a worked-stone celt, but now it is a piece of machete hafted to a handle in the ancient manner. The *jawa* is used for various tasks, but its principal utility is for cutting out honeycombs from tree trunks. Another specialized tool is an ingenious X-shaped device of short poles lashed together (see plate 22). With a pair of these, a man can climb the spiny trunks of tall peach palms to obtain their fruits.

Palms as Food Sources

The individual Yanoama uses a far greater variety of plant species as food than does a "modern" man,[7] and each variety may be consumed in great quantities at the time it is available. Among these vegetable foods that are collected, the autochthonous palms are particularly important.[8] Evidently, palms are among those species that benefit ecologically from Yanoama activities. For one thing, when the forest is cleared for gardens or campsites, palms that are food sources are protected in preference to many other trees. Palms also have an added advantage because they are relatively resistant to damage from the fires set to clear new gardens or to remove tall savanna grasses. One—the peach palm—is planted, principally in garden clearings. Others, like the *seje*, can be seen thriving wild in the dim light of the forest.

Among the various palms, at least two species are used for their tender

Plate 22. A demonstration of how to climb a peach palm tree with a pair of X-shaped platforms. Once these devices have been tied in place at the base of the tree trunk, one is pushed up and the climber stands on it. He then pulls up the other one, standing on it while he pushes up the first one. In this manner he can climb to the clusters of fruit without damaging the tree or injuring himself on the sharp spines of the trunk.

leaf sprouts. The crisp shoots of the needle leaf palm (*bisha* in the Bara-firi dialect) are simply snapped off with the fingers and eaten raw. This palm volunteers in Parima gardens to the point of being a weed. The *palmito*, or *manaca* (*Euterpe oleracea* Mart.), provides much larger leaf shoots. These raw "palm hearts" are widely eaten among peoples of tropical South America (Indians, Creoles, and immigrants), including the Yanoama.[9]

The drupe is the part of the palm generally eaten—the size, flavor, texture, and nutritional value varying greatly among the different species. Usually the layer enclosing each individual seed, or nut, is the part consumed.

The most eagerly sought after fruit is that of the spiny-trunked peach palm (*Guilielma gasipaes* H.B.K.; Bailey), or *rasha*. The Yanoama find its fruit delicious and the yields excellent. This is the palm they plant and the only one consistently considered privately owned. In the highlands, small amounts of fruit are available from January through March. In addition, numerous other palms are presently identifiable, whose edible fruits are also collected. The *albarico* (*Bactris setulosa* Karst.)[10] produces fruits with an edible, gelatinous layer between a hairy outer cover (the epicarp) and a large seed. Two other palms with edible fruits, both popularly called *corozo* in Venezuela, are reported for the area.[11] These are *Aiphanes caryotifolia* (H.B.K.; Wendl.) and *Acrocomia sclerocarpa* (Mart.), with the former preferring considerably higher elevations than the latter. The *cucurito* (*Maximiliana regia* Mart.), one of the tallest of tropical American palms, also yields an attractive, edible fruit.

Two other palms are distinctive for the oily nature of their fruits. The *coroba*, or *yagua* (*Jessenia polycarpa* Karst.), provides an especially oily fleshy layer over each nut. Related to it is the *seje* (*Jessenia bataua* Mart.; Burret.), whose nuts are also covered with a tasty oily flesh. A mature *seje* palm probably yields even more fruits per tree than a peach palm, but a far smaller proportion of each drupe is edible.

The term *moriche* is used popularly in Venezuela to refer to at least three different palms of the upper Orinoco area, all of them of the genus *Mauritia*.[12] Each fruit yields a small amount of nutritive tissue in a thin fibrous layer enclosing its large seed. Other palm fruits, or drupes, collected for their edible portions come from the piassaba (*Leopoldinia piassaba* Wallace; also known as *titía* or chiquichique) and the *cumare* (*Astrocaryum vulgare* Mart.), a palm with a spine-covered trunk, spiny leaf stalks, spiny rachis (stalks), spiny peduncles, and spiny bracts. The eating of nuts from "wild coconut palms" has also been reported among the southern Yanoama.[13] In addition to the palms identified above, for which there is sound evidence of usage as food, it is likely that edible portions of numerous others also figure in the Barafiri diet.[14]

In addition to the palms, other kinds of trees also supply food for the Yanoama diet. Unfortunately, very few of these have been botanically identified, and the Barafiri name is not even available for many of them. In the case of some species, the edible fruits are used, while in other cases it is the seed, or nut, which is eaten. In certain instances, both are used. Flower parts are evidently consumed also. Leaves, stems, and roots have little dietetic utility, even as vegetables.

The fruits of wild guavas (*Psidium* sp.), called *wamorema* in the Barafiri dialect, and certain close relatives are collected. *Guamo* (*Inga* sp.) fruit is also reported.[15] In addition, there are the cherrylike fruits of the *ushi ushi* (a Barafiri term) and the fruits of the *ashowa*, which resemble oxheart cherries.[16] In the case of the latter, the large seed within each fruit is also edible when toasted. Men and boys take baskets up into the *ashowa* trees to collect quantities of this tasty fruit when it is in season.

Another favorite of the Barafiri is the fruit of the fast-growing *kafu* tree, an early volunteer in abandoned garden clearings and an abundant species in parts of the Parima highlands.[17] The fruits have a flavor not unlike ripe figs, but otherwise they are unique. Each consists of a cluster of stems (usually four) approximately twelve inches long, hanging from a common stalk. The stems are covered with a thick layer of gelatinous material containing countless tiny seeds.

A disclike fruit, called *wabu*, is collected in its preferred habitat of the lowlands. *Wabu* is poisonous and must be soaked and cooked before being eaten. The literature on the Yanoama contains numerous references to another fruit poisonous to humans, which is variously called *momo* or *mumu*.[18] The fruits of this particular *Hevea* resemble nuts, since they are encased in hard shells.[19] Both *wabu* and *momo* are distinct from the guavas, *ushi ushi, ashowa*, and *kafu*, all of which can be consumed raw.

Another remarkable food, at least in the Parima highlands of Venezuela, is the *waiore* (in Barafiri). This consists of what appear to be highly perfumed, sweet-flavored parts of flowers.[20] Large clusters of *waiore* are obtained by cutting whole branches from a tree whose leaves and general shape resemble those of the magnolia. Older trees show signs of having been systematically pruned for years in the harvesting of their flowers. Great quantities of *waiore* are consumed when it is available in January or thereabouts.

At least two varieties of cacao (*Theobroma* sp.) are to be found growing wild, sometimes in what might be described as groves. The pods (fruits) are collected, and their sweet flesh sucked or chewed, although not with any particular enthusiasm. Evidently the cacao beans (seeds) serve no purpose.[21]

There are few tree species, apart from the palms, that provide the Yanoama with edible nuts. One of these is the Brazil nut (*Bertholletia excelsa* H.B.K.), whose fruit consists of a large pyxidium that contains fifteen to twenty-five edible seeds. Another is the cashew (*Anacardium occidentale* L.). The small cashew nut, or seed, of each fruit is of no use to the Yanoama, but large amounts of the juicy, sweet-sour cashew fruits are collected in season and eaten raw.[22] Neither of these species is found above 3,000 feet, but both are widely distributed throughout the lowland forests.[23]

Other Plants as Food Sources

A great variety of other plant foods is also collected. On the sunny, well-drained forest-savanna margins, there are wild pineapples (possibly *Ananas ananassiodes*) with a strong astringent flavor. Of the various passifloraceous plants in the Yanoama territory, some produce edible fruits.[24] The fleshy roots of certain wild plants are dug up and roasted. Seeds and mucus from the *Heliconia* inflorescence are also eaten, generally by old men and women. And at least four different kinds of fungi are consumed,[25] particularly certain mushrooms.

Insects as Food Sources

Entomophagy, the eating of insects, is a well-developed Yanoama culture trait. Insect food sources range from large caterpillars to the minute lice parasitic to humans. Certain insect products, such as honey and honeycombs, are also eaten. Among insects that metamorphose, all the stages in the life cycle are represented in the diet: eggs, larvae, pupae, and adults. Insect foods are more important to the Barafiri than some other Yanoama groups, but even they do not use more than a fraction of the many hundreds of insect species in their habitat.[26] Specifically, wide berth is given the big stinging ant called *veinte cuatro*[27] in Venezuelan vernacular. Chigoes (*Tunga penetrans*) are also avoided, as are those poisonous insects deemed useless as food. For the Barafiri "real" foods are garden produce and meat from the hunt, and there is no satisfactory substitute for these. Yet, relatively little animal flesh is eaten, except during ceremonial feasting. In their daily diet, the carbohydrates (provided principally by plantains and such root crops as *ocumo*) are predominant. Consequently, from a nutritional viewpoint, insect foods constitute an important segment of the diet.[28]

Controlled chemical analyses have demonstrated the benefits of honey

Body Components of Selected Insect Food Sources (Compared with Beef)[a]

Insect	Stage	Condition	Moisture	Fats	Proteins
Termite[b]	adult	living	44.5	28.3	23.2
Grasshopper (*Nomadacris septemfasciata*)	adult	fresh	70.6	4.1	18.7
Locust (*Locusta migratoroides*)	adult	fresh	10.5	9.6[d]	46.1[d]
Caterpillar[b]	larva	smoked	15.7	13.7	—
Silkworm[e]	pupa	fresh	60.7	14.2	23.1
Beef (from Dakar area)	—	fresh?	75.2	6.6	16.9

[a]Compiled from Bodenheimer, *Insects as Human Food*, pp. 30–32.
[b]Unidentified West African species.
[c]No specific information provided.
[d]These figures are also given for *Nomadacris*. Cf. Bodenheimer, p. 33.
[e]Unidentified species.

Components (in percent)

Carbohydrates	Minerals	Chitin; Fiber	Ash	Calories (per 100 grams)
—c	—	—	—	347
—	—	4.0	—	—
—	—	12.5	5.0	—
13.9	—	13.5	40.0	258 (digestible)
—	1.5	—	—	207
—	—	—	1.3	127

to the human organism, and they have permitted identification and measurement of the vitamins, fats, minerals (or mineral salts), and proteins to be found in insect food sources. In table 14 some of these data are presented. Clearly, certain insects provide good yields of protein and fats, compared with beef, for example. The analysis of ashes from swarming adult termites, obtained in the African Congo area, shows termites to be "rich in phosphates and potash."[29] Unfortunately, few such specific data are available for tropical American insect species, although basic similarities are presumed to exist between them and the African counterparts for which information is available.

Insect eggs are rarely eaten separately although egg masses are consumed with the adult insect bodies containing them. For example, the adult *bachaco culón*[30] is an ant that is particularly attractive as food, and the swollen, egg-filled abdomens of the females are bitten off, roasted, and eaten. Bee eggs, too, are consumed, along with honey and other matter removed from their hives.

Far more important to the diet are insect larvae, which are nearly always roasted before being eaten. Observers have referred specifically to the "fat larvae" which live in the peach palm and the *bobei*, or *bacaba*, palm (*Oenocarpus bacaba* Mart.) and "are good to eat,"[31] as well as to the eating of a variety of other palmworms particularly common in rotting wood. Termite larvae are a favorite snack and easy to prepare, and the "white larvae of ants" are reported to be "an integral part of the Waika diet."[32] Various kinds of caterpillars are roasted,[33] and the grubs of certain beetles, which resemble "worms," are also consumed. The maggots of at least one type of wasp are presumably available as food "all over Guiana."[34]

The Barafiri apparently concern themselves with few insect species in the pupal state, although one of their favorite insect foods consists of pupae they call *kasha*.[35] The edible portion of each *kasha* is the oily material, of a pasty consistency, contained within a large cocoon up to an inch in length. The individual cocoons are attached to one another in what approximate parallel rows, forming sheets covering up to several square feet, but only one cocoon thick. Over the entire mass is a thin, paperlike layer. These sheets of *kasha* are to be found attached to tree trunks and need only be peeled off by the fortunate person who discovers them. Pieces of the sheet are roasted over hot embers before breaking open the cocoons to eat the contents.

The most widely collected adult insects are probably ants and termites.[36] Sometimes they are taken from their nests, but the large winged ants and termites are most eagerly collected when they swarm on brief "nuptial flights." These are the "sexuals," the queens and drones, whose swollen abdomens—particularly those of the females—are described as being rich in fats and proteins, "in contrast to the much poorer body composition of the neutral castes."[37] When a swarm is observed, the news is spread rapidly by both adults and children. These large insects, clumsy in flight, are quickly collected by the hundreds. Their heads and winged thoraxes are detached at once, and the fat abdomens may be eaten on the spot. Usually, however, they are roasted before being consumed.

It is not unusual for Barafiri to ingest raw the adult mosquitoes, fleas, and lice that they kill on their own bodies or the bodies of close relatives.[38] This is an aspect of personal grooming, however, and these insects constitute a negligible part of the diet.

Insect Products as Food

Honey is a favorite Yanoama food. It was the only concentrated sweet available prior to the introduction of cane sugar products, such as candy. The Barafiri call it *buu*—a word they also use for sugar cane and candy. A wide variety of honey is collected, with differing viscosities, aromas, flavors, and tints, depending upon the source. Most honey seems to be obtained from beehives, although wasps also produce some.[39] Certain types are removed from underground hives, or nests, while others are obtained by cutting into tree trunks with the tomahawklike *jawa*.[40] The amounts of honey taken each time range from a mere handful up to several quarts.

Honey is a nutritious and stimulating food, rich in those sugars (such as dextrose, levulose, and sucrose) that release energy in man. "There is perhaps no other food, excluding stimulating drugs, comparable to honey for the prevention of fatigue or for the restoration of strength after thorough physical exhaustion."[41] Apart from the nutritive value of honey itself, the Yanoama manner of eating it is also important nutritionally. Their custom is to consume honey together with the wax combs, the adult bees, eggs, maggots, pupae, and pollen that might be in the hive. The mixture is often a runny paste, studded with bees in varying stages of the metamorphic process. Except for the wax, these added ingredients are also nourishing. The maggots and pollen are particularly valuable sources of protein, and the pollen also has a high concentration of vitamins.[42]

The Yanoama are like other aboriginals of the South American tropical forests in their love of honey. There is no evidence, however, of any attempts to control the swarming of honey-producing insects or to provide hives for them. The only other edible insect products for which there are data are essentially inorganic structures built by ants and termites. These are variously reported as being clay from dried termite nests, or the tunnels built of mud by ants.[43]

Other Foods Collected

Insects are complemented in the diet by a variety of other arthropods. One of the most consistent references (perhaps because it so shocks writers) is to a particular arachnid, the large hairy spider known popularly in Venezuela as *araña mona*.[44] The bite of this creature is poisonous, and even its hairs can cause pain to the touch, but the white flesh is eaten after roasting the spider whole.[45]

Different crustaceans, including crabs and crawfish,[46] are collected, as are mollusks, such as clams and snails. Some vertebrates are similarly collected for food. These include reptiles, such as lizards, turtles, and snakes,[47] in addition to small alligators of the type called *baba* (*Caiman sclerops*) in Venezuelan vernacular.[48] Reptile eggs are eaten when found. For the larger specimens, weapons are used in making the kill, and in some instances the definition of "collecting" is strained. For example, it is difficult to distinguish between "hunting" a creature like a huge land turtle and "collecting" it. Among the amphibians, frogs and tadpoles are much appreciated. Salamanders and certain toads are eaten, and so are small fishes and eels.[49] Large birds are hunted with bows and arrows, but their young and their eggs—and those of small birds as well—are simply removed from the nests later to be consumed.[50] Most of the food from mammalian sources is obtained by hunting.[51]

The practice of collecting and eating certain natural clays, geophagy, is not unusual. Evidently, the preferred clays are very fine in texture, normally made available by the sorting and depositional actions of running water. Only if such a clay is free of sand and other foreign matter is it considered to be "clean."[52]

Useful Materials Collected

An array of useful materials is collected by the Yanoama for a wide range of purposes other than dietary. These materials are more impressive for their variety than for their volume in most instances. This particular facet of collecting involves plants and plant materials almost exclusively.

Among the plants, the broadleaf evergreen trees furnish much of what is needed. As the source of firewood, they are indispensable, since, in terms of bulk, this is by far the most important material collected.

Plate 23. Juwafusibuwei-teri woman moving through a new garden with a load of firewood. She is about eight months pregnant yet manages this load weighing more than seventy pounds. It is cut to the right lengths for use at her hearth. The ax she used is also stuck into her strong and versatile *wuu* basket.

It is every woman's responsibility to provide the fuel to keep her hearth fire fed, and to accomplish this she cuts firewood every two or three days, if not daily. Sometimes dead trees of the forest are used, but it is far more common for women to cut from the trees felled in the preparation of their family gardens.[53] Cutting firewood requires that a woman wield an ax, since she must sometimes cut up branches and trunks more than a foot in diameter and then split them. Small pieces of kindling are not important to her. When there is enough dead wood to work with, a woman can cut and pack a load in half an hour or so. In the Parima highlands, this job is generally done in the afternoon; daily, sometime before sunset, the last little group of women can be seen trudging in a column along one of the paths to the *shabono* with their loads of firewood. Invariably the wood is packed neatly into their big carrying baskets (*wuu*), the loads ranging from as little as forty pounds to as much as seventy pounds or more (see plate 23). This is independent of the weight of the small children or other burdens a woman also might have in her arms. So little firewood is stored that even in rainy weather this work must continue.

The poles for constructing *shabono* and camp shelters are cut from trees locally available. Wood from the cacao tree is, by tradition, the only kind acceptable for fire-making devices. Other trees provide the bark from which large canoe-shaped containers are sometimes fashioned to hold enormous quantities of mashed plantains and water for a funerary *reajo*. Bark envelopes serve as storage containers for precious feathers, and lowland Yanoama have even used large pieces of thick bark as rafts on which to float down the Río Orinoco.[54] The inner bark, or bast, of certain trees of the linden family[55] is carefully peeled off for various uses. For example, utilitarian hammocks are quickly made from several bast strips one to three inches wide and perhaps five feet long. The strips are tied together at each end with twisted fibers, and the new hammock is ready to be hung up for use (see plate 9). Bast strips also serve as tumplines attached to carrying baskets and other heavy loads (see plates 23 and 24) and as shoulder straps for carrying small children.

Trees provide some of the more important hallucinogenic drugs used by Yanoama men. These drugs belong to a group of strong substances that are taken nasally and are known collectively as *ebena* by the Barafiri. Certain hallucinogenic snuffs are derived from the bark resins of various trees of the genus *Virola*,[56] which are very carefully dried and pulverized. To these resins are sometimes added powdered bark ashes or even powdered leaves,[57] individual men having their own secret formulas for those combinations deemed to produce the most powerful *ebena*. Other snuffs are prepared by toasting and pulverizing beans (seeds) collected from leguminous trees of the genus *Anadenanthera* (*Piptadenia*), such as *A. Peregrina*, to which are often added powdered alkaline

Plate 24. Niyayoba woman returning home after an absence during which she and others visited a distant *shabono* and did some collecting, as well. She carries both of her youngest children and most of her worldly possessions. Behind her is a third child. The load is bulky and cumbersome—palm leaves for roofing repairs, water gourds, assorted baskets, and some food—but not particularly heavy for a Yanoama woman.

substances, such as ashes.[58] These trees, similar to some of the mimosas, are found commonly in arid and semiarid regions of Venezuela and northern Brazil. In the relatively cool, humid Parima highlands, few specimens are evident. It is possible that there is also periodic use of hallucinogenic substances obtained from certain species of *Banisteriopsis*, such as *Banisteria argentea* ([H.B.K.] Spreng.),[59] a woody creeper known as *rejo tieso* in Venezuela. Evidently, nearly all of these materials used to prepare hallucinogens are collected from wild sources, although there are reports of the cultivation of *Anadenanthera* (*Piptadenia*).[60] Some *teri* do not have available in their own territories the resources for preparing all the different kinds of *ebena*, but they can obtain high-grade snuffs through gift exchange or trade with other groups.

A variety of other trees provide useful exudations. For example, at least one species is slashed to induce it to bleed an "oil," which is then collected and mixed with *bixa* coloring in the preparation of decorative unguents. Among the numerous gums that are utilized as adhesives are balata, or *pendare* (obtained from *Manilkara* sp., huge ceibalike trees), *paramán* (*Symphonia globulifera* L.), and latex from various rubber trees (*Hevea* sp.). At least one aromatic resin, collected after it has solidified, is highly combustible and valued as an aid in starting fires under adverse conditions.[61]

Numerous important materials are obtained from the versatile palms. Fronds from the needle-leaf palm, the *yagua*, and the *moriche* are used for thatching roofs; the *moriche* is preferred for this purpose. Wood from the strong, pliant trunks of young peach palms is highly esteemed. Selected pieces are worked into the long Yanoama bows,[62] into *nabrushi* clubs for formalized dueling, and into a special type of arrow point designed for hunting monkeys. Handles for *jawa* are usually made of palmwood, too. Immature leaves from the assai palm (*Euterpe* sp.) are collected for use in feminine adornment. Women wear bunches of these delicate leaflets, along with fresh flowers or aromatic leaves, in their ear-lobe perforations (see plate 5) or attached to arm bands. Coarse fibers are sometimes obtained from the piassaba palm for use as cordage.

Lianas, particularly certain tough, slender, lowland varieties, are collected to be made into sturdy utilitarian baskets.[63] A traditional type of hammock is also made from lengths of liana that have been peeled and split. The technique is the same as that used for the bast strip hammock, but a vine hammock is much more durable and considerably more comfortable.[64] Lianas and fibers from lianas fill a variety of other needs for cordage. Poisons, usually identified as curare, are obtained from various climbing shrubs of the genus *Strychnos*.[65] Men prepare the poison by a process consisting of the "roasting and percolation of barks and roots."[66] While still fresh, the liquid is gently smeared on their peach palm arrowheads.

Herbaceous plants are also useful to the Yanoama in many ways. Aromatic and colored grasses are collected by women for personal decorations, while still other grasses have medicinal functions. Certain leaves of grass with a texture like sandpaper are used by men for the final smoothing of their bows. Other leaves, obtained from a cane plant, have such sharp edges that they are used by the Yanoama to shave their heads and even to cut the umbilical cord at birth.[67] Another herbaceous species of tall grass reportedly yields fibers used in basketry.[68] The enormous leaves of "wild bananas" (*Heliconia* sp.) are freely collected for use as wrapping material and for roofing temporary shelters. At least two bromeliaceous plants yield fine, strong fibers that are skillfully twisted to make bowstrings and are also used for tying together the different parts of arrows. Some of the finest of these fibers, blended with other kinds,[69] are woven together into what appear to be the only true textiles produced in the Yanoama culture: the narrow shoulder strap used by some women when carrying their babies and a type of arm band. Bamboolike plants are another important herbaceous group. Collectively these are popularly referred to in the Venezuelan vernacular as *guasdua*, or *guadua*.[70] Some varieties have such large woody culms, or stems, that a single segment serves a man nicely as a container for extra arrowheads or for his valuable feathers. From the culms of certain others, men cut arrowheads. Hunters prefer heads that will shatter on impact into many slivers, and they carefully select the canes, since among them there is considerable variation in this tendency to shatter. The Barafiri maintain that the best points are obtained from plants that grow at great elevations, that is, above 3,500 feet.

There is very little collection of animals or animal products for purposes other than dietary. Certain wasp and termite nests are so combustible (after removal of the edible insects themselves) that they are used as an aid in starting fires.[71] It is also reported that at least some Yanoama use insects to clean out their ears.[72] A single larva is put into the bothersome ear. Slowly it moves inside toward the tympanic membrane, consuming cerumen as it goes. When filled, it crawls toward the external ear, where it is removed. In serious cases, a person might use two or three of these larvae in succession.

It is obvious that the contemporary Barafiri have no real use for the few mineral resources they once collected. This change is due to acculturation, limited as that might be locally. Clay is no longer needed, since the practice of making their fragile, cuneiform pots has practically disappeared with the advent of metal containers. Stone celts, for *jawa* and hatchets, are useless in comparison with machetes and axes of steel and most of them have been thrown away. Thus, those sites where a man could obtain the blanks that he shaped and polished into celts hold no significance today.

Chapter 7

Hunting

H UNTING is a prestigious and honorable activity. It involves the chase of wild animals by men armed for the purpose of killing them. This is strictly a masculine pursuit, indispensable to the Yanoama life style.[1] All Yanoama are very fond of eating fresh meat, the flesh of animals being a "real" food, like plantains. Their language even has a special term for "meat hunger" as opposed to the word for "hunger" in general. Yet, economically, hunting is entirely subordinated to both horticulture and collecting.[2] It is not unusual for days on end to pass during which no men from a *shabono* are hunting, or when little or no meat is being eaten.

In his daily routine, of course, when a man enters the forest for some reason, he is ever alert to the sights, sounds, and aromas around him. He is always on the lookout for the fresh tracks of forest creatures, their calls, their droppings, or any other sign of their presence. Even a boy old enough to have a functional "toy" bow and arrows is attentive to the possibility of bagging something to satisfy his "meat hunger." Only after he has hunted successfully has he proven his maturity. Any time someone —man, woman, or child—reports having heard or seen signs of game nearby, at least a few men will grab their weapons and be off in pursuit. Brief hunting trips, of a day or so, are sometimes scheduled quite casually by small groups of kinsmen, particularly if they have reason to believe game is in the vicinity of the settlement. They might even go after a specific animal, referring to it by name. These brief hunts provide little more than occasional meat for individual households. The *reajo* ceremonials create the principal demands for meat, and for these feasts fresh meat must be available in respectable—if not imposing—quantities for the hosts and their guests. Hunting parties are expressly constituted for the purpose of meeting these needs for fresh meat.[3]

The Hunting Party

A hunting party might be as small as three or four men or include dozens. However, when a large party leaves together from the *shabono*, they break up into much smaller groups once they get into the hunting grounds and begin to track game. Hunters leave soon after daybreak to use the light of day. Sometimes they follow a circuit that might cover more than fifty miles in five days or so, particularly if their luck is poor and they keep moving with the hope of finding adequate game. Such a long hunting trip normally takes men into remote, uninhabited areas far from any *shabono*, where game is relatively abundant.

On an extended trip, hunters travel light, making their hammocks each night from bast fibers or lianas, just as they build new fires and construct new shelters at each camp. They do not hunt at night, which reduces their chances to kill nocturnal feeders like the tapir. When their route takes them through old gardens, they can sometimes collect food to supplement the kill. A party returns as soon as they have all the meat they can carry back to the *shabono*. Success seems to be largely dependent upon three variables: (*a*) the kind of game they are after, that is, whether or not they are determined to pass up small game in order to concentrate their efforts on such high-prestige animals as the tapir, (*b*) the number of participants and their individual skills and abilities as hunters, and (*c*) chance.

Hunting Gear

The gear used in hunting, like that for other activities, is meager but adequate and does not vary much over the entire Yanoama culture region. Among the Barafiri, each man's equipment consists of a palmwood bow, three or four good arrows (with the different types of arrowheads appropriate for the game he is after), and a quiver (fitted with a skin cover) in which to carry extra arrowheads. When he leaves for the hunt, a man takes with him this equipment, plus a few plantains or some other food. At least one person in a hunting party is likely to bring along a machete or a *jawa*, and someone usually brings a firedrill or matches. A man's bow is considerably longer than he is tall, often reaching a length of more than

Plate 25. Young Jorocoba-teri men with their bows and arrows. Each holds one long arrow (feathered nock end up) along with his bow. The small boys are here only out of curiosity.

six feet (see plate 25). Arrow lengths vary, depending upon the kind of head with which they are designed to be fitted, although all have similar shafts.[4]

The longest arrows, bearing lanceolate heads, range from seven to eight feet. The heads, fashioned from bamboolike *guadua*, are frequently colored red with *bixa* and sometimes bear symbolic designs of black, wavy lines. This is the preferred type of arrowhead for large game, such as forest browsers shot on the ground or felines shot in trees, and for warfare. It makes a large wound, which bleeds considerably, thus permitting the hunter to trail an animal until it drops or until he can shoot it again. An arrow fitted with this kind of head can even be used as a lance for stabbing at the quarry when there is no time to draw a bow. Nearly as long are other arrows, each fitted with a slender hardwood head to which a worked bone is tied in such a way as to form a barb.[5] The use of these arrows is limited largely to birds and other small game shot in trees. The barbed head is intended to remain in the wound, so that even a large bird cannot fly away easily with a long arrow protruding from it. A third type of arrowhead is fitted to the shortest arrow shafts, although these arrows might also be more than six feet in length. This head consists of a slender piece of peach palm, into which are cut a few ringlike grooves around the circumference. Curare poison is smeared on this type of head, which is used for shooting monkeys—or other animals with prehensile tails—in trees. It is ingeniously designed to break off in the prey, along the grooves, so that the arrow shaft will fall to the ground and save the hunter from climbing high into the trees to retrieve it. As the poison is released into the animal's bloodstream, it quickly eliminates the chance of a death grip of paws and tail, and the dying animal falls from the tree rather than attaching itself there.[6]

In craftsmanship there are no specialists. Each man must make his own bow and arrows as best he can,[7] just as each woman is expected to make her own carrying basket. No spare bows are kept, and often a man has no more arrows than he carries with him. These indispensable objects, like most of the rest of their material culture, are made as needed by those who will use them. A man is inseparable from his bow and arrows, and these, along with his quiver, are things that women do not touch. When men from different *shabono* visit, one of their interests is in comparing and exchanging arrowheads. By the hour, they recline in hammocks or squat around a hearth, fondling the different arrowheads and discussing their merits.

Yanoama bows and arrows have been described as being of "exaggerated length" by one scholar,[8] while another writes that the Yanoama have "empirically discovered the ideal balance between size, shape and weight [of their arrows] in relation to the resilience of the bow and their

own muscle power for optimal flight and impact."[9] In fact, an arrow
in flight can be seen to wobble, and some are so long that, when drawn
on the bow, the points literally droop. On forest trails a man holds his
bow and arrows together, resting on his head or shoulder, the points
facing straight ahead. Even so, it takes skillful maneuvering to keep them
from getting caught in lianas and low-growing vegetation. Positioning
such long arrows within the forest is sometimes difficult, and it is indeed
challenging with only this equipment to hit something like a monkey
moving through the leafy treetops more than one hundred feet above
the ground.

Yanoama hunters are masters of the sounds of their habitat, skillfully
duplicating a host of bird and animal calls. They are also remarkably
persistent. Naked among the plants and insects of the forest, in a chill
rain, they will patiently stalk their quarry for hours or remain virtually
immobile as they watch it, oblivious to all else. Suddenly, they shoot,
and then perhaps give chase to the wounded animal for many miles.

Role of the Dog

The Barafiri keep only one domesticated animal, the dog. The possession
of dogs carries prestige, and the affection that most people feel for their
dogs is very deep. Sometimes, like humans, dogs are even mourned at
death.[10] They are not tied or kept on leashes, but wander about freely.
A dog spends much of its life at its owner's hearth; there it sleeps, drinks
from the family water vessels within its reach, sniffs the ashes for food
remnants, and sometimes receives fondling or petting. It never does
a job like protecting the gardens from predators. Dogs are the con-
stant companions of those few fortunate men in a *teri* who own them,
barking out a warning—or at least snarling—when a stranger comes
near. Even so, they are undependable as watchdogs, sometimes missing
the sounds and smells of strangers approaching the *shabono* itself.

Judgments differ greatly as to whether these animals perform any
really significant functions, apart from their companionship and their
dubious role as watchdogs. On the one hand, the Yanoama dog has
been described as "exceedingly active and a good hunter."[11] Yet, its
utility on the hunt is open to serious doubt, even though the Barafiri
themselves might feel that the dog is almost indispensable.[12] For one
thing, the dogs are undisciplined, sometimes following scents or moving
away from the hunting party as they see fit. Often as not, they are behind
the hunters rather than in front of them, barking from time to time, perhaps scaring the game away. The Yanoama recognize the shortcomings
of their dogs as hunters, and they make serious attempts to improve their

abilities. This does not involve training in the Western sense, with systematic instruction and discipline over long periods of time aimed at influencing the responses of the dogs. Rather, it is done through sorcery. One ceremony, designed to sharpen a dog's senses, consists in having a sorcerer gently toss the dog through different wooden hoops fastened between poles set in the ground and decorated to look like arrows. All the while, the sorcerer utters special incantations.[13]

However, in many cases dogs are simply emaciated, ill-tempered curs, so weak from undernourishment and parasites that they can do little more than keep up with their masters while on the hunt. This is probably a principal explanation for their ineffectiveness as hunters. These pathetic creatures get little or no meat—ever. They subsist as best they can on fruit peelings and the few other scraps of food they can scavenge. They are remarkably docile, except with strangers, rarely attempting to steal food. Although these dogs are free to breed as they will, pups are very few, so that dogs are always in short supply. This undernourished condition may well be the cause of their low level of reproductivity.[14]

Mystical Aspects of the Hunt

Among the various economic activities, hunting is distinctive in being so bound up with mysticism. Men and forest creatures are inseparable spiritually; by taking the lives of animals, hunters are obligated to deal directly with them in the spirit realm. Therefore, prior to a hunting trip the men who will participate make ritualistic preparations. In large part, these consist in communications with the spirits and painting the body with appropriate symbols. In the ceremonies hunters frequently identify the specific kind (or kinds) of game animals they expect to kill, and they deal with those spirits in particular. Evidently they are guided by hope, since the usual expectation is to kill tapir, agouti, peccary, or some similarly desirable species. Ritual mock hunts are occasionally performed prior to a real hunt. One man might be a tapir, for example, and the others feign killing him. During this preparatory period, and even on the hunt, men avoid voicing aloud the names of the animals they are after, much as they avoid using their own personal names. Under other circumstances, however, animal names are used freely. Later, after the hunters have left the settlement, their women try to assist them mystically to find and to kill those animals they are after.[15]

Each Yanoama has an alter ego, which is his or her second self, or "mirror soul." The alter ego of a man is frequently embodied in the harpy eagle, a belief manifest in the general avoidance of killing this bird.[16]

No other universal proscriptions are known to exist, although there is a
complex pattern of local taboos on specific creatures. The Coshirowa-teri of the Orinoco lowland, for example, have a taboo on the slaying of deer, since their legends teach them that they are descendants of this creature. High in the Parima massif, the Niyayoba-teri have no compunctions whatsoever about eating deer meat, but traditionally they do not eat jaguar flesh (*Felis onca* or *Panthera onca*). However, the Niyayoba-teri are disinclined to observe their taboo on slaying the jaguar (perhaps because there is less game in the highlands) if it is available and other meat is lacking. The lowland Coshirowa-teri hold to their deer taboo more faithfully.

There are numerous specific restrictions on meat eating by individuals or categories of people in given circumstances, such as children or new fathers.[17] However, these types of restrictions also pertain to vegetable foods, and they do not in themselves proscribe the flesh of a particular animal for an entire community. Sometimes, before an animal is cooked, ritual chanting is done to conciliate its spirit.[18] Skeletal material from slain animals is also saved and displayed, being removed after cooking and eating, so that there is virtually no flesh adhering to it. Bundles of these bones, tied together with fiber, are to be found hanging over many *shabono* hearths. There might be among them tapir skulls, monkey skulls, armadillo carapaces, and the breastbones, skulls, and even beaks of such large birds as the curassow, macaw, and toucan.[19]

Three explanations are given for this predilection to save the bones of their kills. One is rooted in the concepts of an alter ego and the transmutation of the spirit. Thus, it is possible for a man's soul to have been within one of these creatures. Since bones contain the life essence, saving them might save a soul. Another interpretation, closely related to the first, is that from these bones—and particularly the skull—another, identical animal will be regenerated.[20] A third explanation is the one Barafiri are inclined to give when asked directly why bones are kept. It is that these are merely trophies that show how effective a hunter their owner is.[21]

Principal Species Hunted

The game supply varies enormously over the thousands of square miles occupied by the Yanoama. As a general rule, the lowlands are better endowed than the high Barafiri territory, while highland savannas support virtually no game species whatsoever. In the vicinity of established human settlements, game is extremely scarce, having been effectively hunted or frightened off. And hunters quickly dispose of what game there might be found around new *shabono* and gardens. It is the remote, high forests and the old gardens thick with secondary regrowth that provide the habitats attractive to the bulk of the game species. In a sense, many species—even the vertebrates—are not intentionally "hunted," since they are killed for their flesh by men whose real intent when hunting is to kill specimens from but a few of the larger, highly prized species. Similarly, while on a hunting trip, men are continually on the lookout for honey, insects, ripe fruits, and other things that they might collect incidental to the hunt itself. Thus, hunting and collecting as economic activities are effectively meshed.

Among the manifold species[22] hunted, the most esteemed are certain large mammals, such as the tapir, the agouti, and the peccary.[23] However, hunters must often settle for the flesh of birds and monkeys, since these are more numerous and most frequently killed. It is not unusual to find adult tapirs (*Tapirus terrestris*) more than six feet long, and one alone can provide all the meat required for a modest *reajo* ceremonial.[24] Some agouti (*Cuniculus paca*)[25] reportedly attain lengths of more than two feet, and their flesh is said to be particularly tender and delicious. There are at least two classes of peccaries (piglike ungulates) that are hunted. These are the white-lipped peccary (*Tagassu pecari*) and the collared peccary (*Tagassu tajacu*).[26] Hunting these wild pigs can be very dangerous, since the white-lipped species in particular travels in large bands, and males are prone to attack en masse if one of the band is wounded. Some of the white-lipped peccaries reach about three feet in length and a height of about eighteen inches. The flesh of both species is reported to be delicious when roasted.

Other mammals whose flesh is highly regarded include the capybara (*Hydrochaerus hydrochaeris*),[27] armadillos, red squirrels, and the *acure* (or *picure*), a small rodent resembling the agouti.[28] The flesh of anteaters, such as the *oso melero* (*Tamandua tetradactyla*), has a strong odor and an acid taste to which Barafiri are accustomed. The *oso melero* spends much of its time in trees feeding on termites and hives of bees; it averages about fifteen pounds when drawn. Evidently the flesh of sloths, both the two-toed (*Choloepus didactylus*) and the three-toed (*Bradypus tridactylus*), also leaves something to be desired.

While carnivorous felines, such as the ocelot (*Felis pardalis*), jaguar, and puma (*Puma concolor*) are generally avoided,[29] certain other flesh eaters serve as food. These include the weasels (*Tayra barbara*),[30] foxes, skunks (*Conepatus gumillae*), and raccoons (*Procyon* sp.), as well as the kinkajou and the coati, both of which are relatives of the raccoons.[31] In the lowlands, there are also otters (*Pteronura* sp.), or nutria. On occasion, porcupines (*Coendu* sp.), rabbits, and rats are killed when encountered on the hunt, along with marsupials like the opossum (*Didelphis marsupialis*), which has a predilection for avocados. Similarly, lizards are taken, par-

ticularly the highly prized iguana, as well as numerous snake species, including gigantic ones, such as the anaconda (*Eunectes murinus*).

Monkeys are relatively abundant in the forests, and at least fourteen
different kinds can be identified.[32] In size they range from the big
howler monkey (*Alouatta ursina*) through the *marimonda*, *coaiti*, *caparro*,
viudita, and *capuchino*, to the tiny *tití* monkey (*Saimiri sciurea*), which is less
than ten inches long including its tail.[33] The large *marimonda* (*Ateles
belzebuth*) reaches a length of more than five feet (three-fifths of which is
tail) and is said to be almost as tasty as the agoutilike *paca*.[34]

Among the birds sought by hunters, certain large, gallinaceous
species are especially preferred.[35] Of these, the curassows stand out
particularly. One, the *pauji de copete* (*Crax nigra*), attains a total length of
nearly three feet. Curassows inhabit the thick forests of both highlands
and lowlands, rarely coming down out of the trees. A variety of parrots—
particularly macaws, the *guaro*, others of the genus *Amazona*, and even the
noisy little American parakeets (*Aratinga* sp.)—are numerous locally. Occasionally large, storklike birds, cranes, herons, and ducks can be taken
in marshy areas. And the forests harbor edible toucans, trogons famed
for their spectacular plumage, pigeons, and diminutive hummingbirds,[36] along with woodpeckers and birds of prey, such as owls, falcons,
vultures, and eagles.

Disposal of the Kill

Yanoama hunters do not overkill, since there are religious sanctions
against killing animals needlessly. They hunt only to meet their requirements, and all the game that is taken is to be eaten. Every digestible
part of a bird or animal is eaten. Nothing is wasted.[37] In theory the man
who kills an animal owns it, and he will carry it home. However, this is
not always practicable, since several men might have participated in the
kill, or the animal might be a large tapir that is too heavy for one man to
carry. In such cases, the owner, or owners, divides it up as he chooses.

After the kill, the carcass is prepared as soon as convenient.[38] No skin
is removed, or feathers from birds, or even the head, although sometimes viscera and other internal organs might be cut out and wrapped in
fresh leaves. A large animal is cut into chunks, perhaps six or more in
the case of a tapir, to facilitate its transportation. Small animals, or pieces
of big carcasses, are wrapped in fresh green leaves, or at least tied carefully with lianas. Monkeys are trussed up whole. Each of these parcels is
then fitted with some sort of tumpline, and occasionally carrying devices
are plaited for the haul home (see plate 26). Although all the necessary
packaging is done on the spot, Barafiri hunters do not normally cook meat

Plate 26. Niyayoba hunting party returning home with meat for a *reajo* feast. The men carry trussed chunks of tapir carcass.

where an animal was killed unless it will take more than a day or so to get home. On the hunt they limit themselves to small rations, since the meat is to be husbanded for ritual feasting with their kinsmen back at the *shabono*.

Certain parts of some of the animals taken on the hunt have a utility other than dietetic. Feline skins, such as that of the jaguar, are cut off almost whole. A headband, an armband, or a quiver cover of this skin carries with it great prestige. The tails are cut from certain monkeys before they are cooked, and these tails serve as decorative headbands for special occasions.[39] Sometimes pieces of sloth or kinkajou hide are also used as armbands or as covers for quivers.[40] Curassows are often scalped, so that a strip of skin from the top of the head, with all the curly black feathers attached, can be used as an armband. Toucan breasts are similarly removed; small birds with colorful plumage are skinned, sometimes so completely as to resemble the bird in life, with the head, spinal column, wings, and tail in place. Such pieces of natural featherwork are usually suspended from an armband. In all these cases, when skin is removed from birds or other animals, it is not cured or treated. Consequently, it must be regularly replaced, since it becomes brittle, and the feathers or hair fall out. The colorful feathers of all sorts of parrots are removed for use in body ornamentation, and quill feathers from curassows serve in feathering arrows. If, for some reason, a harpy eagle is killed, the downy white feathers are pulled from the body. Before important ceremonials these are attached to the hair of male celebrants. When harpy eagle down is not available, vulture down can be substituted.[41]

There are certain animal parts that also have functions as tools. For example, some monkey bones are used as arrow barbs, agouti teeth are used as gouges or chisels, and peccary jaws serve as planes for smoothing bows. The saving of bones from all sorts of game for mystical, or trophy, purposes has already been discussed.

Acquisition of Pets

Hunters do not kill all the animals they encounter. Frequently, they take home the helpless young of mothers killed or frightened away, and in this manner a wide range of household pets is acquired. Generally, such animals are given to women and children, whereas dogs belong to men. These pets range from tiny hummingbirds to such large birds as curassows and parrots to squirrels, agoutilike *picures*, monkeys, and on rare occasions even baby peccaries.[42] Most of these pets live only briefly, but great affection is shown individuals that survive and learn to live with their masters in a tamed state. In the case of a baby monkey or *picure*, as with a baby dog, a woman might even nurse it at her own breast if it appears necessary or advisable for its well-being.[43] When a particularly beloved pet dies, its body is sometimes cremated.

These pets do not breed in captivity, so they do not enter into a process that might lead to domestication. This is noteworthy, since the Yanoama have available to them several species of wildlife that might offer good potential for domestication. According to one distinguished naturalist the curassow, the peccary, and the kinkajou are all good prospects for domestication.[44] But there is little likelihood of this happening, since even exotic domesticates, like the chicken, are regarded solely as pets and have no other place in the ecosystem. The idea of killing and eating such a pet, or of eating its eggs, is tantamount to savagery. If a rooster is obtained, he is kept as a pet for his "singing." Except for the dog, there is no role for domesticated animals; the Barafiri probably could not supply their dietary requirements anyway.

Fishing

The Yanoama are not oriented toward life on navigable waterways. This traditional indifference to streams and fishing is clear in their lack of specialized fishing techniques, fishing equipment, and craft for water navigation. In a technical sense, they are essentially collectors of aquatic food sources, rather than fishermen. This is particularly evident among the isolated highland populations. When stream levels are low, women and children are able to club fish trapped in small pools and swamps, or to catch them in baskets. They are also very adept at grabbing frogs and other amphibians from the water, patiently waiting for the opportune moment. Sometimes men shoot fish with bow and arrows,[45] and occasionally wicker weirs are constructed across streams. This last method is a group activity in which fish are chased upstream to the weir, where men wait to grab them as they attempt to swim through it.[46] As some *teri* move to the banks of major lowland streams, they have begun to experiment with fishing and the eating of large fish as part of a broad process of acculturation.[47] These particular *teri* are consequently developing an interest in such trade goods as fish hooks and nylon fishing line, as well as dugout canoes.

Chapter 8
The Apportionment and Consumption of Food

T H E great bulk of Yanoama produce is foodstuffs, and most of these are provided by gardening. So far we have been concerned principally with production itself and particularly with horticulture within the Yanoama ecosystem. To put production into perspective as a facet of livelihood activities, attention must be given to the apportionment of produce and its consumption. Production among the highland Yanoama is destined largely for normal daily requirements of the population for food. A second major demand is that of ceremonial feasting. Together these food requirements absorb almost all production.

Ceremonial feasting, like personal gift exchange, is a form of redistribution, since participants are drawn from beyond the host *teri*, and because *teri* reciprocate. Only recently there has developed among some of the less-isolated Barafiri groups a form of exchange that is quite foreign. This is barter with non-Yanoama, principally for trade goods. However, only very insignificant amounts of produce are used for this.

Apportionment and consumption, like production—to the extent that they are separable—take place within the context of functional units that have both economic and social identity. This basic functional unit was introduced in chapter 4.

The Basic Economic Unit

Within a *teri* community there are various basic economic units. These are normally single households consisting of an adult male gardener and his dependent kin; frequently the household is a nuclear family. The economic unit is more clearly apparent as a consumption unit than as a unit of production or apportionment, although it performs all three functions.

The nature of this structure, and the socioeconomic context of gardening, can best be observed by analyzing a sample community. The Jorocoba-teri consist of a single extended family of eighty-four people. The two oldest men, publicly referred to as Irube and Obisai Foo, are

TABLE 15

Lineage Affiliations of Jorocoba-teri Gardeners

	Lineages				
	Coifema Foo[a]		Irube[b] (Lineage III)		Obisai Foo[c]
Kinship Affiliation with Head of Lineage	First Wife (Lineage I)	Second Wife (Lineage II)	First & Second Wives[d]	Third Wife	—
Lineage head	—	—	—	1	—
Married son	3	2	3	—	—
Daughter's husband	2	—	1	—	—
Married grandson[e]	2	—	—	—	—
Granddaughter's husband[f]	1	—	—	—	—
Other	—	—	—	—	1
Total	8	2	4	1	1

[a]Deceased; his two widows were sisters by Yanoama standards.
[b]Actively gardens to support a third wife.
[c]Actively gardens, although unmarried.
[d]Both deceased; these were full sisters, and no distinction is made regarding the biological maternity of their offspring.
[e]One, Brerebimi Feyaroba, lives with Irube's lineage.
[f]This is Jurasimi Feyaroba, who lives with Irube's lineage because of his kinship ties with Criyajoma Feyaroba.

full brothers. A third full brother, Coifema Foo, now deceased, apparently led them in founding the Jorocoba-teri when they fissioned from another *teri* decades ago. There are within the present community two principal lineages and a minor one (see table 15). One important lineage consists of the first wife of Coifema Foo, her children and grandchildren, and people married to them; the other consists of Irube and all those people similarly related directly to him, in addition to his living wife. The minor lineage is composed of the second wife of Coifema Foo, her three children, a daughter-in-law, and a grandchild. The elderly Obisai Foo is the only unmarried adult male of the *teri*. He has no offspring.

There are sixteen adult males among the Jorocoba-teri, and all have gardens of their own.[1] Even a patriarch, such as Irube, still gardens actively to provide for his own nuclear family. In table 15 these men are classified by their lineages, and in this manner the importance of Coifema Foo's older widow—a veritable matriarch—is manifest. Nearly two-thirds of the population of the *teri* belong to her lineage, making her a very influential woman. With two exceptions (a married grandson and a married granddaughter) all of her lineage who pertain to the Jorocoba-teri are housed on one section of the *shabono* (see lineage I, fig. 11).

The number of people directly dependent upon a man for support varies considerably. Of the sixteen men, eight have only one wife apiece, while five have two wives each. Two of the youngest men are in essence divorced and have at least temporarily accepted that state for reasons relating to community harmony. Except for these two,[2] each man is head of one of the fourteen economic units in the *shabono*, as shown in figure 11.

A man with more than one wife is likely to build and maintain a separate household for each wife, but this is not always the case. One man, Iyocosimi Foo (no. 1 in fig. 11), maintains three separate households for his two wives, their children, and other close kin of his. Another man, Buuqui Foo (no. 2), has nine dependents (five children and four adults, including a father-in-law) in addition to himself. He lives with the more attractive of his two wives and her children (no. 2-A), while the older wife, her children, and her father share a shelter just outside the *shabono* proper. Moroqui Foo (no. 4) also maintains two households; he lives in a large shelter with his younger wife and their children, and at some distance is the shelter occupied by his older wife and her infant children (no. 4-B). Brerebimi Feyaroba (no. 14) lives in a single shelter with both his adult wife and a new, child wife, although they keep two hearths. And Criyajoma Feyaroba (no. 13) amiably keeps his adult wife and his child wife at the same hearth.[3]

Of the older people from whom the lineages are derived, Irube (no. 9)

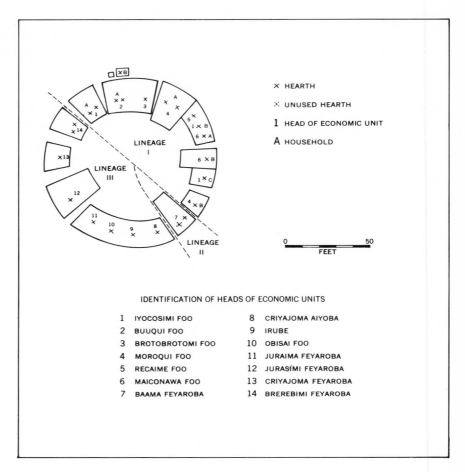

Figure 11. Economic Organization of the Jorocoba-teri

lives with his young wife, her infant son, and his youngest daughter by a deceased older wife. The younger widow of Coifema Foo lives with her entire lineage (no. 7) in a single house. The older widow of Coifema Foo lives in a household, whose nominal head is her grandson, Maiconawa Foo (no. 6). Normally Maiconawa Foo, his wife, and their children live in their own shelter (no. 6-B), and the old woman has a hearth next door (no. 6-A). However, the man is seriously ill, so living patterns are disrupted for the present. Obisai Foo (no. 10) lives with one or two adolescent nephews.

The diversity of detail in the size and composition of households and of the economic units to which they belong is evident. In addition to those people directly dependent upon an adult male, it is not unusual for him to support (at least in part) his wife's parents, particularly if he is newly married. Several Jorocoba-teri men are obligated in this manner, providing garden produce and meat for people within the *teri*, or outside it. Similarly, payments of this kind are being made to the Jorocoba-teri for wives acquired here by Mayobo-teri and Niyayoba-teri men.

Figure 11 identifies all hearths, shelters, and households of the Jorocoba-teri *shabono*, and the adult males who are responsible for the economic welfare of the community. Within the *shabono* the spatial expression of kinship is truly remarkable. The spatial pattern also confirms that the economic structure is deeply rooted in kinship.[4] Thus, the distribution pattern of residences is one of segments that correspond to the lineages identified above. Section I, with 14 hearths, is occupied by the older widow of Coifema Foo and her lineage.[5] In it there are eleven households but only six basic economic units. Section II has only one functional hearth at present and consists of one household and one basic economic unit. It is occupied by the younger widow of Coifema Foo and her line. Section III is occupied by Irube and his lineage.[6] They constitute another six basic economic units, plus that of Obisai Foo (no. 10), who lives with them. All together, however, this part of the *shabono* contains only eight hearths; the households tend also to be smaller than those of Section I, since these men are younger and their offspring are fewer.

Within this *teri*, those of one's own lineage are referred to in a "we" context, as opposed to "them" in another lineage. Likewise, close kinsmen of the same lineage tend to make their gardens together in the same clearings. However, none of this significantly detracts from the overall standards of reciprocity and redistribution within the total *teri* community. In the *teri*, orphans, widows, and the infirm are cared for. Households share their resources when there is real need, providing a high degree of social and economic security. This cohesion is particularly evident when an adult male dies. Soon after his death the growing plants of his gardens are destroyed, along with his other personal possessions and his body itself. This makes his own household(s) utterly dependent upon others for their sustenance (except what they can collect on their own), since there will be no more game and his gardens have been rendered useless. Normally the productive capacity of a community is not significantly reduced by the destruction of one man's gardens, and kinsmen of the deceased and his wife (or wives) can provide complete insurance for his survivors.

In the Yanoama context economic units are not mutually exclusive or competitive. In fact, like the kinship structures in which they are rooted, they overlap within and between *teri*. Bonds of blood and marriage are very strong. Not only do the inhabitants of a *shabono* share common ancestors, but they also practice intermarriage between lineages, thereby constantly fortifying their ties. The *teri* is, after all, a single, extended family. Partly for these reasons, Yanoama economic units are difficult to identify and to fit into our Western constructs.

Ceremonial Feasting

Large amounts of produce are periodically consumed ceremonially. In fact, the demands of ritual feasting may constitute one of the principal reasons for gardening. Invariably the invited guests are kinsmen and kinswomen, rather than "friends" in the Western sense. Feasting functions as a mechanism for reciprocal redistribution of gifts on a regular basis and over extensive areas. A ceremonial feast involves more than a single household or a single economic unit as hosts or as guests. Participants normally include groups of households, or lineages (such as Sections I or III of the Jorocoba-*teri*), from at least two *teri*. Logically, a *reajo* funerary ceremonial for a beloved respected elder with many living descendants might involve scores of people from various *shabono*.

Great prestige is attained by a host group that provides food lavishly for its guests. Hundreds of pounds of plantains are normally required for even a small group, and all of this must come from the gardens of the hosts. The principal aim of hosts is to provide enough food so that they and their guests can sate themselves, perhaps over a period of days. After the feast, there should be sufficient surplus of plantains and meat for guests to take home all they can carry; in this way, guests flatter their hosts for their magnanimity.

Bartering

Apart from traditional, interpersonal, and inter-*teri* gift exchanges, barter with non-Yanoama has been gradually developing locally. This is an activity unfamiliar to the isolated Barafiri, and it has required new attitudes of them. The inducements to learn are clear, since steel tools are universally recognized as useful and desirable, and other trade goods are also widely sought. Many Yanoama respond positively and enthusiastically to such market stimuli if they have reason to trust the foreigners who make the overtures. For Barafiri, even this kind of exchange is essentially personal, since there are no merchants and no political chiefs to command them. There is little to exchange for trade goods except garden produce or labor. As early as the 1920's, the Barafiri were giving cotton thread for metal tools, but this exchange was with other Yanoama who had indirect access to steel tools. Even today some men and women will carry bunches of bananas weighing forty or fifty pounds for miles over mountain trails in order to acquire credit toward manufactured cotton hammocks or steel tools.

However, there is little indiscriminate trading of surplus food; nor do people trade to a point at which they are left needy themselves. Rather, when exchange is anticipated, planting is done for the specific purpose of trading. Useless plants, such as tomatoes, squash, and hybrid corn, are grown only to be exchanged. There is no alternative use for such produce. Exchange is evidently the only effective inducement for the Barafiri to experiment with new garden plants. Thus, the hybrid maize or tomatoes growing in gardens fifteen miles or more from a mission station, or another foreign settlement, are probably destined for barter. Some Barafiri also set out extra plantains and bananas for this purpose. They are capable of using almost any surplus of plantains they do not succeed in trading, but the bananas represent an intentional, market-oriented surplus. Proof of the preplanning for barter lies in the fact that specific plants are set out, or seeds sown, exclusively for the purposes of exchange rather than consumption. Frequently these individual plants are so identified from the time of planting. What is more, when barter with a specific non-Yanoama individual is anticipated, the planting (particularly banana plants) might even be destined for that person and that purpose only. To an outsider, such plants are utterly indistinguishable from all the others in a garden, since they are scattered about among identical plants destined for consumption by the gardener himself.

So far the egalitarianism of Barafiri culture has withstood the challenge inherent in their encounter with commercial exchange. A person is not permitted to accumulate large amounts of wealth in the form of trade goods he cannot use. If he does not redistribute his surplus possessions, he reaps only envy and bitterness rather than respect and prestige. Nor can a lineage or a *teri* benefit from accumulating material wealth. All in all, each *shabono* has largely the same material goods the others do.[7] At death all personal belongings are destroyed, making any accumulations of wealth over the generations impossible. A man can be satisfied if he has his own good ax and another for each of his wives to aid them in the task of cutting firewood, a machete, a dog, and a machine-made hammock.[8] Rarely do worldly aspirations go beyond this level.

Food Consumption and Its Implications

Throughout this study there has been a concern with food: what the

Yanoama consider to be acceptable food, how it is obtained, its nutritional values, and its apportionment. Here the focus is specifically on the consumption of food, including its preparation.

The general healthfulness of the highland Barafiri population, particularly those who have escaped prolonged contact with foreign cultures, has been established. The major source of their nourishment is of vegetable origin, with carbohydrates being obtained principally from plantains and other starchy garden staples, while many fats are provided by palm fruits and nuts. Most protein comes from insect sources and game. There is occasionally a year when food shortages might be experienced for weeks, particularly during November and December. When this occurs, it is a time of concern and people talk about food frequently. But there is no firm evidence that people are frightened. They "recognize and accept periodicity"[9] in much the way other horticultural peoples do.

A multitude of dietary proscriptions are observed, many of them dealing with the consumption of foods of animal origin. These institutionalized sanctions vary regionally as to detail, but they always apply to categories of people—or all people—at specific junctures in their lives. Thus, they apply to men who have just taken the lives of other men, girls at the onset of the first menstruation, pregnant women, new fathers, the ill, children in general, and old people. The sanctions involve both the volume of foods and the kinds of foods and even the intake of water. Some *teri*, and some individuals within a *teri*, adhere to them more fervently than others.

The concept of food surpluses is evidently foreign to the Yanoama, just as are other surpluses. A man has only the bow and those arrows that he needs, and a woman has only the baskets required. To barter one of these items is to leave oneself without a necessity. Available food is eaten or given away. If foods are to be exchanged for trade goods, they are frequently destined for that purpose when the seeds or cuttings are planted. Yet, from a Western viewpoint, there are indeed ample surpluses during at least part of the year: gardens produce a superabundance of ripening plantains, and men haul to the *shabono* far more meat than their families require nutritionally. But there are ceremonial demands on this food. It is to be consumed in feasting, during which time much of it serves as gifts to invited guests. Functionally, then, there are no surpluses (see "Surpluses and Storage," chap. 4).

THE SIGNIFICANCE OF FOOD

Food is extremely important to the Yanoama. Prestige and recognition are attained by those who produce ample food and who share it, but not all edibles are classified as foods in the same sense. There are "real" foods and there are "snacks." Plantains, peach palm fruits, and flesh from some game animals, for example, are among the most coveted of the real foods. Most everything else, particularly collected foods, such as insects, small birds, honey, and fruits, are classified as snack foods, no matter how great the quantities consumed.

Although people spend much of the waking day, and part of the night, snacking as their appetites move them, they also eat meals. The essence of the meal is the manner in which food is consumed, rather than what specifically is eaten. To eat together with family members and kinsmen and to eat different kinds of food together constitutes a meal. Certainly hosts would offend their guests if they did not offer meals based on real foods, although these can be supplemented with foods of the snack category. Plantains and meat legitimize a feast, even if people might also eat things like caterpillars and termites.[10]

Eating is extremely pleasurable, and a good meal, or even a snack, is accompanied by a certain amount of noisy lipsmacking as a sign of satisfaction. The pleasure of eating is heightened when real foods are available in large quantities and when they can be consumed in the fellowship of kinsmen and kinswomen. This is feasting in the fullest sense.

THE SIGNIFICANCE OF COOKING

Among all creatures, man is distinctive because he alone prepares his food through the application of heat; only man eats cooked food. Fire, the *sine qua non* of Yanoama food preparation, has been described as "the most important possession of the Yanoama."[11] Like other culture traits, cooking provides guidelines for comprehension of the ethos of Yanoama culture. In fact, the cooking of food has been equated with culture.[12] The analogy is that to be "cooked" is to be "socialized" and that humans themselves are cooked metaphorically at those critical periods in life when each individual comes into direct conjunction with nature.[13] These are the very times when Yanoama apply the dietary proscriptions discussed above.

The cooking of all real foods is indispensable, and most snack foods are also cooked.[14] Meat must be well cooked,[15] and, similarly, garden staples (plantains, *ocumo*, yams, sweet potatoes, and sweet manioc) are eaten only after having been thoroughly cooked at the hearth fire.[16] Only adult males may make new fire, and they alone own or use firedrills.[17] In contrast, anyone may start fire from the embers of an old one. All but the youngest children know how to cook, and all are free to use fire to cook their foods at almost any time. Individual adults cook for themselves as they are inclined, and even children cook at the family hearth the tidbits they forage. The most valiant hunters and the most fearless warriors cook. When they wake up about dawn, and again at sunset, family members often eat together. Otherwise, snacks account for much of the food intake of the day.

Traditional Yanoama food preparation is so different from ours that the English vocabulary and Western techniques do not really apply to their methods or their concepts of cooking. They do not steam, fry, bake, grill, or broil, as we define these terms. Neither do they cook in the sense of engaging in complex food preparations, such as the manufacture of bitter manioc flour or cakes.[18] Nor do they prepare soups, stews, or other combinations of ingredients that would require recipes. Traditionally, they employ neither spices nor flavorings, except for an infrequent use of small amounts of hot pepper (*Capsicum* sp.).[19] The contempt for salt (sodium chloride) has already been cited in chapter 2. However, there are numerous references in the literature to substitutes for salt,[20] and it is reported by a medical doctor that there is no evidence that the lowland Waika suffer from a salt deficiency.[21]

The Yanoama use three principal methods of cooking, each requiring few utensils or none at all. The most prevalent and simplest is to place foods onto or next to embers of the hearth fire. Another method is to wrap food in green leaves and place the packet onto or next to the embers. Both can be considered forms of roasting, although the latter might possibly qualify as a form of steaming.[22] The most sophisticated technique is that of boiling. Here a food is placed in a pot with water, and the water is kept boiling until the food is well cooked. The receptacle can be a clay pot, an aluminum pot, or even a bark vessel.[23] The food might consist of pieces of a large animal cut to fit the vessel, or a whole animal like a monkey, or peach palm fruits, or peeled plantains. Meat is not skinned or cut up in accord with the anatomical features of the animal.[24] Hair is sometimes singed off, and the feathers are pulled from birds before boiling them. The important thing is that the animal, or chunks of an animal, fit into the pot.

Foods are cooked at the hearth with little preparation. Plantains are peeled before being placed near the embers,[25] while most garden tubers are cooked in their skins. Arthropods, crustaceans, mollusks, reptiles, amphibians, eggs, small fishes and birds, as well as some monkeys, are roasted directly over the hot coals or wrapped in large green leaves first. Boiling is a technique traditionally reserved for male cookery. Thus, when "real" foods—particularly plantains and meat—are to be prepared in the *shabono* for an important ceremonial event, such as a *reajo*, it is men who do the boiling.[26] Before the advent of aluminum cooking pots as trade goods, only the traditional, cuneiform clay pots were used. These pots were scarce and valuable, and each man who owned one was very careful with it.

Cooking, then, is the key to significant sex differentiation in a ritual context. Among the Yanoama, we find the sex roles in cooking to be different from the "common tropical forest pattern [where] women boil, [but] men bake and broil."[27] Yet, the classic Yanoama dichotomy is breaking down, at least where aluminum pots are used for boiling. This is due in part to the extreme portability of aluminum pots in comparison with the heavy, fragile clay vessels. Thus, the new pots are taken on camping trips and used to prepare all manner of snack foods.[28] They are sufficiently commonplace that women sometimes cook in them, and occasionally women even own them. These changes mean that boiling as a method of cooking and the vessels in which boiling is done are becoming secularized and vulgar in comparison with their status only a short time ago.[29]

Cooking is also critically important in any assessment of the role of women. Among the bitter manioc cultivators, for example, a very heavy burden rests upon the women, since it is they alone who must prepare the staple food—manioc cake. It is their duty to maintain the family gardens and to dig, haul, wash, peel, grate, strain, form, and cook the manioc cakes daily for the entire family. When ceremonial feasts are to be held, women have full responsibility for providing sufficient manioc cakes and for producing enormous quantities of mildly alcoholic manioc beer, which are to be consumed with abandon by hosts and guests alike.

Traditionally, a Yanoama woman has none of these jobs. Her most burdensome duties are to keep her household supplied with drinking water and firewood, although she is not exclusively responsible for keeping the fire alive.[30] Most women are far from meticulous in the maintenance of the tiny family living space. Sometimes large amounts of refuse accumulate around the hearth and under the hammocks before anyone bothers to throw it outside the *shabono*. And then, the person who cleans up is as likely to be male as female.[31] What is more, the Yanoama woman does not resemble the Western ideal of the homemaker in her "natural" female role as a fulfilled wife and mother. That domestic personality does not exist: the woman as housekeeper who decorates her home tastefully and keeps it neat, who cooks for her brood, washes their dishes, launders their clothes, and picks up after them. On the contrary, as soon as a child is fully weaned (particularly a boy), it can get along quite well physically without a mother.[32] Finally, unlike the bulk of tropical forest tribes, the Yanoama do not prepare alcoholic drinks, so women never have an opportunity to become drunk.[33] Nor do women normally have access to hallucinogenic drugs, and therefore they pass their lives without knowing the ecstasies and fantasies of macroscopic vision that are experienced by their men.

Chapter 9

Landscape Modification

To the uninitiated, a superficial glance from the air gives the general impression that the Parima highlands are uninhabited. On closer inspection, however, the forest is seen to embrace a patchwork of areas in varying stages of secondary succession, distinguishable by the height, composition, and color of their vegetation. The forest is also interrupted by extensive tracts covered with grassy savannas or ferns. These phenomena are visible evidence of the effectiveness of the occupants of the Parima highlands in significantly modifying the natural landscape. Here the Barafiri have created what is essentially a Yanoama cultural landscape, even if the people themselves cannot be seen from the air.[1]

In like manner the abundant Indian old fields impressed the first European arrivals to the eastern seaboard of the United States. These abandoned gardens were amply reported from Canada through northern Florida, and, in places like western New York state, travelers were left awe-struck by the extent of treeless areas attributed to Indian firing and by the countless old gardens.[2] These areas were so extensive that they could not be explained in terms of the scanty aboriginal population of the time. At least, they could not be explained by observers accustomed to permanent field cultivation in Europe. The effectiveness of that small aboriginal population to modify large areas is inherent in cultivation as practiced in American woodlands by Indian farmers with a deep-seated agricultural tradition. Similarly, the extent of old gardens and savannas in the Parima highlands suggests either a Barafiri tradition of gardening that spans many generations or a very drastic population decline within the past few years. The former is by far the more plausible explanation.

Principally through horticulture, the Barafiri (if not all Yanoama) have succeeded in modifying significantly not only the biological world, but their abiotic surroundings as well. This is a level of attainment attributable to the food-producing level of cultural development, in contrast to that possible by nomadic hunters and gatherers.[3] The world of these highland Yanoama is one of gardens (*ficari taca*), old gardens (*suwabada taca*), and savannas (*borosi*), as well as the forest (*urifi*). The Barafiri thereby offer convincing testimony of the capacity of our neolithic contemporaries to change the face of the earth. The extent to which physical transformation of the environment has occurred and whether the resource base has been significantly altered as a consequence have yet to be established.

Changes Effected in the Habitat

For centuries the Yanoama have occupied the Parima highlands. However, their culture provides no tangible record (see Appendix), and biotic processes have obscured or eradicated the patterns from the past. For these reasons, there is little evidence of former occupancy with which to work.

SOIL CHANGES

Few data are as yet available on the soils of the highland Yanoama habitat, not to mention soil modifications brought about by human occupancy. The results of laboratory analyses of four soil samples (shown in table 16) do provide interesting, if frustratingly limited, information.[4] The compaction and imperviousness of the savanna soil sample is evidenced by a lack of sand. The soil of Cuaisiba-taca, a producing garden, is even more clayey than the savanna, due largely to its peculiar situation on a flood plain.

The newly cleared garden of Wabufita-taca, located on a high slope, has a very sandy soil that is extremely porous, even in comparison with the forest soil from the Niyayoba area. The Wabufita-taca sample is also far less acid than the other samples, probably because of the ash content from recent burning. In short, these data only hint at how the Yanoama have affected soil fertility, structure, and chemistry.

Soils in most producing gardens, like those of the forests, tend to be friable and permeable. The same seems to hold true in old gardens

TABLE 16

201
Analyses of Selected Highland Soil Samples

| | Mechanical Analysis | | | |
Site	Sand (%)	Clay (%)	Silt (%)	pH
Niyayoba savanna	35	48	17	4.6
Niyayoba forest	54	36	10	4.5
Cuaisiba-taca	18	62	20	5.1
Wabufita-taca	62	26	12	6.2

overgrown with secondary forest communities. Soils formed on the igneous rocks and the regolith of the Parima massif appear to be quite resistant to erosion. Gardens show no signs of serious sheet and gully erosion, and streams draining them are not silt laden. In Yanoama horticulture the soil of newly cleared gardens is not left exposed for long, since crop plants and weeds quickly cover most of the surface.

BOTANICAL CHANGES

The most apparent and impressive impact of the Yanoama is botanical, and it is from the air that one obtains an invaluable complement to ground observations. Savanna vegetation characterizes the lower Orinoco basin, the Llanos constituting the largest and best-known South American savanna region north of the equator. Even above Puerto Ayacucho, savanna grasslands are commonplace within many miles of the Río Orinoco. However, beginning some miles below the Casiquiare bifurcation and extending on up into the Parima highlands, the vegetative cover is a thick, broadleaf evergreen forest that is practically unbroken.[5] This is an area virtually devoid of human inhabitants, although it is the sort of forested tropical lowland believed by some to be particularly attractive to aboriginal horticulturalists.[6]

Then, suddenly, after crossing over the forested western edge of the Parima massif, at altitudes above 2,000 feet, there appear extensive savanna areas interspersed with forest. Garden clearings become evident almost as suddenly as the savannas, their distinctive musaceous plantings a deep, shimmering green. Soon *shabono* become distinguishable, but they are much more difficult to find than either savannas or gardens. On closer inspection, the innumerable patches of low secondary forest that mark abandoned garden sites are visible, and a narrow belt of fern savanna lying between the grassy savannas and the adjacent forest can be identified.

Plate 27. Mayobo area from the air, showing interspersed patches of grassy savanna, ferns, old gardens, and forest. Foreground elevation is about 3,500 feet.

Together, gardens, old gardens, and savannas occupy enormous areas of the Parima highlands (see plate 27). In the Niyayoba area, for example, the Niyayoba-u valley and Shokekere Mountain are covered with old gardens and savannas interspersed with irregular patches of forest (see map 9). The same is true of the Jorocoba area and the Mayobo area. In some places the forest appears unaffected (see plate 28), until one looks in another direction (see plate 29).

These major features in the visible record of Yanoama occupancy imprinted on the landscape are a palimpsest challenging interpretation. Clearings in use as *shabono* and gardens present no problem, since they are obviously serving specific functions. Recently abandoned clearings, too, are quickly identifiable. However, certain fern-covered areas, grassy savannas, and low forest offer more of a challenge, and their significance can best be appreciated from within them.

The Forest. From time to time, even in the high forest, one encounters old camp sites. In other places, the forest floor is strewn with the rotting remnants of large charred logs and the stumps of trees, and sometimes even the remains of houses and shelters. Varying stages of forest regrowth are also to be found, as well as cultigens, such as the peach palm, and even solitary giant trees rising above the rest of the forest, attesting to selective cutting at the time of original clearing. An adult Yanoama male can locate and name old gardens and old *shabono*, even in cases

where they are not clearly distinguishable from the surrounding forest.
These exist in great numbers near occupied *shabono* as well as in forests
remote from contemporary settlements. Between the Niyayoba area of
the upper Buuta-u and the Mayobo area of the upper Río Majecodo—
a distance of some fifteen miles on foot—little, if any, virgin forest is encountered. About one-third of the trip by trail, which reaches elevations
well above 3,500 feet, is through grass savannas and fern savannas.

The Fern Savannas. Some grass savannas appear to have a growing edge—
a belt composed largely of ferns, but interspersed with grasses and containing charred tree stumps and other remains of forest. This growth of
ferns is particularly thick on well-drained edges of the grass savanna, but
it is sparse on the low, wet margins. Wild pineapples are also to be found
occasionally where drainage is good and where ferns and grasses are not
so thick as to smother them.[7]

Other tracts of ferns cover many acres and are interspersed with high
forest. This phenomenon can be found locally all the way to the Brazil-
ian-Venezuelan divide and on into the eastern Parima beyond. In some
places the ferns, reaching heights of eight feet and more, are so thick
that they must be cut or beaten down with poles before a barefoot
Yanoama can walk through them. The Barafiri are accustomed to burning fern savannas as it suits their needs, and charred remnants of trees
are not unusual (see plate 30). Where the trunks are standing, they testify
to savanna fires having spread into adjacent forest, killing the trees.[8]

The Grass Savannas. Grass savannas also vary in size and are widely
scattered. They range from many square miles down to a few acres (see
map 9). Their shapes, sometimes with straight edges, and their rather
abrupt, clear-cut limits give the impression that they are not natural.
What is more, as with the fern savannas, no evident correlation exists between their locations and factors of elevation, relief, slope, drainage, soil
type, or other natural phenomena.[9] Savannas are scattered throughout
the highlands on all sorts of surfaces—valley bottoms, mountain sides,
and mountain tops.

The pluvial characteristics of the highland Yanoama habitat, with an
abundant precipitation well distributed throughout the year, are such
that there can be no question that the maintenance of these savannas is
dependent upon regular firing. In fact, the Barafiri periodically burn the
fern and grass savannas when they are dry enough, in order to make travel more comfortable. It is likely that each time the flames reach the forest
more trees are killed, so that the open savannas grow at the expense of
the forest.[10] The Barafiri have a term for the process: *aborosirariyoma*,
which means roughly "to become savanna." The growth rate of the

Plate 28. Newly cleared and partially planted garden clearing of the Jorocoba-teri. This clearing (Boredidire-taca / Canawaubrare-taca) is particularly steep-sided and relatively small, covering a total of about 4.7 acres. It has been cut from the forest in a gorge high on a mountain side.

Plate 29. View from inside the garden clearing in plate 28, looking northwest across the Niyayoba savanna. Scattered through the forested slopes in the distance are the gardens and abandoned gardens of the Niyayoba-teri, the Docodicoro-teri, and the Canashewa-teri, interspersed with patches of fern savanna and grass savanna.

Plate 30. View northeast across the Jorocoba-u valley from the crest of Shokekere Mountain. Note scattering of small savannas and old gardens on the distant slope. In the foreground is part of the fern savanna covering much of the higher parts of Shokekere Mountain, and to the left is the charred trunk of a large tree. Forested until about 1930, this crest was subsequently swept by uncontrolled fires; afterward it became fern covered, or *moromoroma*.

savannas is much greater on well-drained hillsides than in humid places, where the forest stubbornly maintains itself. Along permanent streams at least, a gallery forest is retained.

On the savannas, a humus layer is practically nonexistent. The lateritic soil is compacted and runoff is very rapid.[11] Over the years, some trails have been worn almost a foot into the ground, becoming ruts so deep and narrow that they are difficult to walk in. With a heavy rain, water runs off in sheets, filling the rutted trails and flooding low-lying areas. Savanna creeks become raging torrents that are dangerous to cross. This accelerated runoff is in striking contrast to the forest, where thick layers of spongy humus and topsoil retain much of the rainfall that does not percolate through the soil.[12] On some savannas, particularly on ridges and hilltops, exposed bedrock is commonplace. In other places, pockets of granitic sand can be found among grasses and ferns.

Imperfectly drained areas contain bogs that present problems for the traveler, since they will bear little weight. Where trails cross them, the Yanoama have built ingenious pole bridges (see plate 11). If there are currents of fresh water, groves of *Mauritia* palms can develop, along with a few associated species of birds, insects, and amphibians that live

Plate 31. Grove of *Mauritia* palms and associated flora threading along a creek that passes through a large savanna in Jorocoba-teri territory. An important trail crosses the creek here. Note young man in center foreground.

among the palms and reeds growing in the red-tinted water (see plate 31). Where they have not been destroyed by overuse, these swampy palm groves supply a few edibles and small amounts of roof thatching.

Generally speaking, the savannas are very poor in plant species, and regular firing helps keep that number small. Biotically these savannas can be classified as an ecotone,[13] a zone of struggle between plant communities that is consequently unstable. Although only a limited range of species is represented, the dominant ones vary from savanna to savanna. The most common are very similar to certain species of the Gran Sabana in extreme southeastern Venezuela.[14] These include gramineous plants, such as *Axonopus tamayonis* Lucis, and two sedges (one of them *Oncostylis paradoxa*).[15] Most species—if not all of them—are pyrophytes.

The Parima savannas offer few ecological niches for an autochthonous fauna and none for the Barafiri themselves—convincing evidence of their artificiality.[16] Except for an occasional forest deer killed while crossing the open grasslands, or the rare rabbit shot at the forest-savanna margin, game animals are not taken here. The savannas provide none of the insects that figure largely in the Barafiri diet and few plant foods. Even when *shabono* are constructed here, grasses are not used for thatching. The savannas are also useless for gardening activities. Both grassy areas and those covered with ferns are classified by the Barafiri as "bad for plantains" and as *wanidiwa* ("bad" or "abnormal" places). The thick clumps of sod resist working, and the soils are extremely poor. What is more, there is not enough woody growth to supply ash after burning.[17]

Ecologically, then, the highland Yanoama are not a savanna people. Even in those cases where a settlement is constructed on the savanna, it is still called a *shabono*, or "clearing." In the Barafiri mind, the *urifi* (forest) is diametrically opposed to the *borosi* (savanna).

Factors Producing Landscape Changes

Certain factors can be identified that help explain how the highland Yanoama have been capable of changing their natural environment. The population, numerically significant, occupies such an extensive territory that the result is a statistical mean of only one person for every two square miles. However, two features of this population help account for its effectiveness. First, people are concentrated locally into *shabono*, their total numbers ranging from a few dozen up into the hundreds. Second, these groups are organized, and they are free to shift the areal focus of their activities over extensive territories. Custom dictates that the *shabono* be semipermanent, and thus efforts at exploitation of the environment are concentrated in relatively reduced areas over time periods that can be measured in decades. Consequently, drastic landscape change is possible locally.

Collecting activities produce certain modifications in the forests, particularly in terms of selective cutting. However, these are slight, since the Yanoama do not systematically destroy species. Hunting is also an agency for modification, since, near house sites and camps, game is quickly killed or flees. The principal impact on animal populations is one of redistribution rather than extinction, since far more animals migrate than are killed. The Yanoama as gardener most significantly modifies the natural landscape. With his cutting tools—first made of polished stone and palmwood, now of steel—and fire he destroys the forest.[18] He clears only small parcels at a time, perhaps less than an acre each year for an adult male (probably no more than an average of a square mile annually for all the Venezuelan Barafiri). The Parima highland landscape exhibits the cumulative effects of many generations of gardeners.

In the newly cleared gardens, most cultivars can effectively compete with invading species for a few years at best. Sun-loving volunteers flourish, and fire-tolerant plants also do well. Perennials are set out with the expectation that some will bear after the abandonment of the site. Within a few years a garden clearing becomes a *suwabada taca*, a continuing source of collected foods and materials, as well as a place attractive to game animals. For miles above the juncture of the Shabari-u and the

Jorocoba-u, the slopes on both sides of each valley are thickly dotted with patches of scrubby forest and savanna that are the sites of old gardens and *shabono*. Only a few of these appear on map 9. Similarly, for miles up the Niyayoba-u, on both sides of the valley and even parts of the valley floor, there are countless old gardens identified as having belonged to the Canashewa-teri, the Docodicoro-teri, the Juwafusibuwei-teri, and their predecessors. And an area of hundreds of square miles centering on the Mayobo-u is a mosaic of gardens, scrub forest, savannas, and high forest (see plates 27, 12, and 6).

In just these three small areas, within a time span that can be confirmed as consisting of several generations at least, the sum total of old gardens challenges the imagination. If, during the period of the creation and subsequent abandonment of these gardens, the total population was approximately what it is today (about 520), then at any given time there were probably about 70 acres in production and another 105 of new garden land. Roughly 20 percent of the total population, or nearly one hundred men, were active gardeners.[19] Although most of these old gardens are distant from the areal foci of today's *teri*, there are places like Yoodiba-taca (see map 9) where one can observe the coalescence of new, producing, and abandoned gardens covering tens of acres.

The reversion of a garden clearing to an approximation of the natural climax forest of the Parima highlands requires an indeterminate period, probably several human lifetimes. Since the Yanoama, like other slash-and-burn cultivators, do not devastate large tracts through their horticulture, the remnants of original forest are always available for its reconstruction.[20] Sometimes, however, the forest does not reestablish itself. Then, perhaps because of aggravated leaching or erosion, or because of uncontrolled firing, certain old garden clearings are converted into savannas. Verifiable instances of this can be found in the Niyayoba area. For example, *shabono* and gardens made by the Juwafusibuwei-teri in the 1920's at Docooiwa, about two miles up the Niyayoba-u from the present *shabono*, have subsequently become a grassy savanna. In such a case, land is rendered useless for horticulture, effectively reducing the resource base. Remarkably similar findings have been presented for the New Guinea highlands.[21]

Zones of Impact

Horticultural, collecting, and hunting activities involve different degrees of intensity in the use of the total area accessible to a community, thereby producing zones of differential impact. The wide-ranging, mobile Yanoama hunter travels far from home. But hunting parties are often small groups, who make long trips infrequently and who return as soon as they have killed what animals they can carry. As a consequence these hunting grounds, remote from the widely scattered *shabono* and covering hundreds of square miles, are only lightly affected by human activities. The game supply is critical to Yanoama existence, particularly to ceremonial feasting, and men are willing to travel great distances to obtain meat. Tapir is preferred, of course, but hunters are well satisfied with less. If a group's territory is inadequate in the provision of a specific resource, it can be sought on lands belonging to friendly *teri*.

A significant impact is also made in a zone of intensive foraging within easy reach of the *shabono* and campsite, where fibers, resins, fruits, and nuts are harvested from living plants and where small animals, insects, and the like are taken in volume. Much of what is removed is gradually restored, however, after people move on. In this zone, therefore, human activity is of limited intensity and duration, since there is little destruction of the natural environment. In contrast, near-total modification is achieved in a fragmented zone of intensive use consisting of the *shabono* and the gardens. Not only is there complete removal of the forest, but also, in their gardens, the Yanoama deliberately replace wild species with domesticates. Even though each garden covers only a few acres at most, over the generations enormous expanses are affected. These offer striking contrasts with areas used only for hunting and sporadic collecting, which appear to be largely untouched by man.

Conclusions

The scattered savannas of the Parima highlands bear witness to the impact of the Yanoama on the natural landscape. These savannas appear to have been started through horticulture and to be maintained artificially by the agency of man. Where found, they have a pronounced influence on the horticultural, collecting, and hunting activities of the Yanoama, since they are unsuitable for all these pursuits.

The severity of the human imprint upon the natural landscape is dependent on several variables. For example, although the entire Yanoama territory is chronically humid, the resource base varies somewhat with altitude and relief, so that a variety of microecosystems results. Also, demographic pressure on the local resource base is a function of specific *shabono* populations and the dimensions of the forest resources in their available territories. Consequently, some areas are subjected to more intensive utilization than others. The degree of impact of a population is a function of the duration of their continuous occupancy of an area. This relatively small and stable horticultural population in their isolated culture core region have subjected their tropical highland habitat to locally intensive use over a period that can be measured in centuries. Through this process a distinctive Barafiri-Yanoama cultural landscape has been created and maintained.

Appendix

Studying the Yanoama

S T U D Y of the Yanoama presents a variety of problems for the outsider, most of them inherent to Yanoama culture.[1] The kinds of difficulties, of course, are related to the specific research focus and where it is carried out. In this particular geographic study of unacculturated Barafiri high-landers, three kinds of culture-oriented problems were encountered: usage of personal names, dealing with time already past, and nomenclature of groups.

The first problem lies in the fact that the personal names of adults are secret, although, in fact, most people in a community, even children, know these names.[2] To avoid speaking personal names heavy dependence is placed upon teknonyms derived from adult relationships with the young, since these latter have names that are only temporary and can be used freely. For example, in the case of each of his small children, a man can be referred to as "father of" the specific child. Therefore, he has as many teknonyms as young children.[3] If he has a wife who is still a young girl, he is also known as "husband of" that person. If he has young sisters or brothers, he has another name based on his relationship with each of these, since he is "older brother" of each. To compound the problem, some people have been given Christian names, which they pronounce a variety of ways.[4] Thus, a man working in a garden clearing might say that his own garden belongs to "Older Brother of A." Back at the settlement one of his relatives might identify the same garden as belonging to "Husband of X," which would appear to be a different person, but is, in fact, the same man. A second garden belonging to him might be identified as that of "Flapo" or "Brapo" ("Pablo" in Spanish), or as the garden of "Father of Z." In fact all these references can be to the same person, providing an example of the problems for the outsider wrought by the personal name taboo.

A second major problem is that of studying the past. The Yanoama have no written records, and their very limited material culture is composed largely of perishable objects. Consequently, virtually no archaeological record exists, and very few tangible remains are left when a settlement is abandoned. Vegetation patterns offer about the only concrete source of information on old house sites and abandoned gardens.

The Yanoama do not bury their dead but instead burn the cadaver or the decomposed corpse. The bones are then crushed into a powder and consumed ritually so that no osseous remains are left to give some idea of the physical features, distributions, or densities of previous populations. Moreover, when an adult dies, all his or her personal possessions are destroyed. The few nonperishable objects, such as clay pots and stone tools, are thus quite effectively removed from any potential archaeological record. On rare occasions, a man's house is even destroyed, leaving a gaping hole in the settlement. Communities, or *teri*, seem not to abandon the entire *shabono* settlement because of a death, although a disaster, such as an epidemic, might induce them to do so. The taboo on the use of names of the living is not as stringent as that applied to the dead. People do not talk about the deceased except, sometimes, their bitter enemies, or in terms of abstract spirit beings. It is inconceivable to use the names of one's own deceased relatives.[5]

Such are the problems in study of even the immediate past. They are to be seen in the context of a weakly developed concern with time and the lack of an exact numbering system. Thus, if something did not occur during a person's lifetime, there is no way for him to know precisely when it did happen. Even if he, himself, saw the event he can specify the time only in very general terms.[6] This vagueness and imprecision in time identification and measurement are of no consequence to a Yanoama, so he can hardly be expected to distinguish between the time of his ancestors, his youth, or even his own adolescence. Future time seems not to be clearly divided into an immediate future and a distant one.

A third difficulty is the nomenclature of groups. A great variety of names has been used by writers to refer to specific groups among the Yanoama culture-bearing peoples in general. The names for specific dialect groups, specific residence units, specific kin groups, and peoples living in particular locations have at times been used somewhat indiscriminately, leading to much confusion. There is a threefold explanation for this.

Explorers and others (before there were Yanoama-speaking mis-sionaries) depended very heavily on their guides and Indian informants for identification of groups and the compilation of their other data. Un-fortunately, these informants were non-Yanoama, most commonly Maquiritare (Maiongong) or some other Carib affiliate, who obtained all sorts of misinformation, and invented some as well. For example, *Shirishana* (or, *Shirixana, Shiriana, Shirianna, Xirishana, Kirishana*) is a term frequently used in referring to certain northern Yanoama.[7] The Parima Barafiri seem not to know this word. The term *Guaharibo* (*Guajaribo, Guaharivo, Guariba*), widely used even today as the name for certain Yanoama, is contemptuous. Probably of Carib origin, it is translatable as meaning "savage."[8] In contrast, Yanoama themselves do use the term *Waika* (*Guaica, Guaika, Uaica*), but not as a self-designation. The same can be said for the terms *Shamatari* (*Xamatari*) and *Barafiri* (*Barajiri*, pos-sibly also *Padahuri, Parafuri*, and *Parahuri*), among others.[9]

Practically no highland Yanoama (except those living in association with the Maquiritare) know other American Indian languages, or Spanish, or Portuguese. Consequently, they often completely misunderstand ques-tions asked of them, and answer accordingly. Occasionally they inadvert-ently answer with irrelevancies. Partly for this reason outsiders have sometimes mistaken local kin-based residence units, or *teri*, for much larger "subtribal" or even "tribal" units. The Yanoama language is heavily nasalized, and it is spoken more often than not by an adult with a large wad of tobacco leaves in his mouth. This alone makes it difficult to understand. For the nonlinguist there is the added problem that the distribution of allophones is different from English. Thus, an unas-pirated *t* might be heard as a *d* or as a *t*; *r* and *l* are also interchangeable. Certain highly nasalized final vowels are practically inaudible.[10]

There are several problems incident to the mapping of Yanoama dis-tributions and patterns of circulation. One, not peculiar to this culture area, is the lack of base maps and of cartographic accuracy. Another is the dynamic nature of the *teri* kin groups that constitute local residence units. With births, with deaths, and especially with marriages, the kin-ship composition of any particular *teri* is subject to continuous change, and so are its location and its name. In a sense, then, the *teri* is ephemeral. Those *teri* known to an elderly person in his youth have long since moved; probably they have also fissioned or fused with other groups during the intervening years. There is no escaping this changeability because it is built into the Yanoama way of life. For them it is not the "problem" that confronts a foreign researcher. It does mean that the *teri* concept is more properly applied to the group of people bearing the name at any given time, than it is to the place where they live, even if their name is taken from that place.

Notes

1. Introduction

1. *Yanoama* means "human being," or
"person," as opposed to an animal or a spirit.
More particularly, it refers to a person who
belongs to one of the *teri* kin groups that
speak a comprehensible language (i.e.,
Yanoama) and that otherwise behave like
human beings. Such variants as *Yąnomamö,
Ñaomamö, Yanoamö, Yanumama*, and
Yanomama are used by different authors.
The drawer SQ-18 recently added to the
Human Relations Area Files is titled
Yanoama. Such terms as *Waika, Guaharibo,
Shirishana*, and *Sanemá* (each with
orthographic variations) are also used
widely in referring to Yanoama
culture-bearing groups. These are discussed
in the Appendix. The name *Barafiri*, as
employed in this book, is not an
autodenomination. It is, however, a
Yanoama term. See "Establishing the
Distribution Pattern," chap. 3.

2. Johannes Wilbert favors a figure of
twenty-five thousand or more (*Survivors of
Eldorado*, pp. 15–16). Ernest Cesar Migliazza
uses a figure of twelve thousand
("Yanomama Grammar and Intelligibility,"
p. 15).

3. Both in area and in population, the
Yanoama are by far the largest aboriginal
culture left within that part of South
America drained by the Río Orinoco system.
The *Waika* subgroup has been described as
"one of the densest indigenous populations
of Amazonia" (Janice H. Hopper, ed. and
trans., *Indians of Brazil in the Twentieth
Century*, p. 156).

4. James V. Neel puts it this way, "In a
world in which our heads are spinning
under the impact of information overload,
studies of primitive man provide, above
everything else, perspective" ("Lessons from
a 'Primitive' People," *Science* 170 [1970]:
819).

5. In Brazil, "the [Trans-Amazon]
highway is going to enter the forest carrying
death. More than 20,000 Indians, in all the
region to be cut by the Transamazônica,
according to the delegate of FUNAI
[Fundação Nacional do Indio] in Manaus,
might die with the beginning of road
construction or be condemned to a slow
death, by the diseases of civilized men, in a
period of five years" (Fernando Morais,
Ricardo Contijo, and Roberto de Oliveira
Campos, *Transamazônica*, p. 66; my
translation).

6. This kind of search for cause and effect
(presupposing a predictability in human
voluntary response to natural stimuli) has
proved quite sterile. There is no convincing
evidence that Yanoama culture is a product
of the natural environment.

7. No claim is made here that any of the *Musa* are American in origin, although this might be inferred. The fact is simply that the extremely isolated, conservative, almost totally unacculturated Yanoama rely heavily on plantains for their survival.

8. Julian H. Steward, ed., *Handbook of South American Indians*.

9. George P. Murdock, *Ethnographic Atlas*.

10. This map accompanies Cestmir Loukotka's *Classification of South American Indian Languages*.

11. Many writers use this term. Two books published twenty years apart can be cited as representative: volume 3 of Steward's *Handbook of South American Indians* is titled *The Tropical Forest Tribes*, while Donald W. Lathrap uses the term "Tropical Forest Culture" in his book *The Upper Amazon* (p. 45).

12. Steward, *Handbook*, III, 1 and passim.

13. Irving Goldman, *The Cubeo*, pp. 2–5.

14. Lathrap, *Upper Amazon*, p. 47.

15. In these areas early travelers noted clearly the existence of "enclaves of ruder tribes" of nomads who grew no manioc, built no canoes, and made no pottery. See Robert H. Lowie, "The Tropical Forests: An Introduction," in *Handbook of South American Indians*, ed. Julian H. Steward, III, 2.

16. Fernando Altenfelder Silva, "Cultural Development in Brazil," in *Aboriginal Cultural Development in Latin America*, ed. Betty J. Meggers and Clifford Evans, p. 127.

17. Lathrap points out that tropical forest culture is shared by two very different groups: the riverine people, who "have the best claim to be regarded as typical representatives of Tropical Forest Culture," and the people of interfluvial uplands, some of whom have retained agriculture, and some of whom, presumably, have lost it (*Upper Amazon*, p. 47).

18. Otto Zerries, "Los indios Guaika y su situación cultural: Informe preliminar de la expedición frobenius al alto Orinoco," *Boletín Indigenista Venezolano* 2 (1954): 64; and Inga Steinvorth-Goetz, *Uriji Jami!* p. 14.

19. Julian H. Steward, "South American Cultures: An Interpretative Summary," in *Handbook of South American Indians*, ed. Julian H. Steward, V, 670. The term *Paleo-American* is sometimes applied to hunting cultures, as opposed to *Meso-Indian* cultures based on fishing and specialized gathering. *Neo-Indians* are farmers. In such a classification, the Caribs and Arawaks are Neo-Indians, while the Yanoama are Paleo-Americans (Johannes Wilbert, *Indios de la región Orinoco-Ventuari*, pp. 239–241).

However, in his *Classification of South American Indian Languages*, Loukotka does not classify the Yanoama among the "Paleo-American Tribes."

20. Zerries, "Situación cultural," p. 64.

21. See "Yanoama Origins and Antiquity," chap. 2.

22. Lathrap writes that many of the marginals (including the Shirixana subgroup that he cites specifically on p. 83) inhabiting the high interfluves between major navigable streams of tropical South America are not incipient cultivators, who have only recently adopted horticulture, but rather are in the process of losing it (*Upper Amazon*, pp. 19–34). His whole book deals with the presumed struggle for land, with the weak being pushed from the flood plains up into small tributary streams and highland areas.

2. The Yanoama and Their Milieu

1. In the literature, the Yanoama are frequently referred to as a "tribe." See, e.g., Napoleon A. Chagnon, *Yanomamö*, p. 1; Johannes Wilbert, *Indios de la región Orinoco-Ventuari*, p. 177; and, especially, Napoleon A. Chagnon, "Yanomamö Warfare, Social Organization and Marriage Alliances," p. 43. According to some of Elman R. Service's criteria, they are a "tribe," yet, according to other of his criteria, they are not, principally because the term *tribe* implies adherence to the same leaders (*Primitive Social Organization*, pp. 114–115). Marshall D. Sahlins defines "tribe" in such a way as to make it applicable to the Yanoama (*Tribesmen*, pp. vii–viii). Whether or not we ascribe tribal status to the Yanoama, there is little doubt that they are an ethnolinguistic group with definable culture traits that distinguish them from other populations.

2. By way of contrast, Ernest Cesar Migliazza writes that the Yanoama occupy an area of approximately 100,000 square miles ("Yanomama Grammar and Intelligibility," p. 18).

3. Cestmir Loukotka, however, does support the idea of a fragmented, or discontinuous, Yanoama linguistic region (*Classification of South American Indian Languages*). Cf. map 4.

4. It is not unlike the land of the Hanunóo of the Philippines: "a mountainous, roadless, unsurveyed, pagan domain" (Harold C. Conklin, *Hanunoo Agriculture*, p. 11).

5. "The Yanoama in general . . . are

representatives of the most backward peoples of America and of the entire world" (Wilbert, *Orinoco-Ventuari*, p. 201). Pablo J. Anduze also describes their "backwardness" (*Shailili-ko*, p. 321).

6. Chagnon, *Yanomamö*, p. 1. Chagnon has written that "it may even be said that aggression is the theme of the Yanomamö way of life." As part of their education, "young boys are encouraged to strike their elders." Both quotes from Napoleon A. Chagnon, "Yanomamö Social Organization and Warfare," in "War: The Anthropology of Armed Conflict and Aggression," *Natural History* 76 (1967): 44.

7. Inga Steinvorth-Goetz, *Uriji Jami!* p. 55. The complete passage is a sensitive statement: "What then is it to be Waika? Gentle. Fierce. Tender. Proud. Trusting. Suspicious. Loyal to friend. Deadly to enemy. Quick to laugh. Quick to take offense. Above all, sure of who and what he is, in relation to his fellow man and his environment. To be Waika is to know where one belongs in the universe."

8. He believes that "the *peach palm* is the key theme to begin to understand all the Waika people and each one of its members" (Daniel de Barandiarán, "La fiesta del pijiguao entre los indios Waikas," *El Farol* 28 [1966]: 8).

9. *Ocumo* is a Venezuelan term. The plant is also known as tania, as *yautía* in the Caribbean area, as *taioba* in Brazil, and as coco-yam in West Africa. In this study vegetation is classified according to L. Schnee's *Plantas comunes de Venezuela*, except in those cases where a citation is lacking or his data are incomplete.

10. Otto Zerries identifies the South American tribes that used to practice ritual endocannibalism but describes it as unique among the Guaika [Yanoama] at present ("Los indios Guaika y su situación cultural: Informe preliminar de la expedición frobenius al alto Orinoco," *Boletín Indigenista Venezolano* 2 [1954]: 67–69). The sedentary, riverine, manioc-cultivating Cubeo have been suspected of practicing endocannibalism secretly (See Irving Goldman, *The Cubeo*, pp. 249–250).

11. Zerries, "Situación cultural," p. 75.

12. It is particularly evident on some of the sculpted stone images at San Agustín, as well as pottery and metal artifacts from highland Chibcha sites in other parts of Colombia (see, e.g., Gerardo Reichel-Dolmatoff, *Colombia*). Otto Zerries shows the distribution of the trait in South America (*Waika*, map 19). Some Sirïonó

follow this custom, presumably having gotten it from "Brazilian Indians," according to Allan R. Holmberg (*Nomads of the Long Bow*, pp. 38–39).

13. Zerries, "Situación cultural," p. 75.

14. Prior to the Spanish conquest, the rather sophisticated Arawaks of the Caribbean islands also farmed but had no alcoholic drinks. "Elsewhere in South and Central America all agricultural peoples made fermented drinks . . . and grew certain plants for that purpose. In the absence of alcohol the Island Arawaks were like the Indians of Anglo-America" (Carl O. Sauer, *The Early Spanish Main*, p. 51).

15. He also writes that they do not depilate themselves as do "more civilized" tribes. Perhaps most significant, he explains that the Guaika are essentially seminomadic, with only "incipient agriculture" (Zerries, "Situación cultural," pp. 73–75).

16. Ibid., pp. 67–71. The Yanoama practice of taking powdered hallucinogens via nasal tube is another such trait.

17. At least one linguist believes that Yanoama is not a language but a "language family" composed of at least four major languages and numerous dialects (see Migliazza, "Yanomama Grammar," pp. 26, 33–34). With respect to linguistic affiliation, Migliazza writes that "until linguistic evidence can show the contrary Yanomama [*sic*] must still be considered an isolated family," (p. 26).

18. Steinvorth-Goetz, *Uriji Jami!* p. 128, and Anduze, *Shailili-ko*, p. 321, respectively.

19. A different pattern, based principally on Brazilian sources, is presented in Migliazza, "Yanomama Grammar," p. 4c.

20. Ibid., pp. 47–48. He refers to *wayamo* as the "H (high) language" while the "local native dialects" are "L (low)" (p. 48).

21. Ibid., p. 61.

22. This highland is also believed to be the place where Yanoama found safety while most of the rest of the world was destroyed by a great flood. Only a small group survived "on a summit of the Parima" (Luís Cocco, "Más allá del turismo: Los indios Guaicas," *El Farol* 32 [1970]: 53, n. 7).

23. Migliazza also alludes to this possibility ("Yanomama Grammar," p. 55).

24. The term *Creole* is used in this book as a literal translation of *criollo*. This is a person of the national culture of the modern states of Venezuela or Brazil.

25. They are so called because "antibody studies [have] revealed the virgin status of this population" (James V. Neel, "Some Changing Constraints on the Human

Evolutionary Process," *Proceedings XII International Congress on Genetics* 3 [1969]: 398).

26. The Yanoama and the Xavante (of Brazil) are "examples of the most reasonable approximations [of pre-Columbian Indians] thereto possible at present" (James V. Neel, "Some Aspects of Differential Fertility in Two American Indian Tribes," in *Proceedings of the Eighth International Congress of Anthropological and Ethnological Sciences, 1968 Tokyo and Kyoto*, I, 357).

27. The neighboring Maquiritare were victims of such an *entrada* in 1775 (Marc de Civrieux, *Watunna*, p. 17).

28. The source of the Orinoco and the precise limits with Brazil at that spot were established officially by a Venezuelan-French expedition in 1951 (it took them two months to travel the last sixty miles). See, e.g., Leví Marrero, *Venezuela y sus recursos*, p. 109.

29. Ettore Biocca, *Yanoáma*, p. 12. This book is the uniquely valuable narrative of Helena Valero. Kidnapped by Yanoama in 1937, this remarkable woman lived among them until her escape twenty years later.

30. Antônio Teixeira Guerra, *Estudo geográfico do território do Rio Branco*, p. 165. Subsequently, the name of the federal territory was changed from Rio Branco to Roraima.

31. In Venezuela the Corporation for the Development of the South (CODESUR) has been created within the Ministry of Public Works. Its purposes are to establish the realities of the resource base of extreme southern Venezuela (particularly the Amazonas Federal Territory), to plan its development, and even to undertake some of the development projects. From the sixteenth through the eighteenth centuries the belief existed among certain Europeans and Creoles that there was an immense salt-water lake somewhere in the Guiana highlands between the lower Río Orinoco and the Amazon. This lake was known as Lake Parime, or the White Lake, and on its shore was supposed to rise a fabulous city of gold—Manoa. A few Spaniards tried to find it, but to English-speaking peoples the most famous of the explorers was Sir Walter Raleigh. All attempts to reach this lake (usually via the Río Caroní) were futile. For comprehensive cartographic representation of the legendary lake, see *Cartografía de ultramar*, carpeta I, *América en general*; and *Cartografía histórica de Venezuela, 1635–1946*. For detailed accounts of the lake and attempts to reach it, see Willard M. Wallace,

Sir Walter Raleigh, pp. 108–118; Donald Barr Chidsey, *Sir Walter Raleigh*, pp. 144–146; and David B. Quinn, *Raleigh and the British Empire*, pp. 191–193, 202–203, 245–251.

32. Bobadilla, "without permission from the Governor, left with some soldiers for the headwaters of the Orinoco[in order] to take possession of fugitive Negro slaves which he supposed to be there. He did not succeed in this purpose, since he and his people were attacked by the *Guaika* and *Guaharibo* Indians at the Raudal de Guaharibos" (Civrieux, *Watunna*, p. 16; translation and italics mine). Demetrio Ramos Pérez disputes this, saying that the encounter could not have occurred, since Bobadilla never got beyond the mouth of the Río Ocamo and therefore did not reach the Raudal de los Guaharibos. According to Ramos Pérez, Díez de la Fuente got much farther upstream on the Orinoco than did Bobadilla (*El tratado de límites de 1750 y la expedición de Iturriaga al Orinoco*, pp. 401–402). The first expedition of the Portuguese border commission reached the edge of Yanoama territory in 1787, nearly three centuries after the discovery of the continent (see Zerries, *Waika*, p. 7).

33. "The Indians that I had with me were frightened to death, out of fear of the *Guaribas* Indians, which inhabit these *mountains*, a nation which shows no quarter to any other Indian" (Díez de la Fuente in Ramos Pérez, *Tratado de límites*, p. 401; translation and italics mine).

34. During his prolonged visit at La Esmeralda, Alexander von Humboldt heard all kinds of tales. Evidently he accepted little of this information as truth. He does report (p. 329) that he was told over and over again by the inhabitants of La Esmeralda that no white man had ever gone east of the Raudal de los Guaharibos. Instead of stressing the cruelty of the Yanoama, Humboldt refers to the "frightful slaughter" of "Guaicas" and "Guaharibos" at the Raudal de los Guaharibos and the easy Spanish victory (*Viaje a las regiones equinocciales del nuevo continente*, IV, 315–329).

35. Robert H. Schomburgk, "Report of the Third Expedition into the Interior of Guayana, Comprising the Journey to the Sources of the Essequibo, to the Carumá Mountains, and to Fort San Joaquim, on the Rio Branco, in 1837–1838," *Journal of the Royal Geographical Society* 10 (1840): 221–231.

36. A. Hamilton Rice described one of the "Guaharibos" as a "large, stout, dark,

hideous individual [who] gesticulated violently and kept shouting in an angry manner when his paroxysms of rage subsided sufficiently for him to articulate" ("The Rio Negro, the Casiquiare Canal, and the Upper Orinoco, September 1919–April 1920," *Geographical Journal* 58 [1921]: 340). Between them, Rice and his guides knew only a few words of Yanoama. However, they concluded that the Indians were "cannibals" and were "going to kill and eat [us], notified to us by many of them carrying their hands to their mouths, at the same time making hideous grimaces" (pp. 340–342). We know now that such gesturing was probably the Yanoama manner of asking for gifts of food. It is likely, too, that they were apprehensive and frightened of these intruders, and that because of this their actions were exaggerated. Unfortunately, some of them paid with their lives because Rice and his party misunderstood.

37. A. Hamilton Rice, "The Rio Branco, Uraricuera, and Parima," *Geographical Journal* 71 (1928): 45.

38. Ibid., p. 55.

39. Anduze, *Shailili-ko*, p. 62. Because of this fear, the men went about "armed to the teeth."

40. Cándido Montoya Lirola, *Expedición al Río Paragua*, pp. 129–130.

41. The effective gulf between Creole and Indian is clearly evident in a statement such as this: "On these natives [Guaharibos], just as with the Guaika, rests the responsibility for so many *crimes* committed in the remote and forested regions of *our* Guayana. Possibly, *reprisals*—more or less justified—taken against them have made them even more *savage* and untrusting" (Montoya Lirola, *Río Paragua*, pp. 173–174; translation and italics mine). Even Koch-Grünberg, the highly respected ethnographer, has used surprisingly derogatory expressions when referring to the Brazilian Waika among whom he traveled in 1912. For example, he called them "wild people," "one uglier than the other," "ethnologically . . . the poorest of the poor," and "culturally an utterly inferior [or 'retarded'] society [which is] difficult to rank with their western neighbors, the *intelligent* Taulipang, Makushi, or other tribes, not to mention the Europeans" (Theodor Koch-Grünberg, *Vom Roroima zum Orinoco*, pp. 199–202; translation and italics mine). No writer matches José L. Quílez for sheer bigotry on the subject of the Yanoama in *Los Waikas*.

42. The nonsectarian New Tribes Mission has its headquarters in Woodworth,

Wisconsin. There is a certain resemblance to the Wycliffe Bible Institute in their emphasis on linguistic study as a prelude to missionary field activities.

43. Systematic contact by an agency of the Venezuelan government began with the Malariology Service of the Ministry of Sanitation and Social Assistance (SAS) in May 1958. Their permanent base at the mouth of the Río Mavaca was established soon after that (Dr. Ovideo Catellani [Malariology Service], 1964, personal communication).

44. Among these are the Brazilian posts of the Sociedade Protetora do Indio (SPI) and the recently created Fundação Nacional do Indio (FUNAI), the Salesian Missions of Venezuela, and the Unevangelized Fields Mission in Brazil.

45. A rather complete history of outside contacts with Yanoama groups and of scholarly publications dealing with them can be obtained from Zerries, *Waika*, pp. 7–27; Wilbert, *Orinoco-Ventuari*, pp. 182–189; Chagnon, "Yanomamö Warfare," pp. 45–52; and Migliazza, "Yanomama Grammar," pp. 357–393. In the decade of the 1960's small airplanes became important as a means of getting to areas not accessible by river, or to those places reached by water only with the greatest difficulty. This technological advance has permitted permanent locations, such as missions and government meteorological stations, deep within Yanoama territory.

46. It is speculated that most of the groups following this general route went down the Orinoco once it was reached, rather than upstream (Donald W. Lathrap, *The Upper Amazon*, p. 75).

47. On a more modest scale, it has been suggested that there are "a number of examples" in the tropical forest of South America of "uprooted people" who have given up farming (Goldman, *Cubeo*, p. 7).

48. The major proponent of this hypothesis suggests that "the Piaroa and Yanoama belong to the same and first current of settlers of South America" (Wilbert, *Orinoco-Ventuari*, p. 238).

49. Ibid., p. 240.

50. Between 500 B.C. and A.D. 500, the area the Yanoama now occupy was contained between northward-moving populations of Macro-Arawakans (Lathrap, *Upper Amazon*, p. 77, maps *c* and *d*).

51. Wilbert, *Orinoco-Ventuari*, p. 193. With reference to "macrosiriana" specifically, it is reported that the language has had a minimum of fifty centuries during which to

develop as an internal divergent of some other language (Mauricio Swadesh, *Mapas de clasificación lingüística de México y las Américas*, p. 20).

52. Wilbert, *Orinoco-Ventuari*, p. 240. On p. 193 he groups these contemporary "languages" into two families: (1) the Sanemá, composed of Nabudub, Sanemá, and Pubmatari, with an internal divergence of at least six to seventeen centuries; and (2) the Casapare, composed of Samatari, Waica, and Casapare, with an internal divergence of at least eight to twenty-one centuries. Wilbert reports that all these languages are mutually intelligible although some difficulty is encountered between speakers of certain of them. In a later book much of this detail is lacking, although he continues to suggest that Yanoama might have some relationship with ancient highland Chibchan (Johannes Wilbert, *Survivors of Eldorado*, p. 16).

53. Lathrap, *Upper Amazon*, p. 83.

54. Usually called the "*Di^a* gene." See Walter M. Fitch and James V. Neel, "The Phylogenic Relationships of Some Indian Tribes of Central and South America," *American Journal of Human Genetics* 21 (1969): 393. Since the late 1950's a significant literature on this subject has appeared. See, e.g., Miguel Layrisse, Zulay Layrisse, and Johannes Wilbert, "Blood Group Antigen Tests of the Waica Indians of Venezuela," *Southwest Journal of Anthropology* 18 (1962): 78–93.

55. Presumably these percentages are in terms of numbers of samples, but the author does not so stipulate (Wilbert, *Orinoco-Ventuari*, pp. 198–199, 241–242).

56. In addition to the Yanoama, other South American tribes are said to be "Diego-negative Mongoloid populations." These include the Bari ("wild Motilones"), the Tunebo, and the Warao, according to Wilbert (ibid., p. 198).

57. Fitch and Neel conclude that the data are too limited to prove anything at present. However, in their analysis of twelve tribes—chosen because they are "pure" or "almost pure" (signifying less than 5% non-Indian admixture)—results showed that of all these only the Yanoama were completely negative in the Diego factor ("Phylogenic Relationships," table 1, p. 387).

58. Wilbert correlates this Diego negativity with other features, such as language, dolicocephalic cranial index, and even the lack of agriculture (*Orinoco-Ventuari*, pp. 198–240 passim).

59. A woman's load of firewood can weigh seventy pounds or more, and a man carries to his new gardens considerably heavier loads of plantain suckers.

60. Based on data obtained in the Niyayoba, Jorocoba, and Mayobo areas. The Yanoama have been described as "small and slender, sometimes pygmoid" (Neel, "Human Evolutionary Process," p. 391). Wilbert also describes them as "pigmoides," suggesting that this is probably a "primitive ethnic characteristic" (*Orinoco-Ventuari*, p. 238).

61. Gottfried Polykrates, "Wawanaueteri: Ein Janonami Stamm Nordwestbrasiliens," *Folk* 7 (1965): 129.

62. Ibid. Their hands appear to be small in proportion to the body, and in some cases they can be described as delicate and petite.

63. This first contact was in the Orinoco lowlands, where the use of *bixa* may be more generous than it is in the Parima highlands. Perhaps this is due in part to the abundance of irritating insects in the lowlands, since a thick coating of *bixa* (mixed with saliva or some other moist medium) smeared on the body is thought to provide protection from insects. Conceivably, this mixture also protects from ultraviolet rays.

64. It has been suggested that the common usage of *bixa* by aboriginals of the Caribbean area "possibly gave rise to the term 'red Indians'" (Sauer, *Spanish Main*, p. 56). In Mexico this vegetable coloring matter is *achiote*, in Venezuela it is *onoto*, in Brazil it is *urucú*, and among the Yanoama it is *nana*.

65. James Barker, *Memoria sobre la cultura de los Guaika, Boletín Indigenista Venezolano* 1 (1953): 10. Humboldt wrote of the Guaicas and the Guaharibos as "white" Indians, or "whitish" Indians, expressing the belief that this quality deserved further study (*Viaje*, IV, 317–323).

66. Steinvorth-Goetz describes their toes as "almost prehensile" (*Uriji Jami!* pp. 36, 72).

67. Anduze, *Shailili-ko*, p. 202.

68. Some men also have hair on their lower legs; all men and some women have at least sparse pubic hair, but few adults have axillary hair.

69. Among the "Waika" of the upper Orinoco area, "the Mongolian spot is always present in the new born" (Anduze, *Shailili-ko*, p. 321).

70. This dolicocephalic quality has been linked with Yanoama cultural "marginality." See, e.g., Wilbert, *Orinoco-Ventuari*, p. 239.

71. K. B. Finney, "Préstamos culturales observados entre los Waikas," *Antropológica* 2

(1957): 27–29. The Yanoama simply have no effective craft for navigation, except in areas of close contact with such people as the Maquiritare or with Creoles. In the upper Buuta-u area, dugout canoes are still totally unknown.

72. See "Leadership," chap. 3.

73. Principal among these tools are one kind of fire-making drill, one type of agouti-tooth gouge (or chisel), and the tomahawk, or *jawa*. Crafts include the manufacture of cone-shaped (cuneiform) coiled pots, hammocks of split vine or strips of bast, spun cotton thread, a variety of baskets (said to be "twisted" [Zerries, "Situación cultural," p. 75] or "plaited" [Steinvorth-Goetz, *Uriji Jami!* p. 33], rather than woven), gourd containers, a variety of cordages, bows, arrows, quivers, and arrow points. However, these are not indispensable, according to Helena Valero, who lived with Yanoama for twenty years. She describes Yanoama women biting the heads of fish to kill them, rather than using any kind of implement. Valero herself had no tool but "a piece of bow" during several months that she spent completely alone in the forest (Biocca, *Yanoáma*, pp. 47, 98).

74. The Yanoama have a "religion that regards man as a part of a system" as opposed to ours in which man "is the divinely appointed master of the system" (James V. Neel, "Lessons from a 'Primitive' People," *Science* 170 [1970]: 819). "The Waika do not conceive of a 'God' in the sense of an all-powerful, all-seeing creator deity" (Steinvorth-Goetz, *Uriji Jami!* p. 43). In contrast to preliterate and ancient societies, the modern Western world is one in which "man has been conceptually separated from nature, and God from both" (Alexander Spoehr, "Cultural Differences in the Interpretation of Natural Resources," in *Man's Role in Changing the Face of the Earth*, ed. William L. Thomas et al., pp. 98–99).

75. Thus, the Namoe-teri believed that when the hummingbird was a man he taught the ancestors of the Yanoama how to plant cotton and to spin it into thread. Similarly, the bat taught them about tobacco, ants taught them about maize, and worms are descendants of the people who taught them about *ocumo* (Biocca, *Yanoáma*, pp. 130, 135, 164, 176).

76. Body painting depicts stylizations and abstractions of spirit creatures or specific parts of them. Faithful likeness, as we conceive it, has no significance. Cf. Kaj Birket-Smith, *Primitive Man and His Ways*, p. 26.

77. There are numerous versions of certain basic themes. Those providing the background for this discussion are derived principally from the northern Sanoma (Wilbert, *Orinoco-Ventuari*), the southern Shamatari (Biocca, *Yanoáma*), the Waika of the Orinoco lowlands (Chagnon, *Yanomamö*), and the Parima Barafiri (where my own field work was done).

78. Also found as *Omawe, Omauwa, Omamam, Omao,* and *Omaua.* In order to obtain the blessings enjoyed by the Yanoama of today, spirit ancestors, such as Omawa, had to struggle mightily with mean and stingy spirit beings, who were often ready to devour them. These malevolent beings had to be outsmarted, since they were unwilling to share fire or the garden crop plants that are indispensable to the Yanoama way of life.

79. The Rajara, who sometimes transmutates into an old woman, is described as being nearly one hundred feet long and having no tongue. She is believed to have once lived in a pool at the base of a waterfall on the Shabari-u, not far from the present site of the *shabono* of the Jorocoba-teri. Across the border in the Brazilian Parima, the Rajara is a masculine spirit, who also lives in deep water. There, too, such spirits as Coyerin and Dabarasic are important in any explanation of agricultural origins.

80. Barker, *Cultura de los Guaika*, p. 49.

81. Wilbert suggests that all men are potential shamans (*sablies*) (*Orinoco-Ventuari*, p. 226). Barker observes that most men practice witchcraft (*Cultura de los Guaika*, p. 56), while Chagnon writes that "probably half of the men in each village are shamans" (*Yanomamö*, p. 52). Evidently a distinction should be drawn between those men who experiment and those who are regularly successful.

82. Barker, *Cultura de los Guaika*, p. 40. He further suggests that some men go beyond the realm of religion in their usage of these drugs and become addicted to them (p. 23). In contrast, Ghillean T. Prance found the highland Yanoama he studied to use their narcotics only under "controlled conditions" ("An Ethnobotanical Comparison of Four Tribes of Amazonian Indians," *Acta Amazonica*, in press). In his judgment it is tribes using tobacco-based snuffs that are truly addicted. Perhaps the frequency of usage is directly related to the morale and the emotional tranquility of the community. When they feel insecure, men seek an escape, or contact, with the spirit world

where they might obtain help (cf. "Acculturation"). It has been suggested that there might be a positive correlation between chromosomal damage among the Yanoama and the continuous use of narcotic drugs. See James V. Neel, "Genetic Aspects of the Ecology of Disease in the American Indian," in *The Ongoing Evolution of Latin American Population*, ed. F. A. Salzano, p. 583.

83. Richard Evans Schultes, "Hallucinogens of Plant Origin," *Science* 163 (1969): 248.

84. Ibid. For further detail on Yanoama use of *Virola*, see Richard Evans Schultes, "An Overview of Hallucinogens in the Western Hemisphere," in *Flesh of the Gods*, ed. Peter T. Furst, pp. 41–44.

85. Apparently, to the Yanoama, this is another kind of *ebena*. For example, Helena Valero recalls that "even stronger [than bark *ebena*] is the *epená* which some tribes prepare with the dark seeds of a plant which does not grow very high" (Biocca, *Yanoáma*, p. 147). Similarly, Biocca writes that "*Piptadenia*, *Virola*, etc." are sources of *ebena* (p. 332).

86. Schultes, "Hallucinogens of Plant Origin," p. 249.

87. Intensity and duration of the rituals vary with the age and stature of the deceased and with the circumstances at the time of death or thereafter. For example, during an epidemic, under enemy attack, or during visits, the ceremonies are abbreviated.

88. It is believed by some southern Yanoama that people continue living after death in Thunder's *shabono*, where they do not have to work in gardens or do anything; girls are lovely, flowers nicely scented, and people are beautifully painted. They are always young and never suffer pain (Biocca, *Yanoáma*, pp. 136–138). In another version, the afterlife appears to be very much like life on earth. When hunters do not share meat with Thunder, for example, he roars in anger. Women are said to have their relatives nearby—something they always want in this life (Margaret Jank, 1970, personal communication).

89. The southern Yanoama relate that, if people in this life have been jealous and stingy, they will follow a beautiful path that leads to a trap and fall into a lake of boiling resin (Biocca, *Yanoáma*, pp. 136–138). Cocco defines stinginess (*mezquindad*) as the "vice which is most abhorred." He also provides a brief description of the afterlife for people who have not followed the "single

fundamental commandment" to share and be generous ("Indios Guaicas," p. 53 n. 18).

90. Some Brazilian Parima groups cremate their dead outside the *shabono*.

91. Soon after the death of a woman, for example, a missionary reported that her husband burned all her possessions. "Baskets, pots, sticks, everything had to be broken up and burned" (John Enns, "Further Contact with the Xirianos," *Amazon Challenge* 3 [1960]: 13). One authority suggests that these objects are thereby made available to the deceased. "Young food plants were burned so that the dead would have food where they were going. Young arrow shaft plants were burned so they would have arrows" (James Barker, "Where Is He?" *Headwaters* 29 [1971]: 12).

92. Steinvorth-Goetz, *Uriji Jami!* p. 99.

93. Daniel de Barandiarán, "Vida y muerte entre los indios Sanemá-Yanoama," *Antropológica* 21 (1967): 31; Barandiarán, "Fiesta del pijiguao," p. 15; and Biocca, *Yanoáma*, p. 197. Barker writes that Yanoama mothers threaten naughty children by saying "we won't burn you when you die" (*Cultura de los Guaika*, p. 55). Luís Cocco, a priest, had touching proof of the importance of this incineration of the body and also of the concern that Yanoama can have for foreigners. Convinced that Father Cocco was about to die, the Iyewei-teri offered to burn his body after death "with lots of firewood." They assured him, further, that they would "bring many plantains from the gardens. All of the Iyewei-teri will eat your ashes" (Cocco, "Indios Guaicas," p. 52).

94. Sometimes written as *reaho*, or *reafu*. The pulverized human bone is taken in small doses, since there is a fear that to ingest it in excess might make one ill. Among the Barafiri, bones that are not consumed at a *reajo* or saved for future *reajo* ceremonials might be poured on a fire or put into a hole dug in front of the house of the deceased. We classify the consumption of this powder as endocannibalism. However, the Yanoama do not interpret the rite this way, being horror-stricken at the very idea of cannibalism. Cf. Barker, *Cultura de los Guaika*, pp. 54–55.

95. Adult males invariably drink the liquid, but there are reports that women and children do not (see Cocco, "Indios Guaicas," p. 52). The mother of a cremated infant, or of a young man killed by sorcery or in a raid, will also drink.

96. Barker, *Cultura de los Guaika*, p. 22. People are careful about where they

defecate and even urinate, so as not to contaminate or offend.

97. I have found no evidence that the Barafiri associate either sanctity or evil with particular places, at least in any permanent sense.

98. See "The Parima Barafiri Area," chap. 3. Examples include Shamatari, Barafiri, Shitari, Cadimari, and Cobari (all terminating with the syllable *ri*). Perhaps, too, this applies to the Paquidari, the Padauari, the Karime named by Zerries (*Waika*, pp. 10, 13), and the Pairitiri of Donald Holdridge ("Exploration between the Rio Branco and the Serra Parima," *Geographical Review* 23 [1933]: 380–382).

99. Some examples of position markers, as used in the Venezuelan Parima, include:
"down there" (i.e., "downriver") . . . *cuwa cuboquiri*
"up there" (i.e., "upriver") . . . *cuwa cubojori*
"nearby" . . . *cuwa jarayowa*
"down there nearby" . . . *cuwa curadi*
"far away" . . . *cuwa cuyafufuri*
"beyond it" . . . *cuwa fe doreya*
Jefu is the generic term for "hill." *Jefu baroco* refers to the "front side," "chest," or "facing side" of a hill; while *jefu ta mabucado* means the "backside" or "far side" of a hill (Wallace Jank, December 4, 1970, personal communication). Cf. Migliazza, "Yano-mama Grammar," p. 334, on locative adverbials.

100. Examples to be seen on maps 6 and 9 include the Shabari-u, Jorocoba-u, Niyayoba-u, and Mayobo-u. Stream names and the names of the *teri* living near them tend to be derived from the same root.

101. Thus, in the Mayobo area, for example (see map 6), the Jaya-u, which feeds into the Río Majecodo, is the local *bada-u*; while in the Niyayoba area, the Jorocoba-u is the local *bada-u*; and along the lower Río Mavaca, the Orinoco itself is the *bada-u*.

102. Barker, *Cultura de los Guaika*, p. 57.

103. There are, of course, no such time units as weeks, fortnights, or calendar months.

104. Wallace Jank, 1970, personal communication. The Yanoama are correct, since perihelion does occur during the Venezuelan "dry" season.

105. Barker, *Cultura de los Guaika*, p. 57; Biocca, *Yanoáma*, p. 104. The moon itself is thought to be very small. Thus, Yanoama find it humorous, and even a bit ridiculous, when they are told that men like ourselves and machines have actually been on the moon.

106. Biocca, *Yanoáma*, p. 104.

107. "One" or "alone" is *mori*; "two," "pair," or "couple" is *boreca(bi)*. Anduze says that there is a word for "three" (*Shailili-ko*, p. 254), and Chagnon, too, writes that "the Yanomamö have only three numbers" (*Yanomamö*, p. 74). Migliazza provides additional information on numbering ("Yanomama Grammar," pp. 117–118, 422).

108. Exceptions are to be found among certain groups living on navigable water and among those Yanoama who live in close association with the Carib-Maquiritare of the upper Río Ventuari. In these instances acculturation is relatively advanced, including use of the dugout canoe. The same can be said for "mission Indians."

109. It would appear that by 1960 no *shabono* was still without at least one steel ax, and certain groups were well supplied with them. In some of the most isolated highland *shabono*, however, steel tools are still scarce.

110. The Barafiri of the Parima highlands, where cotton does not grow well, barter for cotton thread with which to make hammocks. The Orinoco lowland Waika, on the contrary, spin coarse thread in quantity, but they use it for indirect barter with the Maquiritare for such things as Maquiritare dugout canoes or cotton hammocks made from Waika thread. When the Yanoama make cotton hammocks, they do it by looping and knotting, rather than weaving. There is some doubt that they weave at all. Cf. Wilbert, *Orinoco-Ventuari*, p. 202, and Zerries, "Situación cultural," p. 75.

111. Steinvorth-Goetz, *Uriji Jami!* pp. 87–91.

112. Particularly waist and leg strings, arm bands or strings, strings crossed over the breast and back, and fringed "aprons" worn by women and girls. See plates 3, 4, and 5.

113. There seem to have been few of these pots, which were used only on special occasions, even before the introduction of metal ones. They were made by forming coils of clay into cone- or wedge-shaped vessels about sixteen to eighteen inches in height. Smooth, but unadorned, they were fired, at least briefly. Some weigh about twenty pounds.

114. Fish hooks are also sought after, but only locally and in small numbers. Those lowland Yanoama who have learned to fish are eager to get hooks. Parima highlanders, on the other hand, do practically no fishing and so show little interest in hooks.

115. Wilbert consistently holds this position: "Among the contemporary Indian

tribes of Venezuela, we can identify the Yanoama of the Territorio Amazonas as having continued the pre-agricultural Paleo-Indian hunting tradition. Only very recently have they adopted horticulture." And "no Yanoama group has practiced horticulture for more than a century . . ." (*Survivors of Eldorado*, pp. 14, 41). Steinvorth-Goetz states that Yanoama "arboriculture [*sic*] goes back a good many years, among some groups possibly as much as a century or more" (*Uriji Jami!* p. 14). Cocco maintains that "plantains have been introduced among the Yanoama no earlier than the 18th century" ("Indios Guaicas," p. 48).

116. Steinvorth-Goetz refers to the "incipient cultivation" of the Yanoama (*Uriji Jami!* p. 14), while Zerries describes the Guaika as "incipient farmers" ("Situación cultural," p. 66).

117. Steinvorth-Goetz, *Uriji Jami!* p. 43. She attributes this suggestion to "Zerries." See also Zerries, *Waika*, pp. 238–239, and Migliazza, "Yanomama Grammar," p. 425 n. 1.

118. Wilbert discusses the developing use of drugs for "recreational" and even "escapist" purposes (*Survivors of Eldorado*, p. 39). Chagnon, describing a lowland population, writes that "the tops of most men's heads are covered with long, ugly [dueling] scars" (*Yanomamö*, p. 119).

119. Another viewpoint has been expressed. Chagnon writes that "the Yanomamö occupy a relatively homogeneous geographical region of low-lying tropical jungle interrupted by densely-wooded hills . . ." ("Yanomamö Warfare," p. 35).

120. For the entire area reliable information is extremely scarce; considerably more data are available for the lowlands accessible by river navigation than for the highlands. Consequently, only gross generalizations are feasible, supplemented by data from microstudies.

121. Many names are used locally for specific parts of this highland belt separating Orinoco from Amazon drainage. Marrero identifies only these four as the principal mountain "ranges" of the Venezuelan-Brazilian border area occupied by the Yanoama (*Venezuela*, p. 19). Pablo Vila states explicitly how inappropriate are many of the toponyms of this area (*Geografía de Venezuela*, I, 59–60).

122. Marrero, *Venezuela*, pp. 130–133.

123. *Tepuy*, or *tepui*, is an aboriginal term (from Pemón, in which it means "moun-

tain") for the tabular formations that characterize the natural landscape of much of the Guayana Shield. They are formed principally under the control of the Roraima sandstones (see Marrero, *Venezuela*, p. 662).

124. Guerra, *Estudo do Rio Branco*, p. 66.

125. In contrast to this usage Steinvorth-Goetz defines *bora* as a "tropical aquatic flora . . . growing in rapids and falls [of the Orinoco] as far as the confluence of the Ugueto," and classifies it as *Apinagia multibrachiata* Van Royen (*Uriji Jami!* p. 155).

126. Marco-Aurelio Vila, *Aspectos geográficos del Territorio Federal Amazonas*, p. 50. Marrero gives a mean altitude of about 360 feet (*Venezuela*, p. 115).

127. Anduze, *Shailili-ko*, map 2.

128. The altitude of the "source" of the Río Orinoco, for example, is officially set at 1,047 meters (3,435 feet).

129. Marrero, *Venezuela*, p. 109.

130. This peneplain is almost indistinguishable from the plains of the Río Orinoco and the Rio Negro. On it erosion has eliminated practically all remains of the Roraima sandstones. The slope is barely six cm. per km., but the Casiquiare Channel manages to draw off at least 20 percent of the flow of the Orinoco (Marrero, *Venezuela*, pp. 114–115). The peneplain is almost uninhabited at present, in large part because it is so swampy and because of the abundance of gnats and other insects there. For more detailed information, see Volkmar Vareschi, *Orinoco Arriba*.

131. Vila, *Territorio Federal Amazonas*, pp. 33–37.

132. Marrero, *Venezuela*, p. 190.

133. Guerra, *Estudo do Rio Branco*, p. 108.

134. Barker, *Cultura de los Guaika*, pp. 6–7.

135. Steinvorth-Goetz, *Uriji Jami!* p. 194. The commonly used terms of "wet" and "dry" seasons have apparently been transferred to this Yanoama habitat from areas of tropical savanna-type climates where they are applicable. In fact, among Creole Venezuelans, the dry season comes during the winter months of the calendar; it is popularly called "summer" because of the relatively higher temperatures in comparison with "winter" (the wet season), which comes during the summer calendar months.

136. Robert H. Schomburgk reported a reading of 56° F at 5:30 A.M. on a February day in 1837, while he was in the high Parima-Pacaraima area. At the maximum elevations of these highlands he reported "lichens" and "reindeer moss" ("Report of the Third Expedition," pp. 233–235).

137. Out on the savannas relative

humidity dropped down to about 40 percent on sunny, windy afternoons.

138. Steinvorth-Goetz, *Uriji Jami!* p. 194. She reports that only at elevations above 2,400 feet does the relative humidity fall below 90 percent.

139. Travelers on the Demini, Toototobi, Padauiri, and Marari (all of which drain the southern slope of the Tapirapeco massif) report greatly fluctuating regimes, with water particularly low in December. The level of the Río Orinoco at Puerto Ayacucho (less than 250 feet above sea level) fluctuates annually by some thirty to thirty-five feet.

140. Measurements were taken (March 1970) in the Niyayoba-u at an elevation of about 2,800 feet, less than two miles above its juncture with the Jorocoba-u. Precipitation was measured at the same location.

141. Throughout most of its length, this river flows through forest or gallery woods. Water in the Orinoco at an elevation of 1,500 feet has been reported at 70° F and at about 2,000 feet at 62° F (Steinvorth-Goetz, *Uriji Jami!* p. 194).

142. Anduze, *Shailili-ko*, pp. 165–167; Vila, *Territorio Federal Amazonas*, pp. 28–29.

143. Anduze, *Shailili-ko*, p. 167.

144. Ibid. Forest soils of the Niyayoba area have a pH of 4.5, indicating considerable acidity. Lathrap takes a dim view of the soils in this general area: "As might be expected, the hard rocks of the Guiana Highlands and the Brazilian Highlands develop only thin soil covers at a very slow rate. The chemical composition of these rocks is such that they weather mainly to pure silicon sands, rather than to soils with an appreciable nutritive content. *Some geographers have dismissed these soils as completely without agricultural value.* There may be limited exceptions to that generalization" (*Upper Amazon*, p. 42; italics mine).

145. It is still believed by some that "the bleached sands of the Guayana and Brazilian shields give rise to rivers with dark brown water, which breaks in golden bubbles over rapids and falls. . . . [These rivers] and the land they drain have such low subsistence potential that they are notorious throughout Amazonia as 'starvation rivers'" (Betty J. Meggers, *Amazonia*, p. 12).

146. Ibid., p. 13. However, she does not include in this category rivers flowing from the Guayana Shield.

147. In fact, there are striking similarities between this selva and mature Pennsylvania woods in the summertime. Particularly, the superficial impressions of sound, smell,

temperature, humidity, and landscape are similar. Even the giant trees of the selva, such as the ceiba (*Ceiba* sp.) and cashew (*Anacardium* sp.), correspond to oaks, while the lianas resemble wild grape vines.

148. The three levels of the selva used here are described by Anduze (*Shailili-ko*, pp. 167–168).

149. *Urifi jami* corresponds to *uriji jami* in the Waika dialect. Steinvorth-Goetz translates *uriji jami* as "an expression used by the Waika Indians of the Upper Orinoco to describe their *way of life* of roaming about freely in the forest" (*Uriji Jami!* p. 2; italics mine).

150. See chap. 9.

151. It has been maintained that the cool weather of high elevations (i.e., above 2,000 or 3,000 feet) severely inhibits growth of banana plants (see N. W. Simmonds, *Bananas*, p. 143).

152. One of these circumstances is cool nights, which undoubtedly affect the growth rates of garden plants.

153. Steinvorth-Goetz writes that as her 1967 expedition got closer to the source of the Orinoco "there was a noticeable decrease in edible plants, especially fruits." Game also decreased. She suggests that the "dearth of wild fruits [might account] for the absence of Indians" in that area (*Uriji Jami!* p. 182).

154. Where possible vertebrate species are classified in this study according to Eduardo Röhl, *Fauna descriptiva de Venezuela*.

155. On the basis of examination of the contents of tapir stomachs, it is believed that, along the Orinoco at elevations above 1,000 feet, aquatic plants (principally one called *bora* and identified as *Apinagia* sp.) constitute "the main diet of tapirs" (Steinvorth-Goetz, *Uriji Jami!* pp. 155, 182).

156. The Edentata order of New World toothless mammals is well represented by a variety of anteaters, as well as armadillos and sloths.

157. The agouti, *lapa* or *paca* (*Cuniculus paca*), has been reported at elevations up to 3,600 feet (Steinvorth-Goetz, *Uriji Jami!* p. 160).

158. This is possibly due to the greater densities of the highland Yanoama populations and to the proportion of the highlands occupied by savannas.

159. Meggers describes "Amazonia" (i.e., *tierra firme*, which includes the Barafiri territory) as a "counterfeit paradise," suggesting that "the equilibrium adaptation achieved by the aboriginal inhabitants" represents full exploitation of the natural

environment. This is not a "land of unrealized promise" in her judgment (*Amazonia*, p. 120).

160. Compare maps 1 and 5 for an appreciation of the correlation between altitude and *shabono* locations. Steinvorth-Goetz discusses the Iyague-teri, who since 1935 have been moving down from their home near the Río Ocamo headwaters at about 3,800 feet. She also captions a photograph "New Yanoama settlement located 4,000 feet above sea level . . ." And, referring to the Jasubue-teri, she writes that "their former home . . . was situated at much higher altitudes, where malaria had not taken hold" (*Uriji Jami!* pp. 18, 25–26, 91). The Brazilian Wawanaue-teri studied by Polykrates lived in a *shabono* built at an elevation of over 3,300 feet and had their gardens at an even greater elevation ("Wawanaueteri," p. 129). Valero, describing her twenty years among isolated Yanoama groups, makes regular reference to a mountainous habitat rather than to hot lowlands (see Biocca, *Yanoáma*, pp. 142, 147, 156, 209–210). A very different position is held by Chagnon, who writes that great elevations are common "in the headwaters of the Orinoco and along the boundaries separating Brazil from Venezuela, but the [Yanoama] Indians prefer to make their villages in the lowlands on small streams, as all of their travelling is done on foot" ("Yanomamö Warfare," p. 35). One of the most intriguing statements to be made relevant to the role of hot, lowland climates is by Meggers. She writes that mildly alcoholic beverages satisfy a "biological need . . . where continued perspiration is necessary to maintain normal bodily temperature" (*Amazonia*, p. 98). *If* she is correct, Yanoama culture evidently has highland origins, because it lacks alcoholic drinks.

161. Robert S. Platt, *Latin America*, p. 487. He writes that "such low-highland areas are described sometimes, in pleasant contrast to both bleak heights above and hot plains below, as lands of perpetual spring, never too cold or too hot for comfort, combining the advantages of agreeable living conditions and prolific plant growth, including both seasonal food crops and tropical perennials" (p. 497). Yet, he states that "outlying parts of the Brazilian highlands and all the Guiana highlands are relatively uninviting unoccupied areas" (p. 498). This same set of habitat zones is used by Betty J. Meggers ("Cultural Development in Latin America: An Interpretative Overview," in *Aboriginal Cultural Development in Latin America*, ed. Betty J. Meggers and Clifford Evans, p. 136). This map, as well as Platt's, is very generalized.

162. H. C. Brookfield and Paula Brown, *Struggle for Land*, p. 161. These references are to elevations of 6,000 to 7,000 feet. They are used to explain why plots can be cultivated for longer periods than in tropical lowlands. The data were obtained from among the Chimbu of New Guinea, whose "traditional core area" is in the highlands (p. 71) and who present certain fascinating parallels with the Yanoama.

163. Biocca, *Yanoáma*, p. 108.

3. Distribution Patterns and Settlement Morphology

1. See, for example, James V. Neel et al., "Notes on the Effect of Measles and Measles Vaccine in a Virgin-Soil Population of South American Indians," *American Journal of Epidemiology* 91 (1970): 422.

2. Cf. "Acculturation," chap. 2. This position contrasts with one recently expressed by Robert L. Carneiro using data from Napoleon A. Chagnon (*Yanomamö*). Carneiro describes the "center of Yanomamö territory" as the area where warfare and violence are more commonplace than on the periphery. The explanation is said to lie in "social circumscription." Because "villages are closer together [in the central area] they tend to impinge on one another more, with the result that warfare is more frequent and intense in the center than in peripheral areas. Moreover, it is more difficult for villages in the nuclear area to escape attack by moving away, since, unlike villages on the periphery, their ability to move is somewhat restricted" ("A Theory of the Origin of the State," *Science* 169 [1970]: 737).

3. Pablo J. Anduze, *Shailili-ko*, p. 248.

4. This no man's land is said to be without trails. Even between the Maquiritare-occupied upper Río Cunucunuma and the upper Río Padamo occupied by Yanoama there is such a no man's land. Both peoples attempt to stay out of this area, entering only if they feel the other will not be there. If they do meet and fight, the Maquiritare usually win, since in addition to bows and arrows they have blowguns and even firearms (ibid.).

5. Robert H. Schomburgk, "Report of the Third Expedition into the Interior of Guayana, Comprising the Journey to the Sources of the Essequibo, to the Carumá

Mountains, and to Fort San Joaquim, on the Rio Branco, in 1837–1838," *Journal of the Royal Geographical Society* 10 (1840): 215–217.

6. Cándido Montoya Lirola, *Expedición al Río Paragua*, p. 130.

7. Inga Steinvorth-Goetz, *Uriji Jami!* p. 195. The game animals in such areas are described as "practically fearless," indicating that little hunting is done there.

8. When Helena Valero was kidnapped in 1937 along the Rio Demití (sometimes Dimití), it was by Yanoama raiders whose home *shabono* was "in the mountains" and at a great distance from the lowland kidnap site. Their temporary camp (where some women, children, and old people waited for the raiders) was itself eleven days from the Demití, and "still a long way from the big village" (Ettore Biocca, *Yanoáma*, pp. 27–28).

9. A systematic air survey might provide the necessary data, if it incorporated all *shabono* and if their dimensions were obtained. Except for the most acculturated, each *teri* has its own *shabono* (or shares one), yet no *teri* group has more than one. As a result, a tally of *shabono* is a tally of *teri* groups. (Among the Barafiri and lowland Waika, field checks have shown that the diameter of a *shabono* is proportional to the number of people who live there, since the circumference reflects the number of hearth fires and, therefore, the number of households.)

10. See *"Shabono* Territory" for data on the man-land ratio of the Jorocoba-teri. The Yanoama are a dense population for a culture that some classify as "preagricultural." Franz Schwanitz suggests, for example, that people with either a hunting or a foraging economy require seven and one-half square miles of territory per person on the average (*The Origin of Cultivated Plants*, p. 1). Yet, the Yanoama are rather sparse for an agricultural population according to figures cited by Karl W. Butzer (*Environment and Archaeology*, p. 457). It is not unlikely, therefore, that they are a horticultural people whose numbers have only recently been reduced. A parallel can be found among the Venezuelan Piaroa, another surviving pre-Arawak culture. This population of bitter-manioc farmers was much more numerous in historic times and occupied a larger territory than it has today.

11. See, e.g., Alfred W. Crosby, Jr., *The Columbian Exchange*, pp. 37 and passim; Murdo J. MacLeod, *Spanish Central America*, p. 16 n. 59; and Paul S. Martin, "The

Discovery of America," *Science* 179 (1973): 970, 974 n. 16.

12. James V. Neel, "Genetic Aspects of the Ecology of Disease in the American Indian," in *The Ongoing Evolution of Latin American Population*, ed. F. A. Salzano, p. 569.

13. James V. Neel, "Lessons from a 'Primitive' People," *Science* 170 (1970): 816. Steinvorth-Goetz, an M.D., reports that among the isolated Jasubue-teri "their health is excellent. They know neither colds nor coughs. The children's noses are never runny, a common condition of Indian children in contact with civilization. There are no skin eruptions—again common in semi-'civilized' settlements" (*Uriji Jami!* pp. 90–91). Helena Valero was told by her Yanoama husband that "white men cause illnesses; if the whites had never existed, diseases would never have existed either" (Biocca, *Yanoáma*, p. 213).

14. Luís Cocco, "Más allá del turismo: Los indios Guaicas," *El Farol* 32 (1970): 53 n. 8.

15. Ibid. No explanation is provided, however, as to why the introduction of agriculture (a much more land-intensive economic system than hunting/fishing/gathering) would have led to significant territorial expansion.

16. Neel, "Ecology of Disease," p. 571; Anduze, *Shaili-ko*, p. 209.

17. Neel, "Ecology of Disease," p. 571.

18. Chigoes (*Tunga penetrans*), for example, are practically ubiquitous. The female buries herself in the human skin, most frequently in the sole of the foot, the toes, or ankles, laying her eggs in a sac. The Yanoama are remarkably adept at removing these sacs whole before the young hatch. For this job they highly prize steel needles.

19. Various levels of violence are socially sanctioned for the resolution of conflict. The most innocuous level is one of name calling, which can escalate among men into a formalized chest-pounding duel, or even through various other levels, before reaching use of the bow and arrows with lethal intent (see n. 136 below).

20. If a *teri* is so harassed by raiding that it is left without enough men to defend itself, let alone to mount its own raiding parties, it is likely to dissolve, with individual members fleeing to friendly *teri* as best they can. There is no evidence, at least among the highland Barafiri, that enemy *teri* attempt to annihilate one another.

21. Steinvorth-Goetz writes that "one is struck again and again by the fact that neither dwelling nor Indians themselves appear dirty" (*Uriji Jami!* p. 108).

22. The Barafiri are not reported to engage in kidnapping with any frequency. According to Napoleon A. Chagnon, however, a major motivation for raiding and warfare is "the woman shortage" ("Yanomamö Warfare, Social Organization and Marriage Alliances," p. 69). Anduze attributes warfare to territorial invasions when game becomes scarce in the territory of particular "tribes" (*Shailili-ko*, p. 321).

23. See Biocca on the psychic influence of these powders, which are called *aroari* by Helena Valero (*Yanoáma*, pp. 173–175).

24. Neel, "Ecology of Disease," p. 565. Malaria is considered post-Columbian, largely because of the "difficulty in finding any other means by which it could have arrived" (G. Robert Coatney et al., *The Primate Malarias*, p. 7).

25. Chagnon, *Yanomamö*, p. 20 n. 2.

26. Dr. Ovideo Catellani, 1964, personal communication.

27. Ibid.

28. Ibid. Evidently both recurrence and reinfection are involved.

29. Reportedly, even infectious (viral) hepatitis has reached part of the Parima highlands (Wallace Jank, 1972, personal communication).

30. Describing the Yanoama during this same epidemic, Dr. Steinvorth-Goetz wrote that "they had absolutely no resistance. Only a very few even developed the characteristic rash, which is a sign of the skin's fight to throw off the disease. Mucous membranes became horribly inflamed, with extreme toxic vomiting and diarrhea. Many had hemorrhaging of the inner walls of the larynx. Many developed pneumonia and died from it. All too often even relatively mild cases failed to respond to penicillin" (*Uriji Jami!* p. 56).

31. Neel et al., "Notes on the Effect of Measles," p. 426.

32. Helena Valero relates how the Yanoama with whom she was living fled in fright when a terrible epidemic hit them in about 1947 (Biocca, *Yanoáma*, pp. 211–213).

33. Johannes Wilbert writes that "the number of their traditional enemies has diminished considerably . . . and they have gained almost 100 kilometers to the north of the Sierra de Pacarima [*sic*]" (*Indios de la región Orinoco-Ventuari*, p. 181).

34. One writer explains that about 1948 the "Guaharibo lost a long and bitter war with the Makiritare" and are now subservient to them (Pedro Jaml, "Expedición de Territorio Amazonas,"

Memoria de la Sociedad de Ciencias Naturales La Salle 18 [1958]: 88).

35. James Barker, *Memoria sobre la cultura de los Guaika*, Boletín Indigenista Venezolano 1 (1953): 4–5.

36. A variety of sources exist, such as Venezuelan government survey teams, Malariology Service personnel, missionaries, ethnologists, and explorers. However, the most important source of information on the areal distribution of Venezuelan Yanoama at the time of writing is James Barker of the New Tribes Mission. He is the principal author of maps 5 and 6.

37. For example, additional *shabono* have been sighted from the air between the upper Río Matacuni and the Ocamo headwaters. Their names and precise locations are unknown at the time of writing, but it can be assumed that they are Cobari. Recent sightings have also been made in portions of the upper Buuta-u (Barafiri dialect area), as well as the upper Río Shucumona.

38. Data supplied by James Barker and Paul Dye of the New Tribes Mission and pilot Dennis Blue. For a different set of dialects, see Ernest Cesar Migliazza, "Yanomama Grammar and Intelligibility," pp. 34–35.

39. The sounds of *f* and *j* are important in the classification of Yanoama dialects. Such words as *uriji*, *Barajiri*, *ojina*, *oji*, and *hecura*, as used by the Waika and Shamatari, become *urifi*, *Barafiri*, *ofina*, *ofi*, and *fecura* when spoken by Barafiri highlanders.

40. Excluding *shabono* whose location is not yet known, the Casapare dialect region, those Yanoama living together with Carib-Maquiritare, and mission villages outside of Yanoama territory. This total of 128 *shabono* differs considerably from 1964 estimates for the same portion of Yanoama territory. At that time there were thought to be 27 settlements south of the Orinoco and about 65 settlements north of the river. The difference is due to increased information rather than to any increase in Yanoama population.

41. Taken to signify "of some years duration," as contrasted with temporary houses ("seasonal") or permanent ones ("lasting for several generations"). See Butzer, *Environment and Archaeology*, p. 341, where these definitions from W. Müller-Wille are used.

42. *Teri* can be both generic and specific, both singular and plural. It refers to the entire kin-derived residence group, as well as to individuals within the group.

43. For further information, see Migliazza, "Yanomama Grammar," p. 32.

44. *Ashi* is "a fruit of the forest which has a thorn on top" (Biocca, *Yanoáma*, pp. 248–249).

45. Conceivably, all names incorporate the concept of place even where this is not explicit. If so, then the Mayobo-teri, for example, are "people of the toucan place," as well as "people of the toucan" (cf. Migliazza, "Yanomama Grammar," p. 32).

46. Barker, *Cultura de los Guaika*, pp. 28, 30.

47. A walk of well over an hour to get from the *shabono* to a garden is not particularly inconvenient to a Yanoama.

48. For example, the *shabono* of the Yoreshiana-teri, the Mayobo-teri, the Arajai-teri, and the Niyayoba area. It is noteworthy that even in such cases, *shabono* are at the savanna-forest edge.

49. For example, the *shabono* of the Jorocoba-teri, the Waracacoyafiba-teri, the Kafucibuwa-teri, the Yaniyaniwa-teri, the Moshimacabaca-teri, and the Shonofedubaca-teri.

50. Gardens are so important to the Yanoama that these might be interpreted as being the focal points of areal functional organization. Barker says that "the center of the area where the Guaika dwell is the conuco [Venezuelan vernacular for swidden plot]. In the forest which surrounds the conuco are located their temporary and semi-permanent villages" (*Cultura de los Guaika*, p. 30).

51. Bronislaw Malinowski, *The Language and Magic of Gardening*, p. 79.

52. I have seen a *shabono* less than fifty feet in diameter, while Gottfried Polykrates reports the *shabono* of the Wawanaue-teri as an oval about 550 feet by 300 feet, with a total population of 312 ("Wawanaueteri: Ein Janonami Stamm Nordwestbrasiliens," *Folk* 7 [1965]: 127–128).

53. See fig. 1, part C. A representative (observed in the Rio Parima headwaters area) is seventy-five feet in diameter and twenty feet high in the center. The roof tapers down to a vertical wall about six feet in height. The central space, free of roof supports, is where ceremonials are performed. See also Steinvorth-Goetz, *Uriji Jami!* pp. 142–146.

54. See fig. 1, part B. This feature is probably related to the chill weather of their high habitat. The dark, closed *maloca* of lowland tribes is designed as much to protect its inhabitants from insects and the heat of the day as to protect from nighttime cold.

55. In areas of acculturation, where there has been close contact with Carib-Maquiritare or missionaries, this is quite evident. Some Yanoama have adopted rectangular, gable-roofed houses with walls. A few are even built with wattle and daub. On occasion, single nuclear families have built such houses for themselves, destroying the traditional intimacy of the *teri* community.

56. Local hardwoods are used, with preference for those most resistant to rot. At the sites of abandoned *shabono*, the upright roof supports are still visible years after all the roofing has disappeared.

57. *Bisha* is the Barafiri word for a type of needle palm. The Jorocoba-teri *shabono* is thatched largely with *Mauritia* obtained from stands of this palm on swampy land near the Jorocoba-u and its tributaries. Repairs, however, are often made with *bisha* palm. The Niyayoba *shabono*, only a few miles away, is thatched almost exclusively with *bisha* palm. Little *Mauritia* is available to these latter people, since they have destroyed most of the trees.

58. See Steinvorth-Goetz, *Uriji Jami!* pp. 20–21, 26–27, and Barker, *Cultura de los Guaika*, p. 28, for details on thatching techniques.

59. Chagnon, *Yanomamö*, p. 26.

60. When the Barafiri Yanoama camp in the forest, they specify such a location as *urifi jami*, or "forest place."

61. Sometimes called *yano*, or *yafi*, or even *nafi*.

62. Also, the back "wall" of a specific house is called *nano*, just as the floor of the house might be *shabono*.

63. Barker, *Cultura de los Guaika*, p. 38.

64. Ibid., p. 37.

65. This applies to the Venezuelan Barafiri. Some highland Yanoama of Brazil include extra space in their *shabono* to accommodate visitors. Also, among the Barafiri, when *teri* return to their *shabono*, even after a prolonged absence, each man has the right to rebuild his house where the old one stood.

66. Cf. Betty J. Meggers, *Amazonia*, p. 98.

67. Barker, *Cultura de los Guaika*, p. 37.

68. Infants sleep with their mothers until they are weaned.

69. In like manner, when Yanoama converse, they feel a need to be close physically. Sometimes they even take hold of each other when talking about important matters.

70. Calculated from the Jorocoba-teri *shabono*. The population, including infants, is about eighty, and the total area of the *shabono* somewhat less than 8,500 square feet. Cf. Patricia Draper, "Crowding among Hunter-Gatherers: The !Kung Bushmen," *Science* 182 (1973): 302.

71. During a period when their kinsmen were visiting the Niyayoba-teri, twenty-five people were seen to have crowded their hammocks in a horizontal distance of about thirty feet.

72. In 1968, for example, the Bishaasa-teri, who were sufficiently acculturated to have built a village of single-family houses, found it necessary also to build a *shabono* since only in such a place could mortuary and other ceremonials be held (Wallace Jank, 1970, personal communication). Helena Valero recalls that even dog burials are made in *shabono* (Biocca, *Yanoáma*, p. 170).

73. Such a palisade is not unlike those built by numerous sedentary aboriginal populations of the Americas. Palisaded settlements of this sort sometimes received the Spanish name *palenque*. See also Lewis H. Morgan, *Houses and House Life of the American Aborigines*.

74. Helena Valero, describing a palisade, recalls that it was built of *pashuba* palm (*Iriartea exorrhiza*) (Biocca, *Yanoáma*, pp. 203, 380).

75. When raiders sneak up to a *shabono* and fire at close range into an unprotected thatch shelter, their chances of hitting the mark are very good. However, with a sturdy palisade, arrows must arc in order to enter the *shabono* at all; thus, the bowman's aim is unsure, and the danger to occupants of the *shabono* is greatly reduced. Yanoama use neither flaming arrows nor fire in their attacks. In the Parima highlands raids on *shabono* are rare. Overt group hostility more commonly takes the form of surprise raids on men in their gardens or on the trail.

76. Describing the Yanoama, Chagnon says that a *shabono* is usually located in "some well-drained portion of the garden" (*Yanomamö*, p. 26). This circumstance, in which *shabono* are within gardens, might characterize certain Yanoama, as well as manioc-cultivating tribes, but not the Barafiri of the Parima highlands.

77. Cf. Biocca, *Yanoáma*, p. 204.

78. There appears to be a positive correlation between the morale of a *teri* and the condition of their *shabono*. For example, if there is a leadership crisis, fear of attack, or insecurity about future fission, little care is paid to maintenance of their settlement.

79. Within the territories of many highland *teri* are savannas covered with ferns and grasses. These are notably insignificant, since they have practically no economic function.

80. See "The Circulatory System" on the functions of trails and bridges.

81. When a man is asked to enumerate the inhabitants of his *shabono*, he might name only the adult males. The rest of the population is to be inferred.

82. "For the village community the Yanoama do recognize a chief" (Johannes Wilbert, *Survivors of Eldorado*, p. 45). The title *tushaua* is said to mean "headman, chief" (Biocca, *Yanoáma*, p. 380). However, *tushaua* (as used in Brazil) is probably a corruption of a non-Yanoama word.

83. Lionel Tiger speculates that this is true of all human societies (*Men in Groups*, p. 60).

84. Much of the conflict between Yanoama is ultimately based upon some act (or supposed act) of sorcery. If a death is attributed to this cause, then vengeance is required. This might take the form of a raid on the *teri* of the sorcerer who is thought to be guilty. From that point on, murder and consequent revenge raids can become parts of a vicious cycle.

85. These decisions involve such mundane things as when to leave the *shabono* for collecting and where to go, the marriage arrangements for a kinswoman, or whether to build a new *shabono*.

86. An old "chief" of the Patanawe-teri has been described (by Helena Valero, who knew him) as a "kind" and "calm" man "who did not believe in killing" (Biocca, *Yanoáma*, pp. 217–218).

87. Quoted by Robert L. Carneiro in "Slash-and-Burn Cultivation among the Kuikuru and Its Implications for Cultural Development in the Amazon Basin," in *The Evolution of Horticultural Systems in Native South America*, ed. Johannes Wilbert, p. 65 n. 7.

88. Population tallies are very difficult to make. If the *teri* is home and entertaining guests, then an excessively high figure is obtained. More commonly, only a part of the population is in the *shabono* at any given time. The others are absent on visits, working their gardens, hunting, or collecting. Sometimes, too, women and children are sent from the *shabono* when foreigners come. Of course, hearths are visible, and these can be counted. Another method is to make a tally of hammocks in

lieu of a head count, since hammocks are left in place unless people expect to be away for a night or more. Even so, this method does not yield the number of children, since infants sleep with their mothers until they are weaned—somewhere between two and four years of age. Since the Yanoama have no precise numbering system, the leader of a *teri* has no way of telling (or even knowing) the number of people in his *shabono*. However, he could easily name everyone.

89. The ages of Yanoama are not available except in cases of certain young people for whom precise records and observations have been kept. All other information is based only upon very gross calculations that take into account the general appearance of a person and detailed observation of such features as the teeth.

90. Neel, "Ecology of Disease," p. 571. Four hundred Yanoama were studied, although the population was not identified as to location. See also James V. Neel, "Some Aspects of Differential Fertility in Two American Indian Tribes," in *Proceedings of the Eighth International Congress of Anthropological and Ethnological Sciences, 1968 Tokyo and Kyoto*, I, 357.

91. *Statistical Abstract of Latin America: 1966*. Brazilian data are for 1960; Venezuelan data are for 1964.

92. James V. Neel, "Some Changing Constraints on the Human Evolutionary Process," *Proceedings XII International Congress on Genetics* 3 (1969): 392.

93. "Feuds over women occur because almost every village has more males than females . . . some villages have a 35 per cent excess of males" (Napoleon A. Chagnon, "The Feast," *Natural History* 77 [1968]: 35). "In some villages the sex ratio may show a 30 per cent excess of males" (Napoleon A. Chagnon, "Yanomamö Social Organization and Warfare," in "War: The Anthropology of Armed Conflict and Aggression," *Natural History* 76 [1967]: 45). About 53 percent of the four hundred Yanoama Neel studied were male ("Ecology of Disease," p. 571).

94. "Throughout the thesis I have emphasized the causal relationship between the shortage of women and the development of hostilities within and between villages. . . . The frequency of hostilities . . . varies directly with the opportunities for males to satisfy their sexual desires in a socially acceptable way" (Chagnon, "Yanomamö Warfare," pp. 197–198). Although this position is not supported by data gathered in the highland core of their territory, it might apply to a lowland zone of acculturation and acute cultural instability.

95. Males can also be classified as *wanidi*. In the instances where this has been observed, it was related to deformities, such as severe crippling. Elsewhere *wanidi* (or *wani*) merely means "bad," without this Barafiri connotation.

96. "In view of the stated practice of killing at birth children with malformations, we have been impressed by the number of individuals with major congenital defects" (Neel, "Ecology of Disease," p. 570).

97. These data were generously supplied by Margaret Jank of the New Tribes Mission.

98. Preston E. James, *Latin America*, pp. 348, 684.

99. When queried on what they would do if twins were born to them, these women respond that they would probably keep only one. The reasoning is that to have two infants at the same time would be "dirty." Their excrement would provide a much bigger problem than does that of a single infant. It would also be ridiculous to nurse two babies and to try to sleep in a small Yanoama hammock with them both.

100. This highland sample gives no indication of widespread female infanticide as reported by others. Chagnon writes, for example, "as is apparent, there are more males in the Yanomamö population than females. This demographic fact results from the practice of selectively killing female babies" (*Yanomamö*, p. 74). Neel calculated that Yanoama infanticide "involves perhaps 15 to 20 percent of all live births" (" 'Primitive' People," p. 816).

101. "In some respects, such as their apparent commitment to population control and their efforts to live in harmony with their ecosystem, they appear somewhat more sophisticated than modern man" (Neel, "Human Evolutionary Process," p. 390).

102. Precise ages are not known, of course. Women placed in this category are believed to be beyond child-bearing age. The sample studied included nearly 375 people.

103. Neel, "Human Evolutionary Process," p. 393.

104. Evidently, systematic disciplining of children is inconceivable to the Yanoama, and so is spanking.

105. The four *teri* occupying the *shabono* were allied in a "war," but only this one fatality occurred during the two-year period.

106. No generalizations are to be

hazarded from these limited data. There do exist, however, specific statements on causes of death among the Yanoama. For example: "Two percent of all adult deaths are due to snake bite; 54 percent are due to malaria, and other epidemic diseases (Chagnon 1966) and 24 percent of adult males die in warfare" (Chagnon, *Yanomamö*, p. 20 n. 2).

107. Neel, "Human Evolutionary Process," p. 393.

108. In one sample population less than 22 percent were older than thirty (Neel, "Ecology of Disease," p. 571).

109. The linguist Migliazza writes *foo* as "fa" and *noo* as "na"("Yanomama Grammar," pp. 267, 325). They might also be written as *föö* and *nöö*. The important feature of each word is the heavy nasalization when it is spoken.

110. See table 15.

111. The Yanoama recognize a strict mother-in-law taboo, which forbids all contact between a man and his wife's mother. He must also avoid his wife's father, although he might supply food to both parents-in-law.

112. See Chagnon, "Yanomamö Warfare" and *Yanomamö*. "The ideal marriage pattern is patrilineage exogamous with a preference for bilateral cross-cousin marriages, but exceptions are not uncommon" (Neel, "Differential Fertility," p. 357). See also John Fred Peters, "Mate Selection among the Shirishana," *Practical Anthropology* 18 (1971): 19–23.

113. Cross cousins are the children of a woman and of her brother; parallel cousins are the children of brothers or of sisters. One's paternal uncles and maternal aunts are his classificatory "fathers" and "mothers" respectively.

114. This Barafiri term also signifies "forest."

115. The density is approximately one person for each three square miles. Cf. Migliazza, who found community ratios of one inhabitant per 9.6 square miles, 1:4.2 square miles, 1:8.4 square miles, 1:8.1 square miles, and, in the upper Buuta-u, 1:0.9 square mile ("Yanomama Grammar," pp. 19–20).

116. See "The Bonds between the *Teri*."

117. This area lies somewhere between the Wabufita-u on the east, the Jorocoba-u on the north, and the Yananicacataja-u on the west.

118. With fusion, land resources might ultimately be pooled. In the case of the four *teri* sharing the Niyayoba *shabono*, each still retains its own territory. However, with

increasing danger from surprise attack, all four cut their new gardens near the *shabono*, in an area theoretically belonging to the Niyayoba-teri.

119. The Yanoama have been described as "travelers who compulsively keep their hands occupied snapping off brush and twigs as they walk" (Chagnon, *Yanomamö*, p. 19). The Parima Barafiri, however, seem not to fit this description. Men make a point of not touching objects on the trail. Normally, a man's hands are on his bow and arrows, which he holds resting on top of his head (or on one shoulder), with the arrows pointing forward. Women on the trail almost always have something to carry. These burdens are supported by carrying straps (or tumplines) upon which a woman often keeps her hands.

120. When women and children accompany men on trips such as this, it takes about twice as long.

121. Steinvorth-Goetz, *Uriji Jami!* p. 136.

122. A. Hamilton Rice, "The Rio Branco, Uraricuera, and Parima," *Geographical Journal* 71 (1928): 49–50.

123. Biocca, *Yanoáma*, p. 155.

124. Chagnon, *Yanomamö*, p. 20.

125. Such women have some sort of kinship bonds with the hostile *teri*. Too old to be attractive as wives and not to be shot since they are females, they are quite safe.

126. One of the men who married into the Niyayoba-teri was originally a Catarowa-teri. The trip between their two *shabono* takes men anywhere from four to six days.

127. Which group he describes as *barafira ducuma*, "having a strong sorcerer." Locations on map 6 are contemporary and therefore do not coincide in all cases with *teri* locations when they were visited. For example: the Irocoroba-teri no longer exist as a separate entity; the Araoba-teri, Yamajarewa-teri, Awayajorowa-teri, Yaniyana-teri, Boreawa-teri, and Braocuwa-teri are new, having either fissioned from existing *teri* or moved into the region recently; the Monotowa-teri, Shonofedubaca-teri, and Moshimacabaca-teri moved to their present locations just prior to 1970.

128. This excludes raiding.

129. That trip was made years ago, on a visit to the Shokeobo-teri. No *teri* now bears that name.

130. Various people from the Catarowa area have visited the Yaniyaniwa-teri, as well as groups in the Mayobo area. These people from the northeast are frequently referred to as Waika by the Venezuelan Barafiri.

131. There are no islands of unfriendly *teri* within that circumscribed area where a man travels. When warfare broke out between the Juwafusibuwei-teri (and their allies) and the Moshimacabaca-teri (and their allies), the latter moved far to the southeast of their enemies, beyond the friendly Mayobo-teri.

132. It is believed that the Barafiri dialect region extends into the upper Rio Parima area of Brazil. However, people of the three *teri* dealt with here know almost nothing of such neighbors. For example, both Ñape Foo and his son believe that, if they were to travel up the Jaya-u, over the divide, and then downslope to the east, they would encounter the Buunasi people. These are said to be very numerous and "enemies" that will kill. (As used in the Brazilian Parima the term *buun* [or *bun*] seems also to refer to a nebulous population.)

133. This is for good reasons: the personnel and budget for the administrative zone are modest, these highlands are remote and sparsely populated, and, until very recently, the Parima highlands were essentially free of malaria.

134. Each spraying team is required to record the date of spraying, the name of the place sprayed, the number of dwellings there, and the population at the time of spraying. In most teams, someone knows rudimentary Yanoama, so that the *teri* names are generally correct. "Dwellings" are sometimes separate structures, or they might be the hearths of a *shabono*. Population figures are based on visible hammocks or on headcounts.

135. "Each village becomes an isolated entity at the peak of the wet season (June). . . . It is only in the dry season that feasts can be held, because travel is difficult or impossible at other times of the year" (Chagnon, *Yanomamö*, pp. 20, 108 n. 14).

136. Helena Valero explains that the Hekurawe-teri "had once lived with the other Karawetari [*sic*]; then they had quarrelled amongst themselves and split up" (Biocca, *Yanoáma*, p. 53). An effective mechanism exists for resolving most conflicts between kinsmen before they reach really dangerous proportions. This consists of formalized male dueling. It is more frequent during inter-*shabono* group visits, but it can also serve to allay intra-*teri* hostilities. The Barafiri recognize various types of dueling, geared to provide for escalating conflict. The most widespread duel, and the one that usually succeeds in alleviating a man's anger over real or supposed offenses against him, consists of chest pounding. Here, one man challenges another to hit his chest with a closed fist. If the man challenged accepts, then he must submit to similar blows. The formalized sequence of beating continues until one man retreats, becomes senseless, or is taken away by his kinsmen. It is not unusual for a "second" to stand in for a man who is losing. Traditionally, more serious conflicts between kinsmen are settled in duels with *nabrushi* (long poles of peach palm wood). Here again, only two individuals are involved, each man striking a blow alternately with the other man. Additional levels of dueling involve chest pounding, using rocks in clenched fists; there is also sideslapping with the flat of machetes or axes. In all the foregoing types of dueling, it is taboo for a man to kill another. Beyond the realm of dueling is the highest level of aggression, which involves the use of the bow and arrow. On those occasions when it is used, death and warfare are likely to result.

137. The Canashewa-teri were once occupants of the valley of the Canashe-u, a small stream that feeds into the Joreaba-u, itself a tributary of the Niyayoba-u (see map 9).

138. The Mayobo-teri were then living in a *shabono* farther north and at a greater elevation than their present home. It was in the headwaters area of the Mayobo-u, at a "place where arrow cane grows."

139. Essentially, the Mayobo-teri appear to consist of two extended families. One of these tends to marry with the Niyayoba-teri and the Canashewa-teri living to their northwest, while the other tends to marry with the Moshimacabaca-teri to their southeast. The first two *teri* are mortal enemies of the Moshimacabaca-teri. Yet, the Mayobo-teri remain neutral.

140. See chap. 9.

141. *Cayuca* is the word for capybara (*Hydrochaerus hydrochaeris*). Many of these gigantic rodents are supposed to have lived in the area at that time. Even the savanna now called Niyayoba Borosi was then Cayuca Borosi.

142. Sometime prior to 1935, a fierce fight occurred on this savanna. It was between the Jorocoba-teri and the Docodicoro-teri, on the one hand, and an alliance of the Yoreshiana-teri and the Boreawa-teri, on the other. Because of that event the savanna became known as the Niyayoba Borosi (literally, "shoot-at-one-another savanna") and the nearby stream became the Niyayoba-u.

143. This is perhaps true also of the Canashewa-teri, the Docodicoro-teri, and the Juwafusibuwei-teri, all of whom now share a single *shabono* with the Niyayoba-teri. Ancestors of these *teri* are said to have once lived at the headwaters of the Niyayoba-u and northwest toward the Comodoroba-teri, although those highlands are uninhabited now. The Niyayoba-teri say that they have "always" lived near the Niyayoba-u, even though it and they have changed names frequently. Evidences of their occupancy of the general area are clearly seen on map 9.

144. This sort of retreat with allies is not unusual. Whenever possible, the move itself is preceded by the preparation of new gardens.

145. As late as 1964, the Yoreshiana-teri were still being referred to as "enemies." However, by 1970, the Jorocoba-teri included the Yoreshiana-teri among their "friends." Like the Mayobo-teri, the Jorocoba-teri now feel sufficiently secure in their peace so that women go about without armed men, and sometimes men will even go to their gardens unarmed.

146. The principal reason, or reasons, for specific *shabono* relocations are difficult to ascertain. However, one is available for the most recent move of the Jorocoba-teri in 1965, when they left their old *shabono* on a small ridge east of the Yoodiba-u in order to build on the west bank of the Jorocoba-u. It is indeed prosaic: one of the elders (Dimanami Foo) decided the old *shabono* had too many chigoes.

147. This would appear to hold for the Orinoco lowlands as well. The Coshirowa-teri, for example, use the word *cuabaowa* for "a man married [into the *shabono*] from outside," and for "an unimportant person." "The founding nucleus of . . . a village consists of two intermarried pairs of brothers and (consanguineally with them unrelated) sisters and their descendants. The two resulting lineages exchange their women, thereby fostering a web of affinal relationships" (Wilbert, *Survivors of Eldorado*, p. 46).

148. Among the Barafiri there is no evident consistency in the matter of where a newly married couple will live. Wilbert writes, however, that "post-nuptial residence is matri-local; the groom joins the household of the bride's parents and renders them brideservice for some time" (ibid., p. 54).

149. Included here are two rather exceptional cases. One involves a Mayobo-teri man who married a Jorocoba-teri woman, moved here, and then got a second wife from still another *teri* (Docodicoro-teri). The second case is that of another Mayobo-teri man who moved in with the Jorocoba-teri when he married a pair of sisters, rather than take them back home with him.

150. It will be remembered that the Shokekere-teri were the immediate predecessors of the Niyayoba-teri. Only the older people from that *teri* are ever identified as Shokekere-teri.

151. Sometime prior to 1940, during a period when the Juwafusibuwei-teri and the Canashewa-teri shared a *shabono* on the Joreaba-u (see map 9), they were known collectively as the Joreaba-teri.

152. News, messages, and special kinds of group requests are transmitted in a very formal, esoteric manner, which has been called a "ceremony . . . of the transmission of messages" (Anduze, *Shailili-ko*, pp. 160–161). Here use is made of the *wayamo*, or formal Yanoama. The news chant is extremely repetitious and so lengthy that an entire night can be occupied by it, with different men (hosts and guests) participating. At dawn the chanting ends abruptly. In this remarkable manner, without the use of proper names except in reference to enemies, a hunt is described, announcements of death are made, the results of a raid conveyed, and invitations extended.

153. Biocca, *Yanoáma*, p. 253. She describes another *reajo* on pp. 181–182.

154. Ibid., p. 215. Tearful participants were numerous; "many came; they came from other tribes." These included people from the original group (the Namoe-teri), as well as the Gnaminawe-teri, the Patanawe-teri, and the Hasubue-teri. The Patanawe-teri, to whom the deceased woman belonged, served as hosts.

155. During an eighteen-month period, only one *showao* was held in the big Niyayoba *shabono*, which houses four friendly *teri*.

4. Yanoama Livelihood

1. The observation was made in chap. 2 that some students of the Yanoama hold to a different viewpoint. They suggest that revolutionary economic changes have occurred recently with the introduction of agriculture. Some of the most unyielding

statements to this effect appear in Johannes Wilbert's *Survivors of Eldorado*, pp. ix, 33–35, 41, and passim.

2. These units are discussed in detail in chap. 8. Included in the category of household are certain other kin groupings of minimal size, such as those where some combination of the elderly, *wanidi*, orphaned children, and single adults might live together sharing a hearth or hearths. These correspond functionally to households but are not necessarily economic units.

3. In this kind of subsistence economy, "a single social unit performs the economic functions relating to production and distribution as well as consumption" (Philip L. Wagner, *The Human Use of the Earth*, p. 65).

4. Such a relationship could be classified as "obligate" (ibid., p. 15).

5. This organization should be viewed as integrated into a larger, total ecosystem, whose dimensions are unknown to the individual Yanoama.

6. In a similar vein, among the Hanunóo in the Philippines, land cannot be "possessed, alienated, or controlled by any member or segment of . . . society" (Harold C. Conklin, *Hanunóo Agriculture*, p. 147). "Traditionally, land and labor are not separated; labor forms part of life, land remains part of nature, life and nature form an articulate whole" (Karl Polanyi, *The Great Transformation*, p. 178).

7. The Yanoama "rely very heavily on cultivated foods: in some areas upwards of 80–90% of their caloric intake comes from garden produce" (Napoleon A. Chagnon, "The Culture-Ecology of Shifting [Pioneering] Cultivation among the Yanomamö Indians," in *Proceedings of the Eighth International Congress of Anthropological and Ethnological Sciences, 1968 Tokyo and Kyoto*, III, 249).

8. See, e.g., James Barker, *Memoria sobre la cultura de los Guaika, Boletín Indigenista Venezolano* 1 (1953): 32, and Ettore Biocca, *Yanoáma*, pp. 209–210.

9. Among others, Conklin has attempted to classify subtypes of shifting cultivation. He concludes that "established, integral swidden agriculture . . . is a *pattern of living* in which everyone in the society participates" (italics mine). His use of the term "established" implies a location fixed in space (Conklin, *Hanunóo*, p. 139). In this sense, the Yanoama can be said to practice an established, integral form of agriculture.

Napoleon A. Chagnon believes that the Yanoama system of shifting cultivation is a "somewhat rare form" because it is "pioneering." See his "Culture-Ecology of Shifting Cultivation," p. 249, and "Yanomamö Warfare, Social Organization and Marriage Alliances," p. 205.

10. Perhaps it might be classified as a "necessary" surplus. See Marvin Harris, "The Economy Has No Surplus?" *American Anthropologist* 61 (1959): 197.

11. *Momo* represents a case in point. These nutlike fruits from trees of the genus *Hevea* are poisonous in their natural state. After the shells are broken, the hard fruits are soaked and rinsed in water to eliminate the toxic substances. Then they can be stored dry (as they are in the Brazilian Parima), or they might be grated on coarse stone to produce a meal that can also be dried and stored (as is done by the Venezuelan Barafiri). With either method *momo* is reported to keep for weeks. See also Biocca, *Yanoáma*, pp. 76–77, on the preparation and storage of this fruit. In the Brazilian Parima some groups preserve small quantities of peeled plantains by roasting or boiling them and later stringing them on vines stretched over their hearth fires.

12. The formal response is a chant reminding the receiver of the gifts and favors that have been provided by the giver. In the host-guest context of social visiting, it is generally the visitors who are expected to ask for gifts and the hosts who are to provide them. Some observers are surprised by the lack of a Yanoama term for "thank you." For example, if given a fish hook, a Yanoama says, "Where is the line to go with it?" To ask for something is to flatter its owner.

13. In 1970 in the Niyayoba area, the Barafiri sought goods from the outside world in the following order of priority: axes, machetes, and aluminum pots; of secondary importance were dyed cotton thread (for hammocks) and dogs. Axes are in a class by themselves, because of their utility in clearing garden sites. In this sense, the ax resembles the spade, which was eagerly accepted by the horticultural Fore people in preference to cloth or metal pots. See Richard E. Sorenson, "Socio-Ecological Change among the Fore of New Guinea," *Current Anthropology* 13 (1972): 367.

14. In the 1920's the Juwafusibuwei-teri obtained their first steel tool, an ax, given them by the Yoreshiana-teri to reciprocate gifts of cotton thread. At that time the

Yoreshiana-teri were themselves short of steel tools. The exchange was related to me in this manner, without mention of individuals, but rather as an exchange between *teri*.

15. It is reported that in a period of a few years about two thousand steel machetes were dispersed throughout Yanoama territory by the Venezuelan Malariology Service. The Service gave them to a few *teri* living along the Orinoco and learned later that these same machetes were appearing among Yanoama in Brazil, far to the east of the Parima massif.

16. Neither Creole nor Carib-Maquiritare traders have effectively penetrated Yanoama territory. For one thing, the Yanoama do not produce valuable trade items, such as manioc flour and cotton hammocks. For another, they are isolated from navigable waterways that are generally frequented by traders and merchants. And the Yanoama are still widely believed to be dangerous, or at least unpredictable.

17. This idea is developed by Anthony Leeds, "Yaruro Incipient Tropical Forest Horticulture—Possibilities and Limits," in *The Evolution of Horticultural Systems in Native South America*, ed. Johannes Wilbert, p. 22.

18. Robert L. Carneiro infers this for the tropical forest peoples of the entire Amazon lowland, writing that "no ecological pressure developed which might have led to the intensification of cultivation" ("Slash-and-Burn Cultivation among the Kuikuru and Its Implications for Cultural Development in the Amazon Basin," in *The Evolution of Horticultural Systems in Native South America*, ed. Johannes Wilbert, p. 62). See also Donald W. Lathrap, *The Upper Amazon*, p. 74.

19. Barker writes that men generally work in their gardens from about 7 or 8 A.M. until about mid-day (*Cultura de los Guaika*, p. 21). Most of his observations were of lowland Yanoama, somewhat acculturated and aware of what was obtainable through bartering their garden surpluses. In the Parima highlands, men were observed to work somewhat less.

20. The Yanoama seem to have more leisure than we permit ourselves, and people can be found resting at any time of the waking day. Yet, when a task is undertaken, a Yanoama persists until he considers the job finished. Both men and women show great stamina when carrying heavy loads on the trail. Men work hard for lengthy periods clearing forest for new gardens, and they move at a grueling pace when on the hunt. The presence of ample leisure has not led to

enterprising inventiveness and revolutionary change. Evidently other stimuli are required. Cf. Carneiro's discussion of leisure among the male Kuikuru, "Cultivation among the Kuikuru," pp. 49, 54.

21. See chap. 9 on the subject of landscape modification.

22. The forest fallow periods used by the Yanoama have not yet been accurately estimated. Data exist for other populations, however. See, e.g., Pierre Gourou, "The Quality of Land Use of Tropical Cultivators," in *Man's Role in Changing the Face of the Earth*, ed. William L. Thomas et al., p. 338. Chagnon reports that the Yanoama "utilize only virgin jungle" ("Culture-Ecology of Shifting Cultivation," p. 252 n. 4).

23. Mario Sanoja, comparing the early (A.D. 1150–1500) inhabitants of the Lake Valencia area of Venezuela with those of the Orinoco, states that "the wild plant and animal food sources were sufficiently abundant to provide a food surplus without intensification of agricultural production, so there was no incentive for the people to look for ways of improving their dominion over nature" ("Cultural Development in Venezuela," in *Aboriginal Cultural Development in Latin America*, ed. Betty J. Meggers and Clifford Evans, p. 74).

24. Affluence is viewed here in a Zen Buddhist context. For people like the Barafiri, "human material wants are finite and few, and technical means unchanging but on the whole adequate" (Marshall D. Sahlins, *Stone Age Economics*, p. 2; he is referring to hunters specifically).

5. Horticulture

1. Cf. Carl O. Sauer, "The Agency of Man on the Earth," in *Man's Role in Changing the Face of the Earth*, ed. William L. Thomas et al., pp. 56–57.

2. In both of these rapidly "modernizing" countries, shifting cultivation continues to be widespread among rural Creole populations. In this book the terms *horticulture* and *gardening* are generally used in preference to foreign words and the rather unwieldy expression *shifting cultivation*.

3. *Ficari taca* is "garden clearing," although *ficari cano* is also used in the Parima highlands.

4. Sauer, "Agency of Man," p. 57.

5. Sometimes, as Barafiri women chant

for the success of their men away on the hunt, they also ask that the plantains in the gardens grow well.

6. With acculturation, and particularly where bitter manioc becomes important as a staple, women can play a larger role.

7. Brazilian Yanoama of the Surucucu area have a similar term to denote a person who is industrious when gardening. The root word is *Coyerin*, a spirit being who "makes the plants grow." A completely different term, *ajodema* (*ohotemu*), refers to a willing worker in contexts other than gardening.

8. In the Orinoco lowlands, some boys only eleven or twelve years old prepare their own small gardens, and even younger boys might set out their own plants in a father's or an older brother's garden (James Barker, *Memoria sobre la cultura de los Guaika, Boletín Indigenista Venezolano* 1 [1953]: 16).

9. This feature applies to the highland Barafiri, if not to other Yanoama.

10. There "a woman's garden is virtually her private domain" (Irving Goldman, *The Cubeo*, p. 30). For an excellent analysis of the feminine and secular nature of Cubeo horticulture, see ibid., pp. 52–53, 58, 63.

11. Helena Valero describes how her group, expecting to get involved in a war, moved far from all other *shabono*. First, however, they made a large new garden at the site, which was three days' travel from the nearest friendly *shabono* (Ettore Biocca, *Yanoáma*, pp. 209–210).

12. Highland Yanoama of the Brazilian Parima refer to places that are good for plantains as being *nuoshea*. There is no information on usage of the term *ishabena* among the Yanoama of the Orinoco lowlands. There, good land for gardening is referred to as *mashita dodijadawa*. In such a place (1) the surface is reasonably flat, (2) the soil contains many large earthworms, (3) there is little wind, and (4) rainfall is abundant (Gary Dawson, 1970, personal communication). Cf. Leopold Pospisil, *Kapauku Papuan Economy*, pp. 86–87, on vegetative cover as a criterion in garden-site selection among New Guinea aboriginals.

13. The word *alemasijenaco* translates to *platanillo* in Spanish. *Platanillo* is "the collective name for various species of *Heliconia*" (L. Schnee, *Plantas comunes de Venezuela, Revista de la Facultad de Agronomía*, Alcance no. 3; p. 513). Only three species are identified in Schnee's exhaustive work: *H. latispatha* Benth., *H. psittacorum* L.f., and *H. Bihai* [sic] L.

14. One informant defined *ishabena* as

"forest where *cowata* will grow." *Cowata* is the Barafiri word for the kind of plantain they most esteem and plant the most of.

15. The Docodicoro-teri of the Niyayoba area are a case in point. They had become so dissatisfied with gardening on the low, alluvial terraces near the safety of the *shabono* that they cleared a large new garden high in the mountains about four miles to the south. This brought them much closer to certain enemies (the Bashobaca-teri), but they took the risk because they felt there was no place closer to the *shabono* that was as good for growing the *cowata* plantain.

16. One of the Jorocoba-teri gardens (Boredidire-taca/Canawaubrare-taca) has been described by some men as "abnormal" (*wanidi*). Its slopes of 35° and 40° are too steep even for most Yanoama. See map 9.

17. Napoleon A. Chagnon writes that among the Yanoama "a garden has a direction—it moves, little by little" (*Yanomamö*, p. 35). However, in the Parima highlands there is no evidence of this. Nor is there evidence that the Barafiri use any analogies between human physiology and their gardens, e.g., that the " 'rectum' (*bei kä bosi*) of the garden is gradually abandoned, and a new 'nose' (*bei kä hushibö*) is added" (ibid., p. 35). In the Parima highlands, the *bei kä bosi* part of a garden is the lower, downslope portion, whether it be a new addition or an old part of the clearing.

18. Helena Valero uses the term in this context, but spells it *teka* (Biocca, *Yanoáma*, p. 205). Inga Steinvorth-Goetz writes that the Yanoama "call their settlements teca, literally hole, in the sense of 'hole cut into the forest.' 'Teca' is added as a suffix to the name of a local group to denote the *settlement*" (*Uriji Jami!* p. 25; italics mine).

19. A garden clearing can also bear the name of the *teri* to which it belongs. Helena Valero identifies gardens in this manner, e.g., "Mahekototeka" belonging to the "Mahekototeri" and "Patanaweteka" belonging to the "Patanaweteri" (Biocca, *Yanoáma*, pp. 176, 205). This sort of terminology is very imprecise, however, since numerous clearings can bear the same appellation. The Barafiri use such a name only if they wish to simplify things for a questioner, since there is usually another distinguishing proper name for every garden clearing.

20. Ibid., p. 110.

21. Barker writes that "the Guaika are continually preparing new 'conucos' " (*Cultura de los Guaika*, p. 31).

22. Barker quotes an old Yanoama

woman of El Platanal (an acculturated settlement in the Orinoco lowlands): "These people of today have it easy: We did not have machetes and axes before. Fire was our principal work implement. We had to carry much firewood to pile around the trees, in order to burn them down" (ibid., pp. 14–15). Ursula M. Cowgill, writing on the agricultural tradition of the Petén Maya, cautions that "it is important to note that the use of stone rather than steel tools would not imply any difference in the total population which could be fed. It only implies that a somewhat smaller proportion of the total labor supply would be available for tasks other than food production. Hester (1952) found that it took twice as long to clear a plot of land using limestone chips as with steel tools. Few operations other than clearing would be much affected by the absence of steel tools" ("An Agricultural Study of the Southern Maya Lowlands," *American Anthropologist* 64 [1962]: 278). Jacques Bordaz discusses the effectiveness of polished celt tools (*Tools of the Old and New Stone Age*, p. 99).

23. Theodor Koch-Grünberg spent a brief period in 1912 visiting a small number of Brazilian Waika. He was a man convinced that agriculture had only recently been introduced to them, along with metal tools. He wrote: "They had no axes to clear forest. A stone ax which I showed them made no impression on them" (*Vom Roroima zum Orinoco*, p. 200). In contrast, Steinvorth-Goetz writes that "before the advent of steel axes, the Yanoama used hatchets of polished black stone, rounded off on both sides and fastened with vines to a notched handle" (*Uriji Jami!* p. 34).

24. This information is attested to in a consistent manner by living Barafiri, who recall the period of their horticulture that predated steel tools. Cf. Allan R. Holmberg, who reports that poles for framing Sirionó communal houses "are cut from nearby trees with machetes, but formerly they were doubtless hacked off with the digging stick" (*Nomads of the Long Bow*, p. 35).

25. Barker writes that small plants are pulled from the ground (*Cultura de los Guaika*, p. 14).

26. These are not usually the largest specimens. Possibly they are left to provide shade or for some mystical purposes.

27. Helena Valero lived with one group that prepared a "big" garden clearing in seven or eight days. However, the job was done under pressure, and they had help from a friendly *teri* (Biocca, *Yanoáma*, pp.

209–210). The Barafiri term for clearing the forest to make gardens is *ficarimo*. It also means "gardening" in a broad sense, since it includes such tasks as planting and weeding.

28. For information on the impact of firing and the merits of double burning, see Emil B. Haney, Jr., "The Nature of Shifting Cultivation in Latin America," pp. 8–9.

29. Perhaps, since some plants grow to a height of twenty-five feet, certain writers erroneously refer to them as "trees." In fact, they are "giant perennial herbs [which] are potentially immortal" (J. J. Ochse et al., *Tropical and Subtropical Agriculture*, I, 376).

30. For a similar observation, see Harold C. Conklin, *Hanunóo Agriculture*, p. 147.

31. Luís Cocco refers to *platanales* ("Más allá del turismo: Los indios Guaicas," *El Farol* 32 [1970]: 51). Steinvorth-Goetz writes of "plantain and banana gardens" and of a "banana grove" (*Uriji Jami!* pp. 14, 40). On the north bank of the upper Río Orinoco, about halfway between the mouth of the Río Mavaca and the Raudal de los Guaharibos, there is a place that for years has borne the name "El Platanal." Evidently, the first Spanish-speaking people to arrive found many plantains growing and named it accordingly. In all likelihood what they encountered was a Yanoama garden.

32. Barker, *Cultura de los Guaika*, p. 14.

33. James V. Neel, "Genetic Aspects of the Ecology of Disease in the American Indian," in *The Ongoing Evolution of Latin American Population*, ed. F. A. Salzano, p. 564.

34. Even the small, frightened group of "Shiriana" that Rice encountered in the uppermost reaches of Brazil's Rio Parima (in April 1925) brought him "several bunches of small miserable-looking wild bananas." This occurred after contact had been made with them, and the Rice party had distributed gifts (A. Hamilton Rice, "The Rio Branco, Uraricuera, and Parima," *Geographical Journal* 71 [1928]: 53).

35. These sources appear in the Bibliography.

36. *Musa paradisiaca* and *Musa sapientum* are so similar botanically that they are not always classified as different species. For example, both the "plantain" and the "banana proper" are classified as *M. paradisiaca* by David R. Harris ("The Ecology of Swidden Cultivation in the Upper Orinoco Rain Forest, Venezuela," *Geographical Review* 61 [1971]: 478). However, plantain and banana are identified as *M. paradisiaca* and *M. sapientum* respectively by Carl L. Johannessen ("The Dispersal of *Musa* in Central America: The

Domestication Process in Action," *Annals of the Association of American Geographers* 60 [1970]: 689–699). No less an authority than N. W. Simmonds maintains that the term *plantain* is almost meaningless because of its varied usages around the world. He uses it "strictly as a cultivar name applied to a group of closely related clones (of which one happens to be identifiable with *Musa paradisiaca* L.)" (*Bananas*, p. 57). Nevertheless, in popular speech the English word *plantain* serves to identify "cooking bananas." Plantains tend to be more starchy than bananas, to have a somewhat drier flesh, and, most important, when used as a human food they are cooked. For these reasons, the words *banana* and *plantain* ought not be used interchangeably, although in much of the literature on the Yanoama this is done, or *banana* is used exclusively. Hans Becher provides a list of names for some of the varieties of bananas grown by the Surára and Pakidái and their counterparts in regional *caboclo* (the vernacular of northeastern Brazil). In this list bananas and plantains are not distinguished in any way, nor are the *caboclo* terms meaningful to most Brazilians ("A importância da banana entre os índios Surára e Pakidái," *Revista de Antropología* 5 [1957]: 193).

37. I am unconvinced that such a universal generic term does exist. However, Cocco writes that *kurata* is the designation for plantains in general ("Indios Guaicas," p. 53). It is his belief that the word is a Carib corruption of the Spanish word *plátano*. Becher, in discussing Brazilian Yanoama whom he calls Surára and Pakidái, states that among these groups the "generic designation for all bananas is kurata" ("Importância da banana," p. 193).

38. The fruit resembles the *resplandor* of Venezuelan vernacular speech, but requires cooking. Pablo J. Anduze classifies it as a banana (*cambur*) (*Shailili-ko*, p. 199).

39. The fruit corresponds roughly to the popular Venezuelan *hartón*, a type of "Horn Plantain" according to Simmonds (*Bananas*, p. 89).

40. Called *rabarimo* (or *rabaimo*) by the Orinoco Waika. It corresponds to the *costeña* of Venezuelan vernacular.

41. This is reported to belong to the type Venezuelans call *manzano* (apple) bananas and some Brazilians call *banana maçã* (see Becher, "Importância da banana," p. 193; Simmonds, *Bananas*, pp. 91, 122; and João Ferreira da Cunha, *Cultura da bananeira*, p. 21).

42. Anduze identifies this as *cambur morado* (*Shailili-ko*, p. 199). It can also be described as a *manzano* type with red fruit.

43. Becher identifies them as "red" and "white" São Tomé respectively ("Importância da banana," p. 193).

44. *Ocumo* is the popular Venezuelan term. Elsewhere in the Caribbean area the terms *yautía* and *tania* are used. The genus *Xanthosoma* (usually *X. sagittifolium*) is native to the West Indies and South America. In contrast, the genus *Colocasia* (to which belong the *taro, danchi*, and *ocumo culín*) is of Old World origin (see, e.g., Schnee, *Plantas comunes*, pp. 444–445). This is probably the *taro* of Napoleon A. Chagnon ("Yanomamö Warfare, Social Organization and Marriage Alliances," p. 35). Other writers are more specific. For example, Biocca identifies the *uhina* of the Yanoama as a *Colocasia* "producing a kind of potato" (*Yanoáma*, p. 380), and Gottfried Polykrates classifies as *Colocasia* the Yanoama *ohiná* (*Wawanaueteri und Pukimapueteri*, p. 125).

45. *Mapuey* in popular Venezuelan speech. Old World yams (*D. alata* and *D. bulbifera*) are also known to Creole Venezuelans, but these are called *ñames*.

46. Schnee, *Plantas comunes*, p. 72.

47. There is disagreement over whether any significant botanical difference exists between sweet and bitter maniocs. Karl H. Schwerin maintains that there is no clear distinction between the two ("Apuntes sobre la Yuca y sus Orígenes," *Boletín Informativo de Antropología* 7 [1970]: 25). Donald W. Lathrap also stresses their similarities. He is satisfied that poisonous manioc is a cultigen developed more recently than the non-poisonous variety (*The Upper Amazon*, p. 49).

48. Bitter-manioc cultivation is of rapidly increasing importance to those Yanoama undergoing acculturation. Even so, it does not usually supplant plantains as the principal food source.

49. The following identify *rasha* as *Bactris*: Barker, *Cultura de los Guaika*, p. 17; Biocca, *Yanoáma*, p. 380; and Otto Zerries, "Los indios Guaika y su situación cultural: Informe preliminar de la expedición frobenius al alto Orinoco," *Boletín Indigenista Venezolano* 2 (1954): 66. However, Steinvorth-Goetz writes that "Pijiguao," "peach palm," and "rasha" are all "Guilelma Gasipaes [sic]" (*Uriji Jami!* p. 30). Schnee classifies the "Pichiguao" as "*Guilielma gasipaes* (H.B.K.) Bailey" (*Plantas comunes*, p. 502).

50. Schnee, *Plantas comunes*, pp. 22, 220, 502, 511.

51. In the highlands, too, they are of minor dietetic importance; much of the peach palm fruit eaten in the high Parima consists of gifts from friendly lowland *teri*. It is to be remembered that most of the Yanoama studied have been lowland groups. Perhaps for this reason the importance of the peach palm has been stressed. See, e.g., Zerries, who writes that "the Guaika seasonally rely heavily on the fruit of the Pijiguao palm" ("Situación cultural," p. 66), and Daniel de Barandiarán, who suggests that the "pijiguao feast" is the most important Yanoama feast and that "the round of these pijiguao feasts among villages continues without interruption for almost three months" ("La fiesta del pijiguao entre los indios Waikas," *El Farol* 28 [1966]: 15). In fact, what Barandiarán seems to be describing is the *reajo*, since he writes of the ritual ingestion of pulverized human bone and says that a "pijiguao feast" might be held without pijiguao, but never "without an exorbitant quantity of plantains" (p. 9).

52. Ochse et al., *Tropical Agriculture*, I, 697.

53. If they are not damaged, papaya plants will fruit for eight to ten years (ibid., p. 593).

54. Ibid., p. 592.

55. Ibid. One such enzyme, papain, is an ingredient of commercial meat tenderizers.

56. Another source of vegetable dyes is a plant called genipap in English. Two species, *Genipa americana* L. and *G. caruto* H.B.K., both known as *caruto* in Venezuela, are widely distributed throughout tropical America (Schnee, *Plantas comunes*, p. 158). There is no evidence, however, that either of these species is planted by the Barafiri.

57. This is usually classified as *Bixa orellana*, although Anduze reports that those he saw in the upper Orinoco area were different from the *orellana* species (*Shailili-ko*, p. 200). If this is the case, the plant cultivated by the Yanoama is not identical to the *onoto* of the Creole Venezuelans. Creole Brazilians know *bixa* as *urucú*.

58. One aromatic grass (*maqui oma shico* in Barafiri) observed in Canawaubrare-taca is said to be rubbed on the body for healing purposes; another is rubbed on arrow points in order to aid in the hunt; yet other herbs, known as *faro*, are powdered and "blown" on enemies. The cyperaceous *aroari* might be included in this last group.

59. Biocca, *Yanoáma*, p. 241.

60. "The Hasubueteri have so many arrows, because in their mountains the canes from which arrows are made grow well, while in the plains of the Namoeteri they do not grow well" (ibid., p. 158). Barker (*Cultura de los Guaika*, p. 33) and Harris ("Ecology of Swidden," p. 480) report it in the Orinoco lowlands. The latter calls the plant "Indian arrowleaf" and identifies it as *"Gynerium sagittatum* (Aubl.) P. Beauv." However, Schnee calls this same plant *caña amarga* or *caña brava*, giving as its Venezuelan habitat "the hot country [*tierra caliente*] along the banks of rivers" (*Plantas comunes*, pp. 133–134). I am inclined to accept that the Barafiri use some species of *Gynerium*, but not necessarily *caña brava*.

61. When the first missionaries reached a newly opened Brazilian government base in the Niyayoba area in 1961, the Barafiri there were growing a few clumps of sugar cane. Obviously they prized it very highly, because one man offered three stalks of cane for a steel ax (Gay Cable, 1971, personal communication).

62. This is remarkable, since the Parima Yanoama are very fond of sweet-tasting foods, including honey, which is a favorite. They endlessly badger visitors for candy, and they enjoy chewing on sugar cane, yet they plant it very little of it.

63. Rice writes of the Yanoama, "Their resemblance to primates was heightened by the swollen, turned outward effect of the lower lip, produced by the maligate or curved plate of coca [*sic*] inserted between the incisors of the inferior maxilla and the mucus membrane of the lower lip" ("Rio Branco," p. 52). He identifies this *coca* as *Erythoxylon coca*. All other sources agree that it is tobacco that is so used, and I identified the garden plant as tobacco. However, the idea suggested by Rice is fascinating, since the highland Yanoama habitat resembles the tropical highlands of western South America where *coca* is widely cultivated. Certain *Erythroxylum*, such as *E. amazonicum* (Peyr.), may exist in the territory occupied by the Yanoama (see Schnee, *Plantas comunes*, p. 105).

64. Barker, *Cultura de los Guaika*, p. 15.

65. Lathrap classifies the perennial cotton bushes of tropical forest cultures as *Gossypium barbadense* (*Upper Amazon*, p. 59). Similarly, Harris identifies the "shrubs of perennial cotton" in a Waika garden of the Orinoco lowlands as "*Gossypium barbadense* L. var. *brasiliense* (Macf.) Hutch" ("Ecology of Swidden," p. 479). Schnee lists three *Gossypium* found in Venezuela that he believes to be exclusively New World cottons: *G. purpurascens* Poir., *G. lapideum*

Tussac. (*Gossypium brasiliense* Macf.) [*sic*], and *G. barbadense* L. (*Plantas comunes*, pp. 27–29).

66. For example, Steinvorth-Goetz, *Uriji Jami!* p. 72; Volkmar Vareschi, *Orinoco Arriba*, p. 158; Gottfried Polykrates, "Wawanaueteri: Ein Janonami Stamm Nordwestbrasiliens," *Folk* 7 (1965): 113; and Zerries, "Situación cultural," p. 71.

67. Barafiri informants also give the names *nijiyoma* and *jorocodo*.

68. Various writers report that the lowland Yanoama have this plant. Steinvorth-Goetz refers simply to "the bottle gourd" (*Uriji Jami!* p. 33). Harris refers to the "bottle gourd (*Langenaria siceraria* [Molina] Standl.)" ("Ecology of Swidden," p. 480).

69. All sorts of confusion result from the application of a few popular names to several species. For example, *taparo* is used synonymously with *totumo* in Venezuela, and *totumo* refers both to *Crescentia cujete* and to *Lagenaria siceraria*. Similarly, Carl O. Sauer points out that, from the times of the earliest European observers in America, the squash (*Cucurbita*), the bottle gourd (*Lagenaria*), and the tree gourd (*Crescentia*) have all been referred to as *calabaza* in Spanish vernacular speech (*The Early Spain Main*, pp. 55).

70. Wallace Jank, 1970, personal communication.

71. Thus, *yono si* is the maize plant, *yono mobo* is maize kernels, *yono mocu* is corn on the cob, and *yono mojii* is corn meal (or corn flakes). This is very similar to the usage of *nashi* as the root word for all references to manioc. In the Orinoco lowlands, particularly in the vicinity of missions and government posts, some Yanoama devote respectable proportions of their gardens to maize. This tends to be the "new" maize, which they are encouraged to use; much of it is destined for barter with the foreigners, who use it as food for themselves or their chickens. Yanoama do not eat it, as a rule, nor are they inclined to keep fowls even in such areas of extreme acculturation.

72. It is conceivable that this is the procedure when planting "new" maize only. Valero, for example, reports religious ritual in the planting of maize among the southern Yanoama. A woman begins the process by soaking a basket of the kernels to be planted in a stream. After three days her body is painted with *bixa*; then she removes the basket of kernels from the water and places it in a shady place. Three days after that the kernels have germinated and people then plant them. During planting, the spirit of the *sauva* ant is invoked, since he taught the Yanoama how to cultivate maize. At the time of planting, too, no one in the *shabono* may eat crocodile (or the maize ears would not have "teeth") or a certain forest tortoise (or the wind would ruin the plants) (Biocca, *Yanoáma*, pp. 164–165).

73. Likewise, the large domesticated Brazilian pineapple (*Ananas comosus* or *A. sativus*) was introduced to the Barafiri soon after 1960. It, too, has disappeared. The only pineapples eaten now are small, wild ones that are gathered in certain savanna areas.

74. Brazilian Yanoama of the Rio Parima headwaters area occasionally use a stafflike palmwood tool (*sejema* or *shocobi*) for this task.

75. Different materials can be used for planting; for example, in the case of bananas, bits of large corms, maidens, sword suckers, water suckers, peepers, and spear points. Further, "for the tropics, the type of sucker used is, within wide limits, unimportant" (Simmonds, *Bananas*, p. 161). Ochse et al. maintain that rhizome pieces are preferred for propagation (*Tropical Agriculture*, I, 376). Cunha suggests that there are two types of transplanting: the use of a piece of rhizome weighing from 1.5 to 2 kgs, and the use of a lateral shoot. The latter, according to Cunha, is more common in small plantings (*Cultura da bananeira*, p. 53).

76. A load can easily weigh eighty pounds. Helena Valero describes vividly the work of transporting heavy loads of these suckers: "So we took those seedlings [suckers]: it was very hard work on those mountains. I walked carrying the burden on my back, with the strip of bark across my forehead, leaning on two sticks so as not to slip. The *tushaua* [headman] carried an enormous basket, full. Thus we walked for three days in order to get to the *roça* that we had prepared" (Biocca, *Yanoáma*, p. 210).

77. See map 13. There is no resemblance to the uniformity of a commercial banana plantation, plants are not set out in rows, different varieties of plantains and bananas are planted together, and the whole area is intercropped with other species.

78. Among the Namoe-teri (prior to 1957) there was a belief that, when the hummingbird taught the Yanoama about cotton, he told them to "sow your seeds so that you get young plants, then plants with fruit, then old plants; in that way you will always have cotton" (Biocca, *Yanoáma*, p. 130).

79. Of the eleven clearings intensively researched for this book, only one relatively flat site (Cuaisiba-taca of the Jorocoba-teri) seems to have been selected with deliberation; the other two (Niyayoba-taca and Waratau-taca of the Niyayoba-teri) were chosen only because the factor of danger weighed so heavily. Polykrates observed that the Wawanaue-teri were cultivating "steep slopes" ("Wawanaueteri," p. 128).

80. The soils exposed by clearing the forest tend to be fertile, friable loams, particularly in the well-drained, higher elevations of the Parima massif, which the Barafiri seem to prefer for their gardens. Of course, sheet erosion sometimes accentuates normal differences between soils in a catena along the continuum of a slope. Only out on the savannas, where they have been stripped by erosion, have soils become hardened and literally lateritic.

81. "As to soil, members of *Musa* will not stand poor drainage but otherwise seem to be tolerant of a virtually infinite range of parent materials, textures, [and] fertilities" (N. W. Simmonds, *The Evolution of the Bananas*, p. 32). Cunha points out that the preferred soils for bananas are clayey-sandy, rich in humus, deep, and well drained (*Cultura da bananeira*, p. 32). The great elevations of many Yanoama gardens, some at or above 1,000 meters, would seem to prohibit successful *Musa* cultivation, but this is not the case. See, e.g., Ochse et al., who say that bananas are not recommended above 1,000 meters (*Tropical Agriculture*, I, 382). Indeed, they are plants characteristic of the *tierra caliente*.

82. This region is sometimes absent in new clearings, since neither crop plants nor weeds have had a chance to develop. Nor is such a region distinguishable in old, abandoned gardens, where entire clearings are overgrown.

83. Harris provides a detailed set of data on phases of regrowth in old gardens of the Orinoco lowland Waika and species characteristic of these early phases of forest regrowth ("Ecology of Swidden," pp. 485–489).

84. In a study of the Tsembaga of New Guinea it was found that "99 per cent by weight of the food consumed is vegetable, [and] the protein intake is high by New Guinea standards." To support this human population "between .15 and .19 acres are put into cultivation per capita per year" (Roy A. Rappaport, "Ritual Regulations of Environmental Relations among a New Guinea People," in *Environment and Cultural Behavior*, ed. Andrew P. Vayda, pp. 186–187).

85. Goldman gives a figure of one acre per family (*Cubeo*, p. 35).

86. Robert L. Carneiro, "Slash-and-Burn Cultivation among the Kuikuru and Its Implications for Cultural Development in the Amazon Basin," in *The Evolution of Horticultural Systems in Native South America*, ed. Johannes Wilbert, pp. 47–48.

87. Harris, "Ecology of Swidden," p. 479.

88. Biocca, *Yanoáma*, p. 130. Bats, too, are attracted to ripe *Musa* (see Simmonds, *Evolution of the Bananas*, p. 33).

89. For example, the concentration of oxalic acid in *Xanthosoma* (*tiquisque* in Nicoya) reportedly keeps pigs away from them (see Philip L. Wagner, *Nicoya*, p. 227).

90. This consistent reference to men as gardeners is deliberate. A woman is not "proper" if she goes to a garden without her husband or other women. It is common knowledge that when a woman goes alone to a garden it is for a liaison.

91. The *shaa* appears to present less of a problem alive than dead, because, when stepped on, the thorns inflict considerable pain and can cause serious wounds leading to infection. This plant resembles the Brazilian *jurubeba* (*Solanaceae*), but it is larger.

92. Barker, *Cultura de los Guaika*, p. 15. There is one report that gardens of the lowland Waika receive an "annual weeding" each March (see Harris, "Ecology of Swidden," p. 480).

93. As a particular kind of garden plant begins to ripen, it becomes conspicuous. For example, from late March through April *bixa* ripens, and then its fresh, bright red-orange color seems to decorate bodies and other objects everywhere.

94. Stealing from a garden is a serious offense even among kinsmen of the same *teri*, and severe punishment is meted out to those who are caught stealing. This sort of thievery can also severely strain relations between *teri* (see Steinvorth-Goetz, *Uriji Jami!* p. 40, and Biocca, *Yanoáma*, pp. 217 and passim). According to Hans Becher, some Yanoama protect their garden produce from theft by "enemy tribes" (*Die Surára und Pakidái*, p. 80). They stick poisoned arrowheads into the ground and cover them with leaves, in such a way that potential thieves will step on them.

95. This particular garden clearing, belonging to the Docodicoro-teri, is located on a flood-plain site adjacent to the Niyayoba-u.

96. Cf. table 11 n. d.

97. The terminology relating to *Musa* plants is potentially confusing. In this study the fruit cluster is referred to as a *bunch* in preference to *stem* or *raceme*. The hands of fruit are attached to an inedible *stem* or *stalk*. The *pseudostem* is exactly that—tightly packed leaf sheaths that resemble a plant stem (for details, see Simmonds, *Bananas*, pp. 19, 40).

98. Of the sixteen plants, bunches of fruit had already formed on eleven of them.

99. The sum of bunches already gathered (16), bunches visibly formed on the plants (9), and mature pseudostems flowering or about to flower (26). Future wind destruction is at least partially compensated for by the sum total of developing suckers, some of which will produce bunches of fruit.

100. This corresponds roughly to a gross annual yield of 6.1 long tons or 6.9 short tons per acre. In comparison, Central American banana plantations average from 3 to 7 tons per acre. Ten to 15 tons is exceptionally good (see Simmonds, *Bananas*, p. 190). The gross annual yield of more than 6 tons of plantains per acre in Barafiri gardens is complemented, of course, by the bananas, tubers, and gourds that are also produced on the same acre.

101. Planting density on commercial banana plantations "ranges very widely within the limits, 150–2,000 plants per acre. . . . In Martinique, the recommended density is 1,000 plants per acre pruned lightly in the ratoons to yield about 1,200 bunches per acre per annum . . . in Jamaica, the usual density is 430 plants per acre pruned . . . to give about 400 bunches per acre per annum (though, in practice, wind and other adverse factors often reduce the yield to 2–300 bunches per acre per annum . . .)" (ibid., pp. 158–159).

102. I had access to only a limited number and variety of bunches of fruit as they were gathered in the gardens. Since the mean weights are based upon these measurements, they must be recognized as rough approximations.

103. Enrique Pérez Arbeláez provides bunch weights obtained in Colombia for a variety of plantains and bananas (*Plantas útiles de Colombia*, p. 530). The range is from fifteen pounds to eighty-four pounds.

104. Based upon a field experiment in which an entire bunch of plantains was peeled. Simmonds reports that, when bananas are green, the weight ratio of pulp to skin varies from 1:2 to 1:6; it sometimes rises to 1:1 in advanced ripeness; and it may reach 3:0 in rotting fruit (*Bananas*, p. 225).

105. Betty J. Meggers, *Amazonia*, pp. 69, 99–100. Goldman writes that manioc takes two years to reach "full maturity" (*Cubeo*, p. 59). Carneiro maintains that manioc tubers reach harvestable size in five to six months but that the Kuikuru prefer to wait eighteen to twenty months before pulling them up ("Cultivation among the Kuikuru," p. 48).

106. In the Parima highlands the peach palm ranks as a minor crop plant. Among the Yanoama of the Orinoco lowlands, however, it is widespread, attractive because of its flavor as well as its high yields. It has been reported, for example, that from its eighth year to about its fiftieth, a peach palm will produce annually from five to six racemes, or clusters, each weighing from twenty to twenty-five pounds (Steinvorth-Goetz, *Uriji Jami!* p. 66).

107. Goldman, *Cubeo*, p. 59.

108. See Simmonds, *Bananas*; Marvin P. Miracle, *Maize in Tropical Africa*; and William T. Sanders and Barbara J. Price, *Mesoamerica*.

109. Simmonds, *Bananas*, p. 256. This is a compromise between the eighty-eight calories and the ninety-four calories given by Watt and Merrill (1950) and by Chatfield (1949) respectively.

110. From 52 percent to 88 percent of all musaceous plants in the Barafiri gardens studied are of the *cowata* type. Cf. tables 7, 8, and 9.

111. Miracle, writing about West Africa, suggests that the caloric yield per hectare of plantains is about three-fourths that of manioc, presumably "sweet" manioc (*Maize*, p. 207). If millet-sorghum have an index of 100 in calorie yield per hectare, manioc has 421, while plantains have 290. For a sample set of consumer units (i.e., the requirements of women, adolescents, children, and the aged, as compared with adult males), see Marshall D. Sahlins, *Stone Age Economics*, p. 115.

112. The high starch content of the principal Yanoama crop plants (i.e., plantains, *ocumo*, yams, sweet potatoes, and sweet manioc) is characteristic of the starch staples of aboriginal Americans, "just as carbohydrate foods are far and away the most important elements in modern agriculture" (Carl O. Sauer, "American Agricultural Origins: A Consideration of Nature and Culture," in *Essays in Anthropology*, pp. 290–291). Yanoama women in their prime tend more toward plumpness than leanness, and one of the traits that makes a woman attractive to men

is being plump. F. S. Bodenheimer believes that plumpness in a population indicates carbohydrates, while meat eaters (hunting populations), who get abundant protein, tend to be lean (*Insects as Human Food*, p. 22).

113. Simmonds, *Bananas*, pp. 256–257, 259.

114. Ibid., p. 261.

115. "There is the interesting finding . . . that the 'Plantain' pulp contained nine times as much ascorbic acid as the 'Banana' " (ibid., p. 260). Pérez Arbeláez writes that "bananas are rich in vitamins A, B, C, and D" (*Plantas útiles*, p. 530).

116. Old gardens are extremely difficult to study. After they have been abandoned for several years, they are almost impossible for a foreigner to identify quickly, particularly from the ground; and the vegetation in them is so thick and thorny as to make them exceedingly disagreeable places in which to work.

117. Napoleon A. Chagnon puts it this way: "the old garden is called 'old woman' (*sua pata*) to emphasize its barrenness" ("The Culture-Ecology of Shifting [Pioneering] Cultivation among the Yanomamö Indians," in *Proceedings of the Eighth International Congress of Anthropological and Ethnological Sciences, 1968 Tokyo and Kyoto*, III, 252 n. 5).

118. For example, the contemporary Jorocoba-teri have innumerable old gardens. Among these, some of the more important are Jorocoba-taca, Dabashinaca-taca, Otomariwa-taca, Ejewanaribue-taca, Naifequebushiri-taca, Widofi-taca, Yeduaja-taca, Oquibiasija-taca, Vifio-taca, Oquimiyari-taca, and Botomanio-taca.

119. This particular garden, used by Tokonaima Foo, is named Oquimiyari-taca. It is located far up the Shabari-u, about two hours' hike from the present site of the Jorocoba-teri *shabono*. In the vicinity of this garden are four other gardens that have been abandoned in sequence since Oquimiyari-taca itself was abandoned. This would make the latter at least eight and perhaps fifteen or more years old. The Jorocoba-teri say they use none of the other old gardens in that area that predate Oquimiyari-taca. The Jorocoba-teri have numerous other abandoned gardens in the upper reaches of the Jorocoba-u. These date from about 1945, when they moved to that area after separating from the Docodicoro-teri. None of these is "used" by the Jorocoba-teri (for plantains), although

they do hunt in them and camp there when collecting other foods and materials.

120. Simmonds, *Bananas*, p. 191.

121. Biocca, *Yanoáma*, pp. 101–104. During the seven months that Helena Valero wandered alone through the forest as a fugitive from the Yanoama, her survival often depended upon foods gathered in these old gardens isolated from any human settlements. Similarly, the Sirionó, for example, are said to "possess many sites containing old gardens, uruku (*Bixa orellana*) trees, calabash trees, etc., to which they may return from time to time in their wanderings" (Holmberg, *Nomads*, p. 48).

122. Cf. Philip L. Wagner, "Natural Vegetation of Middle America," in *Handbook of Middle American Indians*, ed. Robert Wauchope, I, 230–231; Harris, "Ecology of Swidden," p. 486; and P. W. Richards, *The Tropical Rain Forest*, pp. 397–398.

123. Abandoned *shabono* function similarly, but they are much smaller, and their compacted earth inhibits many volunteer plants.

124. In the vicinity of the Shashanawa-teri *shabono* near the Río Orinoco, I explored a patch of jungle that had been a garden about five or six years before. In this low, scrubby woods were scattered logs and stumps in varying degrees of decomposition, as well as peach palms, plantains, *bixa* bushes, and wild *Heliconia* in profusion. Another area, being used as a camp site by the Bishaasa-teri, had been a garden approximately thirty years before. This was an open forest with trees ranging from thirty to fifty feet in height, but not yet attractive for a garden clearing. The site is at least twelve miles by land from their *shabono*.

6. Collecting

1. Where possible, species are identified. None is known to be exclusive to the Yanoama territory.

2. I have observed a positively gleeful group of chattering women and children set out from their *shabono* before dawn with firebrands glowing in the dark. They were responding to special, practically inaudible sounds being made by frogs nearly a mile away. Two hours later they began returning, carrying neatly skinned and beheaded frogs in small leaf packages.

3. Ettore Biocca, *Yanoáma*, p. 101.

4. Low, wet spots in the savanna sometimes contain groves of *Mauritia* palms.

Such places (known as *morichales* in Venezuelan vernacular) are used because edible palm fruits and useful fronds are found in them, as well as frogs, eels, and crabs.

5. In the Parima highlands, the Barafiri even encourage the development of frog populations by providing attractive sites for them. They make small, pondlike excavations in low, swampy areas with their hands and rudimentary tools, such as sticks and machetes. In these the frogs breed and lay eggs. Later, tadpoles and frogs are collected here.

6. It must be remembered that each year there are gardens entering the category of *suwabada taca*, thus the supply of old gardens available to a *teri* is continuously replenished.

7. F. S. Bodenheimer, *Insects as Human Food*, p. 10.

8. Pablo J. Anduze lists nearly sixty different palms found in the Amazonas Federal Territory of Venezuela, suggesting that future collections might lengthen his list considerably. He writes that the uses of the palm are so many that it could be considered "the *arbor vitae* for the people and the fauna of the Territory" (*Shailili-ko*, pp. 371–372).

9. Inga Steinvorth-Goetz, *Uriji Jami!* p. 182. She also reports that the Waika eat the sprouts of the cerbatana palm (*Iriartella setigera* [Mart.] Wendl.) which she says have a nutlike flavor (p. 84).

10. The *albarico* is also known as *macanilla* and as *corozo* among Venezuelan Creoles. Two other palms are also called *corozo* and even scholarly accounts of the vegetation in the Yanoama territory are conflicting in this respect.

11. Anduze, *Shailili-ko*, p. 371, and L. Schnee, *Plantas comunes de Venezuela*, p. 210.

12. *Mauritia aculeata* (H.B.K.), *M. carana* (Wallace), and *M. flexuosa* (L.).

13. These are said to have the "same taste as real coconuts" (Biocca, *Yanoáma*, p. 52). It is doubtful, however, that this is *Cocos nucifera*.

14. Two of these may be the *manaque* (*Oenocarpus minor* Mart.) and the *bobei* (*Oenocarpus bacaba*), both of which produce small dark fruits. Another may be the *barrigón* (*Iriartea ventricosa* Mart.). This tree grows to a height of nearly one hundred feet on a slender trunk that, about halfway up, bulges to more than double the regular diameter. Hence its popular name signifying "big-bellied." At the base of the trunk is a cone of aerial roots, whose point is

several feet from the ground. Other palms, similarly supported upon aerial roots (although considerably shorter than the *barrigón*), also yield potentially edible material in their drupes. These are the *cerbatana* (*Iriartella setigera* [Mart.]; Wendl.) and the *palma de cacho* (*Socratea exorrhiza* [Mart.]; Wendl.).

15. Steinvorth-Goetz, *Uriji Jami!* p. 166. Like the *Cecropia*, this genus is characteristic of secondary forest (see P. W. Richards, *The Tropical Rain Forest*, p. 381).

16. Anduze identifies the lowland Waika *ashawa* [*sic*] as *arbol de frutilla* (*Shailili-ko*, p. 199).

17. There are no reports of this particular *Cecropia* being found at low elevations.

18. *Mumu* is the *conorí* of Brazilian *lingua geral*, according to Helena Valero, who describes it as being "like the fruit of the rubber tree, but of a reddish color" (Biocca, *Yanoáma*, p. 75). Game animals, particularly wild pigs, congregate under *momo* trees to feed on the ripe fruits that fall to the ground.

19. The processing of *momo* into meal is discussed in chap. 4, n. 11.

20. The principal edible part may be the fleshy ovary-receptacle at the base of the pistil.

21. According to Steinvorth-Goetz, the "sweet-tasting, velvety, yellowish-white skin covering the seeds is eaten by the Waika" (*Uriji Jami!* p. 164). In experiments related to the feeding of dairy cattle, it has been shown that cacao pods have approximately the same nutritive value as ears of maize. One hundred kilograms of cacao pod meal (fresh pods, dried and ground into meal) have the same food value as ninety-six to ninety-seven kilograms of chopped ears of maize (J. J. Ochse et al., *Tropical and Subtropical Agriculture*, I, 856).

22. The pear-shaped fruit, or "apple" (the pedicle), is red when ripe. From each fruit, the seed, or cashew nut, is suspended in its own shell. A toxic tissue surrounds the seed, and the unshelled nut must be cooked to drive off the volatile oils before opening it (Ochse et al., *Tropical Agriculture*, I, 524–525). Even smoke containing these oils can be harmful to the eyes.

23. There is no evidence that the Yanoama plant cashews, except for a published statement that cashew trees are "cultivated in the gardens" (Napoleon A. Chagnon, *Yanomamö*, p. 37).

24. A great variety of these fruits, known collectively in Venezuela as *parcha* (*Passiflora*

sp.), are used throughout tropical and subtropical America. Steinvorth-Goetz writes that fifty different kinds of passion flowers are found in Venezuela alone (*Uriji Jami!* p. 171), while Schnee includes eighteen species (*Plantas comunes*, p. 184 and passim).

25. Ghillean T. Prance, "An Ethnobotanical Comparison of Four Tribes of Amazonian Indians," *Acta Amazonica*, in press.

26. Anduze lists some thirty-eight arthropods (with corresponding Waika names) "frequently encountered" in the area of the Upper Orinoco and its headwaters (*Shailili-ko*, pp. 198–199). For information on the dietetic significance of insects to another Venezuelan Indian population, see Kenneth Ruddle, "The Human Use of Insects: Examples from the Yukpa," *Biotropica* 5 (2): 94–101.

27. So named since its bite is said to sting for twenty-four hours. This is probably a species of *Euponera* (Anduze, *Shailili-ko*, p. 198).

28. Bodenheimer writes that tropical diets are greatly deficient in animal components; i.e., wild game is not eaten with much frequency (*Insects*, p. 28). Therefore, he suggests, there is great use of insect food sources: "Comparison with the calorific and nutritive value of other basic items of food leads us to the unavoidable conclusion that insects are most nutritive and only to be compared with the most valuable types of food" (p. 37). In the 1940's, Robert S. Platt pondered the idea that domesticated insects might have produced more for mankind nutritionally than the herbivorous quadrupeds upon which man did ultimately become so dependent (see "Environmentalism versus Geography," *American Journal of Sociology* 53 [1948]: 351–358).

29. Bodenheimer, *Insects*, pp. 29–30. ". . . even the vitamin content of insects may not be negligible . . ." (p. 32).

30. This is a popular Venezuelan term for certain species of *Atta* (Anduze, *Shailili-ko*, p. 198). The large queens of the *Atta* ants, when full of eggs, "taste like condensed milk" (Bodenheimer, *Insects*, pp. 306–307).

31. Biocca, *Yanoáma*, p. 106.

32. Steinvorth-Goetz, *Uriji Jami!* p. 164.

33. Helena Valero describes how certain "butterfly grubs," or "caterpillars," are collected, packaged, and cooked (see Biocca, *Yanoáma*, p. 45). Bodenheimer observes that sometimes care is taken to remove the head and intestines of caterpillars before they are used as human food (*Insects*, p. 307).

34. Bodenheimer, *Insects*, p. 308.

35. Anduze identifies the *kasha* as lepidopterous caterpillars (*gusanos*) belonging to the Noctuidae family of moths (*Shailili-ko*, pp. 198, 213). Among the Barafiri at least, *kasha* also refers to pupae.

36. Helena Valero provides vividly detailed information on collecting and preparing termites as food. In her opinion the *sauba* (*Atta* sp.) ants are particularly good to eat (Biocca, *Yanoáma*, p. 100). Certain large termites (*Termes flavicolle* Pty.) have been reported for the Upper Amazon. When these are used as food, the head and thorax are eaten (Bodenheimer, *Insects*, p. 305).

37. Bodenheimer, *Insects*, p. 13.

38. Lice are reportedly "cracked" between the teeth before being eaten (Steinvorth-Goetz, *Uriji Jami!* p. 72).

39. There are possibly ten or more varieties of bees whose honey the lowland Waika eat, according to James Barker (*Memoria sobre la cultura de los Guaika, Boletín Indigenista Venezolano* 1 [1953]: 12). Bodenheimer refers specifically to the storing of honey by South American social wasps (*Insects*, pp. 37, 315). These are probably *Polybia* wasps, "the largest tropical group of social species . . . most of which are found in Central and South America" (Owain R. Richards, *The Social Insects*, p. 66). A few species of the *Polybia* wasps "have become regular collectors of nectar, like the honey bee" (Richards, *Social Insects*, p. 70).

40. The use of the *jawa* (see fig. 7) for getting at honey in trees is relatively sophisticated. The Sirionó of Bolivia, for example, traditionally got their honey out of tree trunks with only fire and digging sticks as tools (Allan R. Holmberg, *Nomads of the Long Bow*, pp. 66, 268).

41. Bodenheimer, *Insects*, p. 35. Honey is beneficial in other ways. For example, "among the many medicinal virtues of honey its antihaemorrhage and its bactericidal properties are undisputed" (ibid., p. 37).

42. Ibid., p. 36.

43. Biocca, *Yanoáma*, p. 101.

44. This is a species of *Avicularia*, according to Anduze (*Shailili-ko*, p. 198).

45. Biocca, *Yanoáma*, p. 298.

46. There are also references to "shrimps" (ibid., p. 101).

47. Poisonous species, such as rattlesnakes (*Crotalus* sp.), serve as food, and so do constrictors like the anaconda (*Eunectes* sp.). That the latter are eaten is verified by Helena Valero (Biocca, *Yanoáma*, p. 48),

although apparently this is rare. I have no data on Yanoama consumption of annelids, such as leeches, although Steinvorth-Goetz writes that "worms" form a part of the diet (*Uriji Jami!* p. 30).

48. The large caymans, or alligators (*Crocodylus* sp.), of the Orinoco lowlands are utterly foreign to the more isolated highland Barafiri.

49. Fish are traditionally obtained from small streams or pools when water levels are low. They are simply grabbed or caught in baskets, although, on occasion, men might shoot them with bow and arrows. For a lively description of the collecting of small fish, see Biocca, *Yanoáma*, pp. 46–47.

50. Only Steinvorth-Goetz writes that "bird eggs are never eaten" (*Uriji Jami!* p. 30).

51. An exception is the bat, which is eaten when caught but is not hunted per se.

52. One type is described as "white, fine mud" (Biocca, *Yanoáma*, p. 101). Anduze attributes geophagy to a possible lack of minerals in the diet, but his references are to the eating of termite nests. He further suggests that perhaps the Yanoama, seeing animals eat earth at salt licks, think it necessary to imitate them (*Shailili-ko*, p. 217). There is no evidence that these clays are used in lieu of salt (NaCl), although certain wood ashes might serve the purpose.

53. Each woman collects firewood only in her husband's gardens or in others where she has permission to cut, rather than in the place closest to her own hearth. The distances over which these loads are carried range from a few hundred yards to a matter of miles. When meat is to be boiled, men collect the fuel. However, they haul in large branches or trunks, rather than carry baskets of cut firewood (see Barker, *Cultura de los Guaika*, pp. 19, 38).

54. Apparently, the Waika that Alexander von Humboldt met at La Esmeralda (see map 1) in 1799 had reached the place on such rafts. As late as 1958, a few Yanoama were arriving periodically at Tamatama (on the Río Orinoco just upstream from the Casiquiare bifurcation) in this manner. When men used such rafts, they had to walk back home.

55. Collectively, these trees are popularly referred to as *majaguas* in Spanish America. One, the *yáya* of Venezuelan Guayana, is identified as a species of *Guatteria* by Anduze (*Shailili-ko*, p. 200). At least some members of the linden family are known as *envira* in Brazil.

56. Specifically, *V. calophylla, V.*

calophylloidea, and *V. theiodora* (Richard Evans Schultes, "Hallucinogens of Plant Origin," *Science* 163 [1969]: 248). Prance found *V. theiodora* to have a dual use: it serves as both a hallucinogenic snuff and an arrow poison ("Ethnobotanical Comparison of Four Tribes").

57. The bark is *Elizabetha princeps* (Leguminosae) or *Theobroma subincanum* (Sterculiaceae). Occasionally, powdered leaves of *Justicia pectorialis* var. *stenophylla* (Acanthaceae) might also be added (Schultes, "Hallucinogens of Plant Origin," p. 248).

58. Ibid., p. 249.

59. Ibid., p. 250.

60. Ibid., p. 249; see also Biocca, *Yanoáma*, pp. 147–148.

61. The highland Barafiri call this material *waraba coco*. It resembles copal superficially, although it is porous and very lightweight in comparison.

62. With careful use, such a bow can last for years.

63. According to Anduze, at least some of these vines (*bejucos*) are really the roots of different araceous plants. He identifies one of them as *bejuco mamure* (*Shailili-ko*, pp. 220–221).

64. Perhaps one hundred lengths of prepared liana strips (depending upon their coarseness) are bound together at each end and trimmed. These traditional Yanoama hammocks have no transverse members. Steinvorth-Goetz provides a graphic and detailed description of their manufacture (*Uriji Jami!* pp. 28–29).

65. Two of these might be *Strychnos guianensis* and *S. rondeletioides* (Schnee, *Plantas comunes*, pp. 228–229). See also Ettore Biocca, *Viaggi tra gli indi alto Rio Negro–alto Orinoco*, II, 164–183.

66. Biocca, *Yanoáma*, p. 332.

67. Anduze calls it "caña de *Chusquea*" (*Shailili-ko*, p. 261).

68. Ibid., p. 221. The fibers are said to come from the outer layer (*corteza*) of a species of *Ischnosiphon*. This is probably the Venezuelan *casupo*.

69. Malvaceous and annonaceous fibers are so blended (ibid.).

70. These species of *Guadua*, such as *G. latifolia* (H.B.K.), are autochthonous and not to be confused with the Old World *Bambusa*.

71. Biocca, *Yanoáma*, pp. 102, 379. Termite nests are known as *cupim* in the vernacular of northern Brazil.

72. Paul Dye, 1970, personal communication. Evidently there is no concern, as there was with the legendary

earwig, that the creature might burrow through the middle and inner ears and on into the brain, causing excruciating pain.

7. Hunting

1. In support of his argument that the "Guaika" did not traditionally practice agriculture, Otto Zerries stresses a supposed link between their word for "meal" and the word that signifies "to shoot with bow and arrow" ("Los indios Guaika y su situación cultural: Informe preliminar de la expedición frobenius al alto Orinoco," *Boletín Indigenista Venezolano* 2 [1954]: 73). However, students of the Yanoama language do not support this observation. One writer, referring to the "Guaharibos," has expressed the belief that men did not really hunt; instead, "they amused themselves with the forest. . . . They are not hunters, but schoolboys out in the country" (Alain Gheerbrant, *La expedición Orinoco-Amazonas*, p. 293).

2. The horticultural focus of this research—and indeed of Yanoama culture—obviates the need for detailed coverage in this book of hunting. I am aware, however, that there exist rather eloquent statements to the effect that hunting and fishing as significant economic activities of American aboriginals have been dealt with only superficially (see, e.g., Bernard Nietschmann, "Hunting and Fishing Focus among the Miskito Indians, Eastern Nicaragua," *Human Ecology* 1 [1972]: 41–67).

3. This is the "ritual hunt" of Inga Steinvorth-Goetz (*Uriji Jami!* p. 54) and the "organized collective hunt *heni*" of Ernest Cesar Migliazza ("Yanomama Grammar and Intelligibility," p. 401).

4. One end of each arrow shaft is wrapped with fine cord in such a manner as to permit the rapid replacement of arrow points. At the other end, a wooden nock and trimmed feathers are bound to the shaft.

5. The bone is often a sharpened splinter from an arm or leg bone of a monkey (see James Barker, *Memoria sobre la cultura de los Guaika, Boletín Indigenista Venezolano* 1 [1953]: 26).

6. Poisoned arrowheads are also reportedly used when shooting wild boar (Ettore Biocca, *Yanoáma*, p. 183). The poisons used do not affect the edibility of the dead animal's flesh.

7. One tool, a small gouge (or chisel) made by firmly attaching an agouti tooth to a wooden or bone handle, is a universal male possession. Other tools include objects like peccary jawbones. With such equipment, a man shapes his bow and his arrow shafts and works his arrowheads. As in gardening and collecting, acculturation has made virtually no inroads on traditional Barafiri weapons technology and hunting activities. The only evident impact is a replacement of some natural fibers with factory-made cotton thread for fastening arrowheads, nock plugs, and feathers to the arrow shafts.

8. Zerries, "Situación cultural," p. 75. In sheer length, the bows and arrows of the Bolivian Sirionó easily surpass those of the Yanoama. Sirionó bows have average lengths of seven to nine feet, being "perhaps the longest in the world." One of the Sirionó arrow types (with a lanceolate "bamboo" head) averages from eight to ten feet in length, and these arrows are "probably longer than those used by any other known people in the world" (Allan R. Holmberg, *Nomads of the Long Bow*, p. 30).

9. Steinvorth-Goetz, *Uriji Jami!* p. 34.

10. Biocca, *Yanoáma*, pp. 170, 209. Dogs, like little children, are often removed from camera range.

11. Pablo J. Anduze, *Shailili-ko*, p. 214.

12. The Sirionó of Bolivia, who depend heavily on hunting as a principal economic activity, possess no dogs. In fact, "the dog would be of little use to them in hunting in a tangled jungle where the meat supply is mostly shot in trees and where it is not sufficient to feed even themselves, to say nothing of others" (Holmberg, *Nomads*, p. 272). What is more, even "the great hunters of the Upper Paleolithic had no dogs" (Carl O. Sauer, *Agricultural Origins and Dispersals*, p. 29). On several occasions dogs accompanied the Yanoama men who were searching for the fugitive Helena Valero, at least once passing so close to her that she could count the scars on a man's head. Yet, the dogs just went on by. It was the keen senses of the Yanoama, not their dogs, that led to her discovery (Biocca, *Yanoáma*, pp. 118–119). See also Kenneth Iain Taylor, "Sanuma (Yanoama) Food Prohibitions," p. 15.

13. Sometimes preparations of pepper (*Capsicum*) are put into a dog's nostrils in order to sharpen his olfactory powers.

14. The size, colors, markings, even body shapes of Barafiri dogs vary. In general, however, they tend to be of "medium" size with a slender body, long legs, elongated snouts, and large pointed ears. Hair is usually straight and relatively short. Their

origin is uncertain, but considerable antiquity is suggested by these facts: (1) the Yanoama love dogs, all dogs, whether they are their own or brought in by foreigners for barter; (2) they are concerned about the afterlife of dogs, which distinguishes the dog from other animals; and (3) they tend to reject animal domesticates out of hand, since to them there is no merit in raising pigs or fowl and to drink the milk of an animal (such as a cow) is repugnant. Thus, it appears unlikely that the dog, so universally accepted among them, was only recently adopted.

15. "The hunters are magically assisted in the chase with traditional songs and dances performed by those who remain behind in the settlement" (Steinvorth-Goetz, *Uriji Jami!* p. 54). "At night, women and children gather together and dance and sing to propitiate a good hunt" (Luís Cocco, "Más allá del turismo: Los indios Guaicas," *El Farol* 32 [1970]: 52).

16. Taboos on the eating of carnivorous animals (particularly felines) and birds of prey (especially eagles, hawks, and vultures) have been reported by Barker (*Cultura de los Guaika*, p. 11). A contrary observation is that "for these people 'everything from the mosquito on up is fair game' and not in a figurative sense" (Anduze, *Shailili-ko*, p. 203). Both of these writers based their work on Yanoama of the Orinoco lowlands.

17. Among the Namoe-teri a new father "does not eat tapir meat, large wild boar, or monkey, for a long time" (Biocca, *Yanoáma*, p. 161). Niyayoba-teri boys and girls (younger than twelve years or so) are forbidden to eat tapir meat, since it causes pains in their hips or heads or both. This taboo seems to apply to other highland *teri* as well, and, regardless of its physiological merits, it assures more tapir for adults than they might get otherwise.

18. "Before game is cooked and eaten there is often a ritual with much chanting to propitiate the hekura, the spirit or vital essence of the slain animal" (Steinvorth-Goetz, *Uriji Jami!* p. 178).

19. When people travel, even for extended periods, these awkward bundles of fragile bones are about the only possessions left behind in the *shabono*.

20. "The bones and especially the skull [of a slain animal] are carefully preserved, for they are the residing place of the life force and it is from them that the animal will be reborn" (Steinvorth-Goetz, *Uriji Jami!* p. 178).

21. It is probable that this answer is either an oversimplification or one that intentionally evades mention of the mystical aspects of something sacred.

22. There is currently no way of knowing all the species hunted, since zoological and ethnozoological data are still scarce. Even the existing literature contains within it serious inconsistencies in identification and classification.

23. The deer most commonly available to the Barafiri are small forest dwellers frequently referred to in the Venezuelan vernacular as *matacán* deer (*Mazama rufa*). These rarely reach more than two and one-half feet in height. Their flesh, though edible, is more bitter and drier than that of many other deer (see Eduardo Röhl, *Fauna descriptiva de Venezuela*, p. 143).

24. Known as *shama* in Yanoama, this is the largest of the native land animals of tropical America. Tapirs are shy, disinclined to attack unless wounded, and relatively few in number. Their range extends from the hot lowlands up to a reported 8,000 feet (ibid., pp. 135–138).

25. Ibid., pp. 83–84. Agoutis are also classified as *Dasyprocta aguti*, *D. azarae*, and *D. acouchy*, in citations used by Claude Lévi-Strauss (*The Raw and the Cooked*, pp. 129–130). In fact, there is great confusion in the usage of popular names and classifications of the agouti and related genera. For example, the *lapa* might be *Cuniculus paca*, while the *paca* might be classed as *Coelogenys paca*, or *Agouti paca*, or even as a cavy (*Cavia* sp.); and all are said to resemble the *acure* and the *picure*, both of which are species of *Dasyprocta*.

26. These classifications are from Röhl, who gives the range of the white-lipped peccaries as extending up to about 4,500 feet (*Fauna de Venezuela*, pp. 139–142). Lévi-Strauss classifies the white-lipped peccary as *Dicotyles labiatus* and the collared peccary as *D. torquatus* (*Raw and Cooked*, p. 86).

27. This, the world's largest rodent, weighs up to one hundred pounds.

28. I have seen in the Orinoco lowlands a *picure* weighing nearly eighteen pounds drawn. Cf. n. 25 above.

29. There is a report, however, that ocelots "are part of the regular Waika diet" (Steinvorth-Goetz, *Uriji Jami!* p. 160). I have followed the common practice of classifying the ocelot as *Felis pardalis*, while Röhl identifies *F. pardalis* as *manigordo*, *tigrito*, and *onza*, but not *ocelote* (*Fauna de Venezuela*, pp. 100–101).

30. References are to tropical species,

which are often distinct from those of the middle latitudes, although popular names are identical.

31. The kinkajou (*Potos flavus*) is a tree dweller and essentially omnivorous. The coati (*Nasua* sp.) is just one of various long-tailed, fur-bearing flesh eaters of this genus, which are popularly known as *zorro guache* in Venezuela. See Röhl, *Fauna de Venezuela*, pp. 115–117.

32. Anduze, *Shailili-ko*, p. 319.

33. Data on monkeys are principally from Röhl (*Fauna de Venezuela*, pp. 35–58). The *titi* is sometimes said to be of the genus *Callicebus*, although it is the *viudita* that Röhl classifies as *Callicebus torquatus*.

34. Steinvorth-Goetz, *Uriji Jami!* pp. 160, 181. The *marimonda* is also known as the spider monkey. The genus to which it belongs, *Ateles*, is so named to denote that members of this family have only four digits on each hand, lacking a functional opposable digit (Röhl, *Fauna de Venezuela*, p. 49).

35. Anduze provides an "Annotated List of Birds of the Upper Orinoco" in which hundreds of species are named (*Shailili-ko*, pp. 329–351).

36. Small birds are shot with arrows that have special blunted heads or heads supplied with prongs (see Barker, *Cultura de los Guaika*, p. 11).

37. "Waste" is viewed here in the Western sense. However, if a harpy eagle or jaguar is killed, no one is likely to eat the flesh, since the Barafiri are frightened of what the consequence might be.

38. For details on butchering, see Taylor, "Sanuma (Yanoama) Food Prohibitions."

39. The Barafiri call this monkey *wishia*. Anduze identifies it as the *capuchino* (*Shailili-ko*, p. 219).

40. Ibid.

41. Biocca, *Yanoáma*, p. 155.

42. Barker, *Cultura de los Guaika*, pp. 13–14; and Anduze, *Shailili-ko*, p. 255.

43. Barker, *Cultura de los Guaika*, p. 13, and Anduze, *Shailili-ko*, pp. 161, 255. In contrast to this willingness to nurse animals, the Barafiri are repelled by the idea that humans might drink the milk of animals.

44. Röhl writes that the curassow is "easy to domesticate"; that both the white-lipped and the collared peccaries "are easily domesticated, being in this state very affectionate with their masters"; and that the kinkajou "is an animal that easily allows itself to be tamed, especially if they are caught young, and become very affectionate with

their masters" (*Fauna de Venezuela*, pp. 214, 142, 113).

45. In pools and shallow streams, fishing with bow and arrows is feasible, but in large, deep rivers, retrieval is difficult if not impossible. See n. 49, chap. 6.

46. This is the only method for taking fish that requires a somewhat specialized device, namely the weir. Napoleon A. Chagnon writes that a poison is used "to kill fish" (*Yanomamö*, p. 22). Most of the toxic substances used by lowland Yanoama in fishing stun—or even kill—by deoxidizing the water, but there is no evidence that these are used to any extent by the highland Barafiri.

47. Steinvorth-Goetz, *Uriji Jami!* p. 160. There is available a variety of catfish, *bagre*, and piranha, along with sting rays, eels, and porpoises, to name but a few of the aquatic food species.

8. The Apportionment and Consumption of Food

1. Tokonaima Feyaroba, a young Niyayoba-teri, also gardens with the Jorocoba-teri. This is probably a means of paying for his Jorocoba-teri bride, since the couple make their home with the Niyayoba-teri. Most of the personal names used in this book are teknonyms. See the Appendix for an explanation.

2. Neither of these men, Jutemi Feyaroba and Jowarima Feyaroba, had children. Each is currently sharing the quarters of a married full brother and his family. Thus, each of these economic units (nos. 7 and 11 in fig. 11) has two men who garden. This is only a temporary condition.

3. These wives are not sisters. Remarkably, the older wife is from the Docodicoro-teri, while the girl is one of Irube's youngest daughters. Criyajoma Feyaroba himself is Mayobo-teri in origin.

4. The separateness of the roofs over individual hearths or pairs of hearths seems to be largely a matter of personal choice. Each man responsible for constructing a shelter makes the decision as to whether or not his roof will be joined to that of his neighbors.

5. One of her married grandsons, Brerebimi Feyaroba, lives across the *shabono* with his new wife. A granddaughter's husband, Jurasimi Feyaroba, also lives with his close kinsmen (from Mayobo-teri) across the *shabono*, but the granddaughter herself

seems to stay at her mother's hearth frequently.

6. Although all these men have kinship bonds with Irube, in some instances they are quite weak.

7. The *teri* that have established themselves on navigable waterways traveled by foreigners with trade goods do have a potential for accumulating a wealth of such goods. However, because of their ties with other groups—and the resultant pressures for gift exchanges with these kinsmen—they have no significant surpluses of pots, machetes, axes, and beads. The only clearly observable differences between them and more isolated populations are that they manufacture poor quality items (such as arrows) for barter, they wear more clothing (often filthy rags), and they have less fear of foreigners.

8. A man is sufficiently wealthy if he has "a large garden, wife and children, and many machetes and axes" (Pablo J. Anduze, *Shailili-ko*, p. 238).

9. Irving Goldman, *The Cubeo*, p. 51. This attitude is quite different from one associated with hunting and collecting cultures (such as the Sirionó), in which "a concern with food problems will so dominate the society that other aspects of its culture will be little developed" (Allan R. Holmberg, *Nomads of the Long Bow*, p. 261). It can also be contrasted with "prodigality" (Marshall D. Sahlins, *Stone Age Economics*, pp. 30–36).

10. Meat or meatlike things (a category including certain nuts, insects, and mushrooms in some areas) are not to be eaten alone. They are consumed along with food from another category (generally starchy), the most important of which is plantains. The act of eating the two different foods together is *tefiyao* or *difiao*.

11. Inga Steinvorth-Goetz, *Uriji Jami!* p. 24. Here, too, is a Yanoama explanation for the gift of fire. See also Daniel de Barandiarán, "El fuego entre los indios Sanemá-Yanoama," *Antropológica* 22 (1968): 3–64.

12. "In native thought . . . not only does cooking mark the transition from nature to culture, but through it and by means of it, the human state can be defined with all its attributes, even those that, like mortality, might seem to be the most unquestionably natural" (Claude Lévi-Strauss, *The Raw and the Cooked*, p. 164). "With cooking, man renounced the naturalness of eating" (Yi-Fu Tuan, *Man and Nature*, p. 45).

13. Lévi-Strauss, *Raw and Cooked*, p. 336.

14. By way of contrast, among the Hanunóo of the Philippines for example, "only cooked food . . . is considered 'real' food" (Harold C. Conklin, *Hanunóo Agriculture*, p. 29).

15. If meat "is the least bit raw or bloody, the Yanoama becomes disgusted and will not eat it" (Steinvorth-Goetz, *Uriji Jami!* p. 30).

16. Eating foods, such as maize or sweet manioc, raw in the garden is not generally acceptable for adults, although children might do it as a lark.

17. "The making of fire is exclusively the man's province" (Steinvorth-Goetz, *Uriji Jami!* p. 24).

18. The technology of bitter-manioc processing is quite sophisticated, including the specialized grating board (*rallo*), the plaited squeezer (*tipiti* or *sebucán*), and the griddle (*budare*). In contrast, the Barafiri roast their manioc tubers on the embers of the hearth or they boil them. Only very rarely are the tubers grated between small slabs of coarse stone. If there is a choice, they much prefer plantains or even *ocumo* to manioc or manioc products. Acculturated lowland Yanoama, on the other hand, are fond of bitter-manioc flour.

19. Although capsicum is a rarity in the diet of the Barafiri, it is commonly used by the bitter-manioc-cultivating peoples around them.

20. Otto Zerries discusses the usage of *Salzersatz* by South American Indians, including the Yanoama (*Waika*, pp. 79–83). Helena Valero recalls that "to cook worms, snakes and fish, they use salted ashes of a tree which they call *karoriheki* . . . [and] they also use the ashes of a plant that grows in waterfalls and which they call *atahiki*; they burn those leaves, but they prefer very much the ashes of that big tree" (Ettore Biocca, *Yanoáma*, p. 46). "However, as laboratory tests revealed, while it [wood ash] contains many important minerals the ash is virtually lacking in sodium carbonate, the most important constituent of cooking salt" (Steinvorth-Goetz, *Uriji Jami!* p. 33). In most instances these substitutes are described as "salty." Yet, the Yanoama dislike for any salty flavor is so strong that it would appear to preclude this possibility. In North America, aboriginals of Virginia burned the leaves of a plant (evidently a chenopod) to obtain ashes they used as salt (see Carl O. Sauer, *Sixteenth Century North America*, p. 260). Coltsfoot (the *Tussilago farfara* of

Europe and the native North American *Petasites*) leaves can be used similarly.

21. Steinvorth-Goetz, *Uriji Jami!* p. 33.

22. For vivid descriptions of Yanoama cooking methods, see Biocca, *Yanoáma*, pp. 27, 45, 123–124.

23. Ibid., pp. 76–77.

24. Skinning an animal, or even washing the flesh, is thought to remove some of its flavor.

25. Plantains, particularly the *cowata* type, are peeled and roasted while green. Among the different ways of eating plantains around the world, this is unique. For one thing, roasting of plantains appears to be relatively rare; and when *Musa* are roasted, it is usually the peeled ripe fruit (e.g., the "Gonja" clones of Uganda) or the unripe fruit roasted in the skin. In the Pacific, it is peeled green and baked (see N. W. Simmonds, *Bananas*, pp. 261–262).

26. Peeled ripe plantains are boiled, later to be eaten whole or in a thick soup (see "Yanoama and Death," chap. 2). Men also smoke—or cure—meat while on the hunt, but this is uncommon among the Barafiri.

27. Goldman, *Cubeo*, p. 79.

28. For example, *cucurito* (*Maximiliana regia* Mart.) palm fruits are boiled in water until a paste is formed. The bottoms of small gourd vessels are immersed in this paste, which is then licked hot off the gourds.

29. Few if any new cooking techniques, or even dishes, have developed as a result of the adoption of metal cooking pots, even though they make boiling much easier than it used to be.

30. Women's hammocks usually hang at a lower level than those of their men. Ostensibly this is so the women can more easily tend the fires.

31. The only systematic cleaning and repairing of a *shabono* occurs when it is reoccupied after a prolonged absence or just prior to the arrival of guests invited to an important ceremonial. At such times men do much of the work, such as removing trash, pulling weeds, and fixing leaky roofs.

32. For boys, there is a lengthy period when they are still nursing and yet quite independent. By the time a boy is fully weaned (sometime before his fourth year), he can forage with his play pack, cook his share of the family food supply, and generally care for himself. Girls tend to remain near their mothers until marriage, which often occurs well before puberty, tending to a baby brother if there is one.

33. In cultures that know manioc beer, it is often manufactured by women, and they are free to drink it at feasts. Interestingly, all the Arawak and Carib neighbors of the Yanoama practice fermentation, and the Yanoama have available a variety of garden products and forest fruits that could be fermented, as well as bark vessels that would allow volume production.

9. Landscape Modification

1. Under cover of the forest, however, the Yanoama watch those who fly over their territory and report the activity through an effective communications network.

2. Ralph H. Brown, *Historical Geography of the United States*, p. 179. "References to Indian old fields are a part of nearly every contemporary description of the early Colonial period" (p. 13). See, also, Carl O. Sauer, *Sixteenth Century North America*, pp. 57–58.

3. Karl W. Butzer, *Environment and Archaeology*, pp. 457, 470.

4. Grateful thanks are due CODESUR and, particularly, Ing. Nicolás Nyerges and Geóg. Temístocles Rojas for their help in arranging for analyses of these samples.

5. Far to the east, conditions are similar, since the savannas of the upper Rio Branco yield to the tropical forest that covers the lowlands east of the Parima massif.

6. See, e.g., Donald W. Lathrap, *The Upper Amazon*, pp. 19–28.

7. Among the ferns, *Pteridium aquilinum* (or a close relative) predominates. The pineapples are probably *Ananas ananassiodes*. They are peculiar in having a long rhizome above ground and are well adapted to survive periodic burning (Francisco Tamayo, 1970, personal communication; see Francisco Tamayo, "Exploraciones botánicas en el Estado Bolívar," *Boletín de la Sociedad Venezolana de Ciencias Naturales* 22 [1961]: 42).

8. One elderly man can identify specific areas at the edges of the large Niyayoba savanna that were forested in his memory. In some of the places, tangible traces of the forest have long since disappeared.

9. Still, the belief is widely held that these savannas are natural. For the Niyayoba-Mayobo area, for example, reference is made to "patches of natural savannah [*sic*]" (Arthur D. Bloom et al., "Chromosome Aberrations among the Yanomama Indians," *Proceedings of the National Academy of Sciences* 66 [1970]: 920–921).

10. The role of fire in the expansion of savannas is discussed by Carl L. Johannessen in *Savannas of Interior Honduras*, pp. 104–106.

11. For information on soil compaction after forest removal, see Gerardo Budowski, "Tropical Savannas: A Sequence of Forest Felling and Repeated Burnings," *Turrialba* 6 (1956): 23–31.

12. Stream fluctuations of the Niyayoba-u, described in chap. 2, are due in part to the large proportion of the watershed that is covered by savannas.

13. Francisco Tamayo, 1970, personal communication.

14. The term *Gran Sabana* refers to a portion of Venezuela rather than a type of vegetation. This complex area is described by Leví Marrero in *Venezuela y sus recursos*, pp. 125–142 passim.

15. Francisco Tamayo, 1970, personal communication. Various of the species have well-developed fleshy stems, or xylopods, that are adapted to resist fire. Among these, the *Axonopus* is outstanding (see Tamayo, "Exploraciones botánicas," pp. 156–164; and H. H. Bartlett, "Fire, Primitive Agriculture, and Grazing in the Tropics," in *Man's Role in Changing the Face of the Earth*, ed. William L. Thomas et al., pp. 697–698 n. 7).

16. In Panama the recency of savannas is "indicated . . . by a lack of a distinctive fauna" (Charles F. Bennett, *Human Influences on the Zoogeography of Panama*, p. 32). Similarly, "the faunal carrying capacity of the [Orinoco] savannas appears to be quite low in the Cinaruco llanos since foraging foods for larger game animals are sparse" (Anthony Leeds, "Yaruro Incipient Tropical Forest Horticulture—Possibilities and Limits," in *The Evolution of Horticultural Systems in Native South America*, ed. Johannes Wilbert, p. 17). A very different conclusion is reached by Butzer in his discussion of meat sources (from hoofed mammals) for early hunter-gatherer populations. He notes that, while the tropical rain forest has a very low ungulate biomass (kg/km²), "the tropical savannas stand out as optimal areas" (*Environment and Archaeology*, pp. 144–145). It must be noted, however, that *all* of his examples from the tropics are African.

17. Cf. Bartlett, "Fire, Primitive Agriculture, and Grazing in the Tropics," pp. 693–694 n. 4.

18. The highland Yanoama do not use fire intentionally to create savannas with the idea that this might improve their collecting or provide better grazing land for game.

Nor is there evidence of the use of fire in hunting.

19. These figures are means derived from data on the Jorocoba-teri and the Niyayoba-teri. See "Garden Size," chap. 5.

20. See A. Gómez-Pompa, C. Vázquez-Yanes, and S. Guevara, "The Tropical Rain Forest: A Nonrenewable Resource," *Science* 177 (1972): 763.

21. See, for example, Richard E. Sorenson, "Socio-Ecological Change among the Fore of New Guinea," *Current Anthropology* 13 (1972): 349–372. He writes that savanna "takes the place of abandoned gardens and hamlet sites" (p. 354).

Appendix

1. Or, conversely, inherent in the culture of the outsider. In one scholarly book on the Yanoama a chapter is devoted to the subject of doing fieldwork among them. The author reports that he was initially horrified by the "naked, filthy, hideous men [and by] the stench of the decaying vegetation and filth," and that he "had to become very much like the Yanomamö to be able to get along with them on their terms: sly, aggressive, and intimidating" (Napoleon A. Chagnon, *Yanomamö*, pp. 5, 9).

2. Secretiveness of names is far more common in the isolated Parima highlands than in the lowlands to the east and west, where it is gradually breaking down. Examples of personal names of adult males include "Deer Eye," "Lip," "Stinking," and "Alligator Dung." "Ocelot Dung" is the name of one young Barafiri girl, and "Testicles," the name of a little boy. Alcida Rita Ramos writes of patronyms, lineage names, and sib names, as well as personal names and teknonyms ("The Social System of the Sanuma of Northern Brazil," pp. 161–172).

3. Parenthood is not based on biological children alone, since a child's real mother and his maternal aunts can be his "mothers," just as his biological father and his paternal uncles can be his "fathers." There are also instances (such as Ñape Foo or Obisai Foo) where the offspring suggested by a name are nonexistent.

4. A foreign name, like Pablo or Enrique, is highly regarded as a valuable personal possession.

5. Allegorical references are permitted. Thus, "the gourd is smashed" can symbolize a death.

6. For example, there is a period "before

he remembers," which began after his birth and existed before his recollection; there are periods in his life that can be indicated by raising the hand to an approximation of his height at the time of some event; there are also periods defined in terms of important happenings in his life, such as the acquisition of a wife, the birth of a specific child, or the weaning of a child (although these people can be referred to only if they are still alive).

7. Johannes Wilbert writes that *Shirishana* is equivalent to howler monkey (*Indios de la región Orinoco-Ventuari*, p. 177). Pablo J. Anduze has information from Maquiritare Indians that *Shiriana*, a name used by Carib peoples, is contemptuous (*Shailili-ko*, p. 191 n. 25). Ernest Cesar Migliazza explains, however, that "the word Shiriana" is an internal denomination, "opposite to the term 'waika' " ("Yanomama Grammar and Intelligibility," p. 30).

8. A. Hamilton Rice used terms like this freely. He believed that "the bold and warlike Guaharibos [lived] on the west side of the Parima Serra" and that the Shirianas, "poor, under-sized, inoffensive creatures," lived on the eastern slopes of the Parima highlands ("The Rio Branco, Uraricuera, and Parima," *Geographical Journal* 71 [1928]: 55).

9. See Migliazza, "Yanomama Grammar," pp. 25–32.

10. Some Barafiri find it rude for strangers to ask questions. As a guide to the kinds of information he seeks from another, a person himself should first give precisely those kinds of information voluntarily.

Glossary

aiyoba: older brother; older brother of.

banana: *Musa sapientum*; *Musa* whose fruit is usually eaten raw.

Barafiri: dialect group of the central Parima highlands; sometimes "people to the east"; neither of these used as a self-designation.

bixa: *Bixa* sp.; small tree whose seeds yield a red dye; also known as *achiote*, *onoto*, and *urucú*.

celt: an ax blade of stone, without perforations or grooves for hafting.

chigoe: *Tunga penetrans*, a type of flea, the female of which buries itself in the skin of men and animals.

clone: the progeny of a single plant, vegetatively reproduced.

corm: the fleshy, bulblike base of a plant stem.

cowata: the most prevalent type of plantain cultivated by the Barafiri.

cowata uba: boiled ripe plantains in a liquid; to this liquid is added pulverized human bone for ritual ingestion.

Creole: a person of the national culture of the modern states of Venezuela and Brazil.

culm: the jointed and usually hollow stem characteristic of certain giant grasses.

dude taca: a newly prepared garden.

ebena: general term for hallucinogenic snuffs.

feyaroba: husband; husband of.

ficari: garden.

foo: father; father of.

Guaika: see Waika.

ishabena:	the condition of being apt for growing crops, particularly plantains; an area with this quality.
jawa:	tomahawklike cutting tool.
kafu:	a highland *Cecropia*; the edible fruit of such a tree.
lineage:	those people directly descendant from a specific individual.
maloca:	Brazilian vernacular term for "communal house."
Mauritia:	a genus of water-loving palms, popularly known as *moriche* and *buriti* in Venezuela and Brazil, respectively.
momo:	highland species of *Hevea*; the poisonous but edible fruit of this tree.
Musa:	genus of perennial herbs to which belong the bananas and plantains.
naba:	foreigner; foreign.
noo:	mother; mother of.
ocumo:	Venezuelan vernacular for certain *Xanthosoma*, comparable to *tania*, *yautía*, and *taioba*.
Parima:	mountainous region shared by the Amazonas Federal Territory of Venezuela and the Roraima Federal Territory of Brazil.
peach palm:	*Guilielma* sp.; the *pijiguao* of Venezuelans and the *pupunha* of Brazilians; sometimes "pejibaye" in English.
plantain:	*Musa paradisiaca*; the cooking banana.
pseudostem:	tightly packed leaf sheaths of the *Musa*, resembling a plant stem.
rasha:	peach palm.
reajo:	funerary ritual, culminating with the ingestion of pulverized human bone in a plantain soup.
rhizome:	rootlike subterranean stem of a plant.
shabono:	discrete, roughly circular community settlement; literally, the cleared central space of such a settlement.
sucker:	lateral shoot of a *Musa* plant, especially one with its own corm and capable of bearing fruit.
suwabada taca:	abandoned garden; old garden.
taca:	clearing in the forest; a suffix in garden names.
teri:	a kin group (generally an extended family), which has or once had its own community residence; "people" or "people of" when used as a suffix.
u:	water; liquid; "stream" when used as a suffix.
urifi:	forest; territory.
Waika:	dialect group of the Orinoco lowlands, but not a self-designation; sometimes "dangerous."
wanidi:	abnormal; bad; ugly.
wayamo:	a formal version of the Yanoama language, chanted by adult males during ritualized occasions.
wuu:	large basket used by women for carrying heavy loads.
Xanthosoma:	genus to which belong certain native American cultigens bearing edible tuberous roots.
Yanoama:	human being; person; people; the inhabitants of an extensive area centering on the Parima highlands of southeastern Venezuela and adjacent Brazil; also Yanomama and Yanomamö.

Bibliography

Adamo, Francesco. "Note antropogeografiche sugli Yanoáma." *Annali di Ricerche e Studi di Geografia* 25 (1969): 1–28.

Albuquerque, Milton de. *A mandioca na Amazônia*. Belém: Superintendência do Desenvolvimento da Amazônia (Ministério do Interior), 1969.

Altenfelder Silva, Fernando. "Cultural Development in Brazil." In *Aboriginal Cultural Development in Latin America: An Interpretative Review*, edited by Betty J. Meggers and Clifford Evans, pp. 119–127. Smithsonian Miscellaneous Collections, vol. 146, no. 1. Washington, D.C.: Smithsonian Institution, 1963.

Anduze, Pablo J. *Shailili-ko: Descubrimiento de las Fuentes del Orinoco*. Caracas: Talleres Gráficos Ilustraciones, 1960.

Arends, Tulio; Brewer, G.; Chagnon, N.; Gallango, M. L.; Gershowitz, H.; Layrisse, M.; Neel, J.; Shreffler, D.; Tashian, R.; and Weitkamp, L. "Intratribal Genetic Differentiation among the Yanomama Indians of Southern Venezuela." *Proceedings of the National Academy of Sciences* 57 (1967): 1252–1259.

Barandiarán, Daniel de. "Agricultura y recolección entre los Indios Sanemá-Yanoama, o el hacha de piedra y la psicología paleolítica de los Mismos." *Antropológica* 19 (1967): 24–50.

—————[Aushi Walalam]. "La fiesta del pijiguao entre los indios Waikas." *El Farol* 28 (1966): 8–15.

—————. "El fuego entre los indios Sanemá-Yanoama." *Antropológica* 22 (1968): 3–64.

—————. "Vida y muerte entre los indios Sanemá-Yanoama." *Antropológica* 21 (1967): 1–65.

Barker, James. *Memoria sobre la cultura de los Guaika. Boletín Indigenista Venezolano* 1 (1953). [Entire issue]

—————. "Where Is He?" *Headwaters* 29 (1971): 11–13. [Venezuelan Field Paper, New Tribes Mission]

Bartlett, H. H. "Fire, Primitive Agriculture, and Grazing in the Tropics." In *Man's Role in Changing the Face of the Earth*, edited by William L. Thomas et al., pp. 692–720. Chicago: University of Chicago Press, 1956.

Becher, Hans. "A importância da banana entre os indios Surára e Pakidái." *Revista de Antropología* 5 (1957): 192–194.

—————. *Die Surára und Pakidái: Zwei Yanonami-Stämme in Nordwestbrasilien*. Hamburg: Kommissionsverlag Cram, de Gruyter & Co., 1960.

Beek, Klaas Jan, and Bramao, D. Luis. "Nature and Geography of South American Soils." In *Biogeography and Ecology in South America*, edited by E. J. Fittkau, J. Illies, H. Klinge, G. H. Schwabe, and H. Sioli, pp. 82–112. Monographiae Biologicae, edited by P. Van Oye, vol. 18. The Hague: Dr. W. Junk Publishers, 1969.

Bennett, Charles F. *Human Influences on the Zoogeography of Panama*. University of California Publications, Ibero-Americana, no. 51. Berkeley, 1968.

Biocca, Ettore. *Viaggi tra gli indi alto Rio Negro–alto Orinoco*. 4 vols. Rome: Consiglio Nazionale delle Ricerche, 1965.

——. *Yanoáma: The Narrative of a White Girl* [Helena Valero] *Kidnapped by Amazonian Indians*. New York: E. P. Dutton, 1970.

Birket-Smith, Kaj. *Primitive Man and His Ways*. New York: New American Library, Mentor Books, 1963.

Blackwood, Beatrice. *The Technology of a Modern Stone Age People in New Guinea*. Oxford: Oxford University Press, 1950.

Bloom, Arthur D.; Neel, James V.; Choi, Kyoo W.; Idia, Shozo; and Chagnon, Napoleon. "Chromosome Aberrations among the Yanomama Indians." *Proceedings of the National Academy of Sciences* 66 (1970): 920–927.

Bodenheimer, F. S. *Insects as Human Food: A Chapter of the Ecology of Man*. The Hague: Dr. W. Junk Publishers, 1951.

Bordaz, Jacques. *Tools of the Old and New Stone Age*. Garden City, N.Y.: Natural History Press, 1970.

Brookfield, H. C. "The Chimbu: A Highland People in New Guinea." In *Geography as Human Ecology: Methodology by Example*, edited by S. R. Eyre and G. R. J. Jones, pp. 174–198. New York: St. Martin's Press, 1965.

Brookfield, H. C., and Brown, Paula. *Struggle for Land: Agriculture and Group Territories among the Chimbu of the New Guinea Highlands*. London: Oxford University Press, 1963.

Brookfield, H. C., and Hart, Doreen. *Melanesia: A Geographical Interpretation of an Island World*. London: Methuen, 1971.

Brown, Ralph H. *Historical Geography of the United States*. New York: Harcourt, Brace, 1948.

Budowski, Gerardo. "Tropical Savannas: A Sequence of Forest Felling and Repeated Burnings." *Turrialba* 6 (1956): 23–31.

Butzer, Karl W. *Environment and Archaeology*. Chicago: Aldine, 1964.

Carneiro, Robert L. "Slash-and-Burn Cultivation among the Kuikuru and Its Implications for Cultural Development in the Amazon Basin." In *The Evolution of Horticultural Systems in Native South America: Causes and Consequences*, edited by Johannes Wilbert, pp. 47–67. Caracas: Sociedad de Ciencias Naturales La Salle, 1961.

——. "A Theory of the Origin of the State." *Science* 169 (1970): 733–738.

Cartografía de ultramar. Carpeta I. *América en general*. Madrid: Imprenta del Servicio Geográfico del Ejército, 1949.

Cartografía histórica de Venezuela, 1635–1946. Presentada en la IV Asamblea del Instituto Panamericano de Geografía e Historia por la Comisión Venezolana. Caracas, 1946.

Chagnon, Napoleon A. "The Culture-Ecology of Shifting (Pioneering) Cultivation among the Yanomamö Indians." In *Proceedings of the Eighth International Congress of Anthropological and Ethnological Sciences, 1968 Tokyo and Kyoto*, III, 249–255. Tokyo: Science Council of Japan, 1969.

——. "The Feast." *Natural History* 77 (1968): 34–41.

——. *Yanomamö: The Fierce People*. New York: Holt, Rinehart and Winston, 1968.

——. "Yanomamö Social Organization and Warfare" in "War: The Anthropology of Armed Conflict and Aggression." *Natural History* 76 (1967): 44–48.

——. "Yanomamö Warfare, Social Organization and Marriage Alliances." Ph.D. dissertation, University of Michigan, 1966.

Chidsey, Donald Barr. *Sir Walter Raleigh*. New York: John Day, 1931.

Civrieux, Marc de. *Watunna: Mitología Makiritare*. Caracas: Monte Avila Editores, 1970.

Coatney, G. Robert; Collins, William E.; Warren, McWilson; and Contacos, Peter G. *The Primate Malarias*. Bethesda, Md.: National Institutes of Health, 1971.

Cocco, Luís. "Más allá del turismo: Los indios Guaicas." *El Farol* 32 (1970): 42–53.

Conklin, Harold C. *Hanunóo Agriculture*. FAO Forestry Development Paper, no. 12. Rome: Food and Agriculture Organization, 1957.

Cowgill, Ursula M. "An Agricultural Study of the Southern Maya Lowlands." *American Anthropologist* 64 (1962): 273–286.

Crosby, Alfred W., Jr. *The Columbian Exchange: Biological and Cultural Consequences of 1492*. Westport, Conn.: Greenwood Publishing Co., 1972.

Cruxent, J. M. "Técnica prehistórica para cortar árboles." *Boletín Informativo de Antropología* 7 (1970): 22.

Cunha, João Ferreira da. *Cultura da bananeira*. Rio de Janeiro: Ministério da Agricultura, Serviço de Informação Agrícola, 1948.

Dahlgren, B. E., and Standley, Paul. *Index of American Palms*. Chicago: Field Museum of Museum of Natural History, 1959.

Draper, Patricia. "Crowding among Hunter-Gatherers: The !Kung Bushmen." *Science* 182 (1973): 301–303.

Enns, John. "Further Contact with the Xirianos." *Amazon Challenge* 3 (1960): 13. [Brazilian Field Paper, New Tribes Mission]

Finney, K. B. "Préstamos culturales observados entre los Waikas." *Antropológica* 2 (1957): 27–29.

Fitch, Walter M., and Neel, James V. "The Phylogenic Relationships of Some Indian Tribes of Central and South America." *American Journal of Human Genetics* 21 (1969): 384–397.

Forge, Anthony. "Normative factors in the settlement size of Neolithic cultivators (New Guinea)." In *Man, Settlement and Urbanism*, edited by Peter J. Ucko, Ruth Tringham, and G. W. Dimbleby, pp. 363–376. Cambridge, Mass.: Schenkman Publishing Co., 1972.

Gheerbrant, Alain. *La expedición Orinoco-Amazonas*. Buenos Aires: Librería Hachette, 1957.

Goldman, Irving. *The Cubeo: Indians of the Northwest Amazon*. Illinois Studies in Anthropology, no. 2. Urbana: University of Illinois Press, 1963.

Gómez-Pompa, A.; Vázquez-Yanes, C.; and Guevara, S. "The Tropical Rain Forest: A Nonrenewable Resource." *Science* 177 (1972): 762–765.

Gourou, Pierre. "The Quality of Land Use of Tropical Cultivators." In *Man's Role in Changing the Face of the Earth*, edited by William L. Thomas et al., pp. 336–349. Chicago: University of Chicago Press, 1956.

Guerra, Antônio Teixeira. *Estudo geográfico do território do Rio Branco*. Rio de Janeiro: Instituto Brasileiro de Geografía e Estatística, Conselho Nacional de Geografía, 1957.

Haney, Emil B., Jr. "The Nature of Shifting Cultivation in Latin America." Mimeographed. L.T.C., no. 45. Madison: University of Wisconsin, Land Tenure Center, 1968.

Harris, David R. "The Ecology of Swidden Cultivation in the Upper Orinoco Rain Forest, Venezuela." *Geographical Review* 61 (1971): 475–495.

———. "The Origins of Agriculture in the Tropics." *American Scientist* 60 (1972): 180–193.

Harris, Marvin. "The Economy Has No Surplus?" *American Anthropologist* 61 (1959): 185–199.

Heidenreich, Conrad. *Huronia: A History and Geography of the Huron Indians 1600–1650*. Toronto: Historical Sites Branch, Ontario Ministry of Natural Resources, 1971.

Hills, T. L., and Randall, R. E., eds. *The Ecology of the Forest/Savanna Boundary*. Proceedings of the International Geographical Union Humid Tropics Symposium, Venezuela, 1964. Montreal: McGill University, Department of Geography, 1968.

Holdridge, Donald. "Exploration between the Rio Branco and the Serra Parima." *Geographical Review* 23 (1933): 372–384.

Holmberg, Allan R. *Nomads of the Long Bow*. Garden City, N.Y.: Natural History Press, 1969.

Hopper, Janice H., ed. and trans. *Indians of Brazil in the Twentieth Century*. Washington, D.C.: Institute for Cross-Cultural Research, 1967.

Humboldt, Alexander von. *Viaje a las regiones equinocciales del nuevo continente*. 5 vols. Caracas: Ministerio de Educación, Dirección de Cultura y Bellas Artes, n.d.

James, Preston E. *Latin America*. 4th ed. New York: Odyssey Press, 1969.

Jaml, Pedro. "Expedición de Territorio Amazonas." *Memoria de la Sociedad de Ciencias Naturales La Salle* 18 (1958): 77–89.

Jensen, Lloyd B. *Man's Foods*. Champaign, Ill.: Garrard Press, 1953.

Johannessen, Carl L. "The Dispersal of *Musa* in Central America: The Domestication Process in Action." *Annals of the Association of American Geographers* 60 (1970): 689–699.

———. *Savannas of Interior Honduras*. University of California Publications, Ibero-Americana, no. 46. Berkeley, 1963.

Jones, William O. *Manioc in Africa*. Stanford: Stanford University Press, 1959.

Koch-Grünberg, Theodor. *Vom Roroima zum Orinoco*. Berlin: Dietrich Reimer (Ernst Vohsen), 1917.

Lathrap, Donald W. *The Upper Amazon*. New York: Praeger, 1970.

Layrisse, Miguel; Layrisse, Zulay; and Wilbert, Johannes. "Blood Group Antigen Tests of the Waica Indians of Venezuela." *Southwest Journal of Anthropology* 18 (1962): 78–93.

Leeds, Anthony. "Yaruro Incipient Tropical Forest Horticulture—Possibilities and Limits." In *The Evolution of Horticultural Systems in Native South America: Causes and Consequences*, edited by Johannes Wilbert, pp. 13–46. Caracas: Sociedad de Ciencias Naturales La Salle, 1961.

Lévi-Strauss, Claude. *The Raw and the Cooked*. Translated by John and Doreen Weightman. New York: Harper and Row, 1969.

Loukotka, Cestmir. *Classification of South American Indian Languages*. Latin American Center, Reference Series, vol. 7. Los Angeles: University of California, 1968.

Lowie, Robert H. "The Tropical Forests: An Introduction." In *Handbook of South American Indians*, edited by Julian H. Steward, III, 1–57. Bureau of American Ethnology Bulletin, no. 143. Washington, D.C.: Smithsonian Institution, 1949.

MacLeod, Murdo J. *Spanish Central America: A Socioeconomic History, 1520–1720*. Berkeley: University of California Press, 1973.

Malinowski, Bronislaw. *The Language and Magic of Gardening*. Bloomington: Indiana University Press, 1965.

Marrero, Leví. *Venezuela y sus recursos*. Caracas: Cultural Venezolana, 1964.

Martin, Paul S. "The Discovery of America." *Science* 179 (1973): 969–974.

Meggers, Betty J. *Amazonia: Man and Nature in a Counterfeit Paradise*. Chicago: Aldine-Atherton, 1971.

———. "Cultural Development in Latin America: An Interpretative Overview." In *Aboriginal Cultural Development in Latin America: An Interpretative Review*, edited by Betty J. Meggers and Clifford Evans, pp. 131–145. Smithsonian Miscellaneous Collections, vol. 146, no. 1. Washington, D.C.: Smithsonian Institution, 1963.

Migliazza, Ernest Cesar. "Yanomama Grammar and Intelligibility." Ph.D. dissertation, Indiana University, 1972.

Miracle, Marvin P. *Maize in Tropical Africa*. Madison: University of Wisconsin Press, 1966.

Montgomery, Evelyn Ina. *With the Shiriana in Brazil*. Dubuque, Iowa: Kendall-Hunt, 1970.

Montoya Lirola, Cándido. *Expedición al Río Paragua*. Caracas: Ministerio de Minas e Hidrocarburos, Dirección de Investigaciones Químicas, 1958.

Morais, Fernando; Contijo, Ricardo; and Oliveira Campos, Roberto de. *Transamazônica*. São Paulo: Editôra Brasiliense, 1970.

Morgan, Lewis H. *Houses and House Life of the American Aborigines*. 1881. Reprint. Chicago: University of Chicago Press, 1965.

Murdock, George P. *Ethnographic Atlas*. Pittsburgh: University of Pittsburgh Press, 1967.

Neel, James V. "Genetic Aspects of the Ecology of Disease in the American Indian." In *The Ongoing Evolution of Latin American Population*, edited by F. A. Salzano, pp. 561–590. Springfield, Ill.: C. C. Thomas, 1971.

———. "Lessons from a 'Primitive' People." *Science* 170 (1970): 815–822.

———. "Some Aspects of Differential Fertility in Two American Indian Tribes." In *Proceedings of the Eighth International Congress of Anthropological and Ethnological Sciences, 1968 Tokyo and Kyoto*, I, 356–361. Tokyo: Science Council of Japan, 1969.

———. "Some Changing Constraints on the Human Evolutionary Process." *Proceedings XII International Congress on Genetics* 3 (1969): 389–403.

Neel, James V.; Centerwall, Willard R.; Chagnon, Napoleon A.; and Casey, Helen L. "Notes on the Effect of Measles and Measles Vaccine in a Virgin-Soil Population of South American Indians." *American Journal of Epidemiology* 91 (1970): 418–429.

Nietschmann, Bernard. "Hunting and Fishing Focus among the Miskito Indians, Eastern Nicaragua." *Human Ecology* 1 (1972): 41–67.

Ochse, J. J.; Souler, M. J., Jr.; Dijkman, M. J.; and Wehlburg, C. *Tropical and Subtropical Agriculture*. 2 vols. New York: Macmillan, 1961.

Patiño, Víctor Manuel. *Historia de la actividad agropecuaria en América equinoccial*. Cali, Colombia: Imprenta Departamental, 1965.

———. *Plantas cultivadas y animales domésticos en América equinoccial*. Vol. 2, *Plantas Alimenticias*. Cali, Colombia: Imprenta Departamental, 1964.

————. "Plátanos y bananos en América equinoccial." *Revista Colombiana de Antropología* 7 (1958): 295–337.

Pérez Arbeláez, Enrique. *Plantas útiles de Colombia*. Madrid: Sucesores de Rivadeneyra, 1956.

Peters, John Fred. "Mate Selection among the Shirishana." *Practical Anthropology* 18 (1971): 19–23.

Platt, Robert S. "Environmentalism versus Geography." *American Journal of Sociology* 53 (1948): 351–358.

————. *Latin America: Countrysides and United Regions*. New York: McGraw-Hill, 1942.

Polanyi, Karl. *The Great Transformation*. 1944. Reprint. Boston: Beacon Press, 1957.

Polykrates, Gottfried. "Wawanaueteri: Ein Janonami Stamm Nordwestbrasiliens." *Folk* 7 (1965): 125–152.

————. *Wawanaueteri und Pukimapueteri*. Ethnographical Series, vol. 13. Copenhagen: National Museum of Denmark, 1969.

Pospisil, Leopold. *Kapauku Papuan Economy*. Yale University Publications in Anthropology, no. 67. New Haven: Yale University, 1963.

Prance, Ghillean T. "An Ethnobotanical Comparison of Four Tribes of Amazonian Indians." *Acta Amazonica*, in press.

Quílez, José L. *Los Waikas: O mil años atrás*. Madrid: Ediciones Iberoamericanas, 1968.

Quin, P. J. *Foods and Feeding Habits of the Pedi*. Johannesburg: Witwatersrand University Press, 1959.

Quinn, David B. *Raleigh and the British Empire*. New York: Macmillan, 1949.

Ramos, Alcida Rita. "The Social System of the Sanuma of Northern Brazil." Ph.D. dissertation, University of Wisconsin, 1972.

Ramos Pérez, Demetrio. *El tratado de límites de 1750 y la expedición de Iturriaga al Orinoco*. Madrid: Consejo Superior de Investigaciones Científicas, Instituto "Juan Sebastián Elcano," 1946.

Rappaport, Roy A. "Ritual Regulations of Environmental Relations among a New Guinea People." In *Environment and Cultural Behavior*, edited by Andrew P. Vayda, pp. 181–201. Garden City, N.Y.: Natural History Press, 1969.

Reichel-Dolmatoff, Gerardo. "The Agricultural Basis of the Sub-Andean Chiefdoms of Colombia." In *The Evolution of Horticultural Systems in Native South America: Causes and Consequences*, edited by Johannes Wilbert, pp. 83–100. Caracas: Sociedad de Ciencias Naturales La Salle, 1961.

————. *Colombia*. London: Thames and Hudson, 1965.

Rice, A. Hamilton. "The Rio Branco, Uraricuera, and Parima." *Geographical Journal* 71 (1928). [Privately reprinted; pagination cited in notes from this edition]

————. "The Rio Negro, the Casiquiare Canal, and the Upper Orinoco, September 1919–April 1920." *Geographical Journal* 58 (1921): 321–344.

Richards, Owain R. *The Social Insects*. New York: Philosophical Library, 1953.

Richards, P. W. *The Tropical Rain Forest: An Ecological Study*. Cambridge: At the University Press, 1952. Reprinted 1966.

Röhl, Eduardo. *Fauna descriptiva de Venezuela: Vertebrados*. Madrid: Nuevas Gráficas, 1959.

Ruddle, Kenneth. "The Human Use of Insects: Examples from the Yukpa." *Biotropica* 5 (2): 94–101.

Sahlins, Marshall D. *Stone Age Economics*. Chicago: Aldine-Atherton, 1972.

————. *Tribesmen*. Englewood Cliffs, N.J.: Prentice-Hall, 1968.

Sanders, William T., and Price, Barbara J. *Mesoamerica: The Evolution of a Civilization*. New York: Random House, 1968.

Sanoja, Mario. "Cultural Development in Venezuela." In *Aboriginal Cultural Development in Latin America: An Interpretative Review*, edited by Betty J. Meggers and Clifford Evans, pp. 67–76. Smithsonian Miscellaneous Collections, vol. 146, no. 1. Washington, D.C.: Smithsonian Institution, 1963.

Sarmiento, Guillermo, and Monasterio, Maximina. *Ecología de las sabanas de América tropical: Análisis macro-ecológico de los llanos de Calabozo, Venezuela*. Mérida, Venezuela: Cuadernos Geográficos, 1971.

Sauer, Carl O. "The Agency of Man on the Earth." In *Man's Role in Changing the Face of the Earth*, edited by William L. Thomas et al., pp. 49–69. Chicago: University of Chicago Press, 1956.

————. *Agricultural Origins and Dispersals*. New York: American Geographical Society, 1952.

————. "American Agricultural Origins: A Consideration of Nature and Culture." In *Essays in Anthropology* [Presented to A. L. Kroeber]. Berkeley: University of California Press, 1936.

————. "Cultivated Plants of South and Central America." In *Handbook of South American Indians*, edited by Julian H. Steward, VI, 487–543. Bureau of American Ethnology Bulletin, no. 143. Washington, D.C.: Smithsonian Institution, 1949.

————. *The Early Spanish Main.* Berkeley: University of California Press, 1969.

————. *Sixteenth Century North America.* Berkeley: University of California Press, 1971.

Schnee, L. *Plantas comunes de Venezuela. Revista de la Facultad de Agronomía.* Alcance, no. 3. Caracas: Universidad Central de Venezuela, 1960. [Entire issue]

Schomburgk, Robert H. "Report of the Third Expedition into the Interior of Guayana, Comprising the Journey to the Sources of the Essequibo, to the Carumá Mountains, and to Fort San Joaquim, on the Rio Branco, in 1837–1838." *Journal of the Royal Geographical Society* 10 (1840): 191–247.

Schultes, Richard Evans. "The Botanical Origins of South American Snuffs." In *Ethnopharmacologic Search for Psychoactive Drugs*, edited by Daniel H. Efron, Bo Holmstedt, and Nathan S. Kline, pp. 291–306. USPHS Publication, no. 1645. Washington, D.C.: U.S. Public Health Service, 1967.

————. "Hallucinogens of Plant Origin." *Science* 163 (1969): 245–254.

————. "An Overview of Hallucinogens in the Western Hemisphere." In *Flesh of the Gods: The Ritual Use of Hallucinogens*, edited by Peter T. Furst, pp. 3–54. New York: Praeger, 1972.

Schwanitz, Franz. *The Origin of Cultivated Plants.* Cambridge: Harvard University Press, 1966.

Schwerin, Karl H. "Apuntes sobre la Yuca y sus Orígenes." *Boletín Informativo de Antropología* 7 (1970): 23–27.

Service, Elman R. *Primitive Social Organization.* New York: Random House, 1962.

Simmonds, N. W. *Bananas.* 2d ed. London: Longmans Group, 1966.

————. *The Evolution of the Bananas.* London: Longmans, Green, 1962.

Sorenson, Richard E. "Socio-Ecological Change among the Fore of New Guinea." *Current Anthropology* 13 (1972): 342–372.

Spoehr, Alexander. "Cultural Differences in the Interpretation of Natural Resources." In *Man's Role in Changing the Face of the Earth*, edited by William L. Thomas et al., pp. 93–102. Chicago: University of Chicago Press, 1956.

Statistical Abstract of Latin America: 1966. Los Angeles: University of California at Los Angeles, 1967.

Steinvorth-Goetz, Inga. *Uriji Jami! Life and Belief of the Forest Waika in the Upper Orinoco.* Translated by Peter T. Furst. Caracas: Asociación Cultural Humboldt, 1969.

Steward, Julian H., ed. *Handbook of South American Indians.* Bureau of American Ethnology Bulletin, no. 143. 7 vols. Washington, D.C.: Smithsonian Institution, 1949.

————. "South American Cultures: An Interpretative Summary." In *Handbook of South American Indians*, edited by Julian H. Steward, V, 669–772. Bureau of American Ethnology Bulletin, no. 143. Washington, D.C.: Smithsonian Institution, 1949.

Swadesh, Mauricio. *Mapas de clasificación lingüística de México y las Américas.* Mexico City: Universidad Nacional Autónoma, Cuadernos del Instituto de Historia, 1959.

Tamayo, Francisco. "Exploraciones botánicas en el Estado Bolívar." *Boletín de la Sociedad Venezolana de Ciencias Naturales* 22 (1961): 25–180.

————. *Los Llanos de Venezuela.* Caracas: Instituto Pedagógico, 1961.

Taylor, Kenneth Iain. "Sanuma (Yanoama) Food Prohibitions." Ph.D. dissertation, University of Wisconsin, 1972.

Tiger, Lionel. *Men in Groups.* New York: Random House, 1969.

Tuan, Yi-Fu. *Man and Nature.* Commission on College Geography, Resource Paper, no. 10. Washington, D.C.: Association of American Geographers, 1971.

Valero, Helena. *See* Biocca, Ettore. *Yanoáma.*

Vareschi, Volkmar. *Orinoco Arriba.* Caracas: Lectura, 1959.

Vila, Marco-Aurelio. *Aspectos geográficos del Territorio Federal Amazonas.* Monografías Económicas Estadales. Caracas: Corporación Venezolana de Fomento, 1964.

Vila, Pablo. *Geografía de Venezuela: El territorio nacional y su ambiente físico.* Geografía de Venezuela, vol. 1. Caracas: Ministerio de Educación, 1960.

Vila, Pablo; Brito Figueroa, F.; Cárdenas, A. L.; and Carpio, Rubén. *Geografía de Venezuela: El paisaje natural y el paisaje humanizado*. Geografía de Venezuela, vol. 2. Caracas: Ministerio de Educación, 1965.

Waddell, Eric W. *The Mound Builders: Agricultural Practices, Environment, and Society in the Central Highlands of New Guinea*. American Ethnological Society Monograph, no. 53. Seattle: University of Washington Press, 1972.

Wagner, Philip L. *The Human Use of the Earth*. Glencoe, Ill.: Free Press, 1960.

———. "Natural Vegetation of Middle America." In *Handbook of Middle American Indians*, edited by Robert Wauchope, I, 216–264. Austin: University of Texas Press, 1964.

———. *Nicoya: A Cultural Geography*. Berkeley: University of California Publications in Geography, 1958.

Wallace, Willard M. *Sir Walter Raleigh*. Princeton, N.J.: Princeton University Press, 1959.

Watters, F. F. "The Nature of Shifting Cultivation." *Pacific Viewpoint* 1 (1960): 59–99.

Wilbert, Johannes. *Indios de la región Orinoco-Ventuari*. Published for "Fundación La Salle de Ciencias Naturales." Caracas: Editorial Sucre, 1963.

———. *Survivors of Eldorado*. New York: Praeger, 1972.

Zerries, Otto. "Los indios Guaika y su situación cultural: Informe preliminar de la expedición frobenius al alto Orinoco." *Boletín Indigenista Venezolano* 2 (1954): 61–76.

———. *Waika*. Munich: Klaus Renner Verlag, 1964.

Index